PHANTOM PAST, INDIGENOUS PRESENCE

PHANTOM
PAST
INDIGENOUS
PRESENCE

Native Ghosts in North American Culture and History

Edited & with an introduction by Colleen E. Boyd & Coll Thrush

UNIVERSITY OF NEBRASKA PRESS | LINCOLN AND LONDON

Publication of this volume was assisted by a grant from Ball State
University.

Library of Congress Cataloging-in-Publication Data
Phantom past, indigenous presence: native ghosts in North
American culture and history / edited and with an introduction
by Colleen E. Boyd and Coll Thrush.
p. cm.
Includes bibliographical references and index.
ISBN 978-0-8032-1137-7 (pbk.: alk. paper)
1. Indian mythology—North America. 2. Indians of North
America—Religion. 3. Ghosts—North America. 4. Ghosts in
literature. 5. Indians in literature. I. Boyd, Colleen E. II. Thrush,
Coll-Peter, 1970–
E98.R3P493 2011
398.208997—dc22
2011001180

Set in Sabon and Meta by Bob Reitz. Designed by A. Shahan.

Contents

Illustrations

Table

Introduction

Bringing Ghosts to Ground

COLLEEN E. BOYD AND COLL THRUSH

It is a story that is familiar to most modern North Americans. When unexplained, sinister, or violent things happen in the landscapes and communities we inhabit, one explanation seems to satisfy us more than many others. Whether accounting for the haunted house down the dirt lane, the spectral woods behind the subdivision, or the seemingly cursed stretch of highway up the canyon, one kind of story in particular helps us make sense of these places: *Didn't you know? It was built on an Indian burial ground.* It is the stuff of countless local legends told around campfires and at teenage slumber parties, a persistent and ubiquitous vernacular of titillation and otherness.

Beginning in the last decades of the twentieth century, this motif has been a tried-and-true element of the cultural industry. In *The Amityville Horror*, the cursed house that famously sat astride the boundary between fact and fiction in the 1970s also sat upon land where Shinnecock Indians were said to have left the sick to die by exposure to the elements. (Rather conveniently, the house also had a gateway to hell in the basement.) In Stephen King's best-selling *Pet Sematary* (1983), the "real cemetery," where those lain to rest rise again, is not the place where locals inter their pets, but rather is beyond it, over a dangerous deadfall, farther into the woods, where the Mi'kmaq people allegedly buried their dead. In the 1990s the breakthrough horror of *The Blair Witch Project*—a film that intentionally blurred the line between truth- and tale-telling—included a scene in which the three young, doomed filmmakers stumble across mysterious cairns in the foreboding woods of Maryland, immediately understood by both characters and audience as a Native cemetery. In the new millennium—and somewhat less ominously—even the two-dimensional residents of South Park, Colorado, "break on through to the other side," as when Kyle purchases a goldfish at the Indian Burial Ground Pet Store and in doing so opens a portal into an alternate universe.

Such tales of Indian burial grounds are but one subspecies of Indigenous haunting in North American culture. Alongside accounts featuring Native cemeteries, there exist, for example, countless stories of actual Indian apparitions. Aboriginal ghosts shimmer and shock on urban golf courses in the United States and warn of disaster and death in Canadian mining towns; they wreak havoc on campus in *Buffy the Vampire Slayer* and impart wisdom to vision-questing, galaxy-hopping descendants on *Star Trek: Voyager*. Together with tales of Indian burial grounds—and numberless other varieties of revenants and wraiths of all ethnicities, and the popular obsession with vampires, zombies, and other forms of the living dead—such ghosts suggest that the social theorist Slavoj Žižek is correct when he claims that the undead are "the fundamental fantasy of contemporary mass culture."[1]

But Žižek is no historian, and his claim sells its subject short. Stories of Native ghosts and of places haunted by their Indigenous pasts are not simply the result of postwar suburban anomie and do not belong only to the era of reality TV and horror films. Ghosts—and in particular, the ghosts of Indians—have been an important element of colonial fantasy ever since Europeans (and, in particular, people from the British Isles) first arrived in North America. They have a long and deep history in both the United States and Canada, in both local folklore and national literatures. While often viewed as romantic remnants of "traditional" Indigenous cultures or as the nostalgic detritus of "local" history, Native ghosts have in fact shaped and informed colonizing encounters in significant ways, becoming stock characters in a quotidian North American drama of displacement, transformation, and belonging. The Puritans of New England, for example, saw living Indigenous people as demonic presences inhabiting the howling wilderness, and the Indigenous dead were almost as bad. During the European Enlightenment, colonial observers often described Native peoples as inherently irrational and superstitious, qualities they also attributed to Native spirits. And in the nineteenth century, North American writers, in the process of displacing Indigenous cultures, created national cultures by employing the spectral Native as a powerful trope of terror and lament. Thus, Indian ghosts appear in the writings of iconic American authors such as Washington Irving, James Fenimore Cooper, Herman Melville, and Edgar Allen Poe.[2] Meanwhile, one of the most popular characters of the stage in the nineteenth-century United States was the ghost of the executed Wampanoag leader Metacom ("King Philip"), whose jeremiad against the sins of the nation sent shivers down the spines of thousands upon thousands of men and women attending nightly performances.[3]

As scholars of this "Indian uncanny" have illustrated, stories of Native ghosts—whether in print or on screen, whether in the eighteenth century or the twenty-first—perform a wide range of cultural and political work. First, they express the moral anxieties and uncertainties provoked by the dispossession of a place's Indigenous inhabitants. Second, and almost paradoxically, Indian ghost stories harness very real Indigenous beliefs in the power and potency of the dead, and then cast those beliefs as irrational "superstition" that must give way, like the believers themselves, to rational "progress." Third, and often ironically, Native hauntings disrupt dominant and official historical narratives as expressions of liminality that transcend fixed boundaries of time and space. For all their ubiquity and legibility, Indigenous ghosts are remarkably complex facets of the experience of colonialism and highlight the ways in which knowledge of place and past are constructed, produced, revealed, and contested. Drawing to a large extent on Sigmund Freud's notion of the *unheimlich* (literally, "un-home-y"; more gracefully, "uncanny"), scholars of ghosts and hauntings have made a persuasive case for the utility of such stories for thinking about the rhetoric of colonialism and the process of identity-making in settler societies. As Renée Bergland writes, "The American subject is obsessed with an originary sin against Native people that both engenders that subject and irrevocably stains it. Native American ghosts haunt American literature because the American nation is compelled to return again and again to an encounter that makes it both sorry and happy, a defiled grave upon which it must continually rebuild the American subject."[4] The presence of Aboriginal ghosts in Canadian literature, meanwhile, suggests that Indigenous hauntings are central, then, to a particular kind of *North American* subjectivity.[5]

While drawing on the insights of such literary studies, *Phantom Pasts, Indigenous Presence* takes a different approach. Writing in the 1970s, the San Juan Pueblo intellectual Alfonso Ortiz wrote that "historians need to develop a sensitivity to certain tribal traditions that have a bearing on a people's past, present, and aspirations for the future, to wit, on their history, which have no meaning apart from where they occur."[6] Perhaps because his call came on the eve of "the linguistic turn," which has placed such emphasis on narrative and rhetoric, for the most part scholars have yet to rise to Ortiz's challenge. All too often, analyses of colonialism emphasize only the symbolic or discursive aspects of settler societies—for example, tales of Indian ghosts—while spending relatively little time exploring the physical landscapes those discourses inhabit, or the surviving Indigenous bodies and minds that often continue to, in turn, inhabit those landscapes. In her work on ghosts in the Hudson Valley of New York, Judith Richardson has critiqued this disembodied and "dis-placed" approach to hauntings:

> Although [literary] studies begin to approach the real-life implications of haunting as social memory, and of ghosts as social artifacts and tools, their findings still tend to hover in rarified literary and theoretical spheres. They connect ghosts to issues of broad social significance—nationhood, ethnicity, gender. But they rarely touch ground. By contrast, this book explores how hauntings rise from and operate in particular everyday worlds; it builds arguments, quite literally, from the ground up, cordoning off a territory and a stretch of time, and examining hauntings as they work *in place*.[7]

The essays in *Phantom Pasts, Indigenous Presence*, then, reach beyond literary representations to ground Native hauntings in their cultural, political, social, historical, and environmental contexts. From our backgrounds in history, anthropology, Native studies, and other disciplines, we extend the discussion beyond the realm of the primarily imaginative and immaterial into the world of storied places and embodied practices. In doing so, we are also responding to the insistence of scholars, such as the Canadian geographer Cole Harris, who argue that we must look past the narrative and discursive practices of colonialism, which have so often dominated the literature, to examine the praxis of resettlement: the everyday technologies, elite and vernacular, that make colonialism work, such as mapping, the law, violence, and ecology.[8] If, as Renée Bergland has argued, ghost stories are "first and foremost . . . a technique of removal,"[9] then this volume begins to make the connections between such stories and the actual practices of removal and dispossession.

In their work on hauntings in the modern imagination, Peter Buse and Andrew Stott have noted that "the Enlightenment never succeeds entirely in exorcising its own ghosts,"[10] and in a similar fashion, the Indigenous removal toward which scholars such as Bergland gesture is rarely complete. Simply put, in the same way that many "primitive" aspects of European cultures, including beliefs in spirits and hauntings, have survived the onslaught of Enlightenment rationalism, Native peoples, despite the best efforts of colonizers, have often survived into the present. If anything, literary scholars have tended to overstate the power of the discourses of haunting, limiting Indigenous agency even if from an authorial position of sympathy or alliance. In Bergland's case, for example, she argues that even when Native Americans used ghostly narratives to resist the haunted yet aggressively expansive nationalism of the United States, "they gained rhetorical power at the cost of relinquishing everything else."[11]

In this collection, in contrast, Indigenous people are more than metaphors in the settler imagination, or silenced victims of removal. Rather, they are active participants in the shaping of uncanny narratives as a form of both resistance and persistence. We focus in particular on two aspects of what Gerald Vizenor has called "survivance," a term that refers to the survival and endurance of Indian people through the repudiation of colonial dominance. We pay special attention both to the maintenance of Indigenous historical consciousness and Indigenous identities enacted through narrative and to the territoriality maintained through physical and intellectual connections to ancestral places.[12] In this way, *Phantom Pasts, Indigenous Presence* seeks to engage the ongoing political, social, and economic struggles of Native peoples for recognition, autonomy, and territory. What is remarkable about ghosts is that they are often so central to these struggles, even if they exist at the margins of legitimate political debate. As Michael Mayerfeld Bell has argued, "Our sense of the rightful possession of a place depends in part upon our sense of the ghosts that possess it, and the connections of different people to those ghosts. . . . Ghosts are political. The possession of a place by ghosts thus is not a non-material phenomenon."[13] The hauntings explored herein, therefore, are not ephemeral; they are fundamental.

That Indigenous ghosts populate much of North America is without question; take, for example, the two very different parts of the continent where the editors of this volume happen to reside: the midwestern heartland of the United States and the southwestern corner of Canada.

Sitting at the crossroad of a network of sinewy rivers connecting the upper Midwest to the Mississippi River valley, Indiana was the *pays d'en haut* and homeland of the Miami Confederacy, which entered into commerce first with French and British fur traders and later with the Americans from the new United States. Today it can be difficult to locate the ghosts of the past—any past—in central Indiana. Family farms and small-town charm have been displaced by large-scale agribusiness and Wal-mart, the inevitable signs of globalizing "progress." Yet just below the "golden arches" and other symbols of modernity lurks a darker and more dangerous history. At Conner's Prairie, for example, a popular "living" history museum visited by thousands of school children each year, there are whispered memories that skirt the edges of official park history and local cultural memory. The original homesteader, William Conner, for whom the prairie is named, sent his Miami wife and children off along the "Trail of Tears," while he stayed behind to help build a new state. Indiana demographics bear testimony to the ghostly remnants of removal history today; there are no recognized reservations within state borders, although the non-recognized Miami Indians of Indiana occupy their headquarters in Peru, and the Pokegon Band of Potawatami Indians, a recognized nation, have acquired a small amount of trust land in northern Indiana.

In Indiana, Indian hauntings represent Native peoples as eternally "other." At Mounds State Park near Anderson, for example, "little people" called Pugwudgies are said to live in the forests surrounding the prehistoric ceremonial mounds. Near Batesville, the ghost of an Indian woman, said to be a witch, returns to haunt the St. Louis Cemetery.[14] In the city of Muncie, the "Middletown" of Helen and Robert Lynds' famous 1920s study, Native peoples haunt the banks of the White River. Where the Minnetrista cultural center now stands and where early twentieth-century industrial leaders built their family mansions, nineteenth-century settlers and missionaries once encountered Algonquian-speaking Indians, and on cold autumn nights, or so the story goes, the tortured screams of kidnapped settlers may be heard begging for mercy from their Indian captors. (Sometimes the story includes a newly converted Indian Christian murdered by his own savage kinsmen.)[15] Meanwhile, the ghosts of William Henry Harrison's militia are said to march to their doom to the sounds of rolling drums and "hundreds of marching feet" each November in a spectral reenactment of the 1811 Battle of Tippecanoe, fought between U.S. soldiers and Indigenous warriors of the Shawnee and other groups. And still other stories underscore the blended histories of Native Americans and African Americans in Indiana: a "slave woman," for instance, calling upon a "local shaman" to put a curse on the master that beat her husband to death.[16] The message of such stories is clear: living Natives threatened the survival of new settler communities determined to carve a presence in colonized landscapes, and their removal through so-called Indian Wars and forced marches to Indian Territory is remembered as tragic *and* justified, fearsome *and* inevitable. And the remembering is done in no small part through ghost stories.

The history of colonialism in British Columbia bears little immediate resemblance to that of Indiana: the first encounters between Indigenous peoples and the newcomers came far later than in the *pays d'en haut*, and the frontier of resettlement on the Northwest Coast was Victorian, industrial, and relentlessly modern. Meanwhile, unlike in Indiana, which saw most of its Native population displaced, in British Columbia Aboriginal peoples are still very much present; indeed, the province is a global hotspot for Indigenous rights, given that the vast majority of it has never been ceded by treaty, a process which has only recently begun. Not surprisingly, British Columbia has many Native ghosts.

In and around Vancouver, Indigenous history and landscapes are central to local stories of the supernatural. In one suburb in the 1970s, for instance, a white child developed a relationship with a poltergeist, and both local First Nations people and members of a Vancouver psychic society identified the boy's house as having been built on a Coast Salish burial ground.[17] Nearby, a shingle-bolt cutter living in a shack on the slopes of Grouse Mountain in the early twentieth century was haunted by a disembodied head; one recent retelling of the visitation invokes the history of epidemics that killed much of the local Indigenous population but suggests that "an ancient tribal battle" might also explain the specter.[18] A similar tale, referring to a "vicious battle" between the local Squamish people and Haida slavers from the north, describes odd experiences of a red mist hanging over a local highway and an "inexplicable force" moving cars as they pass through the area. "Perhaps," notes one writer, "that battle has somehow permanently scarred the area's psychic atmosphere."[19] The film and television industry, such an important part of the Vancouver economy, also has participated in this kind of storytelling; the actress Gillian Anderson recounted that the house she lived in while filming *The X-Files* was near a First Nations cemetery and that "it was creepy" and she "felt like there was someone attached" to her, a situation that was only remedied by a smudging ceremony.[20]

Indeed, throughout British Columbia, Native ghosts haunt settler places built in Indigenous landscapes. In the provincial capital of Victoria on Vancouver Island, the ghost of a fur trader's Native wife haunted a heritage house beginning in the 1880s; the haunting did not end until a headless female skeleton was unearthed in the garden in the mid-twentieth century. (Again, a battle between rival Native communities was said to have taken place in the vicinity.)[21] Elsewhere in the islands, a bloody, axe-wielding Indian haunts a house in downtown Nanaimo;[22] a museum in Ladysmith is disturbed by the spirit of a Native woman whose remains were once on display there;[23] the construction of the now-historic Craigflower School in the second decade of the twentieth century unearthed an Indian burial ground, leading to troubling and inexplicable phenomena;[24] and sites of "gruesome and tragic" battles between Indigenous communities have resulted in spectral visitations on Pender and Valdez islands.[25] In the remote mountains of the interior, meanwhile, one of the most famous hauntings in Canadian history involves a curse laid on the mining town of Fernie by a Ktunaxa leader in the late nineteenth century—symbolized by a spectral "ghost rider" on the face of a mountain rising above town—which has been used to explain everything from devastating floods and fires to mine accidents, the Great Depression, and conflicts between immigrant communities in the town.[26] Clearly, for all the historical differences between the Midwest and the Northwest Coast, certain common themes prevail. As in any Stephen King novel, the lands in central Indiana and British Columbia are dotted with haunted burial grounds, signifying what Peter Nabokov asserts about "the power of ancestral bones to mobilize emotions."[27] Similarly, the history of North America is shaded by the spirits of settlers and Indians who reenact conflict in stories told to justify and explain certain outcomes; regardless of location, settler society depends upon the acquisition of Indian ghosts. There is a case to be made, in fact, that the ghosts of British Columbia and Indiana, for all their regional valences, are part of a broader European history of haunting. Indeed, ghosts are part and parcel, and perhaps even a defining characteristic, of the British colonial footprint around the world, evidenced by their importance in the imaginaries of postcolonial nations such as Australia and New Zealand, in addition to Canada and the United States, all with their origins primarily in Anglo-Celtic migration and resettlement.[28]

And if we turn to the history of ghosts in Britain, and in Europe more generally, we find that hauntings have in fact always been tied to material circumstances: to changes in the land, to social revolutions, and to histories of conflict. In medieval England, for example, where there was a deep belief in reciprocity between the living and the dead, ghosts often appeared to speak out against murderers, to aggrieve the redistribution of wealth, or to condemn the destruction of ancestral burial grounds.[29] Meanwhile, conflicts between the Crown and the Church over property took the form of battles over the concept of *mortmain* (literally, "dead hand"), through which ecclesiastical authorities' right to real property was often described as a form of haunting, a posthumous, anachronistic lien of the dead upon the living.[30] As medieval European epistemologies later gave way to the Renaissance and Enlightenment, and to murderous religious schisms, questions about ghosts and the walking dead (were they demons or not? should rituals be conducted to prevent them?), which had been normal topics of medieval debate, became a significant point of conflict between Protestants and Catholics.[31] In Britain, such conflicts—and the institutional upheavals that resulted from them, such as the dissolution of the monasteries—left haunting echoes across the island–nation's landscape in the form of headless monks, spectral nuns, and cursed priests' hiding places, which feature in much of local folklore.[32] In a way that is reminiscent of many Indigenous beliefs regarding the continued presence of the dead in ancestral landscapes, the British worldview in particular seemed to require ghosts as anchors of history, self, and community.

With the massive social changes of the Enlightenment—new narrative structures of rationality, difference, and mechanistic thought, for example, but also new technologies and economic relations—the ghosts of Europe changed as well. As Keith Thomas first noted in the 1970s, ghosts that had once appeared in order to protest injustice, and which often "belonged" to particular families and places, began to fade in importance as migration and displacement accelerated in the face of social and economic changes. Later scholars such as Terry Castle and Renée Bergland have argued that this transition involved ghosts, in their typically contradictory and polyvalent way, becoming both more internalized (reflecting the idea of a modern individual psychology) and more broadly communal (heralding the rise of the nation–state and nationalisms).[33] With the advent of print culture and consumerism more generally, the literature of the supernatural—including what would eventually become known as the Gothic—became a new venue for ideas about relations between the living and the dead, which, as Julian Wolfreys has argued, were also ways to talk about more-concrete matters of everyday reality: the famous haunting of London's Cock Lane or the Gothic writings of a Radcliffe or Walpole could be tools for thinking about political leadership, the perils of capitalism, religious authority, and other disruptions of the eighteenth and nineteenth centuries.[34] Meanwhile, in colonial settings such as North America, Indigenous ghosts could serve as stand-ins for European ancestral dead, providing a spectral genealogy linking settlers to new places. For all their immateriality, hauntings were very much about the tangible world they disturbed.

That the "modern" era would not be able to lay ghosts to rest—indeed, that the modern era instead seemed to produce ever more hauntings—seems both improbable and contradictory. But the founding of "ghost societies" in Europe and North America, the rise of scientific paranormal research, and the explosion of a popular genre of ghost stories in the Victorian and Edwardian eras on both sides of the Atlantic all spoke to the seemingly anachronistic power of hauntings to express both exteriorized longings for a preindustrial, folkloric past and the anxieties of an atomistic, increasingly diverse world composed of individuals with interiorized psychologies.[35] Such movements were often closely tied to very real struggles for social and economic power; in the case of the spiritualism craze of the late nineteenth and early twentieth centuries, scholars such as Alex Owen and Ann Braude have described the ways in which spiritualists used the prevailing language of the day, positivist scientism, to seek out logical evidence of "spirit matter," and women were central to this process, challenging male domination of both science and religion.[36]

In a parallel development, the rise of anthropology was tied directly to Victorian concerns regarding religion and spirituality.

Indeed, early social theorists such as Edward Tylor and Lewis Henry Morgan, "grandfathers" of the discipline, based their findings on surveys and information recorded by missionaries, among others, who were stationed around the globe. A classic example of the Victorian era's comparative method, so favored by Tylor, Morgan, and others, was James Frazer's astounding twelve-volume work *The Golden Bough*. Published first in 1890, and abridged to a single volume in 1922, Frazer's encyclopedia of cross-cultural beliefs, customs, and practices attempted to present a broad comparison of the beliefs and institutions of all humankind, from magic and religion to human sacrifice and fertility rites and beyond. Not surprisingly, among the beliefs and customs covered at length in *The Golden Bough* are those related to impulses and anxieties, providing a framework for locating the irrational, including "superstitions" concerning ghosts and the afterlife, in social others, whether they be the "underclass" at the core of empire or the "savages" at its margins. It became commonplace for early ethnographers to include sections devoted to superstitions and beliefs that marked Indigenous peoples as savage, mysterious, and less sophisticated.

In the twentieth century, "holdouts" of "primitive" "folk" belief—or, more accurately, persistent vernacular epistemologies—combined with the narrative structures of colonialism such as Indian hauntings, new theories of self such as collective memory and psychoanalysis, and new "haunted media" such as radio and film to ensure that the past and the unreal survived into the present and disturbed the real.[37] In fact, it is the atemporality of hauntings, their out-of-time-ness, that has made them such powerful constellations of story and experience throughout linear time. Buse and Stott go so far as to say that "anachronism might well be the defining feature of ghosts, now and in the past, because haunting, by its very structure, implies a deformation of linear temporality: there may be no proper time for ghosts."[38]

And in this respect, ghosts are very much like Indigenous peoples: neither was expected to survive modernity's ascent. The notion that Indigenous peoples were incapable of, or even incompatible with, modernity was manifested through diverse means by settlers, colonial officials, and cosmopolitan cogitators. These practices ranged from enslavement and genocidal violence to religious and cultural assimilation, from the doctrines of the noble savage and *terra nullius* to discourses of authenticity and policies of blood quantum. And yet Native peoples, individually and collectively, have often survived, and with them, their ways of understanding the relevance of the dead to the living. Many contemporary practitioners of Indigenous religions continue to evoke the threads that bind humans to spirit—the living to the dead—through belief and ritual: the most personal belongings of the recently deceased in Coast Salish communities, for example, are burned, along with food and drink, so the deceased will be sustained as they begin their journey to the land of the dead.[39] Diné (Navajo) people, meanwhile, avoid at all costs any contact with the deceased person's belongings or physical remains in order to protect the living from dangerous encounters with the spirits of the dead.[40] Such beliefs and practices, far from being superstitious or antiquated, are in fact means by which Indigenous people maintain social order through practices of reverence and care, and by which they commemorate their own survival in the face of seemingly endless physical and cultural onslaughts.

Many Indigenous beliefs are akin in some ways to the older European traditions that have also persisted—the reciprocity between the present and the past, the linking of ancestry to place, and so on—but there are also key differences, arising from the individual and collective experience of colonialism. Kathleen Brogan has examined the fiction of minority authors, arguing that such writers use ghost stories to deal with the erasure of their communities' collective memory and to highlight their own subjectivity within a society that claims, superficially at least, to value difference. In the novel *Tracks*, for example, the Ojibwe author Louise Erdrich introduces contemporary readers to the Wendigo or Cannibal spirit, using fiction to contextualize her cultural awareness of disease, loss, and spectral horrors for turn-of-the-century Natives in the Great Lakes region. "We started dying before the snow and like the snow, we continued to fall. . . . The water there was surrounded by the highest oaks, by woods inhabited by ghosts," her haunting story of death and survival begins.[41] According to Brogan, the ghost stories of Native American authors such as Erdrich, Leslie Marmon Silko, and others, whether employing timeless images such as the Wendigo or invoking more recent history such as the Ghost Dance, "re-create ethnic identity through an imaginative recuperation of the past and . . . press this new version of the past into the present."[42] Not surprisingly, ties to the land have often been central to this process, with sacred geographies, sites of historical conflict, and places that are haunted by the past being employed to weave powerful accounts of survival and persistence. In telling ghost stories to the colonizer, Indigenous writers claim one of the most powerful North American narrative tropes and use it for their own ends, replacing settler guilt with Indigenous mourning, and imagined spectral ancestries with actual genealogies embedded in the land. These ghosts are political, as ghosts almost always are.[43]

It is possible, however, to overstate the difference between Indigenous and European notions of haunting, or to draw too sharp a line between Native and settler histories. Indeed, if the scholarship of the past two decades has shown us anything, it is that colonial and Indigenous societies have always interacted in complicated ways, often producing hybrid identities, practices, and cultures, and that efforts to create boundaries such as "race" often have devastating effects on those with limited social or political power, such as Indigenous peoples.[44] Such framings also tend to write Native peoples out of the history of the modern world. Recent scholarship, for instance, has shown that the scientific traditions of the Enlightenment are often held up as the antonym to both Indigenous belief systems and beliefs in such things as ghosts. Ironically, such ideas arose in no small part out of the very exchange of knowledge between colonial centers such as London and Paris and, among other things, the embodied environmental knowledge of Indigenous peoples in the colonies.[45] It is in this spirit—the notion that Indigenous people have been constitutive agents in the construction of settler modernity—that *Phantom Pasts, Indigenous Presence* is offered. An interdisciplinary critique of the previous emphasis on literary analyses of Indian ghosts, it is also an Indigenist critique of teleological narratives of dispossession and extinction. Simply put, the survival of both ghosts and Native peoples suggests that for all their power, colonial accounts of progress—whether triumphal or lamenting—are in themselves just another kind of fiction.

The first three essays in our collection build on the extant scholarship on Indigenous ghosts, which emphasizes analysis of literary representations, by highlighting the kinds of grounding we call for more generally in *Phantom Pasts, Indigenous Presence*. All three essays set literary representations within local contexts of landscape and history rather than in more-abstract spaces and categories such as "nation" or "race"; in each case, what matters are the physical spaces in which these representations occur, the material objects that are deployed as evidence, and the specific, local "back stories" that undergird forms of resistance. The discourses of the uncanny, these authors argue, are best understood in the context of territoriality and materiality. Two of the essays in this section also pay particular attention to Native people's own representational strategies and life experiences, rather than simply focusing on the colonial imagination. Together, the three essays set the tone for the pieces that follow.

Michelle Burnham begins from the insights of scholars such as Kathleen Brogan and offers compelling analysis of one Indigenous author's deployment of haunting narratives. Sherman Alexie's novel *Indian Killer* weaves a dark tale of a serial murderer who takes the lives of college professors, shock jockeys, and others in and around Seattle. (The killer may or may not be an Indian; Alexie deliberately withholds from the reader the pleasure of certainty.) Burnham argues that *Indian Killer* marks the arrival of an "Indigenous gothic" by challenging self-indulgent liberal attitudes toward Indians in addition to the thinly veiled arrogance that is central to the project of telling stories about Indians. The ironically named John Smith, Burnham argues, is an "Indian Frankenstein" haunting both the poorly lit parking lots of the Pacific Northwest and the imagination of the reader. Instead of the traditional American gothic, in which non-Native readers simultaneously mourn and appropriate the Indian, Burnham's Indigenous gothic is an "ethics of disturbance" that requires a "compensatory loss of self" on the part of its audience—a price many readers have been unwilling to pay, given the number of reviewers cited by Burnham who have dismissed, critiqued, or been deeply troubled by Alexie's characters' (and Alexie's own) anger. Burnham also places *Indian Killer* within a broader comparative context that includes both Jewish and African histories. Most intriguingly, she also connects *Indian Killer* to the prophetic religious movements that were particular to the peoples of the Columbia Plateau in the nineteenth century, including Alexie's own Spokane and Coeur d'Alene ancestors. In doing so, she sets the stage for a common theme in *Phantom Pasts, Indigenous Presence*: the connections between representations of Indian ghosts and actual histories of Native–newcomer encounters.

Geneva Gano's essay continues this theme of grounded hauntings in history through an examination of the work of the early twentieth-century poet Robinson Jeffers. Gano focuses on the efforts of the California poet to craft a national narrative out of two kinds of horror: that of his local place's colonial past, in which both Spaniards and Americans engaged in genocide against the Ohlone and Esselen peoples, and that of his international present, in which millions were being drawn into the maelstrom of the rather optimistically named "war to end all wars." Like many young liberal intellectuals and cultural workers of his generation—from his fellow writer Hart Crane to the dancer and choreographer Martha Graham—Jeffers sought to create an authentic, ethical, and vibrant American identity in response to that of the seemingly degenerate, war-hungry, and moribund societies of Europe. And so he turned to a vision of the Indigenous past, and in particular to the imagined and real histories of the Native peoples of the California coast, whose stone tools and arrowheads he found in the earth surrounding his Carmel retreat. Gano pays special attention to Jeffers's remarkable 1923 poem "Tamar," in which a rural settler family engages in a séance that both reveals shocking family secrets and is hijacked by ghostly Indian voices, with tragic and horrible consequences. Jeffers's graphic images of rape, incest, and violent death were simultaneously racist and expiatory, elegiac and aggressive, reflecting the complexities and internal inconsistencies of settler society's attempts to make a usable history out of its colonial past. In the end, "Tamar" was in effect a House of Usher for a modern America, with vengeful Indian ghosts literally bringing the house down.

Coll Thrush, a historian, puts a finer point on the methodological and interpretive approach of *Phantom Pasts, Indigenous Presence* by arguing that popular accounts of Indian ghosts in Seattle illustrate the degree to which urban and Indigenous histories, rather than being mutually exclusive, are in fact mutually constitutive, and the ways in which ghost stories can provide access to very real pasts. Using vernacular stories of ghostly shamans dancing on golf courses, spectral prostitutes reenacting their own murders, Indian "princesses" appearing and disappearing in the corridors of a public market, and urban residents of many periods and stripes imagining the landscape of the Indigenous dead, Thrush makes a case that such tales, while reflective of larger patterns in the colonial imagination of haunting, are also clues to specific local histories. He suggests that, when placed in conversation with fine-grained social and environmental history, hauntings are a kind of historical evidence in their own right, gesturing toward salient conflicts and trends in the local past. Seattle's Indian ghosts, for example, speak to specific issues with which the city's residents, both Indigenous and newcomer, concerned themselves: the proper use of sacred sites, the question of "vice" and urban disorder, anti-modernist longings for a romantic pre-urban past, and present-day Native struggles for federal recognition. Thrush also raises a set of questions that, in many ways, are in the background of every essay in this book: Can places really have spirits, which then act upon the lives that encounter them? Do nonliving (or nonhuman) forces truly have agency? Is the past ever really past?

The second trio of essays looks closely at particular historical encounters between Indigenous and colonial societies, and the roles that the Native dead and their spaces and places played in the drama of conquest and survival. Adam John Waterman's essay on the corpse and grave of Black Hawk, a Sauk military leader who died in 1833 in what is now Scott County, Iowa, tells one of the more disturbing stories in this collection. Maintaining his reputation as an assertive, outspoken critic of the newcomers trickling into his people's territory, Black Hawk sought to make his grave speak just as he had. In keeping with Sauk tradition, his was an open-air burial, in which the decay of both body and grave structure would be a ritual in its own right, actively (and literally) linking him and his people to the ground on which he lay. Meanwhile, objects interred with him, such as medals and weapons, represented the political and military relationships he had cultivated during his lifetime. Within a year of his burial, however, Black Hawk's body was gone, and it is here that the story takes a gruesome turn. A local doctor—a man who can be described only as a ghoul—took both the head and body, boiled them clean of flesh, and delivered them into the hands of a nineteenth-century America obsessed with noble savages and that most macabre wing of scientific racism, phrenology. Waterman argues convincingly that, just as it had been for surviving Sauks, Black Hawk's body became an "affective anchor" for settler society, and his grave a locus of orientation—literally, as it was used to take the first land survey bearings in the area. Waterman's account continues with a discussion of the growing confusion over who stole the body and when they stole it, reflecting the ways in which Black Hawk the man had been, at least in part, transformed into Black Hawk the symbol. The disturbing image of Black Hawk's widow finally retrieving her husband's remains also reminds us that behind colonial fantasies are very real and very intimate Indigenous histories. The ghosts that populate this collection (and while Waterman's story is technically about a corpse, and not a ghost per se, it is nonetheless a kind of haunting) come from somewhere. And the very fact that Black Hawk was interred with ceremonies indicative of his Sauk heritage demonstrates that nineteenth-century Indians were well aware of the effect their "afterlife" would have on those who came after, Native and non-Native alike.

Turning our attention for the first time to Canada, Lisa Philips and Allan K. McDougall trace the cultural genealogy of "The Baldoon Mystery," a series of strange occurrences that plagued a Scottish settler family in the 1820s: animals injured, objects moved, and other occurrences most of us might now recognize as a poltergeist, thanks in no small part to Steven Spielberg. Philips and McDougall examine the various theories that were proposed for the events, among them Old World witchcraft, "jealous" Indians, smugglers, and fairies of both Indigenous and Scottish origin. From local histories written in the nineteenth century to folk songs and plays in the twentieth (and even blogs in the twenty-first), the authors show the kinds of slippages, elisions, and contemporary prejudices that often make the thing we call history so very different from the actual past. They also note two important trends. First, as the Baldoon Mystery became better known throughout Canada, it tended to become unmoored from the specifics of time and place, eventually becoming generic Canadian folklore as opposed to a locally grounded event. Second, versions of the story that did remain attentive to local details often involved standard-issue narratives of the hardy and often victim-ized pioneers, or compared the story to contemporary accounts of supernatural phenomena. Both trends, the authors note, had in common the tendency to avoid discussion of Indigenous people except as vengeful ghosts or purveyors of witchcraft—odd, given that the original events occurred among territories initially reserved for Potawatomie, Ojibwe, and other Indigenous communities that had supported the British in the War of 1812. In a sense, Philips and McDougall read the Baldoon story backward, reconnecting a piece of generic Canadiana with its specific historical origins in the complex encounters between Natives and newcomers on what had once been the "middle ground." Through their very detailed textual analyses of a single event's tellings, they illustrate the subtle and often contradictory ways in which the histories of actual Indigenous peoples are routinely displaced (and, as they suggest, dis-placed) by narratives of Indian ghosts.

Returning to the United States, Sarah Kavanagh's account of the intensely local, but also intrinsically nationalized, story of Indian Hill Cemetery in Middletown, Connecticut, illustrates the extent to which the territories of the dead could inform relations between Native and newcomer. To the Indigenous Wangunk people, the hill was known as Wune Wahjet, and it remained important to them—as reserved land, as a gathering place, and as sacred space—for at least two hundred years after the beginning of white resettlement. Meanwhile, the white residents of Middletown, while priding themselves on the relatively peaceful relationships they enjoyed with their Native neighbors, nonetheless expressed deep anxieties about the "frenzied powwows" and other events that had occurred on what they called "Indian Hill," happenings that both shocked the community's sense of propriety and reminded them of Indigenous claims to territory. By the middle of the nineteenth century, when Indigenous connections to Wune Wahjet had apparently been sundered for good, the residents of Middletown found themselves faced with a new concern: without Indians, and the generative frontier they represented, the area's *future* was now at risk. In short, the frontier had left New England behind, threatening to draw the community's young people and vital energy away to the west. To allay those fears, they reasserted and preserved the story of the frontier in the landscape by consecrating a new cemetery whose name referred to the Wangunk but whose construction removed them—quite literally, in the form of their exhumed and discarded dead—from the landscape. Through a close reading of local sources, such as the consecration speech of Rev. Stephen Olin (the first president of Wesleyan College, where the Senior Honors thesis upon which this chapter is based was written), Kavanagh draws connections between local mythologies such as that of the "Sachem Ghost" and broader national contexts of the rural cemetery movement, the monument-building craze, and the project of patriotism. The story of Wune Wahjet/Indian Hill Cemetery highlights the conflation of both presence and absence, and of both the local and the national, that is at the heart of the cultural logics of haunting. It also draws attention to the complex relationship of encounters between diverse human societies and the landscape, made manifest in iron gates, stone monuments, cellars full of bones, and freshly dug graves.

The final group of essays, four in all, take up the question of the ongoing presence of the ancestral dead in present-day Native communities, and the ways in the which the legacies of colonialism inform the so-called postcolonial present. Each essay also engages the ways that scholars work with communities in which the dead (and in a more general sense, the past) are a dominant force in the present. Colleen Boyd's contribution begins with a foul smell and a veiled reference to Sasquatch on the banks of the Elwha River in Washington State, and then continues as an examination of the ways in which supposedly "marginal" or "irrational" things such as ghosts and spirits are not only central to Indigenous communities' lived realities, but can also have dramatic effects on the aspirations of settler society. In the case of the Lower Elwha Klallam, a Coast Salish community into which Boyd married and where she has conducted anthropological fieldwork since 1992, ghosts and spirits of diverse kinds are part of everyday life, just as everyday life is part of the spirit world: one elder noted in the early twentieth century, for example, that the land of the dead now had cars and storefronts. Such realities came to the forefront when *Tse-whit-zen*, a Klallam village more than two millennia old, was uncovered, along with more than three hundred ancestral burials, during construction along the Port Angeles waterfront. Boyd shares in detail the experiences of Elwha Klallam people, many of whom became involved in the recovery of their ancestors' remains. These included both ritual measures such as smudging and the wearing of red ochre, in addition to encounters that can be described only as uncanny; how a living Native fisherman came to find the grave of a dead Native fisherman, for example, is one of the most startling images in this volume. Drawing on her own family's Irish Catholic traditions and "superstitions," Boyd suggests that we rethink the hard line that previous generations of scholars have drawn between knowledge and belief and self and other. She ends with thoughts on the ethics of collaboration between Indigenous communities and non-Indigenous scholars, providing a perfect segue to our final set of essays.

Victoria Freeman's interviews with Indigenous people living in Toronto provide the basis for a contribution that challenges many of the more facile ideas about Native relationships with territory, which assume a static historical and geographical presence, and illuminates the relationship between perceived historical absence and the very real presences of ancestors in the landscape. She shows us the ways in which the Aboriginal community has laid claim to spaces and places within the fabric of Canada's largest city: planting a white pine on Spirit Island in honor of the prophecy of the Great Peace, for example, or making offerings of tobacco at the site of a Wendat ossuary (and several haunted houses) during a bus tour. In this "global" city that has no official First Nations territories within its boundaries, and which has no well-articulated mainstream sense of its own past, urban Indigenous people routinely speak of ancestral spirits in the landscape. Often, these spirits are understood as belonging to a complicated set of identities (or rather, Indigeneities): the Mississauga who originally inhabited the place, the Haudenosaunee and others who expanded into it later, or ancestors from distant traditional territories whose descendants now call the city home. What Freeman argues is that this deployment of the notion of ancestry, phrased in the language of ghosts and spirits and in notions of cyclical return, is a powerful alternative historical consciousness in the city, often built out of direct bodily experiences and intuitive encounters with urban places. For Freeman herself, a non-Native native Torontonian, her work in the community has rendered the city powerfully unfamiliar, creating a "double vision" of competing historical consciousnesses: one about the embodied, diverse ancestral connections to place, in which even the name Toronto itself is believed to carry spiritual power into the present, and the other about a city concerned only with progress, in which Native peoples are a spectral absence.

Cynthia Landrum builds a link between haunted ground, material culture, and undead histories. Her arresting essay on the transference of power between places and material objects reminds us that, like the shape-shifters she evokes, the power of the uncanny to haunt the living shifts locales when objects, in this case museum pieces set for repatriation, are revealed. Landrum shifts between the Great Plains and a story that surely still haunts North Americans—the 1890 Massacre at Wounded Knee—and the Smithsonian Institution, where, bizarrely, many of the material cultural remains of the Ghost Dance—the event that triggered the killings of Lakota men, women, and children in 1890—have been housed. Just as modern-

day Lakota people continue to process Wounded Knee in 1890 "as
if it just happened," guards and other employees of the Smithsonian are forced to reckon with the spirits of Great Plains peoples
whose ancestors remain attached to powerful objects housed in
America's museum and now haunt its halls. Landrum's essay asks us
to consider how objects can be the vehicles through which power is
transferred between places—collapsing the distances between space,
time, and cultures.

The anthropologist Jill Grady rounds out the volume by asking some of the really big questions in her analysis of present-day
interactions of Indigenous ancestors with their living descendants
and with the functionaries of settler society. While documenting and
mapping traditional cultural properties for the Stillaguamish Tribe of
Washington State, Grady experienced firsthand the tensions between
what she calls a "discourse of the dead"—a positivistic cataloging
of Indigenous "reality" through dead bodies, documents produced
by dead settlers, and the oral traditions of dead Indians—and the
living connections some present-day Native people share with their
ancestors. Perhaps more than any other essay in this collection,
Grady's shows us the boundaries of the professionally acceptable.
What does a contract anthropologist do, for example, when faced
with an elder's "powerful feelings" about the presence of ancestors
in a place not documented through archival records or oral tradition? Should she simply assign ancestral spirits a GPS coordinate,
add it to the GIS database, and be done with it? If so, what might a
funding agency or co-managing entity have to say about that? How
should (or better yet, how *can*) government agencies respond to an
elder's "powerful feelings" about a place? As scholars, practitioners, and advocates, just how far can we take this whole haunting
thing? (In the case of the government agency, read on to see what
happened.) Grady also warns us to avoid reading such encounters
merely as rhetorical forms of subaltern resistance or as subconscious
expressions of the anguish of the colonized; among the Stillaguamish
and other Coast Salish peoples, reciprocal relationships with and
responsibilities to the ancestors (and their remains) existed long
before either Freud or Foucault. Lastly, Grady's essay also gestures

toward one of the central ironies of North America's obsession with the "Indian uncanny": Indigenous burial grounds and ghosts populate the colonial imagination, almost in an inverse relationship to the degree to which settler societies have treated the actual Indigenous dead with dignity. For every ghost story committed to film or shared on a moonlit night around a campfire, there are countless desecrated graves. Literary hauntings, meanwhile, are easily outnumbered by the bodies of ancestors lying in captivity at the Smithsonian or the Museum of Civilization.

Phantom Pasts, Indigenous Presence has its origin in a blizzard of email exchanges in 2003, when the editors of this volume—an anthropologist and a historian, both fascinated by the North American obsession with dead Indians—concluded that it was time for North American scholars beyond the literary realm to broach the subject of Native ghosts. Out of this informal exchange of ideas came a session organized for the 2004 annual meeting of the American Society for Ethnohistory titled "Cultural Haunting as Historical Encounter: The Ethnohistory of the Uncanny." While the panel was a success, we were at times scared to proceed to the next phase, despite interest from publishers, not because we necessarily feared ghosts themselves, but because we were uncertain how the academy would react to efforts to seriously explore why so many people believe so strongly that North America is such a haunted place. Many of us found it curious that scholars who work with Indigenous communities find themselves listening to stories about ghosts and spirits (and in some cases encountering those entities themselves) but only a very few incorporate such experiences into their published scholarship in explicit, meaningful ways. As Jill Grady and others ask in these pages, what do we as academics *do* with ghosts? How seriously should we take these beliefs, and what are the risks associated with proceeding in our professional lives as though ancestral spirits and other hauntings are real social, political, and historical entities? After all, even that stalwart Enlightenment skeptic Samuel Johnson famously quipped, "It is undecided whether or not there has ever been an instance of the spirit of any person appearing after dead.

All argument is against it; but all belief is for it."[46] And yet, as the Australian Indigenous studies scholar Peter Read has noted, the most common response to his own work on hauntings and landscape has been, "We are all for free speech, as long as you don't get weird on us."[47]

In fact, most scholars writing on ghosts and the supernatural generally dismiss specters as little more than anti-colonial metaphors and psychological manifestations of the repressed, or evade altogether the question of whether spirits are real. Buse and Stott, for example, write that "proving or disproving the existence of ghosts is a fruitless exercise," going on to say that "it is more rewarding to diagnose the persistence of the trope of spectrality in culture."[48] In her work on British spiritualism, meanwhile, Alex Owen inquires into her own subjectivity vis-à-vis the supernatural: "What was I to do about the spirits? Should I research the social implications of women's spiritualist beliefs and leave it at that, or should I grasp the nettle and try to make sense of the fact that thousands of individuals firmly believed that they saw, touched, and spoke to the real thing—a discarnate entity, a commentator upon, and survivor of, the dark and fearful travails of the dead?" Mostly, however, Owen avoids "grasping the nettle" and leaves her own questions unanswered, offering three possible explanations for spiritualists' experiences with the dead: deliberate fraud, unconscious production and projection, and "causal mechanisms which fall outside our current understanding of the workings of natural law." On this last point, however, Owen disclaims that it "remains mere conjecture on [her] part and plays no theoretical role in the book."[49] In these statements, Buse, Stott, and Owen, like the majority of scholarly writers working on ghosts and hauntings—and interestingly, like most of the popular writers who compile collections of ghost stories for wider audiences—punt. They avoid taking a stand on their own belief systems and, we might imagine in at least some cases, their own subjective experiences.

This demurral regarding the dead, when considered in the context of Indian ghosts and hauntings, is squarely at odds with the increasingly compelling consensus regarding the need for academic scholarship to take Indigenous epistemologies and ways of knowing and being seriously. Often writing from the margins of mainstream scholarship, but increasingly achieving an audience in our postmodern and postcolonial moment, scholars such as Devon Mihesuah, Angela Cavender Wilson, Taiaiake Alfred, Rauna Kaukkonen, and Linda Tuhiwai-Smith, most of them of Indigenous heritage, have called for academe to engage seriously the ways in which Indigenous peoples, individually and communally, understand power, place, time, and other basic constructions of reality.[50] But when it comes to actually believing in the reality of subjective experiences of things such as nonhuman sentience, prophecy and dreams, or communication with the dead, scholars tend toward reticence and postmodern deconstruction at best, or outright dismissal at worst. At least in anthropology, a handful of scholars have begun to "come out" about the extraordinary and often—at least according to Western epistemologies—inexplicable experiences they have had while conducting fieldwork: cases of interspecies communication, entanglements with magic, and yes, encounters with spirits.[51] For those of us who work primarily in archives rather than in communities, such experiences are perhaps less direct, but the sources, if read with care and attention to Indigenous epistemologies, also suggest the presence of extraordinary forces. The question remains, then, of what exactly to do with such experiences and forces. As Bruce Granville Miller and Jean-Guy Goulet have written,

> Transformative events lived with others in their world cannot be wished away. Our hosts know this and we do too. They expect us to take seriously what we have lived with them and have learned from them. In other words, the expectation is that we rise to the challenge of effective and respectful cross-cultural communication. We are called to transcend our own ethnocentrism and to explore forms of knowledge production and knowledge dissemination that serve the best interests of our hosts and our profession.[52]

That said, what then? Do we keep stories of such experiences, whether had in the field or found in the archive, quiet? Do we save them only for post-conference panel schmoozing and tale-telling? Do we share them with students? Dare we publish about them?

We did not ask the authors in this volume to take a stand on such questions, and on the core issue of whether or not they each believe ghosts and hauntings to be real. But Miller and Goulet's statement suggests that a new sort of humility is in order. Peter Read, who writes on Aboriginal issues and the question of haunting in the Australian context, suggests that perhaps scholars do not have any particular claim on truth: "What limitations we western scholars place upon ourselves! Priding ourselves on our open-ended and fearless academic enquiries, how narrow must we seem to South Sea Islanders in our refusal to admit even the remotest possibility that a coconut that fell on the head of an evil sorcerer did so by design. Such immense spiritual reserves and resources, imaginings, intuitions, certainties and divinations about spiritual place, I suspect, must dwell in the land. About them I know almost nothing."[53] Similarly, the religious studies scholar Robert Orsi warns against seeing humans as somehow unique or privileged—a worldview very much at odds with most Indigenous societies, who see nonhuman peoples as kin or even as superiors—and cautions us against seeing spirits as mere "social facts," since to do so perhaps misses the lived reality of the peoples we write with and about.[54]

So perhaps our professions and disciplines have much to learn from accounts of "non-ordinary reality" such as those of ghosts and hauntings. But perhaps more importantly, taking Indigenous hauntings and ghosts seriously involves taking Indigenous peoples and their histories seriously, with ramifications for the present and future of Native and settler societies alike. In the context of, for example, the First Nations treaty process in British Columbia or the recognition of genocide in Australia, ghosts and hauntings—as expressions of Indigenous histories and connections to place and past—can be of critical importance. What harm does it cause, given the imbalance of power that still exists between Indigenous communities and colonial nation–states, to create space in our work for the possibility that the dead do continue to influence the lives of the living? Does our potential professional discomfort outweigh our oft-stated commitments to respect the peoples on whose lives and histories we build our careers?

Granted, there are other risks—most notably, that bringing to light Indigenous understandings of spirit will serve only to undermine (or as some scholars might say, "spectralize") Indigenous legal and political claims by playing into the long-standing stereotype of Indigenous peoples as irrational, anti-intellectual, or superstitious. Ken Gelder and Jane M. Jacobs have written about this tension in Australia in the wake of the landmark 1992 *Mabo* decision about Aboriginal land rights:

> An Aboriginal claim to land is quite literally a claim concerning unfinished business, a claim which enables what should have been laid to rest to overflow into the otherwise "homely" realm of modernity. In this moment of decolonization, what is "ours" is also potentially, or even always already, "theirs"—an aspect of the ongoing recovery of Aboriginal identity in the modern scene of postcolonial Australia. The past returns to the present . . . [and] an Aboriginal claim for land or for a sacred site (especially when it happens to be rich in mineral deposits) is often represented . . . as something the nation cannot afford: a "luxury."[55]

Particularly when, in settler societies, ghosts are largely the stuff of cable television and Halloween haunted houses rather than the subject of deeply held belief and long-standing ceremony, taking Indigenous ghosts seriously may serve only to segregate Indigenous people themselves from political and legal power, with very concrete consequences. But hauntings, if anything, are never simple in their meaning or effect, and so they also hold promise. For all their avoidance of the reality of ghosts, Buse and Stott offer an articulate position on the relevance of the spirits of the dead, writing, "Ghosts are a problem for historicism precisely because they disrupt our sense of a linear teleology in which the consecutive movement of history passes untroubled through the generations. . . . [G]hosts are anachronism *par excellence*, the appearance of something in a time in which they clearly do not belong. But ghosts do not represent just reminders of the past . . . they very often demand something of the future."[56] Here, then, it must be said again: ghosts are political. And what are they political about? The cultural and historical experience of colonialism, for one thing, and just as important, the places and territories they inhabit.

Perhaps nothing symbolizes this grounded, embodied, emplaced interpenetration of past and present, and the survival of both Indigenous peoples and ghostly narratives, than the image on the front cover of this volume. In 1998 the Canadian artist Marianne Nicolson, a member of the Dzawada'enuxw Tribe of the Kwakw*aka*'wakw nation, gained international attention when she rappelled down a sheer rock cliff in Kingcome Inlet on the central British Columbia coast to paint an enormous pictograph on the stone. The image, the first of its kind painted in the region for more than half a century, symbolized the survival of her people in the territory around their ancestral community of Gwa'yi.[57] Ten years later, Nicolson created a site-specific installation in downtown Vancouver, transforming the façade of the Vancouver Art Gallery with Kwakw*aka*'wakw imagery. At night, orcas, the two-headed sea serpent Sisiutl, and other totemic figures are projected in stark red and white onto the columns and lintels of the neoclassical structure, surrounding a skeletal human figure. During the day, this ghostly image is framed by a prayer in Kwak'wala and in English translation:

Giga, Lilo'linuxw! Suma'<u>a</u>s ganutɫida 'nala dɫuwi' 'nalida ganutɫe', la<u>x</u> gad 'Walas Gukw.
Wosida ga<u>x</u>anu'<u>x</u>w Ha'yaɫiligas <u>k</u>as wa'xidage'os <u>k</u>a <u>k</u>'waligalitɫe'sa na<u>x</u>wa!
Come, Ghosts! You, whose night is day and whose day is night, in this Great House.
I beg you, Great Healer, to take pity on us and restore us to life!

This is a powerful assertion of Nicolson's cultural heritage and its traditions regarding the ancestral dead. More pointedly, though, *House of Ghosts* claims place: before it became the Vancouver Art Gallery, the building on which the prayer is projected was once a courthouse and jail, where Nicolson's own Kwakw*aka*'wakw people, like other First Nations people in British Columbia, were tried and incarcerated during the three-quarters of a century when the potlatch was outlawed. By literally reinscribing the place where her ancestors and their beliefs were denigrated, criminalized, and punished, Nicolson's work is both a call for, and evidence of, the reincarnation of Indigenous lifeways in a colonized place. It is a ghostly anachronism at its finest: a colonial courthouse transformed into a house of ghosts, where the living and the dead encounter each other.

It is in encounters, then—between Native and settler, between the past and present, between scholars and subjects—that ghosts and hauntings do some of their best work. They are categorically *not* luxuries, and they have bearing on our shared lives. Peter Read writes lucidly about the relationship between specters and the hope of a better future: "At this point in our history, guilt, apologies, compensation, retribution and expiation form part of the inescapable burden of the colonizers. So are these hauntings part of the burden, and will remain so until raised, probably by the Indigenous people themselves. Decolonization, like reconciliation, is a matter for both sides."[58]

Tales of hauntings, like the ones collected in *Phantom Pasts, Indigenous Presence*, suggest that what so often seem like either grim tales of terror or whimsical fictions of fancy, can in fact offer insights into some of the most pressing issues in North American society today. As Katherine Rowe has noted, in ghost stories "the grip of the past requites the desire it creates by reassuring us that the past is as obsessed with us as we are with it."[59] We hope, then, that the essays presented here, if conceived partly in desire and obsession, may also provide reassurance that there is much work yet to be done.

NOTES

1. Slavoj Žižek, *Looking Awry: An Introduction to Jacques Lacan through Popular Culture* (Cambridge: MIT Press, 1993), 22.

2. Renée L. Bergland, *The National Uncanny: Indian Ghosts and American Subjects* (Hanover NH: University Press of New England, 1999).

3. For performances of Metacom, see Jill Lepore, *The Name of War: King Philip's War and the Origins of American Identity* (New York: Knopf, 1998).

4. Bergland, *National Uncanny*, 22.

5. For Canadian ghost stories, see John Robert Colombo, *The Big Book of Canadian Ghost Stories* (Toronto: Dundurn, 2008), and Marlene Goldman and Joanne Saul, "Talking with Ghosts: Haunting in Canadian Cultural Production," *University of Toronto Quarterly* 75, no. 2 (2006): 645–55.

6. Alfonso Ortiz, "Some Concerns Central to the Writing of 'Indian' History," *Indian Historian* (Winter 1977): 20. Quoted in Peter Nabokov, *A Forest of Time: American Indian Ways of History* (Cambridge: Cambridge University Press, 2002), 131–32.

7. Judith Richardson, *Possessions: The History and Uses of Haunting in the Hudson Valley* (Cambridge MA: Harvard University Press, 2003), 4.

8. Cole Harris, "How Did Colonialism Dispossess? Comments from an Edge of Empire," *Annals of the Association of American Geographers* 94, no. 1 (2004): 165–82.

9. Bergland, *National Uncanny*, 4.

10. Peter Buse and Andrew Stott, "Introduction: A Future for Haunting," in *Ghosts: Deconstruction, Psychoanalysis, History*, ed. Peter Buse and Andrew Stott (London: MacMillan, 1999), 5.

11. Bergland, *National Uncanny*, 3–4.

12. Gerald Vizenor, *Survivance: Narratives of Native Presence* (Lincoln: University of Nebraska Press, 2008).

13. Michael Mayerfeld Bell, "The Ghosts of Place," *Theory and Society* 26 (1997): 832.

14. "Haunted Places of Indiana," http://www.angelfire.com/theforce/haunted/hauntedplacesofindiana.htm, accessed December 2, 2008.

15. C. Boyd, Anonymous Informant, personal communication, Ball State University, 2004.

16. "Haunted Places of Indiana."

17. Barbara Smith, *Ghost Stories and Mysterious Creatures of British Columbia* (Edmonton: Lone Pine, 1999), 22–24; Robert C. Belyk, *Ghosts: True Stories from British Columbia* (Ganges BC: Horsdal & Schubart, 1990), 106–9; and Jo-Anne Christensen, *Ghost Stories of British Columbia* (Toronto: Hounslow, 1996), 145–48. Contemporary accounts of this haunting appeared in both of Vancouver's daily newspapers, the *Sun* and *Province*, on December 23, 1976.

18. Belyk, *Ghosts*, 135–36.

19. Smith, *Ghost Stories*, 185–86, and Belyk, *Ghosts*, 91.

20. Smith, *Ghost Stories*, 193.

21. Smith, *Ghost Stories*, 63–66; John Robert Colombo, *Ghost Stories of Canada* (Toronto: Dundurn, 2000), 171–72; Belyk, *Ghosts*, 10–20; and Christensen, *Ghost Stories of British Columbia*, 92–94.

22. Belyk, *Ghosts*, 134–35.

23. Smith, *Ghost Stories*, 61–62, and Christensen, *Ghost Stories of British Columbia*, 21–22.

24. Belyk, *Ghost Stories*, 69–75.

25. Colombo, *Ghost Stories of Canada*, 177–79; Smith, *Ghost Stories*, 84; and Belyk, *Ghosts*, 94–96. The original source for this story is Jack Scott, "The Night I Began to Believe in Ghosts," *Vancouver Sun*, August 28, 1971; reprinted in *Great Scott!: A Collection of the Best Newspaper Columns* (Victoria BC: Sono Nis, 1985).

26. The basic storyline of the curse is provided in Smith, *Ghost Stories*, 128–30. For a scholarly analysis of the curse and its legacies, see Leslie A. Robertson, *Imagining Difference: Legend, Curse, and Spectacle in a Canadian Mining Town* (Vancouver: UBC Press, 2005).

27. Nabokov, *Forest of Time*, 148.

28. For two examples from Australia, see Peter Read, *Haunted Earth* (Sydney: University of New South Wales Press, 2003), and Ken Gelder and Jane M. Jacobs, *Uncanny Australia: Sacredness and Identity in a Postcolonial Nation* (Melbourne: Melbourne University Press, 1998).

29. Keith Thomas, *Religion and the Decline of Magic* (New York: Scribner, 1971).

30. Katherine Rowe, *Dead Hands: Fictions of Agency, Renaissance to Modern* (Stanford CA: Stanford University Press, 1999), 118.

31. Darren Oldridge, *Strange Histories: The Trial of the Pig, the Walking Dead, and Other Matters of Fact from the Medieval and Renaissance Worlds* (London: Routledge, 2007), 67–70.

32. For a recent encyclopedic treatment of the subject, see Jennifer Westwood and Jacqueline Simpson, *The Lore of the Land: A Guide to England's Legends, from Spring-Heeled Jack to the Witches of Warboys* (New York: Penguin Books, 2006).

33. Bergland, *National Uncanny*, 8–9; and Terry Castle, *The Female Thermometer: 18th-Century Culture and the Invention of the Uncanny* (Oxford: Oxford University Press, 1995).

34. E. J. Clery, *The Rise of Supernatural Fiction, 1762–1800* (Cambridge: Cambridge University Press, 1995).

35. Elton E. Smith and Robert Haas, eds., *The Haunted Mind: The Supernatural in Victorian Literature* (Lanham MD: Scarecrow, 1999), viii.

36. Alex Owen, *The Darkened Room: Women, Power, and Spiritualism in Late Nineteenth Century England* (London: Virago, 1989); Alex Owen, *The Place of Enchantment: British Occultism and the Culture of the Modern* (Chicago: University of Chicago Press, 2004), 7–8; and Ann Braude, *Radical Spirits: Spiritualism and Women's Rights in Nineteenth-Century America* (Bloomington: Indiana University Press, 1989).

37. Colin Davis, *Haunted Subjects: Deconstruction, Psychoanalysis, and*

the Return of the Dead (London: Palgrave Macmillan, 2007), and Marina Warner, *Phantasmagoria: Spirit Visions, Metaphors, and Media into the Twenty-first Century* (Oxford: Oxford University Press, 2006).

38. Buse and Stott, *Ghosts*, 1.

39. See Colleen Boyd's contribution to this volume for more on this tradition.

40. Barry Holt, "A Cultural Resource Management Dilemma: Anasazi Ruins and the Navajo," *American Antiquity* 48, no. 3 (1983), 594–99.

41. Louise Erdrich, *Tracks* (New York: HarperCollins, 1988), 1–3.

42. Kathleen Brogan, *Cultural Haunting: Ghosts and Ethnicity in Recent American Literature* (Charlottesville: University Press of Virginia, 1998), 4, 27, 30–60.

43. For two recent studies of Indigenous writers' use of connections to territory, see Lee Schweninger, *Listening to the Land: Native American Literary Responses to the Landscape* (Athens: University of Georgia Press, 2008), and Lindsey Claire Smith, *Indians, Environment, and Identity on the Borders of American Literature: From Faulkner and Morrison to Walker and Silko* (London: Palgrave Macmillan, 2008).

44. For some of the best discussions of Indigenous cultural hybridity across the past three and a half centuries, see Richard White, *The Middle Ground: Indians, Empires, and Republics on the Great Lakes, 1650–1815* (Cambridge: Cambridge University Press, 1991); Paige Raibmon, *Authentic Indians: Episodes of Encounter from the Late-Nineteenth-Century Northwest Coast* (Durham NC: Duke University Press, 2005); and Philip J. Deloria, *Indians in Unexpected Places* (Lawrence: University Press of Kansas, 2004). For two histories examining the imposition of racial categories on Indigenous peoples and families, see Bonita Lawrence, *"Real" Indians and Others: Mixed-Blood Urban Native Peoples and Indigenous Nationhood* (Lincoln: University of Nebraska Press, 2004), and Claudio Saunt, *Black, White, and Indian: Race and the Unmaking of an American Family* (New York: Oxford University Press, 2005).

45. See Susan Scott Parrish, *American Curiosity: Cultures of Natural History in the Colonial British Atlantic World* (Chapel Hill: University of North Carolina Press, 2006).

46. From the April 3, 1778, entry in James Boswell's oft-reprinted *Life of Johnson*.

47. Peter Read, *Haunted Earth* (Sydney: University of New South Wales Press, 2003), 29.

48. Buse and Stott, *Ghosts*, 2–3.

49. Owen, *Darkened Room*, xviii–xx.

50. For some of the best examples of this scholarship, see Devon Abbott Mihesuah and Angela Cavender Wilson, *Indigenizing the Academy: Trans-*

forming Scholarship and Empowering Communities (Lincoln: University of Nebraska Press, 2004), Rauna Kuokkanen, *Reshaping the University: Responsibility, Indigenous Epistemes, and the Logic of the Gift* (Vancouver: UBC Press, 2007); and Linda Tuhiwai Smith, *Decolonizing Methodologies: Research and Indigenous Peoples* (London: Zed, 1999).

51. For examples, see Edith Turner, with William Blodgett, Singleton Kahona, and Fideli Benwa, *Experiencing Ritual: A New Interpretation of African Healing* (Philadelphia: University of Pennsylvania Press, 1992); *Being Changed: The Anthropology of Extraordinary Experience*, ed. David E. Young and Jean-Guy Goulet (Peterborough ON: Broadview, 1994); and *Extraordinary Anthropology: Transformations in the Field*, ed. Jean-Guy Goulet and Bruce Granville Miller (Lincoln: University of Nebraska Press, 2007).

52. Goulet and Miller, *Extraordinary Anthropology*, 7.

53. Read, *Haunted Earth*, 41.

54. Robert Orsi, *Between Heaven and Earth: The Religious Worlds People Make and the Scholars Who Study Them* (Princeton: Princeton University Press, 2005), 150.

55. Ken Gelder and Jane M. Jacobs, "The Postcolonial Ghost Story," in Buse and Stott, *Ghosts*, 181.

56. Buse and Stott, *Ghosts*, 14.

57. For an account of Nicolson's commemoration of Gwa'yi, see Judith Williams, *Two Wolves at the Dawn of Time: Kingcome Inlet Pictographs, 1893–1998* (Vancouver: New Star, 2001).

58. Read, *Haunted Earth*, 58.

59. Rowe, *Dead Hands*, 117.

PHANTOM PAST, INDIGENOUS PRESENCE

PART 1

METHODOLOGIES

1

Sherman Alexie's *Indian Killer* as Indigenous Gothic

MICHELLE BURNHAM

In Sherman Alexie's controversial 1996 novel *Indian Killer*, a six-year-old boy named Mark Jones, "the first-born son of a white family" (192), is kidnapped from his bedroom by someone identified only as "the killer." The killer, who possesses a knife inlaid with turquoise stones that has already been used to stab and scalp a white, male victim, leaves after the crime a calling-card of blood-stained white owl feathers. Intent on completing "a powerful ceremony that would change the world" (192), the killer remains not only menacingly anonymous and indecipherable, even to the very conclusion of Alexie's book, but is described as a "shadow" (71) that shifts between human and bird or spirit form, able to glide into and out of trees, and to enter and exit inhabited homes undetected. More than anything, perhaps, the killer seems to *be* the darkness itself, as the following passage suggests: "Mark Jones woke up in a very dark place but knew instantly that somebody was sitting near him. The frightened little boy tried to talk and to move, but found he was gagged and his arms were tied behind his back. He struggled against the ropes. The killer reached out and touched him. Mark couldn't see the killer, but felt something familiar, and almost comforting, in the touch" (191). Inside a terrifying darkness, a gagged, bound, and blinded white American boy comes into contact with a touch that is uncanny in its strange familiarity. That haunting brush with faceless otherness is, I argue, absolutely central to the anti-liberal literary and cultural politics of *Indian Killer*, a book that compels its readers into an experience of contact surprisingly similar to that of

Mark Jones. In place of access to Indian experience or identity that many readers might seek, the book *Indian Killer* offers its readers a disorienting encounter with nothingness and unknowability.

Alexie radically reformulates the politics of gothic sensation as these have historically functioned and been understood within the Euro-American literary tradition. I bring Alexie's novel together with Emmanuel Levinas's philosophical work on alterity and ethics to begin to imagine the terms of an Indigenous gothic. The inchoate Indian killer appears as a product of the genocidal violence that has characterized the long history of Native American contact with Europeans—a kind of Indian Frankenstein figure, a mysterious double whose palindromic name simultaneously invokes both its creators (those who have been killers of Indians, and of their stories) and their creations (both the Indian dead who traverse the land as vengeful ghosts, and counterfeit stories about Indians, which return as vengeful ghostwriting).

Indian Killer is a novel marked, in many ways, by a series of stalkings, by a succession of characters who are or feel themselves to be followed by absolutely menacing but utterly invisible figures. The guilt-ridden liberal college student David Rogers senses with a suddenly shaking fear that he is being followed across a casino parking lot (Alexie 1996, 108); the racist right-wing radio talk show host Truck Schultz finds himself "surrounded by a strangely dark and dense fog" and believes that he is being pursued by the Indian killer (293–94); the University of Washington professor Dr. Clarence Mather hears a "rattling" sound while in the basement of the anthropology building where the bones of Chief Seattle are stored in a box, and becomes convinced that "something was chasing him, was right behind him, reaching for his neck" (140). Each of these scenes contains in different ways explicit echoes of a mid-nineteenth-century speech attributed to Chief Seattle, the Indian namesake of the city in which *Indian Killer* takes place. In the speech, Seattle reportedly warned,

> The Indians' night promises to be dark. . . . [W]hen the last Red
> Man shall have perished, and the memory of my tribe shall have

become a myth among the White Men, these shores will swarm
with the invisible dead of my tribe, and when your children think
themselves alone in the field, the store, the shop, upon the highway, or in the silence of the pathless woods, they will not be alone.
. . . The White Man will never be alone.

Let him be just and deal kindly with my people, for the dead
are not powerless. (Vanderwerth 1971, 118–22)[1]

Indian Killer would seem to materialize the content of this speech
when Mather delusionally imagines he is being pursued by the ghost
of Seattle's stolen remains, just as the abduction of Mark Jones by
the Indian killer seems an event that makes good on Chief Seattle's
threatening vision of "children" who mistakenly "think themselves
alone" when they are in fact surrounded by potentially vengeful
ghosts of the Indian dead.

But it is crucial to note that Chief Seattle's speech is itself a kind
of ghost; exposed as an inauthentic product of several generations
of white ghostwriters, it is now recognized as one of many "Indian
speeches" largely manufactured, distributed, and consumed by
whites. By materializing the speech's calm vengeance around the
figure of the Indian killer (who might either be a killer of Indians, or
a killer who is Indian), Alexie is crafting an Indigenously gothicized
version of such literary appropriations and offering it in menacing form to those very readers who take delight in consuming the
mournful narratives of Indian disappearance that such texts depend
on. Rather than counter manufactured Indianness with "authentic"
Indianness, his book instead sets loose the ghosts that populate the
production of Indian identity within American history and literature. When readers confront the dark and vengeful space embodied
by the Indian killer, they confront an absent presence that underscores all that they do not know about Indians. This confrontation
demands and initiates, however, a terrifying erosion of the foundations of liberal selfhood. One of the most overlooked meanings of
the book's title may well then be that *Indian Killer* kills any certainty
or knowledge readers may have claimed or hoped to possess about
Indian identity, and that it provokes in turn a devastating crisis in
self-knowledge.

Alexie's narrative mobilizes two kinds of ghosts at once—the ghosts of the Native American dead, and the ghosts of their stories.[2] Both of these ghosts are exposed as the products of a genocidal violence that consists not only of America's long history of appropriating Indigenous lands and cultures, but of what might be called the soft violence of more recent white liberalism. *Indian Killer* thus constitutes an anti-liberal project that turns these colonialist productions against their creators in a kind of Indianized Frankenstein story. I read *Indian Killer* as an instance of Indigenous gothic that destabilizes as it lays bare the racial, historical, and affective investments of the American tradition of the gothic—thus turning this tradition, too, against its creators. Readers' sensations of delightful terror have of course been central to the tradition of the gothic, but I adapt here the work of the Jewish philosopher Emmanuel Levinas to argue for another kind of gothic that is explicitly grounded in an acknowledgment rather than a disavowal of genocide. Whereas traditional American gothic serves a colonialist politics of mourning that pleasurably reinforces the very self that its frightening narratives appear to put at risk, Sherman Alexie's Indigenous gothic refuses such absolution and produces in readers instead a disorienting loss of self that serves an anti-liberal politics and, ultimately, an anti-colonialist ethics.

Although critics have most often positioned *Indian Killer* within the genre of the detective story or the mystery novel, situating the book within the tradition of the gothic might best make sense of the popular critical response to it, since it has received the most mixed reviews of any of Alexie's books to date. Whatever praise the novel initially received tended to be combined with some measure of discomfort, disdain, or dismissal—invariably in response to the book's expression or representation of anger. Indeed, virtually every objection to or critique of the novel is explicitly linked to its so-called anger. The best known of these responses is the *Time* magazine review subtitled "Rage Sours the Eloquent Novel *Indian Killer*," which remarks that "Alexie's tale is septic with what clearly seems to be his own unappeasable fury"—a fury to which the reviewer can only imagine responding with a dismissive "Right. Understood. Take a number. Get in line" (Skow 1996, 88). The *Rocky Mountain News* reviewer criticizes Alexie's "general depiction of most whites in this book [as] revolting—crude, bigoted, pompous, cowardly caricatures" (Mitchell 1996, 31D), a position later taken in a *New York Times* article by Timothy Egan (1998). Richard Nicholls, in an earlier *New York Times Book Review*, tempers his praise for the novel with the observation that it is "difficult not to make the novel seem more angry than reflective" (1996, 4), while the reviewer for *Booklist* argues that "anger is rarely an endearing trait—it tends to flatten over the most well-rounded characters—and this novel is populated almost completely by angry people" (Ott 1996, 5).[3]

These critics assume or imply that good literature cannot also be angry; that assumption in turn betrays these reviewers' consistent discomfort with and defensive avoidance of the political and historical conditions of such anger, as Alexie himself observes.[4] Alexie points to this symptomatic avoidance when, asked about such critical feedback, he observes that "it's a condescending treatment of political rage or political anger," adding, "That same reviewer [in *Time* magazine], with a novel by Elie Wiesel or Primo Levi, he wouldn't say that. Certain white critics and audience people's responses to the anger, it was depressing for me. They didn't examine the anger. They were merely afraid of it, and then dismissed it out of that fear" (Donadoni 1998).

Several literary critical efforts to "examine the anger" in *Indian Killer* have since emerged, but most of them still find the book flawed or ineffective in one way or another, and its anger unassimilable. Ron McFarland, for instance, characterizes the "combativeness" of Alexie's work as "polemic" in the sense that it is "at war" (1997, 27) with stereotypes of Native Americans—although this agenda does not, McFarland notes, "make his anger exactly palatable" (28). Louis Owens argues that Alexie's fiction is in fact filled with stereotypes; he dismisses the protagonist of *Indian Killer* as a prototype of the "helpless, romantic victim still in the process of vanishing just as he is supposed to do" (1998, 77) and faults the book overall for being inhabited by "Indians who repetitiously protest the exploitation and appropriation of their cultures while exhibiting almost no traces at all of the cultures supposedly being appropriated" (78). Patrice Hollrah, while significantly recognizing the character Marie Polatkin's aggressiveness as the assertion of "an agenda of tribal intellectual sovereignty" (2001, 27) against "the colonizing act of telling the reading public what Indians are 'really' like" (30), nevertheless goes on to question Alexie's refusal to propose a solution for this problem.[5] Perhaps most perplexingly, Stuart Christie identifies the novel's violence as "merely one manifestation of a collective cultural madness" (2001, 19 n.34) and excoriates Alexie for belittling and undermining the plight of homeless schizophrenics by treating his protagonist's insanity as an empty metaphor for postmodern cultural dislocation.

Alexie directly associates his book's anger with the colonial experience of American Indians, observing, "I'm a colonized man . . . we're a colonized people. This *is* South Africa here. . . . The United States *is* a colony, and I'm always going to write like one who is colonized, and that's with a lot of anger" (Giles 1996). Even those critics who recognize Native anger in *Indian Killer* as anti-colonialist expression go on to dismiss its strategies or assumptions as ineffective—perhaps because they are unable to assimilate anger within dominant liberal conceptions of an anti-violent or antiracist politics. In this essay, I argue that *Indian Killer* is better understood as an Indigenous anti-colonial gothic that disables the racial and affective logic of traditional gothic, and in doing so, invites readers to enter into proximity with an other who they are not only unable to domesticate or mourn but also are unable to know. The dismissive or hostile critical reactions surveyed above illustrate what Alexie identifies as the "fear" with which many readers respond to such unknowability. In fact, by casting Alexie as an "angry Indian" and his book as an "angry novel" these same critics may be attempting to claim a definitive knowledge of him and of his text that both author and work radically deny.[6] Thus, when Stuart Christie complains that the tone and style of *Indian Killer* disable "any nascent cross-cultural sympathy" (2001, 10), he mistakes as a failing what very well may be the main point and effect of *Indian Killer*.

Scenes such as the abduction of the young boy Mark Jones, with which this essay begins, evoke the familiar terrain of the gothic. Central to that tradition is the production of the sensation of the sublime through a spectatorial relation that is subtly exposed in *Indian Killer* as racialized. The sublime, as Edmund Burke described it in his 1757 treatise on the sublime and the beautiful, results when viewers or readers sympathetically identify with characters who are in situations of extreme danger, and most dramatically with figures who face the terrifyingly real possibility of death. Burke insists that this sympathetic experience of pain or fear is, however, a source of pleasure for spectators, for "we have a degree of delight, and that no small one, in the real misfortunes and pains of others"; we experience pleasure in response to terror when such terror "does not press too close" (1990, 42). The sublime is a kind of pain that is experienced as pleasure because the spectator is protected by some measure of distance from the actual source of pain itself: these feelings "are delightful when we have an idea of pain and danger, without being actually in such circumstances" (47).

This sensation of the sublime is very much dependent on relations of similarity, as Burke makes clear: "When two distinct objects have a resemblance, we are struck, we attend to them, and we are pleased. The mind of man has naturally a far greater alacrity and satisfaction in tracing resemblances than in searching for differences" (1990, 17). When the Indian killer selects his victims, the killer does so with a deliberate awareness of its identificatory effects on a predominantly white audience. Deciding to kidnap the boy Mark Jones is, the killer knows, "the first dance of a powerful ceremony that would change the world" since "the world would shudder when a white boy was sacrificed" (192). *Indian Killer* upsets the racialized division of affect that characterizes sublime spectatorship in conventional American gothic because its plot does not allow for the retaliatory violence against the killer with which such novels traditionally conclude; indeed, it does not even allow for the identification of this killer as anything other than *something its readers cannot know*.[7] Unless readers succeed in identifying with the killer (who threatens vengeance up to the very end of the book, despite the fact that he

9

returns Mark to his sleeping mother after cutting out—in an act like that of counting coup—a piece of fabric from the boy's superhero pajamas), they are denied the recuperative delight that traditionally accompanies sublime fear in the white gothic.

Freud's notion of the uncanny (or *unheimlich*) as a sensation of strange familiarity experienced in response to an exposed secret that ought to have remained hidden has likewise long been central to theories of gothic literature. Recent work on American gothic, taking its cue from Toni Morrison's *Playing in the Dark* (1992), recognizes the historical experiences of slavery and genocide as the repressed (and exposed) secret that is central to the workings of sensation within American gothic. In *Gothic America*, for instance, Teresa Goddu argues that American gothic tales consistently relate and repress the history of violence against African and Native Americans, negotiating "the historical horrors that make national identity possible yet must be repressed in order to sustain it" (1997, 10). Renée Bergland's *National Uncanny* (2000) focuses more specifically on the presence of Native American specters in American literature but argues similarly for the gothic construction of an American national identity: "Native American ghosts haunt American literature because the American nation is compelled to return again and again to an encounter that makes it both sorry and happy, a defiled grave upon which it must continually rebuild the American subject" (22).

Both Goddu and Bergland focus predominantly on literature written by white authors for largely white audiences, and implicitly identify American gothic as a white nationalist gothic in which, as Toni Morrison observed, white American subjects are haunted by the return of the nation's repressed historical violence against nonwhite others. At the end of her book, Goddu turns, however, to African American uses of gothic to "haunt back" (1997, 132) at the nation, as Bergland turns at the end of hers to Native American revisions of the trope of the Indian ghost. Kathleen Brogan has focused exclusively on contemporary ethnic American literary uses of ghosts in what she calls narratives of "cultural haunting" that become for many writers of color a means of reconnecting the present to an ancestral past and of expressing "concerns about assimilation and cultural identity"

(1998, 16). Sherman Alexie's *Indian Killer* might be positioned within this alternative ethnic tradition of the gothic, except that its project aims less at an eventual integration that might "put the dead to rest" (Brogan 1998, 22) than at a disintegration of the foundations of the spectatorial self on which gothic sensation depends.

In order to begin to conceptualize the political and affective work of gothic sensation in *Indian Killer*, I bring such concepts as the uncanny and the sublime into dialogue with other theoretical and cultural sources for thinking about an anti-colonial gothic—including Emmanuel Levinas's work on alterity and, later in this essay, invocations of the dead within hybrid Native American religious traditions, especially from the Plateau region. Levinas's work is of value in this regard because his formulation of the encounter with the other eliminates that margin of protection or safety enjoyed by the subject as a result of his or her distance from actual pain (assumed by the sublime) or from a repressed history or memory (central to the psychoanalytic concept of the uncanny). That protective distance is, moreover, essential to liberal sentimental models of otherness, which posit and celebrate the self's sympathetic access and response to an other, as if the other were something that "we can assimilate through enjoyment" (Levinas 1978; 1989, 43). Levinas adamantly refuses such constructions and instead insists:

> The relationship with the other is not an idyllic and harmonious relationship of communion, or a sympathy through which we put ourselves in the other's place; we recognize the other as resembling us, but exterior to us; the relationship with the other is a relationship with a Mystery. The other's entire being is constituted by its exteriority, or rather its alterity, for exteriority is a property of space and leads the subject back to itself through light.
>
> Consequently only a being whose solitude has reached a crispation through suffering, and in relation to death, takes its place on a ground where the relationship with the other becomes possible. (Levinas 1989, 43)

For Levinas, only a self that has in some measure lost possession of itself is able to come into relationship with the other. Any encounter that permits the self to return to rather than abandon itself will fail to recognize otherness.

Sherman Alexie has often mocked and critiqued white liberal appropriations of Native American culture and spirituality, a project continued in *Indian Killer*, whose narrative robs readers of the safety necessary to sustain their sense of self afforded by the racial terms of identification that subtend the tradition of the American gothic. Alexie forces readers to experience not a pleasurable haunting but a disturbing threat. Levinas admits that one common response to this fearful experience of a loss of self is violence, a response played out in various ways in the novel by the incendiary right-wing radio host Truck Schultz and the disaffected fraternity brother Aaron Rogers—and a response that might well be reflected in some of the critical responses to the book discussed earlier. Levinas's reflections on ethics and otherness allow for a theory of an other gothic, one that disables the affective terms that govern the recuperative politics of traditional gothic representations of colonial and ethnic violence and that offers, in turn, an alternative ethics of gothic sensation.

Uncanny doubles typical of the gothic appear throughout *Indian Killer*, but these doubles everywhere expose the violent erasures on which identity depends in the context of internal colonialism. The kidnapping of the boy Mark Jones, for instance, mirrors the novel's opening scene, in which a nameless newborn baby of undocumented tribal origins is stolen from his Indian mother and transported by helicopter into the waiting arms of the wealthy white woman, Olivia Smith, who has adopted him. One effect of pairing these two events is to utterly complicate their apparent moral and emotional difference, for it suggests that both young boys come into contact with a terrifying yet familiar other, that the adoption (in its surreal description of the "helicopter gunman" firing on the reservation "[as] if there [were] a war beginning" [Alexie 1996, 6]) is as much an act of violence and terror as the kidnapping, which, with its surprising account of the killer "gently lifting the boy from the bed" (153), sounds rather like an act of affection and care. As if this origin story did not sufficiently convey the emptiness on which John Smith's identity rests, that emptiness is further symbolized by the utter commonness of his generic Anglo-American name and by the ironic fact that he shares that name with the early English colonist long mythologized for his fictionalized love for the Native woman Pocahontas and for his self-promotional writings that have so often served as a foundational narrative for an "American" national identity.

But if John Smith's adoption mirrors the abduction of Mark Jones (who also has a generic Anglo-American name), Smith is even more explicitly a double for the character Jack Wilson, a white man who ironically shares *his* generic name with Wovoka—the Ghost Dance prophet associated with the uprising and violence at Wounded Knee, who renamed himself Jack Wilson after being adopted into a white family.[8] Literary doubles typically reflect what is repressed in each other, and these two characters are revealed to be selves equally founded on nothing, on stories invented to take the place of a devastating lack of knowledge. The novel's Jack Wilson is a best-selling mystery writer and former cop who passes himself off as a member of a no-longer-existing Shilshomish tribe and whose books, according to the Spokane student activist Marie Polatkin, are "killing Indian books" (Alexie 1996, 68). Whereas the white Jack constructs an imagined and profitable Native genealogy for himself, the Indian John sustains dispossession and losses of origin so profound that his position as a construction worker on Seattle skyscrapers perfectly illustrates his own suspended and dangerous distance from the ground of his own history and self. Indeed, it is precisely because of his profound self-alienation that Smith, a man who "had no definition for what he was" (276), is such a phantom figure in the text.

While critics and reviewers consistently identify John Smith as insane or schizophrenic, he might more accurately be described as a ghost, for his radical self-abandonment brings him into a closeness to death. His dis-ease is positioned in the novel as the effect of cultural genocide rather than of an individual psychopathology.[9] As Marie Polatkin says, "John was dead from the start" (Alexie 1996, 417); he is earlier described as a man who feels "less than real" (17). But as a ghost, John Smith is also the phantom product of white liberalism's soft violence.[10] Adopted at birth by a wealthy white couple who seek to provide him with stability, love, and resources for learning about Indians, Smith is nevertheless a man without an identity, in a condition of permanent alienation. Wilson, on the other hand, who "grew up white and orphaned" and was passed around between "eleven foster families," succeeds precisely where Smith fails, by creating an Indian identity for himself based on the images he finds in books (157). Much like Smith, Wilson fantasizes about someday finding the family that he has invented for himself, and struggles and fails to be accepted by the local Indian community. While both figures are presented as suspects in the Indian Killer case, the menace embodied by the Indian killer is represented by the two men as a doubled pair—dispossession and appropriation, ghost and ghostwriter—who end the novel in a struggle at the top of Seattle's last skyscraper, suspended at an immeasurable distance from the ground of their own identities.

The doubles in Alexie's Indigenous gothic reveal the haunting erasures created by America's history of colonization and genocide. In interviews and literary work, Alexie has discussed the Indigenous holocaust by repeatedly drawing explicit parallels between the historical experiences of Indians and Jews. A poem in *First Indian on the Moon* titled "The Game between the Jews and the Indians Is Tied Going into the Bottom of the Ninth Inning" aligns the two communities as victims of genocidal violence, and the poem "Inside Dachau," which appears in *Summer of Black Widows*, argues, according to one critic, that "America needs to acknowledge and construct monuments to the massacres and genocide of Indians" (Grassian 2005, 140). In her subtle reading of that poem, Laura Arnold Liebman maintains that the poem's speaker acknowledges his ignorance of and incommensurability with victims of the Nazi concentration camp, but that the poem ultimately seeks resolution and healing through a "bridge of difference" (2005, 552–57). *Indian Killer* eschews this elegiac mode for the gothic, however, and stages a meeting between self and other not on a sustaining horizontal bridge of difference but in a terrifying vertical space of darkness.

When Alexie complains that reviewers would not so easily dismiss in books by Primo Levi or Elie Wiesel the anger they disliked in *Indian Killer*, he is, of course, arguing that the extermination of Indians in America must be recognized alongside the atrocities of the Jewish Holocaust and South African apartheid, and that this rage needs to be recognized as a valid response to sustained ethnic violence.[11]

The Indigenous gothic of *Indian Killer* exposes the genocidal violence on which traditional gothic and its delighted audience feeds, and it moreover compels an experience of loss that is fundamental to an alternative encounter with the other. In *Existence and Existents*, a book he conceived during his internment by Nazis during World War II, Levinas describes the terror of night in a way that echoes Alexie's description of the proximity between the killer and the killer's actual and potential victims: "When the forms of things are dissolved in the night, the darkness of the night, which is neither an object nor the quality of an object, invades like a presence. In the night, where we are riven to it, we are not dealing with anything. . . . There is no longer *this* or *that*; there is not "something." But this universal absence is in its turn a presence, an absolutely unavoidable presence. . . . Its anonymity is essential" (1978, 52).

The darkness of night generates an insecurity that, Levinas insists, "does not come from the things of the day world which the night conceals" but "is due just to the fact that nothing approaches, nothing comes, nothing threatens." He continues, "This silence, this tranquility, this void of sensations constitutes a mute, absolutely indeterminate menace. The indeterminateness constitutes its acuteness" (53–54). The strangely tranquil horror described by Levinas and conjured by Alexie is very different from a fear of death (remember, for example, that the "frightened" and "gagged" Mark Jones responds by feeling "something familiar, and almost comforting" in the touch of the killer), very different from a fear that is generated around a desire to protect and preserve the self associated with traditional gothic and the sensations of the sublime or the uncanny. The horror described by Levinas designates instead a "stripping" of the self so profound that "the subject is depersonalized" and death actually becomes impossible (56). Within this framework, horror is generated not by the threat of death but by the experience of nonexistence.

Yet it is only within such a terrifying experience that, for Levinas, an ethical encounter with the other is possible. Levinas insists that this encounter with the other can happen in a meaningful way only if the self is "itself submerged by the night, invaded, depersonalized, stifled by it" (53). To the extent that the Indigenous gothic of Alexie's *Indian Killer* invites its readers into an indeterminate darkness inhabited by the absent presence of Native ghosts and Native stories and encourages a fearful collapse of self and knowledge, what makes the book disturbing is precisely what might make it ethical in this Levinasian sense, for ethics derive, for Levinas, from "an encounter with the Other which puts the self into question" (Davis 1996, 5). *Indian Killer* erases rather than produces certainty, it empties out rather than accumulates knowledge, it releases rather than endorses readers' understanding of what it might mean to be "Indian" or even of what it might mean to "be." In the process of encountering such absences, the colonialist self—which depends for its own self-definition on the marginalization of those it oppresses—is forced to vanish.

Indian Killer challenges literary convention by refusing to identify "the killer," but even when it temptingly and tauntingly presents potential suspects or candidates—including the erotically paired figures of John Smith and Jack Wilson—it deliberately exposes the identity of those characters as utterly obscure. I have suggested that by continually reminding us that we do not know, the novel *Indian Killer* might itself be seen as a killer of the word "Indian" and all that word might mean or has come to mean, of all that non-Indians think they know or hope they will learn when they see the word. The character who best represents the self-assured colonialist possession of knowledge about the other is the liberal university professor Dr. Clarence Mather (who also serves as a kind of political double for the conservative racist Truck Schultz, who is equally assured of his "knowledge" that Indians are, essentially, still savages).

The chapter titled "Deconstruction" is one of several set in Mather's

Introduction to Native American Literature class, where the student Marie Polatkin is provoked by Mather's contrast of the Indian killer to Jack Wilson's "fictional alter ego, Aristotle Little Hawk" (Alexie 1996, 246) and by Mather's pretensions to know what "being Indian" means. She challenges Mather's certainty that either Jack Wilson or the Indian killer is in fact Indian, asking, "You think you know more about being Indian than Indians do, don't you? Just because you read all those books about Indians, most of them written by white people. By guys like Jack Wilson." The uncertainty, she points out, is in the very name, since "calling him the Indian Killer doesn't make any sense." She adds, "If it was an Indian doing the killing, then wouldn't he be called the Killer Indian? I mean, Custer was an Indian killer, not a killer Indian." Marie asks Mather—clearly an updated version of Cotton Mather, the colonial New England Puritan divine who sought to "save" many young women from their possession by Indians or by witchcraft—to confront his own assumptions when she says of herself, "I'm not an Indian warrior chief. I'm not some demure little Indian woman healer talking spider this, spider that, am I? I'm not babbling about the four directions. Or the two-legged, four-legged, and winged" (247).

Marie is not only challenging Mather's claims to knowledge, but also aiming to leave him in a conceptual darkness as profound as that he experiences upon losing consciousness when, believing that he is being pursued by the killer, he runs headfirst into a pipe in the basement of his building. She tells him, "You love Indians so much you think you're excluded from our hatred" (Alexie 1996, 313). She later informs him, "If the Ghost Dance worked, there would be no exceptions. All you white people would disappear. All of you. If those dead Indians came back to life, they wouldn't crawl into a sweathouse with you. They wouldn't smoke the pipe with you. They wouldn't go to the movies and munch popcorn with you. They'd kill you. They'd gut you and eat your heart" (314). Marie's exchange with Mather resembles John Smith's with Jack Wilson, when John terrifies Jack out of possession of his self and into an encounter with the blank and frightening emptiness of what he does not know about the other and, therefore, what he does not know about himself.

Although her terrain is not explicitly the gothic, Sharon Holland has recently argued that black subjectivity inhabits a space of death. Like Goddu and Bergland, Holland (2000) builds on the work of Toni Morrison, who insists, in *Playing in the Dark*, "Invisible things are not necessarily 'not-there'; . . . a void may be empty, but is not a vacuum. In addition, certain absences are so stressed, so ornate, so planned, they call attention to themselves; arrest us with intentionality and purpose, like neighborhoods that are defined by the population held away from them" (1992, 11).[12] We might use Morrison's insight to think not just about the crowded absences within particular texts but about those crowded absences within literary genres or traditions. For instance, we can see traditional American gothic, in Morrison's terms, as a kind of generic "neighborhood" dependent for its pleasurably haunting effects on the nonwhite populations held away from it (or killed off within its pages). Holland's study locates the raised bodies and voices of the dead in literary and cultural productions by African Americans and Native Americans and provocatively suggests, "Perhaps *some* people are ready to die because the space imagined—the place of death—is not a dead space but a living space; perhaps, even with the advent of imperialism and nationalisms, a bit of the power of Indigenous thought—the importance of the dead in life—has seeped into an otherwise finite and closed space. People do not die, therefore, for a national invention, but they die so that they might be able to attach themselves to an idea of life before the alien invaders" (2000, 26). I would add that it may also well be that this space of death is for the disempowered a far safer space than the space of the living in which to express rage. *Indian Killer* thus joins the kinds of texts Holland examines to animate this alternative neighborhood, to give shape and form to this phantom backdrop to dominant history and traditional gothic.

But Alexie is not just replying to a European tradition of the gothic with an Indigenous reversal; he is also invoking throughout his novel the religious traditions that developed in the post-contact period among Native American tribes in the Plateau region. Many of the religious traditions that have developed in the region of what is now eastern Washington, northern Idaho, and western

Montana, where the Spokane and Coeur d'Alene tribes are located, depend on a powerfully spiritualized realm that connects the living with the dead. Traditions such as the Prophet Dance, the Washat or Seven Drum religion, and the Feather cult all point toward the world-transforming possibilities of raising the dead. The Prophet Dance, for instance, involves a circular dance around a leader who "made prophecies obtained in visions usually experienced during 'death-like trance states,' followed by a reawakening or 'rebirth'" (Walker Jr. and Schuster 1998, 500).[13] Within the Washat religion, the Wanapam religious leader Smohalla prophesied "a revitalization of tribal cultures in which the dead would be brought back to life and Whites would be banished from Indian lands" (501), much like the Ghost Dance of the Plains Indians. The Feather cult was founded by a Klikitat Indian named Jake Hunt out of the experience of mourning the death of his wife and desiring to revive her from the dead. The cult is described as "an ecstatic healing sect, with ritual and ideology influenced by both shamanism and the Washat religion" and in which "curing was accomplished by possession of spirit power, manifested by a rapid spinning movement, with eagle feathers held aloft" (511). Cultural beliefs among the Coeur d'Alene Indians likewise suggest that the dead continue to inhabit the space of the living, since "after death, a person's spirit survived to become a ghost that remained near the grave, wandered its accustomed places, and tried to visit people it had known" (Palmer 1998, 319).

These post-contact Plateau religious traditions establish not a boundary but a passageway between life and death, or, perhaps more accurately, conceive of life and death as folded within and over each other in a way that enables the dead to have material effects on the living and in the present. Of course, when Alexie has publicly identified himself with a religion it has been with none of these but rather as a "Spokane Indian Catholic" (Highway 1997). Yet the Catholic Christianity that has influenced and informed Alexie certainly has its own religious accounts about the power of figures who return from the dead and has its own practices that connect the living with the dead.[14] Although the novel integrates these various and already hybridized religious histories, it would seem to be the Native religious and spiritual traditions and their alliance with the better-known Ghost Dance that animate the performance at the very end of *Indian Killer*. The book's brief final chapter, titled "A Creation Story," takes place in a "cemetery on an Indian reservation" (Alexie 1996, 419), where the following ominous gathering commences:

> The killer spins in circles and, with each revolution, another owl floats in from the darkness and takes its place in the tree. Dark blossom after dark blossom. The killer sings and dances for hours, days. Other Indians arrive and quickly learn the song. A dozen Indians, then hundreds, and more, all learning the same song, the exact dance. The killer dances and will not tire. The killer knows this dance is over five hundred years old. The killer believes in all masks, in this wooden mask. The killer gazes skyward and screeches. With this mask, with this mystery, the killer can dance forever. The killer plans on dancing forever. The killer never falls. The moon never falls. The tree grows heavy with owls. (420)

At its conclusion, *Indian Killer* leaves its readers positioned, as if they were the boy Mark Jones, within a menacing and indeterminate darkness inhabited by a faceless killer. But the empty features of the Indian killer are a response to the same colonialist story of theft that the forced adoption of John Smith and the fictional adoption of Jack Wilson both tell.

The well-meaning Daniel and Olivia Smith, the eager-to-belong Jack Wilson, and the self-satisfied Clarence Mather might all be seen as colonialist ghostwriters whose efforts—motivated by a disavowed liberal indulgence—kill, more than they sustain, Indians. Wilson is writing a novel called *Indian Killer* that he believes will "finally reveal to the world what it truly meant to be Indian" (Alexie 1996, 338) but that he is meaningfully unable to write. Alexie's novel called *Indian Killer* deliberately refuses its readers the knowledge they desire about Indians, which so many books ghostwritten by whites promise to deliver to them, just as it deliberately refuses the affective pleasure that the conclusions to conventional gothic novels provide. In place of the pleasurable haunting of the white liberal gothic, *Indian Killer* offers a menacing darkness, a terrifying indeterminacy, a present absence that invokes the return of the dead promised by many Plateau-region religious traditions and characterized by an anger that is explicitly positioned as the product of a continental history that has itself been septic with anti-Indian rage. By inviting its readers into an encounter with the other that requires a compensatory loss of self, *Indian Killer* marks the arrival of an Indigenous gothic.

NOTES

I thank Juliana Chang, Kate Morris, and Jennifer Trainor for their helpful readings of and responses to earlier drafts of this article.

1. See Reneé Bergland for a discussion of this speech in the context of native hauntings within the white national imaginary.

2. See Stokes for a brief discussion of Alexie's treatment of "story-colonizing by non-Native writers" (2002, 45–46).

3. With the exception of the review by Owens, these reviews are all by white critics. While Owens sharply criticizes the book and aligns himself with other Native critics (such as Gloria Bird and Elizabeth Cook-Lynn) in finding Alexie's work problematic, his position does not represent any "unified" Native response. Indeed, Alexie's own comments about Indian responses to *Indian Killer* are, perhaps purposefully, contradictory. In one 1998 interview he is asked, "What about Indian readers?" He replies, "They were into it. It was the first time somebody sort of put on paper the feelings we have" (Donadoni 1998). In another review (Campbell 2003), on the other hand, he is quoted as saying that *Indian Killer* "sold by far the least of all [his] books," adding, "Indians didn't like it."

4. It is rare to come across any account of or interview with Alexie that does not refer to this anger. The *New York Times*, in a brief 1997 piece, for instance, observed in an interview with Alexie, "You're clearly angry, especially at whites who try to 'connect' by immersing themselves in Indian culture" ("Questions," 1997). See Dean for another discussion of this critical response to the novel (2008, 32), and Van Styvendale for a discussion of the role of anger within the novel (2008, 210–12).

5. In particular, Hollrah argues that Alexie's stated "desires to reach a larger audience, get attention, and at the same time realistically expect that white scholars will not write about his works as they teach them in Native American literature classes" are contradictory and "unlikely to happen simultaneously in the near future" (2001, 32). She bemoans his refusal to "offer any solutions or suggestions for white scholars" (32)—although we

might well read his silence on that issue as its own pointed anti-colonial tactic. Alexie has elsewhere suggested that whites writing about Native Americans produce "books by members of the privileged, of the powerful, writing about the culture that has been colonized" and explicitly need to identify their work as colonial (Fraser 2001).

6. I am indebted to Juliana Chang for her insightful observation that anger can serve as a "rubric by which to know the Other."

7. See Chen for a brief discussion of how *Indian Killer* "challenges the assumptions and desires of a readership trained to read for points of identification rather than alienation" (2005, 164). I discovered Chen's essay, which brings Alexie and Levinas into dialogue around the question of the ethics of reading, while completing my own.

8. For other accounts of Smith and Wilson as doubles, see Grassian (2005, 121) and Fritsch and Gymnich (2003, 216). For an analysis of doubles in Alexie's *Reservation Blues*, see Jorgensen (1997).

9. Cyrus Patell has argued that this novel dramatizes "an idea articulated by Frantz Fanon in *The Wretched of the Earth*: that colonizers inflict cultural damage upon those whose lands and minds they invade" (1997, 4).

10. Smith might be seen as a "monstrous" product of such Frankensteinian desire. Interestingly enough, Alexie puts such an observation into ironic terms when he has the novel's conservative and incendiary radio talk show host Truck Schultz insist during an on-air racist rant that "we've created a monster"—although Truck believes this monster has been created by "coddl[ing] Indians too long" instead of "terminat[ing] Indian tribes from the very beginning" and "assimilat[ing them] into normal society long ago" (Alexie 1996, 209).

11. See, for instance, the interview with Fraser (2001) where Alexie aligns the United States and South Africa, claiming "the only difference is about 50 years, not even that much."

12. Holland (2000), like Goddu (1997) and Bergland (2000), refers to Morrison's lecture "Unspeakable Things Unspoken," which later developed into *Playing in the Dark* (1992), from which I quote here.

13. Anthropologists disagree about whether these features of the Prophet Dance represented a response to the conditions of disease, depopulation, and socioeconomic disorganization brought about by European contact or whether they represent a development of traditional Salish culture (Walker Jr. and Schuster 1998, 500).

14. Consider, for instance, the figure of Father Duncan, the Indian Jesuit priest who has disappeared but whom John sees, in visionary dreams, walking across a desert—a landscape that symbolizes the no-man's-land of identity that he (like John) inhabits. When queried by a young John, Father Duncan identifies himself doubly, with both the victims and the perpetrators,

in a stained-glass-window image that depicts the violent abuse of Indians by the Jesuits. For a brief discussion of Alexie's Catholicism, see Blumberg (2000, 133).

WORKS CITED

Alexie, Sherman. 1996. *Indian Killer*. New York: Warner Books.

Bergland, Renée L. 2000. *The National Uncanny: Indian Ghosts and American Subjects*. Hanover NH: University Press of New England.

Blumberg, Janet. 2000. "Sherman Alexie: Walking with Skeletons." In *Literature and the Renewal of the Public Sphere*, ed. Susan VanZanten Gallagher and M. D. Walhout, 122–38. New York: St. Martin's.

Brogan, Kathleen. 1998. *Cultural Haunting: Ghosts and Ethnicity in Recent American Literature*. Charlottesville: University of Virginia Press.

Burke, Edmund. 1990. *A Philosophical Enquiry into the Origin of Our Ideas of the Sublime and Beautiful*. Ed. Adam Phillips. Oxford: Oxford University Press. (Orig. pub. 1757.)

Campbell, Duncan. 2003. "Voice of the New Tribes." Review of Sherman Alexie's *Indian Killer*. *Guardian Unlimited*, January 4.

Chen, Tina. 2005. "Towards an Ethics of Knowledge." *MELUS* 30 (2): 157–73.

Christie, Stuart. 2001. "Renaissance Man: The Tribal 'Schizophrenic' in Sherman Alexie's *Indian Killer*." *American Indian Culture and Research Journal* 25 (4): 1–19.

Davis, Colin. 1996. *Levinas: An Introduction*. Notre Dame IN: University of Notre Dame Press.

Dean, Janet. 2008. "The Violence of Collection: *Indian Killer*'s Archives." *Studies in American Indian Literatures* 20, no. 3 (Fall): 29–51.

Donadoni, Serena. 1998. "Talking with the Writer: Way beyond Tonto." *Metrotimes*, July 8. http://www.metrotimes.com/movies/filmarchive/18/41/smokesb.html.

Egan, Timothy. 1998. "An Indian without Reservations." *New York Times*, January 18, 191.

Fraser, Joelle. 2001. "Sherman Alexie's *Iowa Review* Interview." Repr. from *Iowa Review*. http://www.english.uiuc.edu/maps/poets/a_f/alexie/fraser.htm.

Fritsch, Esther, and Marion Gymnich. 2003. "'Crime Spirit': The Significance of Dreams and Ghosts in Three Contemporary Native American Crime Novels." In *Sleuthing Ethnicity: The Detective in Multiethnic Crime Fiction*, ed. Dorothea Fischer-Hornung and Monika Mueller, 204–23. Madison NJ: Fairleigh Dickinson University Press.

Giles, Gretchen. 1996. "Seeing Red: Author Sherman Alexie Is One Angry

Young Man." *Metroactive*, October 3. http://www.metroactive.com/papers/sonoma/10.03.96/books-9640.html.

Goddu, Teresa. 1997. *Gothic America: Narrative, History, and Nation.* New York: Columbia University Press.

Grassian, Daniel. 2005. *Understanding Sherman Alexie.* Columbia: University of South Carolina Press.

Highway, Tomson. 1997. "Spokane Words: Tomson Highway Raps with Sherman Alexie." *Aboriginal Voices* 4, no. 1 (January–March): 36–41.

Holland, Sharon. 2000. *Raising the Dead: Reading of Death and (Black) Subjectivity.* Durham NC: Duke University Press.

Hollrah, Patrice. 2001. "Sherman Alexie's Challenge to the Academy's Teaching of Native American Literature, Non-Native Writers, and Critics." *Studies in American Indian Literature* 13, nos. 2–3 (Summer–Fall): 23–35.

Jorgensen, Karen. 1997. "White Shadows: The Use of Doppelgängers in Sherman Alexie's *Reservation Blues*." *Studies in American Indian Literatures* 9, no. 4 (Winter): 19–25.

Levinas, Emmanuel. 1978. *Existence and Existents.* Trans. Alphonso Lingis. Pittsburgh PA: Duquesne University Press.

———. 1989. *The Levinas Reader.* Ed. Seán Hand. Oxford: Blackwell.

Liebman, Laura Arnold. 2005. "A Bridge of Difference: Sherman Alexie and the Politics of Mourning." *American Literature* 77 (3): 541–61.

McFarland, Ron. 1997. "Sherman Alexie's Polemical Stories." *Studies in American Indian Literatures* 9, no. 4 (Winter): 27–38.

Mitchell, Justin. 1996. "Well-Crafted Thriller Riveting, but Caricatures of Whites Jarring." *Rocky Mountain News*, October 20, 31D.

Morrison, Toni. 1992. *Playing in the Dark: Whiteness and the Literary Imagination.* New York: Random House.

Nicholls, Richard E. 1996. "Skin Games." *New York Times Book Review*, November 24, 34.

Ott, Bill. 1996. "Review of Sherman Alexie, *Indian Killer*." *Booklist* 93, no. 1 (September 1): 5.

Owens, Louis. 1998. *Mixedblood Messages: Literature, Film, Family, Place.* Norman: University of Oklahoma Press.

Palmer, Gary. 1998. "Coeur D'Alene." In Walker, *Plateau*, 313–26.

Patell, Cyrus R. K. 1997. "The Violence of Hybridity in Silko and Alexie." *Journal of the American Studies of Turkey* 6:3–9.

"Questions for: Sherman Alexie." *New York Times Magazine*, January 5, 8.

Ross, John Alan. "Spokane." In Walker, *Plateau*, 271–82.

Skow, John. 1996. "Lost Heritage: Rage Sours the Eloquent Novel *Indian Killer*." *Time Magazine* 148, no. 19 (October 21): 88.

Stokes, Karah. 2002. "'Was Jesus an Indian?': Fighting Stories with Stories in Sherman Alexie's *Indian Killer.*" *Kentucky Philological Review* 16:44–47.

Vanderwerth, W. C., ed. 1971. *Indian Oratory: Famous Speeches by Noted Indian Chieftains.* Norman: University of Oklahoma Press.

Van Styvendale, Nancy. 2008. "The Trans/Historicity of Trauma in Jeannette Armstrong's *Slash* and Sherman Alexie's *Indian Killer.*" *Studies in the Novel* 40, nos. 1–2 (Spring–Summer): 203–23.

Walker, Deward E., Jr., ed. 1998. *Plateau.* Vol. 12 of *Handbook of North American Indians*, ed. William C. Sturtevant. Washington DC: Smithsonian Institution.

———, and Helen H. Schuster. 1998. "Religious Movements." In Walker, *Plateau,* 499–514.

2

Violence on the Home Front in Robinson Jeffers's "Tamar"

GENEVA M. GANO

World War I was not "the Good War." Americans in general were reluctant to become involved in what was widely viewed as a "European war" (Wilson's successful presidential campaign slogan in 1916 was "He kept us out of war"), and the draft did not help foster general enthusiasm for it. Among artists and intellectuals, the war was even less popular. Randolph Bourne, an influential writer and critic associated with the radical little magazine *Seven Arts*, declared that "war is the health of the state," and Jane Addams, the progressive reformer and peace activist, maintained that war in general is destructive to democracy. Modernists, including Ezra Pound, Ernest Hemingway, Willa Cather, and others, wrote about it repeatedly, portraying it as the culmination of a bankrupt Western culture.

As a group, the American avant-garde sought to understand the relationship of the nation's present to its past, especially its violent colonial past. As John T. Matthews has shown in other American writings from the period, "The prospect of American engagement more immediately became an opportunity to address pre-existing problems on the home front."[1] The genocidal dispossession of Native peoples, as a number of Americans were coming to acknowledge, was one such "pre-existing problem," a blot on the nation's history that could not be ignored, that had to be reckoned with.

Robinson Jeffers, hailed in the 1920s as "the most impressive poet the U.S. [had] yet produced," was an unlikely antiwar activist. By all accounts, he was a reticent man, unwilling to speak out about contemporary political problems and much more content to write about the beauty of the Big Sur region on the California coast. Yet Jeffers's response to the devastation of World War I was especially profound. In his writing, he imagines the war as an instance of divine punishment for the nation's collective sins: the extreme violence of Anglo-American imperialism was finally being punished by the ghosts of Native peoples taking their vengeance. That is to say, the episodes of horrifying violence in World War I were ones for which the United States was culpable.

Jeffers's sensational narrative poem, "Tamar" (1923), set at the beginning of the war, interrogates the relationship of the present to the past in a number of ways. This interrogation is most pointed in the poem's climactic scene, when Indian ghosts interrupt a séance in which the title character attempts to contact her dead aunt. The ghosts force Tamar to adhere to "Indian customs" that require her to strip naked, dance in Indian fashion, and submit to a sexual ritual. This essay considers the implications of the scene, focusing in particular on its racial and national meaning in a post-World War I context. I argue that for Jeffers, the story of California's Native Americans and the story of America's World War I dead are analogous in that both represent the nation's legacy of injustices. In "Tamar," the Great War can be seen as an instance of cosmic redress, serving as a potent reminder of the sins of our fathers, the horrors of the nation's past that we have hidden and repressed.

"Tamar" and other poems from Jeffers's first commercial volume, *Roan Stallion, Tamar, and Other Poems* (1925), were widely acknowledged to "reverberate with echoes of the horrors in which humanity was submerged" during the war.[2] Some of these poems refer to the war explicitly, in their titles, such as "Woodrow Wilson (February, 1924)" and "The Truce and the Peace (November, 1918)." Others register the effects of the war more subtly, such as the short lyric "Natural Music," in which the human terror of "the storm of the sick nations" impedes the ability to hear the "one language" of nature (*Collected Poems* [CP] 1:6). "The Coast-Range Christ," one of Jeffers's earliest narratives to be included, takes as its subject a draft dodger. The poem from the volume that would become his best known, "Shine, Perishing Republic," begins with a reference to American involvement in the war:

> While this America settles in the mould of its vulgarity,
>   heavily thickening to empire,
> And protest, only a bubble in the molten mass, pops and
>   sighs out, and the mass hardens,
>
> I sadly smiling remember that the flower fades to make fruit,
>   the fruit rots to make earth.[3]

The poem's speaker concludes his counsel by advising his sons to "distance" themselves from America and its sins, declaring that "corruption / never has been compulsory," a reference, perhaps, to compulsory military service, instituted for the first time in U.S. history during World War I. The volume's success—both commercial and critical—attests to the sympathy his antiwar, even anti-nationalist, views evoked.[4]

Jeffers's assessment of the war as a catastrophe, and his sense that the past may hold clues to the problems of the present, was shared by other artists and intellectuals at the time. Though initial opposition to U.S. involvement in World War I was widespread, most Americans were brought on board in support of it once the United States joined the Allied forces on the battlefields of Europe. In the years following the war, however, U.S. nationalism raged, the League of Nations collapsed, and the progressive and radical Left staggered under overwhelming repression. In this context, artists and intellectuals in particular began to challenge the hegemonic meaning of the war as evidence of humanistic progress toward good.[5] Reassessing the meaning of the war—and the U.S. leadership that led its citizenry into war—prompted a reconsideration of U.S. history in general. The always-important celebration of "Indigenous" themes in history, ones that traced the development of a distinctively non-European, "American" character, was pursued with a new vigor. This was especially urgent for Americans who did not want to imagine their country going the way of the morally—and, now, economically—bankrupt countries of Europe, and who preferred to think of the United States as an exceptional nation.

A typical expression of Americanism in the arts might be found in a letter from Edgar Lee Masters to Robinson Jeffers in December 1927. Masters, who had made a pilgrimage to Carmel to meet Jeffers and who corresponded with him occasionally, wrote to him about his "favorite subject of the greatness of American literature to be." This literature would, predictably enough, specifically address what Masters considered to be American themes, set in the distinctively American West. As Masters wrote to Jeffers: "I began to think of you, and to wish that you would try some of these things—somehow—someway—if it comes to you—hoping that it will come to you. There's the gold rush; there's the Mormon movement; there's Kit Carson and Daniel Boone, and many more. What are Miles Standish, or hired men or Miniver Cheevy or others to such characters and stories, belonging as they do to the magical expansion of the country, the republic when it began to feel its oats?"[6]

Jeffers never directly took up Masters's suggestion—at least not with the same intentions: in Jeffers's estimation, U.S. history, and the expansion of the country in particular, was riddled not with magic but with shameful and immoral acts. We might consider his 1928 poem, "A Redeemer," as a response of sorts to Masters's request. In this poem, one of Jeffers's heroes, a hermit and self-styled savior of mankind, sums up a very different vision of U.S. history than that of Masters:

> They have done what never was done before. Not as a
>   people takes a land to love it and be fed,
> A little, according to need and love, and again a little;
>   sparing the country tribes, mixing
> Their blood with theirs, their minds with all the rocks and
>   rivers, their flesh with the soil; no, without hunger
> Wasting the world and your own labor, without love
>   possessing, not even your hands to the dirt but plows
> Like the blades of knives; heartless machines; houses of steel;
>   using and despising the patient earth . . .

> Oh as a rich man eats a forest for profit and a field for
>   vanity, so you came west and raped
> The continent and brushed its people to death. Without
>   need, the weak skirmishing hunters, and without mercy.[7]

When compared to Masters's celebration of Boone, Carson, and the like, "A Redeemer" reads like revisionist history.

Masters and Jeffers represent extreme, opposing versions of a more widespread reexamination of U.S. history by artists and intellectuals at this time. Many felt pride in the nation while being uncomfortable with the familiar stories and characters of American history that celebrated U.S. expansion, financial power, and technological innovation. Chief among them was Van Wyck Brooks, whose 1918 essay in the *Dial*, "On Creating a Usable Past," argued that the traditional institutions charged with making the national past known and relevant, the universities, had failed young Americans by providing them with examples of capitalist success instead of artistic and spiritual heroism.

Though Brooks himself did not turn to American Indians as examples of genuine native authenticity (like Masters, he remembered only Anglo-American heroes), a number of similarly minded "Young Americans" did. These included Waldo Frank, whose *Our America* (1919) traced to Indigenous peoples an alternate lineage of American culture ; William Carlos Williams, who wrote his own history of the Americas, one that dealt heavily with Europeans' encounters with Native Americans, *In the American Grain* (1925); and Hart Crane, who wrote *The Bridge* (1930), a poetic exploration of national history along the same lines.[8] One of the most influential of these reassessments of U.S. literary and cultural history, *Studies in Classic American Literature* (1923), was penned by the Englishman D. H. Lawrence, whose deep interest in the subject (not to mention his residency near Taos, New Mexico, during the 1920s) might qualify him as an "honorary American."[9] Lawrence counseled Americans to "listen to [their] own," to glean artistic inspiration from American sources, including "the Red Indian, the Aztec, the Maya, [and] the Incas."[10]

The search for an authentic national history upon which to base new forms of art was mingled with the primitivist celebration of Indigenous arts and lifestyles.[11] On the one hand, the "Young Americans" admired Indians because they seemed to possess that which modern Americans felt they didn't have, including spirituality, community, tradition, and a deeply felt connection with their homeland. They located within Native American bodies, arts, culture, and religion the foundational elements of an authentic, "Indigenous" American culture.[12] As "substitute ancestors," Indians provided these liberal young intellectuals with an alternate lineage from which they could imagine themselves to have descended.[13] Ironically, even though the "Young Americans" thought of themselves as admirers and supporters of Indians, their celebration of Indians arose from a nationalist impulse: they "claimed continuity with a culture on whose destruction their country had been built."[14]

Jeffers differed from the Young Americans in that he hardly believed that Indians—or, better put, the idea of Indians—might help redeem the souls of white Americans in the present. In the poem "New Mexican Mountain," Jeffers considers the relationship between Taos Indians performing the Corn Dance and the white Americans, including himself, who watch.

> I watch the Indians dancing to help the young corn at Taos
>   pueblo. The old men squat in a ring
> And make the song, the young women with fat bare arms,
>   and a few shame-faced young men, shuffle the dance.
>
> The lean-muscled young men are naked to the narrow loins,
>   their breasts and backs daubed with white clay,
> Two eagle feathers plume the black heads. They dance
>   with reluctance, they are growing civilized; the old men
>   persuade them.
> . . . .
> These tourists have eyes, the hundred watching the dance,
>   white Americans, hungrily too, with reverence, not
>   laughter;

> Pilgrims from civilization, anxiously seeking beauty, religion,
> poetry; pilgrims from the vacuum.
>
> People from cities, anxious to be human again. Poor show
> how they suck you empty! The Indians are emptied,
> And certainly there was never religion enough, nor beauty
> nor poetry here . . . to fill Americans.[15]

The "reluctant" "shuffle" of the young men is a symptom of "growing civilized"; that is, more like the Americans who have come to watch. The phrase "pilgrims from civilization," which Jeffers changes within the same line to "pilgrims from the vacuum," indicates the bitter irony of the word "civilization": it is the so-called civilized that seek redemption in the highest forms of culture—"beauty, religion, poetry"—from the so-called savages. And there can be no question that the Americans, not the Indians, are the actual savages. Vampire-like, the Americans "hungrily" suck the life from the Indians until they are emptied. Their needs are insatiable: "Certainly there was never religion enough, nor beauty nor poetry here . . . to fill Americans." If any doubts remain that becoming Americanized, which is here akin to becoming "civilized," is itself an unenviable prospect, the poem concludes by asserting that "civilization is a transient sickness."

While Jeffers frequently broods on Indians who have been murdered and dispossessed in the past, in this poem he considers the situation of living Indians in the present. Yet even these Indians, having contracted the debilitating disease of civilization, seem more dead than alive. In contrast to the Americans, whose hunger transforms the usually passive role of watching to an "anxious" attempt to satiate their hunger, the (reluctantly) dancing Indians have been reduced to a passive, zombie-like state. This contrast is reflected in the poem's grammar, as the poet apostrophizes, "Poor show, how [the Americans] suck you empty!" accusing the Americans of actively, if not necessarily malevolently, trying to fill themselves with what they think the Indians have. The Indians, on the other hand, are revealed as victims. Immediately following this statement, the poet describes the Indians with the passive-verb construction, "The Indians are emptied," evacuating them as well of a living, resisting agency.

At the cost of rendering the Indians passively (though not sentimentally), Jeffers stresses the evil of the European Americans, responsible for the genocide of Native Americans and the destruction of their cultures in the first place. "A Redeemer" expresses a sense that white Americans needed to atone for what they had already taken from Indians. The title character imagines himself as a Christ-like savior who suffers for the actions of white Americans, going so far as to pierce the palms of his hands in imitation of the stigmata of crucifixion: "There never . . . was any people earned so much ruin. / I love them, I am trying to suffer for them." While nothing in his writings suggests that Jeffers loved his fellow Americans as such, the sense of guilt for the American extermination of Indian peoples that the man expresses is registered in a number of Jeffers's poems, including an unpublished poem from 1921, "Shells":

> The Mission Spaniards
> Came and enslaved, Spain's soldiers came and murdered
> Or bastardized, and we God's choice of slayers
> Who first debauch and then exterminate
> Tribe after tribe following the evening star
> Have nearly ill-finished what Spain ill-began.[16]

The dripping sarcasm of the phrase "God's choice of slayers" indicates Jeffers's revulsion at the actions of "God's chosen people"; his pronoun "we" in the same sentence acknowledges the acts as part of a horrible national legacy that he, too, has inherited.

Jeffers's sensational, career-making narrative poem "Tamar" details the fall of the house of Cauldwell, in which a family isolated on the rural California coast confronts its past, only to be torn apart by revelations of incest that reverberate through the family line. The extreme violence of the poem, the dream visions and otherworldly happenings that punctuate it throughout, and its ominous wartime setting give it an unforgettable, nightmarish feeling. It is literally a story of domestic collapse: the poem concludes with the Cauldwell home in flames and the family trapped within, the burning rafters falling inward, and the floor shifting beneath their feet. The four-line coda assures us that all have perished:

> Grass grows where the flame flowered;
> A hollowed lawn strewn with a few black stones
> And the brick of broken chimneys; all about there
> The old trees, some of them scarred with fire, endure
>   the sea-wind.[17]

The poem's underlying World War I context suggests that this narrative of domestic apocalypse may be read as an allegorical critique of U.S. involvement in the war, even though the poem's representative American soldier, Lee Cauldwell, never actually makes it to the wartime front. Indeed, he thinks fondly of war as an escape from a nightmarish world at home:

> Slowly, he had taken five drinks in Monterey
> And saw his tragedy of love, sin and war
> At the disinterested romantic angle
> Misted with not unpleasing melancholy,
> Over with, new adventure ahead, a perilous cruise
> On the other ocean, and a great play of guns
> On the other shore. (CP 1:68)

To this childish fantasy his aunt caustically provides a dose of realism, though whom it is directed toward is ambiguous: "A man that's ready to cross land and water / To set the world in order can't be expected / To leave his house in order" (CP 1:68).

Of course, the "house" to which Aunt Stella refers is the Cauldwell home and the family it shelters. But in setting the house in opposition to "the world," which is tellingly located across the Atlantic, Aunt Stella indicates that the house also serves as a synecdoche for the nation. A symbolic reading of the house is encouraged early in the poem, as the patriarch Old David Cauldwell observes that "it seemed that nightmare / Within the house answered to storm without" (CP 1:21). Though, in this instance, the "storm without" is literally a tempest that is racking the Big Sur headlands, we need look no further than Jeffers's poem "Natural Music" (published in the same volume as "Tamar") to connect "the storm of the sick nations" to World War I.[18] In closing the gap between what is "within the house" and what is "without," Jeffers minimizes distinctions that might be made between the United States and the other nations involved in the war. Though "Tamar" registers his antiwar sentiments, Jeffers was not typical of isolationists, who tended to defend their position by noting that the United States was historically and geographically distinct from Europe. To Jeffers the climate of the United States in the twentieth century was not exceptional among nations but every bit as liable to unrest as the European one that was "storm[ing] without" the national and continental borders.

Because the house signifies both the nation and the family home, the Cauldwells can be understood as a representative (if not exactly typical) American family. The Cauldwells' sins and sicknesses, then, point toward those of the nation, which conceives of itself as the culmination of Western culture as a whole. Not restricted solely to a perverse family at the continent's end, this sickness is actually quite widespread. In this light, Tamar's observation, just before seducing her brother, that their feelings and actions can be explained by their shared heritage and environment is especially chilling: they grew up in "the withered house / Of an old man and a withered woman and an idiot woman," she says. "No wonder if we go mad, no wonder" (CP 1:24). Her rationale applies to a whole generation that has inherited its illnesses, indeed to a whole Western civilization on the skids.

To read the poem this way is to consider the nightmarish scene that opens "Tamar" as particularly suggestive:

A night the half-moon was like a dancing-girl,
No, like a drunkard's last half-dollar
Shoved on the polished bar of the eastern hill-range,
Young Cauldwell rode his pony along the sea-cliff;

When she stopped, spurred; when she trembled, drove
The teeth of the little jagged wheels so deep
They tasted blood; the mare with four slim hooves
On a foot of ground pivoted like a top,
Jumped from the crumble of sod, went down, caught,
    slipped;
Then, the quick frenzy finished, stiffening herself
Slid with drunken rider down the ledges,
Shot from sheer rock and broke
Her life out on the rounded tidal boulders. (CP 1:18)

Set in December 1916, just as the United States was teetering toward involvement in World War I, the poem presents young Cauldwell's fall as a nation's fall. The excessive violence of the spurring and the decadence suggested by the images of "dancing-girl" and "drunkard" result in the mare's death, a senseless waste of life that foreshadows that which the war will demand. In an allegorical reading, representative Americans such as Lee Cauldwell do not merely blunder innocently into the deadly fray, but are drawn inevitably into the war through the results of their own actions in the present and the past. Similarly, neither Tamar nor her brother is wholly culpable for their sin or capable of preventing it, as it is "fore-dated" (CP 1:33) by the sins of an older generation. Allegorically speaking (since the family stands as a synecdoche for the nation), the narrative refuses to lay blame for the nation's current problems on the modern generation. The problems of the present, Jeffers suggests, are American inheritances, long-standing and—perhaps—even inevitable. The chickens, as Malcolm X (or Ward Churchill) put it, have come home to roost.

In "Tamar," Jeffers considers inheritance—both national and familial—at length. Most intimately, this involves the title character's discovery of the family legacy of incest: she finds out that her sexual relationship with her brother was preceded by her father's sexual relationship with his sister, her Aunt Helen. Tamar turns to the past for answers to the predicaments of the present when, secretly pregnant with her brother's child and carrying on a sexual relationship with her neighbor, she decides to consult the dead. Accompanied by her Aunt Stella, a medium, Tamar goes to the beach one August night in order to communicate with her deceased Aunt Helen through a séance.

At this point, the narrative, already unconventional because it graphically depicts sexual seduction and broaches the taboo topic of incest, becomes quite bizarre. Her family's secrets are not the only sordid stories Tamar discovers. As the séance reveals, her familial past is inseparable from the national past. Tamar not only is visited by the spirit of her dead aunt, but also inadvertently conjures the ghosts of those civilizations that made their homes on the Big Sur coast. As a precondition to the discovery of her familial heritage, Tamar Cauldwell must reckon with the literal "spirits" of place: the "unavenged" ghosts of the "lost hunters / Our fathers hunted," as Jeffers puts it in "The Torch-Bearer's Race," the poem that immediately precedes "Tamar" in the published collection.[19] Tamar is possessed by the spirits, first dancing naked then submitting to multiple rapes by them. The past directly affects the present and future: Tamar's consort with the dead results in a miscarriage, ensuring that a future generation will not go on to propagate the evils of the past.

This is a complicated, if fascinating, moment in the poem, not least because the Indian ghosts seem gratuitous and sensationalistic: their appearance in the poem does not serve any apparent narrative purpose; their power and violence is extreme, overshadowing even the poem's graphic accounts of incest; and they seem to distract from the poem's other concerns, including the effects of modernization and the world war on a remote community in California and the complex relationship between humans and the natural world. No explanation is given in the text for the Indians' intercession in Tamar's search for answers to questions about her family's past, making the ghosts seem little more than unexplainable specters of Jeffers's own mind, vivid and imaginative at best, racist and sordid at worst. It is little wonder that few critics have attempted to account for the presence and actions of the Indian ghosts. Yet the scene, I think, is crucial to an understanding of Jeffers's conception of an American national inheritance and the special place that Indians have in it. In

"Tamar" the appearance of Indian ghosts links contemporary acts of American imperialism in World War I to the violent legacy of the nation's colonial history, ultimately enabling Jeffers to critique American brutalities in both the past and the present.

Jeffers's interest in genealogy—especially the genealogy of place—is evident in this poem and elsewhere. In a letter to his bibliographer, Sidney Alberts, Jeffers meditated on the genealogy of the foundations of his home in Carmel, which he built with stones he had hauled up from the tideline, writing, "The soil that I dig up here to plant trees or lay foundation-stones is full of Indian leavings, sea-shells and flint scrapers; and the crack-voiced churchbells that we hear in the evening were hung in their tower when this was Spanish country. Where not only generations but races drizzle away so fast, one wonders the more urgently what it is for, and whether this beautiful earth is amused or sorry at the procession of her possessors."[20]

This procession is first invoked in "Tamar" when Tamar has a dream or vision of the dead. In this vision, first brown-skinned families, then Spaniards, then English speakers, including her own mother, "came down the river and wandered through the wood to the sea, and hearing the universal music / Went where it led them and were nothing" (CP 1:34–35).

As her dream-vision foreshadows, Tamar encounters the voices of other peoples who have lived in the region before she makes contact with her Aunt Helen. As Victoria Freeman observes in her essay in this volume, such ghostly spirits "signify much more than individual ancestors; they embody the continuity of the people as a whole" (225). The first spirit to speak through the medium is a man who speaks in Spanish, the Spaniards being among those who immediately preceded the Anglos in inhabiting the region. He asks, "Que quieres pobrecita?" to which Tamar replies, "Morir" (CP 1:43), then adds, "Es porque no entiendo, / Anything but ingles." The intrusion into the poem of untranslated Spanish underscores the cultural difference between Tamar and the man: his language is an index of his otherness, which is "anything but ingles." Her words reveal just how important it is that she learn to understand (*entender*) that which is radically other; indeed, she already has begun to do so. Despite her claim not to understand his words, she replies intelligibly, and the combination of English and Spanish in which she responds further minimizes the differences between them. Both other and yet somehow the same, the Spanish-speaking ghost serves here as a mediating or transitioning figure between the Indians and the Americans. In fact, the Americans have more in common with the Spanish than they might think, as the poem "Shells" indicates when it equates the acts of the Mission Spaniards with those of the Americans.

A more radical education in cultural understanding is yet to come for Tamar. The next voice that emerges from Stella's mouth is unrendered in the narrative: it is so foreign that its representation is neither inscribed nor imagined in the text of the poem. Fortunately for Tamar (and for us), a translator speaks through Stella: "An Indian. He says that his people feasted here and sang to their Gods and the tall Gods came walking / Between the tide-marks on the rocks; he says to strip and dance and he will sing, and his Gods / Come walking." He explains, "the pregnant women / Would always dance here and the shore belongs to his people's ghosts nor will they endure another / Unless they are pleased" (CP 1:44). Though living Indians have been supplanted by Mexicans and then Americans, the ghosts of the Ohlone Indians continue to be able to claim possession over the land and demand that their successors conform to their cultural traditions. This *genius loci* has otherworldly powers; indeed, powers that can invert the contemporary cultural conditions to not only reveal those originary possessors of the place, but to reinvest them with authoritative power.[21]

Tamar's response to the Indian is more violent than her response to the Spanish speaker: she tells him that she "will not" dance, and to "go away" multiple times. At the same time,

> Her hands accepting alien life and a strange will undid the
>   fastenings of her garments.
> She panted to control them, tears ran down her cheeks, the
>   male voice chanted
> Hoarse discords from the old woman's body. (CP 1:44)

At this moment in the narrative, Tamar crosses the cultural divide, dancing as instructed. Though Tamar mentally resists the Native American "spirit of the place," "all her body / Obeyed it," and "invited the spirits of the night" (CP 1:45). The ghosts, in turn, "came swaggering along the tide-marks unto Tamar, to use her / Shamefully and return from her, gross and replete shadows" (CP 1:45). Recalling the actions of Americans in "A Redeemer," in which it is Americans, not Indians, who assert their dominance by "using and despising" and "rap[ing]" the Indians and their land, in the séance the roles are reversed. As the object of the Indian ghosts' revenge, Tamar is identified with America—not the continent, but with the Anglo people who imagine themselves to be God's chosen people.[22] In this sacred space, along the tideline, a past in which Native Americans were culturally dominant is, as C. Jill Grady and Colleen Boyd propose in this volume, "anchored and authenticate[d]" by ghostly encounters (Boyd, 186). Jeffers proposes that such a past persists in the present, and, as the poem indicates when Tamar loses the Anglo-American child she is carrying, that it continues to assert its original authority in the future as well. At this point in the poem, such a subversion of cultural power is no longer rejected by Tamar; as her dance indicates, she has already shed her American identity for an Indian one.

As Tamar becomes identified with the Native American women she (apparently) is channeling, the Western metrical tradition is abandoned in favor of free verse. The visual appearance of the poem reflects the shift as the lines become shorter and more irregular.

> So Tamar weeping
> Slipped every sheath down to her feet, the spirit of the place
> Ruling her, she and the evening star sharing the darkness,
> And danced on the naked shore
> Where a pale couch of sand covered the rocks,
> Danced with slow steps and streaming hair,
> Dark and slender
> Against the pallid sea-gleam, slender and maidenly
> Dancing and weeping . . .

It seemed to her that all her body
Was touched and troubled with polluting presences
Invisible, and whatever had happened to her from her two
    lovers
She had been until that hour inviolately a virgin,
Whom now the desires of dead men and dead Gods and a
    dead tribe
Used for their common prey . . . dancing and weeping,
Slender and maidenly . . . The chant was changed,
And Tamar's body responded to the change, her spirit
Wailing within her. (CP 1:44–45)

Tamar's "slow steps and streaming hair" recall conventional images of the "dark and slender" Indian maiden, which is reinforced with the repetition of the words "slender and maidenly." The repetition of "danced" and "dancing" invoke the sound of the drum, the dactyl and trochee in the phrase "dancing and weeping" mimicking the beat. The ellipses further signify something—we don't know what, since it is elided—alien to the Western tradition, as alien and uninscribable as the words of the Indian's ghostly speech.

    The shift in the poem's formal strategies indicates a shift in Tamar's racial and national allegiance. This occurs through the act of the sexual dance in which she undergoes a bodily transformation from typical American to one "driven westward . . . [to] hang at the land's hem."[23] The idea that dance might serve as a vehicle for cultural transformation—and particularly an act through which Anglo-Americans could "break free" from their own, repressive cultural traditions—was a fairly widespread one in the United States at the time Jeffers was writing.[24] The founders of "exotic" dance in America, Ruth St. Denis and Ted Shawn, operated the Los Angeles—based dance company, Denishawn, which was known for performing dances (and wearing costumes) that were inspired by American Indians.[25] Denishawn's most famous prodigy, Martha Graham, believed that while dancing she felt her body become the site of cultural and national transition and transformation: "There are always ancestral footsteps behind me, pushing me, when I am creating a new dance, and gestures are flowing through me. . . . You get to the point where your body is something else and it takes on a world of cultures from the past."[26] Between the wars, modern dance such as that epitomized by Graham became, as Susan Manning asserts, an "arena for the forging of national identity" (CP 1:36), which was, in turn, inseparable from racial identity.[27]

More literally than Graham, Tamar becomes possessed by otherworldly "cultures from the past"; when Native American ghosts, embodying "the spirit of the place," "rul[e] her": her body defies her mind, truly becoming "something else." In this poem, dance enables "the imaginary boundary between self and Other [to be understood as] not just fluid and dynamic but actually as permeable."[28] As the dance historian Ramsay Burt suggests, "Because dance uses the body as its primary means of expression, early modern dancers using 'primitive' dance material literally embodied this ambivalence when their encounters with the Other led to loss of self as their bodies became the alien bodies of these Other."[29] Tamar, that is, "becomes" Indian. The "polluting presences" of the Native American ghosts that "touched and troubled" "all her body" register Tamar's sense of (and revulsion toward) the national and racial difference that Indian bodies signify. "Anxiety over national boundaries (cultural, geographical) was equated [during the interwar period] with concern over bodily boundaries, pollution and degeneration," Burt writes. "Dance, whose primary means of communication is of course the body, therefore became a locus of anxieties over loss of national and racial identity as a consequence of the impact of modernity."[30] The Indian ghosts' sexual violation of Tamar's bodily boundaries in the dance prompt her own national and racial crossings.

Until the moment of miscegenous contact in the dance, Tamar remains, "whatever had happened to her from her two lovers, . . . inviolately a virgin." That is, Tamar's "virginity" depends on the kind of sexual experience she has, with a clear line drawn between interracial and intraracial sex. If, as Walter Benn Michaels proposes of other works of modern American literature, the wish to maintain the racial purity of the nation and family is signaled by a character's incestuous desires, Tamar's desire for her brother early in the narrative can be said to reflect her racial and national introversion, her essential (Anglo) Americanness.[31] Because Indians are quite clearly portrayed here as racial and cultural others, the sexual content of the dance can be understood to serve as a foil to Tamar's prior sexual relationship with her brother. Her transformation from Anglo-American virgin to sensual Indian maiden to "wanton," "beastlike" savage is a supreme act of cultural and racial crossing. It marks the conclusion not only of her racial introversion but of her childhood as well.[32]

At first, Tamar is broken. Her Aunt Helen finds her "humbler" than she was. She remarks, "She has been humbled, my little Tamar. And not so clean as the first lover left you, Tamar" (CP 1:46). For Helen, incest maintains one's "purity," whereas the "fouling" Tamar endures makes her despicable. This suggests that, for Helen, Tamar's uncleanliness is a result not of having sexual relations in general, but of the specifically racial crossing that the dance signifies. Her disdainful refrain, "you danced, Tamar" (CP 1:48), laden with racist meaning, is the great insult she hurls at her niece. "As for me, I chose rather to die" (CP 1:46). Though initially resistant to dancing and overwhelmed by a sense of the "pollut[ion]" of the Indian ghosts, Tamar comes to understand her experience as an empowering and purifying one. She is not humbled, but becomes defiant, standing "naked and not ashamed" (CP 1:57). Further, she maintains, "We pure have power," a very different idea of purity than Helen's version of it.

Tamar miscarries her brother's child after the dance, ensuring an end to the legacy of introversion that plagues the Cauldwell family. With the loss of her child, Tamar is freed to sever social ties with her family, culture, and nation. After the dance, Tamar no longer refers to Helen as her "aunt," but as her "father's bitch" (CP 1:47). In the scenes that follow, she rejects her brother and father as well. In her first interaction with Lee after the séance, she is enraged by his insistence that she is his sister: "What can I say except I love you, sister?" "Why do you call me sister, / Not Tamar?" (CP 1:53). In addition, she orders Old Cauldwell, "Tell God we have revoked relationship in this house, he is not / Your son nor you my father" (CP 1:62).

43

Inasmuch as the family stands in for the nation, Tamar's denial of family allegiance may be understood as a denial of national allegiance. As it often is in Jeffers's poetry, this is figured in "Tamar" as geographic distance. Taunting her brother and "standing dark against the west in the window" of the west-facing bedroom, she declares, "My brother can you feel how happy I am but how far off too? / ... / ... if I were standing back of the evening crimson on a mountain in Asia / All the fool shames you can whip up into a filth of words would not be farther off me, / Nor any fear of anything" (CP 1:74). "Far off" in the west (from the perspective of the California coast, Asia is the Far West), Tamar is free from family and nation.

A later poem, titled "Come Little Birds" (1940), clarifies the séance scene in "Tamar" as both an indictment of America's attempts at Native American genocide and an instance of antinational, antiwar resistance. This shorter poem recalls "Tamar" topically, in that its subject is a séance that takes place near the mouth of the Sur River. A more direct reference to "Tamar" comes at the end of the lyric, when Tamar Cauldwell appears in the poem as a spirit who has been called forth. She runs toward the poet–speaker and says, "I am Tamar Cauldwell from Lobos: write my story. Tell them / I have my desire."[33] In this poem, a procession of spirits emerges during the séance, but they are not specters of America's violent colonial past; they are ghosts from the more recent imperial present. They are soldiers from the Great War who have something to communicate:

> ... one leaned toward me
> Saying "Tell my mother." "What?" I said. "Tell her I was well enough
> Before that old buzzard waked me. I died in the base-
>   hospital—" Another of the forms crossed him and said
> "God curse every man that makes war or plans it." (This was in nineteen twenty, about two years
> After the armistice.) "God curse every congressman that voted it, God curse Wilson."[34]

The soldiers replace the Indian ghosts as the "unavenged" spirits who had been wronged by Americans; their condemnation of the war and the leaders of the American government make explicit the anti-nationalism that is implicit in "Tamar."

Admittedly, the unquiet spirits these poems feature are unlikely equivalents, representing the objects and agents of U.S. imperial violence. Yet while we routinely think of the common soldier as a symbol for the U.S. military and its policies, the synthesis of soldier and policy was perhaps, at the time, less secure than it may now seem. In part, this was due to the institution of the draft in 1917, which forced young men to serve in the war regardless of their inclinations. But it was also due to the fact that the notion was widespread at the time—even beyond the Socialist circles that most loudly proclaimed the idea—that the United States was drawn into the war by the power and money of hawkish, wealthy capitalists, not by a true consideration of the interests of the wider American public.[35] That is to say, the common soldier could be seen as a victim of a compromised national government that used its military to back the business interests of the powerful elite. In substituting soldiers for Indians in his later poem, Jeffers implies that the ghosts of California's Native Americans and the ghosts of U.S. soldiers in World War I are both victims of the nation's imperialist bloodlust.

The spirit of Tamar Cauldwell makes a third appearance in Jeffers's "Apology for Bad Dreams" (1925), linking it to the other two poems. In this poem we are reminded again of the Big Sur coast's Indian past and the ghosts that remain as souvenirs: "All the soil is thick with shells, the tide-rock feasts of a dead people. / Here the granite flanks are scarred with ancient fire, the ghosts of the tribe / Crouch in the nights beside the ghost of a fire." "Apology for Bad Dreams" explicitly tells us what the Indian ghosts should mean to "we living" now:

> These have paid something for the future
> Luck of the country, while we living keep old griefs in
>   memory: though God's
> Envy is not a likely fountain of ruin, to forget evils calls
>   down

> Sudden reminders from the cloud: remembered deaths be
> our redeemers.[36]

The commonly held view that Indians are a "dead people," having vanished from the land in all but spirit, is a useful one to Jeffers, though not because such a notion renders Indians impotent or irrelevant in the present. Indeed, when Jeffers invokes ghosts in poems throughout his career—including, frequently, his own ghost—he imbues them with a special power, authority, perspective, and wisdom at which the living can only grasp.[37] As "Apology for Bad Dreams" and "Tamar" show, the spirits of the dead intervene in the events of the present, even calling forth "sudden reminders" of retribution.

In imagining the ghosts of dead Indians as the potential "redeemers" of living Americans—the statement "remembered deaths be our redeemers" is more of a plea than a command—Jeffers clarifies and delimits his interest in Indians. They are crucial primarily because they serve as figures of chastening and warning to modern-day Americans who may otherwise be too confident about their status as exceptional people. This is evident in a later poem, "Hands" (1928), which contemplates the meaning of the handprints left by aboriginal peoples in a cave near Tassajara, also in the region. After proposing that they could have been intended for "Religion or magic, or made their tracings / In the idleness of art," Jeffers concludes that they

> . . . are now like a sealed message
> Saying: "Look: we also were human; we had hands, not
>   paws. All hail
> You people with the cleverer hands, our supplanters
> In the beautiful country; enjoy her a season, her beauty, and
>   come down
> And be supplanted; for you also are human."[38]

One of Jeffers's purposes here seems to be to stress the humanity of the Essalen Indians and level the differences between them and the "cleverer" people, which he achieves through the repetition of the word "human" and the wry claim that "we had hands, not paws." The conclusion of this short poem forces us to reconsider the sincerity of the word "cleverer," since, in the light of the similar fates of Indian and white peoples, the word is evacuated of meaning. Just so, we should reread the command "All hail" as ironic, if not sarcastic, for the same reasons. By acknowledging that the handprints of the Essalen Indians meant something unique to them that is inaccessible to him, Jeffers grants them a complex subjectivity: we can hardly expect or even desire that Jeffers might presume to know their "true" meaning. Even so, his contemplation of the meaning for the Essalen is cursory. In emphasizing the meaning the hand paintings seem to have for Anglo-Americans, the "supplanters," Jeffers relegates Indians (or the idea of Indians) to a symbolic status that may be instructive—should they be humble enough to understand it as such—to white Americans in the present and future. Ultimately, even though "Hands" attempts to dismantle racist hierarchies that proposed that "primitives" such as Indians were subhuman and that the white Americans to whom the poem is addressed were of a "cleverer" species, the poem's emphasis on what white people can learn from Indian artifacts reveals the limits of Jeffers's intellectual engagement of Indians.

Why consider Indians at all, then? Are they really necessary to Jeffers's conceptions of the American past, present, and future? "Jeffers was not a cultural relativist or even much interested in Native America, but he had a sense of justice and fate. He saw that an amputated past not only starves the present but poisons it," writes David Rains Wallace. "The phantasmagorias of his narratives are the fevers and exhalations of that poison."[39] Jeffers's career-long attempt to "keep old griefs in memory" by returning to the scene of conquest, genocide, and attempted extermination in his poems indicates that his interest in Native America was probably more extensive than Wallace acknowledges.[40] Still, Wallace's underlying point is an important one: Indians, as the victims of a violent and unjust American people in the past, were central figures in Jeffers's conception of the nightmarish present. The present horrors—the world war being the most terrific example of these—are absolutely inseparable from the horrors of the past.

The very act of confronting the familial and national past—espe-cially its Indian past—may be interpreted as a threat to U.S. nationalism in the present: it destabilizes "the dominant culture['s] construct[ion of] . . . nationalisms as stable and timeless ideas" by reminding us of the area's pre-American history. It also records Indian resistance to incorporation into the nation.[41] According to Benedict Anderson, a national project of collective forgetting of such ancient (or, in the case of California, not-so-ancient) bloody enterprises as the U.S. military annexation of northern Mexico and the attempted extermination of the West's native peoples is a "prime contemporary civic duty."[42] Contra prevailing contemporary con-figurations of American Indians that would describe them as having "vanished" in some nebulous, inevitable fashion, Jeffers emphasizes that they have been, as Freeman points out, "actively dispossessed" by white Americans (222, in this volume). On a national level, at least, remembering these evils constitutes an act of treason.

Threatening though it may be, "keep[ing] old griefs in memory" does not seem, in Jeffers's view, to sufficiently atone for our national sins. Tamar's very intimate understanding of the brutalities of Ameri-can conquest is not completed with the end of the dance, after which she may return to her life as it was. The evils of the past are not safely confined to history and memory but threaten the present and even (as Jeffers puts it in "Apology for Bad Dreams") "the future luck of the country." In "Tamar," this threat is delivered upon: the Indian ghosts' "sudden reminder" of their "old griefs" results in Tamar's miscar-riage and in the destruction of the house and all of its occupants. The violence the Indian ghosts wreak upon Tamar and her family goes beyond a mere "reminder" of the brutalities they endured. Instead, she is on the receiving end of a divine retribution, paid in kind.

The retribution the Indian ghosts dole out is only a fragment of what Indians had received at the hands of Americans in the past: their treatment of Tamar is symbolic rather than comprehensive. Tamar herself—after "becoming" Indian in the poem's climax—is the source of the cosmic justice that is visited upon America. That an Anglo-American of Calvinist heritage such as Jeffers might issue a jeremiad in poetic form, warning that the nation must pay for its

sins, is unsurprising. Yet Jeffers, a pantheist of sorts, definitively parts
ways here with his Calvinist forebears. While these thought Indians
to be the minions of Satan, Jeffers establishes them as the agents of a
divine—though not Christian—justice.[43] The purifying fire that Tamar
calls forth at the poem's conclusion, while aligned with the Christian
apocalypse, promises no redemption for the family's souls: as Old
Cauldwell projects, there will be nothing waiting for them but "eternal
death, eternal wrath, eternal torture, eternity, eternity, eternity" after
the judgment (CP 1:73). The final words Tamar utters in the poem
definitively link the apocalypse with the Great War, redefining the
war as punishment, an act of divine judgment, not one of American
triumph. Mocking her soldier-to-be brother, she asks, "Did you think
you would go / Laughing through France?" (CP 1:97).

Both the poet and the title character confront this past and
reap the results. Initially, Jeffers (and "Tamar" in particular) was
applauded, as his sentiments seemed to reflect the spirit of the age.
In her important volume, *The New Poetry* (1932), Harriet Monroe
judged that "the post-war disillusion that almost smothered our
youngest generation, the black pessimism that was the first reaction to the realization that science and machinery, undirected, were
leading us into a blind alley, and the sharp revulsion from the performances of democracy—all these attitudes find congenial echoes in
the poems of Jeffers."[44] But by the late 1930s, as the nation geared
up for a second world war, Jeffers's anti-American feelings fell out
of favor, and, as James Shebl and others have shown, his career suffered for it.[45] Tamar's bodily assumption of the role of the mediator
of colonial struggle enables her to understand the devastation of U.S.
imperialism; this new knowledge spurs both her attempt to prevent
her brother from going to war, and her broader rejection of familial
and national bonds. Tamar's single-minded desire to burn the family
home down to its foundation is driven, at least in part, by her act of
confronting and acknowledging the nation's own faulty foundations.

NOTES

*I would like to thank the Harry Ransom Humanities Research Center at
the University of Texas at Austin and the Henry E. Huntington Library,*

49

San Marino, California, for supporting the research for this project. I also thank the editors of this volume, Coll Thrush and Colleen Boyd, for their wise guidance during the revision process, and the members of the Robinson Jeffers Association, who heard a presentation based on the research for this essay and contributed valuable feedback.

1. John T. Matthews, "American Writing of the Great War," *Cambridge Companion to the Literature of the First War*, ed. Vincent Sherry (Cambridge: Cambridge University Press, 2005), 217.

2. Charles Cestre, "A Review of *Roan Stallion, Tamar, and Other Poems*," *La Revue Anglo-Americaine* 4, no. 6 (August 1927): 489–502, trans. L. C. Powell, Robinson Jeffers Collection, Harry Ransom Center, University of Texas at Austin.

3. Robinson Jeffers, *The Collected Poetry of Robinson Jeffers*, ed. Tim Hunt, (Stanford CA: Stanford University Press, 2000), 1:15.

4. Within the first eight years after the publication of *Roan Stallion, Tamar, and Other Poems* by Boni & Liveright in 1925, the collection went through eleven printings. See Tim Hunt, "Introduction," in Jeffers, *Collected Poetry*, 1:xxv.

5. See Thomas Fleming, *The Illusion of Victory: America in World War I* (New York: Basic Books, 2003); David M. Kennedy, *Over Here: The First World War and American Society* (Oxford: Oxford University Press, 1980); Cecilia Elizabeth O'Leary, *To Die For: The Paradox of American Patriotism* (Princeton: Princeton University Press, 1999).

6. Edgar Lee Masters to Robinson Jeffers, December 8, 1927, Robinson Jeffers Collection.

7. Jeffers, *Collected Poetry*, 1:406–7.

8. Waldo Frank, *Our America* (New York: Boni & Liveright, 1919); William Carlos Williams, *In the American Grain* (New York: New Directions, 1925); Hart Crane, *The Bridge, A Poem* (New York: Liveright, 1930).

9. D. H. Lawrence, *Studies in Classic American Literature*, ed. Ezra Greenspan, Lindeth Vasey, and John Worthen (Cambridge: Cambridge University Press, 2003).

10. D. H. Lawrence, "America, Listen to Your Own," in *Phoenix: The Posthumous Papers of D. H. Lawrence*, ed. Edward D. McDonald (New York: Viking, 1936), 90.

11. This complex entanglement of nationalist and racialist thought was not unique to the early twentieth century; indeed, as numerous scholars have shown, white Americans have alternately celebrated and despised Native Americans according to nationalistic needs. Outside of literary studies, these include Helen Carr, *Inventing the American Primitive: Politics, Gender, and the Representation of Native American Literary Traditions, 1789–1936*, (Cork, Ireland: Cork University Press, 1989); Philip J. Deloria, *Playing*

Indian (New Haven CT: Yale University Press, 1998); and Brian W. Dippie, *The Vanishing American: White Attitudes and U.S. Indian Policy* (Lawrence: University Press of Kansas, 1991). Literary analyses have included Renée L. Bergland, *The National Uncanny: Indian Ghosts and American Subjects* (Hanover NH: Dartmouth College Press, 2000); John J. Kucich, *Ghostly Communion: Cross-Cultural Spiritualism in Nineteenth-Century American Literature* (Hanover NH: Dartmouth College Press, 2004); Jeffrey Weinstock, ed., *Spectral America: Phantoms and the National Imagination* (Madison: University of Wisconsin Press, 2004).

12. D. H. Lawrence, "Review of William Carlos Williams's *In the American Grain*," *The Nation* (April 14, 1926); Repr. *Phoenix*, 334

13. Werner Sollors, ed., *The Invention of Ethnicity* (New York: Oxford University Press, 1989); Walter Benn Michaels, *Our America: Nativism, Modernism, and Pluralism* (Durham NC: Duke University Press, 1995).

14. The close ideological relationship between cultural nationalism and cultural imperialism—responsible, at least in part, for the "murder" in the first place—caused "deep political problems for white Americans who claimed continuity with a culture on whose destruction their country had been built" (Carr, *Inventing the American Primitive*, 212).

15. Jeffers, *Collected Poetry*, 2:158.

16. Jeffers, *Collected Poetry*, 4:500–1.

17. Jeffers, *Collected Poetry*, 1:89. Subsequent references to "Tamar" will be cited parenthetically in the text.

18. Jeffers, *Collected Poetry*, 1:6.

19. "The Torch-Bearer's Race," Jeffers, *Collected Poetry*, 1:99.

20. Cited in S. S. Alberts, *A Bibliography of the Works of Robinson Jeffers*, (New York: Random House, 1933), 51.

21. The powers of sacred place are described in Belden C. Lane's *Landscapes of the Sacred: Geography and Narrative in American Spirituality* (New York: Paulist, 1988); and Peter Nabokov's *Where the Lightning Strikes: The Lives of American Indian Sacred Places* (New York: Viking, 2006).

22. As Lawrence Clark Powell puts it, Tamar is a "symbol of the race which drove them from their lands"; L. C. Powell, *Robinson Jeffers: The Man and His Work* (Pasadena CA: San Pasqual, 1940), 69.

23. "The Torch-Bearer's Race," in Jeffers, *Collected Poetry*, 1:99.

24. Jack Anderson, *Art without Boundaries* (Iowa City: University of Iowa Press, 1997); Ramsay Burt, *Alien Bodies: Representations of Modernity, "Race," and Nation in Early Modern Dance* (London: Routledge, 1998); Julia L. Foulkes, *Modern Bodies: Dance and American Modernism from Martha Graham to Alvin Ailey* (Chapel Hill: University of North Carolina Press, 2002); Mark Franko, "Nation, Class and Ethnicities in the Mod-

ern Dance of the 1930s," *Theatre Journal* 49, no. 4 (1997): 475–91; Susan Manning, *Modern Dance, Negro Dance: Race in Motion* (Minneapolis: University of Minnesota Press, 2004).

25. Una Jeffers's references to Denishawn and Ruth St. Denis in her correspondence with Hazel Pinkham indicates her familiarity with modern dance and this company in particular; Una Jeffers to Hazel Pinkham, n.d. [October 7, 1920], Una Jeffers File, Robinson Jeffers Collection. Though he doesn't mention the company in his own writings, Robinson Jeffers was surely aware of the company's doings as well. More directly, his interest in dance must be inferred from his many poems of the period that refer to dance and dancing.

26. Martha Graham, *Blood Memory* (New York: Doubleday, 1991), 13.

27. Susan Manning, "Modernist Dogma and Post-Modern Rhetoric: A Response to Sally Banes' 'Terpsichore in Sneakers,'" *Drama Review* 32, no. 4 (Winter 1988): 36. Burt, *Alien Bodies*; Franko, "Nation, Class and Ethnicities."

28. Ramsay Burt argues that Graham's piece, "Primitive Mysteries," does this as well (Burt, *Alien Bodies*, 189).

29. Burt, *Alien Bodies*, 165.

30. Burt, *Alien Bodies*, 16.

31. Jeffers's comments on his use of the incest theme seem to accord with this interpretation. He writes, "Incest seems to me a fairly appropriate symbol of the immoderate racial introversion which needs pointing out and protesting against"; Robinson Jeffers to George West, January 22, 1926, *The Selected Letters of Robinson Jeffers, 1897–1962*, ed. Ann N. Ridgeway (Baltimore MD: Johns Hopkins Press, 1968), 59. Though Jeffers uses the term "racial" in a broad sense (meaning "human race" rather than "white race"), the procession of races he invokes in "Tamar" and elsewhere indicates that he simultaneously imagines "racial introversion" in a more specifically ethnic and cultural sense.

32. Michaels argues that Tamar and Lee's incestuous relationship is analogous to her sexual contact with the Indians, seeing both as manifestations of a desire for American purity (Michaels, *Our America*, 100).

33. Jeffers, *Collected Poetry*, 3:9.

34. Jeffers, *Collected Poetry*, 3:7.

35. Kennedy, *Over Here*; O'Leary, *To Die For*.

36. Jeffers, *Collected Poetry*, 1:210.

37. Jeffers frequently invokes his own ghost, as in "The Cycle"; and those of ancient English lore, as in "Ghosts in England" ("The Cycle," in Jeffers, *Collected Poetry*, 1:14; "Ghosts in England," in Jeffers, *Collected Poetry*, 2:123–24).

38. Jeffers, *Collected Poetry*, 2:4.

39. David Rains Wallace, "What Ever Happened to Robinson Jeffers?" *Los Angeles Times Book Review* (October 29, 2000): 6.

40. Jeffers wrote poems about Indians—both living (as in "New Mexican Mountain") and dead (as in "Tamar" and "Hands")—and, like many artists in the 1920s, witnessed Indian dances in New Mexico. He also became familiar with living and past Native American traditions through conversations with his neighbor and friend, the anthropologist and linguist Jaime de Angulo; the writer and Indian enthusiast Mary Austin; and later, his son Garth, who received a bachelor's degree in Indigenous anthropology from the University of California.

41. Werner Sollors, "Introduction: The Invention of Ethnicity," in *The Invention of Ethnicity*, ed. Werner Sollors (New York: Oxford University Press, 1989), xiii–xiv.

42. Benedict Anderson, *Imagined Communities*, rev. ed. (New York: Verso, 1991), 200.

43. Bergland, *National Uncanny*.

44. Harriet Monroe and Alice Corbin Henderson, eds., *The New Poetry: An Anthology of Twentieth-Century Verse in English* (New York: Macmillan, 1932), 632.

45. James Shebl, *In This Wild Water: The Suppressed Poems of Robinson Jeffers* (Pasadena CA: Ward Ritchie, 1976).

3
Hauntings as Histories
Indigenous Ghosts and the Urban Past in Seattle

COLL THRUSH

Do places have spirits?

Another way to frame this question is to ask whether places—physical locations and the multiple human histories embedded in them—have distinct identities and are capable of agency. Can a single place be home to a certain kind of history, persistent and cohesive, even across boundaries of time and cultural regime? Can the nonhuman, in the form of organisms, climate, or other entities, define the shape of a place and even its meaning? Can remnants of past societies—ruins, ecological footprints, artifacts—"speak" in active ways for the histories they represent? And can we include the dead, or apparitions of the dead, in this agency? Affirmative answers to these questions have come from many quarters; in this essay, I would like to consider three of them as a way to frame ghosts and hauntings as articulations of place-bound histories in urban space, or as I have called them elsewhere, place-stories.

The idea that particular locations have both identity and agency is central to Indigenous epistemologies of place, in which sites not only have meaning but volition, acting upon the lives of human (and other) peoples. For example, in his collaborations with the Apache of the White Mountain Reservation, the anthropologist Keith Basso found that they understand the landscape as an active force in their individual and collective lives: as one elder described it, geography "stalked" people with stories. These stories—of creation, of distant ancestors human and otherwise, of historical figures, of gossip—give meaning to Apache lives to the extent that entire conversations can be held using only place names. Such connections between lifeway and place are not metaphorical; they are literal.[1] Similarly, Julie Cruikshank learned in her work with Athapaskan and other Indigenous peoples in the Yukon Territory that glaciers can in fact "listen." The rivers of ice, local Indigenous people believe, surge and obliterate, retreat and disappear in response to human behavior—something that, as Cruikshank suggests, we might want to think more about in our age of industrially induced climate change.[2] And from her work among the Coast Salish peoples of British Columbia and Washington, Crisca Bierwert has noted the dialogic nature of Indigenous relationships with places: "The concept of place . . . can imply binary complementarities, like provider and receiver. Place can also subsume reciprocals, like domain and residents. And place can also be collectively created; those who frequent a place become part of one another's ambiance of that place."[3]

Each of these scholars, like the communities they work with, assert that landscapes are ultimately moral arbiters in their own right, responding to and shaping proper and improper human behaviors. Peter Nabokov summarizes a career's worth of work with Native peoples in the United States in terms of what he has learned about how landscapes relate to Indigenous senses of self, community, and past: "The full-bodied role of nonbuilt environments in American Indian history is more than painted canvas backdrops for human events. Mountains, canyons, springs, rivers, and trees often enjoyed the capacity for volition and intentionality. They demanded allegiance to and remembrance of their significance as full players in tribal passages through time. Regardless of when a group historically came to occupy a locale, it commonly felt compelled to construe some "primordial tie" to the topography it hereafter called home."[4] The key phrase here is "full players." For Indigenous societies—not just in the United States, but around the world—springs have intent, canyons have motivations. In other words, places are sentient and have historical agency in their own right, affirmed by generations of embodied human experience.

If the deep inhabitance represented by Indigenous histories provides one window into spirits of place, then another kind of his-

tory, the history of cities, suggests another. Arising as much out
of performance art and leftist politics as from historical scholarship per se, the loose constellation of practices and perspectives
known as psychogeography, first articulated in Paris and London
but increasingly influential in urban thinking around the world, is
predicated upon the notion that urban landscapes contain patterns
of meaning that persist through historical time and that the places
that make up those patterns have distinct identities that shape the
human activities that inhabit them.[5] As the London author (and erst-
while psychogeographer) Peter Ackroyd has written, such patterns
are "territorial clusters," which he defines as "a congregation of
aligned forces, by coincidence or design, remaining active within the
neighborhood of a very few streets." Examples in London's urban
fabric include sites known for political radicalism, places marred
by recurring outbreaks of violence across centuries and millennia,
and even the locations of mundane activities such as the making of
cheese.[6] Such places are not immune to human influence, however;
rather, they resemble the chronotopes of Mikhail Bakhtin, which
he describes as "points in the geography of a community where . . .
time takes on flesh and becomes visible for human contemplation,"
"Likewise," he says, "space becomes charged and responsive to
the movements of time and history and the enduring character of
a people," adding, "Chronotopes thus stand as monuments to the
community itself, as symbols of it, as forces operating to shape
its members' images of themselves."[7] Like Apache, Athapaskan,
or Coast Salish geographies that guide—but are also transformed
by—human behavior, psychogeographies are neither totalizing nor
static but exist in dialogue with culture and history.

But what do Indigenous and urban epistemologies, sentient
landscapes and psychogeographies, really have to do with each
other? Indigenous and urban histories around the world have been
estranged from each other; perhaps nowhere is this truer than in
North America, where Indians and cities exist at opposite ends of
the settler imagination: one represents the past, the other the future.
For all their differences, the last Mohicans or the Beothuks, final
showdowns at Wounded Knees, and lone Ishis wandering out of

the California foothills are variations on the same theme: the inevitable disappearance of Indigenous peoples before the onslaught of modernity, represented above all else by cities. This is true of popular culture, but the academic world, with its dearth of research on urban Indigenous histories—and with the almost total absence of scholarship on the relationship between urbanity and Indigeneity—has given legitimacy to the idea that Indigenous peoples and urban places are somehow mutually exclusive.

Yet, there is an undeniable connection between Indigenous and urban histories: they have occurred in the same locations. And so there is another line of historical inquiry that offers insight into the question of whether places have spirits: environmental history, which is concerned with physical and ideological transformations of particular locations. Among environmental historians, it is standard operating procedure to ascribe agency—usually unthinking agency, but agency nonetheless—to the natural world. Hurricanes depopulate cities; microbes facilitate colonization; wolves refuse to stay inside national parks. Particular places act upon history through their geology, biology, climate, or other inherent physical characteristics, even if they can in turn be transformed by human activity. Similarly, many environmental historians, following the lead of Annales scholars such as Fernand Braudel, work on a scale much larger than the human lifespan in which individual human decisions, even collectively, seem little more than a tiny, faint buzzing against the backdrop of enormous, and often slow-moving, environmental forces.

This essay brings together these three kinds of history, each with its own openness to the possibility that particular locations have both identity and agency, by telling place-based stories of an urban environment that grew up in an Indigenous landscape: Seattle, the largest city on the Northwest Coast of North America, constructed in the Indigenous territories of the Inside People, the Duwamish Coast Salish. Brought into conversation through attention to the transformations of local places, the urban and Indigenous histories of Seattle show that such histories are not mutually exclusive; rather, urban and Indigenous histories—like urbanity and Indigeneity—are in fact mutually constitutive. The particular genre of place-stories emphasized here are those of Indian ghosts: specters of shamans and chiefs, princesses and prostitutes, that are part of Seattle's urban folklore. In addition to highlighting the connections between urban and Indigenous histories that are articulated through place, Seattle's stories of Native ghosts, while reflecting cultural tropes about haunting and colonialism that are ubiquitous in the imagination of North America's settler societies, also resonate with the locally grounded specifics of historical Indigenous–newcomer relationships. In other words, examining ghost stories can be a sort of place-based methodology, in which hauntings gesture toward salient conflicts and patterns in the history of conquest. A ghost, in effect, is a place's past speaking to its—and our—present.

A misanthrope named Joshua Winfield, his already-meager patience with humanity worn thin by the throngs of New England, migrates to Washington Territory in 1874. There, he stakes a claim in a dark, dank hollow some distance from the little sawmill town of Seattle, in what would someday become the city's Mount Baker neighborhood. The site he has chosen is a Duwamish burial ground, still visited by the descendants of the deceased, but this fact does not deter him—in fact, it spurs him all the more forcefully out of characteristic spite. Some nights, though, he finds himself taking refuge, sweat-drenched and resentful, in the cabin of a young couple down the forest path. He loathes telling them of the whispers and fluttering sounds in his rafters, or of the chanting and the shuffling of feet outside his door. These same neighbors will later find him cold and dead on the floor of his little cabin in the hollow, a look of abject terror frozen on his face. He was frightened into eternity by something, *and his neighbors have a good idea what. Or so the story goes.*[8]

In 1911, city workers excavating the grade for a new playground in the Alki Beach neighborhood, near the strand where a small party of Midwesterners straggled ashore in 1851, uncovered human remains. Based on the objects interred with the bodies, it was clear that they had disturbed an Indian cemetery. Word of the discovery spread quickly throughout Seattle, including among local Indigenous people, who feared that a new outbreak of Coming-Out-All-Over (smallpox) might be released by the disturbance: the cemetery was known in local oral tradition, and the dead resting there were understood to have been victims of the epidemics that had ravaged the region in the nineteenth century. They shared their fears with ethnographers working in the area, resurrecting an Indigenous past that lay just beneath the thin veneer of Seattle's urban history.[9] Like their Coast Salish relatives throughout the region, and like many societies around the world, the Duwamish believed that the human dead, like the nonhuman peoples and other spirit forces that inhabited the landscape, could have dramatic effects on the living. In general, the Indigenous peoples of Puget Sound segregated their dead from their living: spatially, by locating cemeteries away from communities; spiritually, by limiting the handling of human remains to certain individuals who carried particular spirit powers, like Wolf, that protected them; and even linguistically, by avoiding use of the deceased's name, or even words that sounded like it, for an extended period of time after death. And among the Indigenous people of Puget Sound, the phantasms most feared were those of the recent dead or of kin; these ghosts vexed the living and put them in great danger, particularly in the rainy winter months when spiritual forces were at their zenith. The ghosts of strangers, on the other hand, were far less dangerous. The greater its entanglement with the living, it was thought, the greater a phantom's power.[10]

These beliefs, carried into the twentieth century by Duwamish people who remained in and around Seattle as it grew, meant that new hauntings could be made possible by events such as the disturbance at the Alki Beach playground. And the events at Alki were hardly unique: throughout Seattle's history, urban development often disturbed the Indigenous dead. No one seems to know what became of the human remains that once filled canoes and cedar boxes high in the branches of trees on tiny Foster Island in Lake Washington; the cemetery was destroyed by logging in the 1870s and a knot of freeway on-ramps traverses the area today.[11] Similar disinterments occurred elsewhere; in the 1880s, for example, bodies wrapped in cedar bark were routinely exhumed during the city's northward expansion into what would become known as the Belltown neighborhood.[12] Whether an Indigenous cemetery actually existed in the Mount Baker neighborhood where Joshua Winfield squatted and died is unknown (indeed, whether Winfield himself ever existed is not entirely clear). Even if his story is apocryphal, it nonetheless both reflects the stock "Indian burial ground" narrative common to many settler societies and resonates with the actual histories of burials and disturbances in the Indigenous territories that became Seattle. The presence of the Indigenous dead, both in settler and Native minds and on the land, suggests that urban and Indigenous histories are not separate but simultaneous.

Near the Duwamish River—or more accurately, near what used to be the Duwamish River; now it is known as the Duwamish Waterway, since it barely looks or works like a river anymore—there is a golf course. On dark nights since at least the 1960s, members and neighbors have seen a naked figure who does a shuffling dance punctuated by leaps and turns on the tightly clipped green and between the strategically placed trees before he suddenly disappears. Ask anyone who has seen him, and they'll tell you: it's the ghost of an Indian medicine man. No surprise there—what else could it be?

In the fall of 1851, a canoe with five occupants slowly made its way up a river on the eastern shore of Puget Sound. The names of two of the men, both Indigenous and serving as guides, are unknown; the other three were Americans named John Low, Leander Terry, and David Denny, who had come in search of places to settle. The river would soon be known as the Duwamish. Had the Americans been able to converse with their guides in Whulshootseed, the local Indigenous language,[13] instead of a crude combination of hand signs and Chinook Jargon (the region's lingua franca) as they moved along the river's tortuous bends, they might have learned the names of landmarks along the way: Canoe Opening, Backwater, Little Bends at the Tail End. They might have learned names derived from the river's abundance: Fish Drying Rack, Much Paddle-Wood, Aerial Duck Net

Place. Their guides might not, however, have mentioned other sites: a boulder covered in shamans' carvings, the home of a malevolent spirit that took the form of a fingerless hand rising from the water, the petrified ruins of a supernatural fish weir. Even if they had spoken of such places, they—both the guides and the places—would surely have been misunderstood: the settlers and their guides spoke two mutually unintelligible languages of landscape. Where Indigenous people saw spirits and nets and carving wood—the wealth of the land as it was and had always been—Denny and the others saw the wealth of the land as it could and would be, expressed in words such as *arable, improvement,* and *export.*[14]

By Duwamish reckoning, nonhuman forces inhabiting the land and water made life possible, and whether they knew it or not, the settlers who would soon arrive would also be shaped by these spirits in the landscape. Just offshore from where the Alki playground would eventually be built and the smallpox victims disturbed, a spirit that gave great wealth and fishing skills lived in a longhouse beneath the waters of Puget Sound, over whose roof salmon schooled. In other places that would become part of Seattle, Thunderbirds nested, bestowing the power of oratory and political acumen. Both the salmon caught and sold to settlers, and the speeches given during treaty negotiations on Front Street, were evidence that the numinous Indigenous landscape informed and affected life in the young sawmill outpost of Seattle.[15]

One of the most powerful elements of the Duwamish landscape was Changes-Its-Face. A serpent of enormous proportions, often described as having antlers like an elk and being capable of seeing in all directions, Changes-Its-Face was both admired and feared for the powers it gave to Coast Salish shamans. Changes-Its-Face lived in at least two places in what would become Seattle, and almost certainly played a central role in the spiritual and medical practices of local Indigenous communities.[16] For the men and women who had responsibilities for doctoring, the arrival of newcomers like the three Americans in the canoe would have dramatic consequences as new diseases such as Coming-Out-All-Over ravaged Indigenous communities in the region. Accounts from the 1850s suggest that such outbreaks often led to shaman-killings, the doctors' ministrations now seeming to do as much harm as good. Combined with the new technologies and religious entities that accompanied settlers, the epidemics reframed the powers in the landscape and the people whose careers arose from those powers. Changes in the land itself could also affect shamans; one stream in what became the neighborhood of Ballard, for example, was home to a spirit that helped shamans retrieve the souls of ill people from the land of the dead. After less than two decades of American settlement, the stream had been fouled by cattle, and in 1880 a doctor whose power likely originated there hung himself nearby. Similarly, in the early twentieth century one Duwamish man told an anthropologist that a Changes-Its-Face had departed from its home on the Lake Washington shoreline in response to urban development.[17]

The dancing shaman on the golf course, then, can be understood as more than a figment of the settler imagination, more than simply a local iteration of other "medicine men" and "witch doctors" of colonial folklore. He also provokes inquiry into Duwamish relationships with nonhuman forces in the landscape, into the history of health and illness in local Indigenous communities, and into the very real costs of resettlement for practitioners of traditional doctoring. The golf course where he dances is in the headwaters of a stream valley known as Sweat House in the local Whulshootseed language, a term referring to a practice that maintained physical and spiritual well-being. According to some local Duwamish people, the valley of Sweat House contained a cemetery; it is also within sight of the Duwamish River and the spiritual sites that Low and Terry and Denny were canoed past in 1851. Indeed, the geography of Seattle's Indian ghosts is largely congruent with the Indigenous geographies that predated the city: they are seen primarily near places where Indigenous inhabitance was the most dense and storied. Such congruence suggests that ghosts can tell us something real about the local, and in this case urban and Indigenous, past.[18]

The Pike Place Market, a jumbled warren of shops and restaurants founded in the early twentieth century, tumbles down the old coastal bluffs to what was once a cobbled beach. Here, cruiseshipsful of tourists stand and wait for a local to buy a salmon from the famous fish-throwing mongers, or crowd in to have their photo taken in front of the very first Starbucks. In the Down Under, the lower floors of the market, a strange presence has been felt and sometimes even seen. It takes the form of an Indian woman in braids and shawl, projecting a feeling of serenity or bathed in a warm, golden light. There are a number of theories about who she is; the most popular is that she is Princess Angeline, the daughter of Chief Seattle. Whoever she is, though, her appearance, some would warn you, is not only a visitation by a kindly spirit—but can also be an omen of impending death, as might be the appearance of an Irish banshee. You can see through her. If you speak to her, she vanishes.

When new settlers arrived in Seattle during its first years, they were often shocked by the numbers of Indigenous people present in the embryonic settlement. Alonzo Russell came in 1853 and recalled years later that "like any boy of fourteen" his "first impressions of Seattle were of the Thousands of Indians standing by."[19] Numerous such accounts exist, penned by settlers who obviously thought they were coming to a little piece of New England or the Midwest on Puget Sound but, upon arrival, found something else entirely. David Kellogg, who also came in the 1850s, recalled later that Seattle was "really more Indian than White!"[20] Indigenous people came to Seattle to seek out new resources such as Western medicines, hoop skirts, or Jesus Christ; to conduct ceremonies and engage in diplomacy with their new neighbors; or, mostly, to work. Without the labor of Indigenous people—as millworkers and laundresses, clam-diggers and house-builders, prostitutes and potato farmers—Seattle would have been just another failed frontier townsite. The necessity of Indigenous labor mitigated the racism of the period, resulting in ambivalent policies such as Ordinance No. 5, enacted when the town incorporated in 1865, which ruled that no Indians could live within the town limits—unless they were employed and housed by a white person.[21]

For many elite families in Seattle, both Indigenous and settler, there were practical reasons to maintain close alliances, despite efforts by the federal government to relocate all Indigenous people to new reservations. In the first years of Seattle's existence, for example, Saneewa, a leader of the Snoqualmie people whose territories lay to the east, regularly visited Arthur Denny, arguably the most powerful man in Seattle and the one credited with its founding, and the relationship was mutually beneficial. As the headman of a community located at the western entrance to the lowest pass across the Cascades, Saneewa provided crucial information about the route, and Denny would be among the first to map that route for a wagon road, calling it Snoqualmie Pass. As for Saneewa, he and many of his people were able to remain in their homeland thanks in part to relationships they built with settler "headmen" such as Denny. In this case, urban and Indigenous ambitions coincided.[22]

Arthur Denny and his family had even closer relations with the family of Seeathl,[23] also known as Chief Seattle, a leader of Duwamish and Suquamish heritage who facilitated the town's founding and who procured Indigenous laborers for settlers. Although Seeathl died in 1866, his family continued to have a strong presence in town, the most notable example being his daughter Kikisebloo or "Princess Angeline." Present at the arrival of the settlers in 1851 and allied closely with the Dennys and other upper-class families, Kikisebloo was a fixture of Seattle society for another half-century. Simultaneously noblewoman and drudge, she elicited a wide range of reactions from settlers. Some revered her as a symbol of the romantic past, case in point being her much ballyhooed introduction to the visiting U.S. president Benjamin Harrison in 1891. Others, however, saw her as an unattractive feature of the urban landscape. Only four years before her death in 1896, one local observer described the "Shantytown" neighborhood around Kikisebloo's home: "What a blemish on this fair and growing city is that particular locality, where scores of shanties, lean-tos, and sheds, holding a heterogeneous mass of humanity, are huddled together—little children with old faces, unkempt men and women, dirty dogs, stray cats, the sewage from unclean sewers pouring down contagion and filth, moral and physical ill-being—all down that hillside, where the tumble-down

dwellings are piled in many cases one over the other."[24] Many settlers, particularly those interested in development, saw Kikisebloo
and other Indigenous people living in town as part of an urban
underclass marked by "moral and physical ill-being," which in turn
marked urban spaces as being in need of what would someday be
called urban renewal.

That the apparition in the Pike Place Market store might be
Kikisebloo makes sense; the city's first public sanitary market was
constructed literally on top of her old neighborhood, less than a
generation after her death. ("Sanitary," in this context, suggests not
just hygiene, but also class and ethnic "cleansing.") And while the
economic contributions of Indigenous people to Seattle's growth
have largely been forgotten, the idea that Kikisebloo might still
wander her old haunts suggests a folk memory of her presence in
the urban landscape, and the ambiguities of the Pike Place Market's
spectral visitation—warm serenity or omen of death—reflect the
ambivalence felt by settler society toward Indigenous people who
insisted on being part of town life. Simultaneously royalty and rev-
enant, emblematic in life and death of both a lost Arcadia and urban
disorder, her ghost speaks to the ambiguities of settler experiences
with and attitudes toward Indigenous peoples and places.

*Located just south of the city along the Duwamish, Georgetown is
an old neighborhood, with Victorian homes tucked amid the airfields
and foundries. One of the grandest of the old houses, known as "the
Castle," did duty as a bordello, a gambling den, and a boarding-
house before falling into disrepair. In the last years of the twentieth
century, an art dealer bought the Castle and began renovating it.
He soon learned he was not alone: disembodied screams, shouts of
"Manny, no!" and loud crashes reverberated from an upstairs room
on some nights. Seeking answers from neighbors and former owners,
he learned that strange things had been taking place in the house for
decades. Then, by chance, he came across a newspaper clipping from
1899, when the house was still a brothel. One night, a young Indian
woman had been murdered in the upstairs bedroom from which the
sounds emanated. Her killer? Why, someone named Manny, of course.*

Elite settler families such as the Dennys had close ties to elite Duwamish families such as that of Seeathl and Kikisebloo, but there was one line they apparently did not cross: they never let those relationships become sexual. That was something "lower-class" people did, and such relationships vexed many town leaders, who thought they brought out the worst traits of both cultures. There was even a term for settler men who had relations, and families, with Indigenous women: *squaw men,* a term that merged powerful ideas about race, class, and gender. To many upper-class settlers, race-mixing caused only chaos and grief, and needed to be prevented. Throughout the 1850s, 1860s, and 1870s, the territorial legislature enacted laws that voided Indian–white marriages, prevented "half-breeds" from voting, or outlawed the inheriting of property by mixed-heritage descendants. Meanwhile, in Seattle and elsewhere, entrepreneurs began to import large groups of single white women who would, by their very presence, fix the "Indian problem." Indigenous women in Seattle, meanwhile, were routinely characterized as prostitutes and associated with the "Lava Beds," the red-light district on the tide flats south of town. In the 1870s Seattle's newspapers printed editorial after editorial warning that Native women would in fact destroy the town, either by drunkenly setting it ablaze or by introducing smallpox or other diseases. Indigenous women and "squaw men" were understood as threats to urban order, and even to the future of the city itself, and means both legal and otherwise were used to limit the presence of Indigenous people in town.[25]

In the twentieth century, one of the primary debates in Seattle, and one on which political careers would turn, centered on the question of the "open town." Would Seattle tolerate vice, or even encourage it by creating an official red-light district? Or would city leaders drive all immorality out of town, relegating the gambling dens and brothels and speakeasies to, literally, marginal status? Such questions, the subject of intense and sometimes violent disagreement, shaped urban politics even though their origins in Indigenous history had been largely forgotten.[26] At the same time, Indians and Indian-ness remained markers of urban disorder. For the poet Richard Hugo, growing up during the Depression in the working-class neighborhoods along the Duwamish River, Native neighbors signified his own inferiority. He wrote that middle-class neighborhoods had "towered over the sources of felt debasement, the filthy, loud belching steel mill, the oily slow river, the immigrants hanging on to their odd ways, Indians getting drunk in the unswept taverns." Nearby, the Hooverville constructed on the filled tide flats was described by some observers in "Indian" terms: the hovels were like those of "the Siberian Chukchee," and prostitutes visiting the encampment were "squaws," whether they were Indigenous or not. Into the late twentieth century, Native people in the city would signify places in need of renewal, particularly in neighborhoods such as the historic Pioneer Square district—the place where the term "skid road" was coined—that had become "Indian territory" and the core of an urban Indigenous community.[27]

The 1899 news clipping about Manny and the murdered girl in the Georgetown brothel is perhaps apocryphal, but the ghost story connected to it nonetheless reflects the fact that Indigenous people—and Indigenous women in particular—were both central to the town's growth and perceived by some settlers as threats to that growth. The ghost of an Indigenous prostitute, not far from the old Lava Beds, speaks to the ways in which class, gender, and race—and conflicting ideas about "vice," and urban order—have been inscribed on the urban landscape, whether in the form of Kiki-sebloo's "shantytown," the "squaws" of Hooverville, or Skid Road as "Indian territory." Even as formerly down-and-out districts such as Georgetown, once associated with poverty and Indigeneity, are refurbished and gentrified, they continue to be haunted by the specters of encounter and exploitation.

Among the upland bogs full of cranberries and marsh tea, a small spring wells up, its iron-rich water staining the clay around it. Native people burned the clay and mixed it with bear grease to create a cinnabar-red ceremonial paint. By 1909, the year of Seattle's first world's fair, the springs are surrounded by a new park and a suburban neighborhood connected to the city by electric trolley. One of the development's promoters, imagining the ghost of an Indian returning to the springs, warns that the uniformed caretaker will escort the specter out of the park, onto the cement sidewalks, and into the glare of the electric lights. After all, "this is the twentieth century, and to move on is the edict for all of us." The name of the neighborhood, however, will remain Licton Springs, "licton" being a version of the Indigenous word for the pigment once collected there.[28]

Seattle is a bad place to build a city, all steep hills of crumbling sand and clay, tide flats and twisting rivers, hilltop peat bogs and plunging ravines, and with a major earthquake fault straight across its middle. But built it was, and the Indigenous landscape that the Duwamish and the earliest settlers knew has been transformed almost beyond recognition. Once, four rivers joined to become the Duwamish; today, only one flows to Seattle's Elliott Bay—the rest have been diverted or extinguished. The Duwamish estuary is now a major container port; Lake Washington is twenty feet lower and connected to Puget Sound by locks and a canal; several of Seattle's hills have been washed away with water cannons. Although Seattle is one of the few large cities one moves *to* in order to get "closer to nature," its history is one of environmental discontinuity.[29]

For the Duwamish and other local Indigenous people, the transformation of Seattle's landscapes was the means of their dispossession. Beginning in the 1850s settlers routinely razed Native longhouses to claim the cleared ground and "help" Indians move along to the new reservations, but as late as the 1890s some distinctly Indigenous communities remained in and around Seattle, their residents participating as best they could in the local economy while maintaining connections to place. In the early twentieth century, however, the process of dispossession accelerated so that by the 1920s it was virtually impossible for Indigenous people to live in Indigenous ways in Seattle: the eelgrass salmon nurseries and clam beaches were gone, as were the camas-bulb prairies and cranberry bogs. Although some people of Indigenous heritage survived by fitting in to modern urban life, for many, relocation to a reservation was the best option. For those who stayed, eking out an Indigenous living among the wharves and factories, the price was often high: in 1920 one Native couple starved to death on the Duwamish River, within sight of downtown.[30]

None of this happened invisibly. While neither the ship canal engineers' reports nor the city's plans for the filling of tidelands mention Indigenous people, engineers and planners would have known about the struggles of the Duwamish to survive in the changing landscape. Seattle's "last Indians," as those still living in Indigenous ways were portrayed, were front-page news, their travails appearing regularly, often with photographs, in the city's newspapers. The men who transformed the city must have been more than aware of what was happening to these people, but to them the outcome seemed inevitable. Rife with phrases such as "fast falling bands," "citizens of yesterday," or other variations on the trope of the "vanishing race," accounts of Indigenous people in Seattle's landscape were urban tautologies, just-so stories about the incompatibility of Indians with cities—and thus the past with the future.[31]

Seattle's ghost stories, many of which likely began coalescing into local folklore soon after the city's environmental transformation, were one vehicle used to make sense out of this social and environmental change. As such, they were one of the technologies of colonialism, in that they both executed and excused the transformation of Indigenous places into urban places. The imagined ghost at Licton Springs was but one example. When the new residential plat was unveiled just in time for Seattle's metropolitan "coming-out party," the Alaska-Yukon-Pacific Exposition, it was the connection to the Indigenous past that made Licton Springs desirable. Using "legends of our Indian tribes now extinct" to sell streetcar-suburb homesites made perfect sense in Seattle, where actual Indigenous people seemed to be on their way out, save for "here or there a relic."[32] As "great throngs" rode new trolleys to Licton Springs, few of them ever expected Indigenous people to return to the site. Just in case, however, the preemptive strike against Indigenous haunting envisioned in the story of the caretaker and the Indian ghost suggested that there was no room for Indigenous people—alive or undead—at Licton Springs (or anywhere else in Seattle). If most ghost stories allow the settler simultaneously to assuage his or her guilt over conquest and to claim territory through the construction of local knowledge, the story of ghost-expulsion at the springs takes it a step further. It is the narrative of urban conquest at its most muscular and exorcismic: not only are Indians impossible in the modern city; so, too, are their dead. Or so it seemed at the time.

The valley of the Duwamish River is transformed almost beyond recognition; many Seattleites don't even know their city has a river. Yet, among the concrete plants and steel mills, the container ports and the warehouse stores, there remain a handful of "original" places, including the last surviving bend of the river. Here and at other places near the river, members of the Duwamish tribe continue to acknowledge their dead, conducting sacred burnings on the banks amid the industrial sprawl. Even downtown, beneath Pioneer Square, modern-day Indian people engage the Indigenous dead, performing healing ceremonies among the old storefronts and alleys of the Seattle Underground, dim light descending through glass blocks in the sidewalks overhead. And sometimes Indigenous ancestors rise back to the surface in basements and backyards and building sites, their bones and the stories attached to them rising also into the consciousness of urban people, Indigenous and otherwise, who then conduct rituals, Indigenous or otherwise, to lay those bones—but not the stories—to rest.[33]

In 1925 an anonymous booster scripted one of the thousands of promotional brochures that beckoned visitors and investors to Seattle. He began with his own encounter with the city: "First impression! As I found her[,] so will I always think of Seattle. As young and eager. Life still the great unexplored; living still the great adventure. With no old past to stop and worship; no dead men's bones to reckon with; no traditions chained to her ankles." This was the story of the modern era, and of the American nation: the past was irrelevant (although it had been a great adventure), and a bright future lay ahead of the city and nation. No old bones.[34]

Not so; just ask Jan Deeds and Ron Mandt, who in the late

1990s uncovered the bones of an Indigenous family beneath their basement in West Seattle while doing renovations prior to selling their home. After frantic calls to city officials and local tribes and thousands of dollars paid to privately hired archaeologists (and after a buyer backed out of the deal), the family was finally reburied ceremonially in situ to minimize spiritual disturbance, in keeping with tribal wishes. The encounter between modern-day homeowners and the Indigenous past (and present) showed that there are, in fact, old bones to reckon with in Seattle. As in earlier periods, urban development had disturbed the Indigenous dead in Seattle, but in the late twentieth century, there was an important difference: the Indigenous living used such moments as opportunities to articulate their continuing claims to place. And in even greater contrast with earlier periods, they were usually heard.[35]

Few processes of dispossession are ever complete, and despite all the changes that had transformed Seattle's environment, a handful of Duwamish people continued to call the city home in the early twentieth century. Many of them flew "below the radar," largely invisible to their non-Indian neighbors but known to themselves and each other through kinship networks and oral tradition. Officially, the Duwamish Tribe does not exist; a federal ruling in the 1970s determined that they were legally extinct, citing an alleged ten-year break in tribal leadership that dated to the years when Seattle's environmental transformations were at their most traumatic. Nonetheless, the Duwamish have maintained a presence within Seattle and have established cultural, if not necessarily legal, authority over the city. One of the keys to that new authority was the excavation of several archaeological sites in the urban landscape. The Duwamish used such moments to draw attention to their own struggles and to an Indigenous counter-narrative to the city's booster narrative of urban development. When a Port of Seattle bulldozer desecrated an ancient village site on the Duwamish River in 1975, the tribal chairwoman Cecile Maxwell told local press, "We have no culture left, no history left. That's because we have no land base." In response, one journalist noted that Europeans were in the "dark ages" when the longhouses on the riverbank were built and that "perhaps a thousand years from now, Indians [would] discover the decaying remains of the Space Needle," while the editors of the *Seattle Times* wrote that Arthur Denny and other of the city's founders were "Johnny and Janie-come-latelies." Since the 1970s other archaeological discoveries have provided moments in which Duwamish tribal members used the city's increasingly multicultural and eco-friendly persona to articulate the costs of urban conquest. Meanwhile, local tribes with legal authority over the city, including descendants of Duwamish people who had left Seattle decades before, also exerted their power over the urban landscape, both in terms of claims to archaeological sites and, perhaps most importantly, to the imperiled salmon stocks that continued to survive amid all the changes in the local environment.[36]

The reassertion of Indigenous histories within the urban landscape has been accompanied by increasingly public Duwamish ceremonies acknowledging ancestral ties to the landscape, including the burnings for dead along the river and in the Underground. As Peter Nabokov has written, rituals such as these are ways of resisting dominant narratives of the past, renewing identities and social relationships, and satirizing or indicting power.[37] In the case of Seattle, they have helped overturn the city's self-congratulatory place-story of unfettered development and have replaced it with a more ambivalent, complex place-story that includes accounts of dispossession and survival. Such place-stories were a central feature of the 2001 sesquicentennial of Seattle's founding, which included numerous high-profile events at which Duwamish and other Indigenous people told their own versions of the city's past.[38]

Urban development, by its very definition, unearths its own past; in shovels of earth and oral tradition, in ghost stories and place names, Seattle's Indigenous history erupts into the unstable present. In a city so often focused only on the present or the future, the past appears unexpectedly. The reemergence of an Indigenous family's bones in a city basement, for example, recalls Michel de Certeau's description of "wild objects," ancient structures that survived the modernization of Paris: "These seemingly sleepy, old-fashioned things, defaced houses, closed-down factories, the debris of shipwrecked histories still today raise up the ruins of an unknown, strange city. They burst forth within the modernist, massive, homogenous city like slips of the tongue from an unknown, perhaps unconscious, language. They surprise."[39] De Certeau continues by questioning whether such "slips of the tongue" can speak to us in the present, and suggests that if they can, what they have to say is primarily of therapeutic value to modern city dwellers troubled by postmodern urban anomie. In the case of Seattle, though, the "debris of shipwrecked histories," such as bones in the basement, also gives voice to modern Indigenous people and their very specific, concrete claims upon urban places. As a result, through burnings for the dead and healing ceremonies, the Duwamish and other Indigenous people have introduced settler society to yet another kind of haunting, and initiated a new, collective awareness of Indigenous landscapes of the dead and the living.

There is a man in my office who reeks of cigarettes. He's Googled me and, like Joshua Winfield, he is troubled. There is something in his University District apartment, and he wants me to tell him what it is. "Were there any Indian burial grounds in the area?" he asks, because he thinks it could be human. At the same time, he wants to know what kinds of things haunted the "people who lived here before," because what he's encountered might also not be human. He used to work for the university; he claims they fired him because he was too much of a union man. I have a sense there may be other reasons as well. As he talks for nearly two hours, I am reminded of the time a newspaper reporter, compiling a guide to Halloween-weekend haunted houses, called to ask me if one in particular was on top of a Native cemetery, as its organizers claimed. In Seattle both frightened people and purveyors of fright ask the same question: What, and who, was here before us?

Seattle's best-known ghost story is a speech Seeathl, the Duwamish leader who had been so closely allied with some of the most powerful and influential settlers, allegedly gave during treaty discussions in the 1850s. It ends with a haunting: "At night when the streets of your cities and villages will be silent and you think them deserted, they will throng with returning hosts that once filled and still love this beautiful land. The white man will never be alone. Let him be just and deal kindly with my people, for the dead are not power-less. Dead—did I say? There is no death, only a change of worlds."

According to the *Seattle Times* writer Eric Scigliano, the Chief Seattle Speech is a "ghost story like no other," warning modern-day urbanites to "tread lightly and treat the land softly." He adds, "You never know who might be watching—from above, or even nearer."[40] But like any good haunting, the speech cannot be proven. It first appeared in print more than three decades after Seeathl put his mark on the Treaty of Point Elliott and bears no small resemblance to Vic-torian prose lamenting the passing of "Lo, the Poor Indian." There is no question that Seeathl spoke eloquently at the treaty proceed-ings—he carried Thunder as a spirit helper, giving him the power of oratory—but his exact words are lost. Nevertheless, the speech has become a "fifth gospel" of Native rights and environmentalism for its indictment of colonialism's effects on Indigenous peoples and the environment. Somewhere between fiction and fact, however, its uses have often had little to do with the real man named Seeathl, but with concerns of the present, whether among urban environmentalists, progressive Christians, or even modern-day tribal communities.[41]

The speech attributed to Seeathl is not unique; it is merely one example of the local impulse to craft urban narratives using Indian imagery. As scores of thousands of newcomers arrived in the city in the 1890s and after, the descendants of Seattle's pioneers found themselves haunted by the very urban changes they had helped mid-wife, and told stories about Indians to express their anxieties. In her 1909 memoir *Blazing the Way*, Emily Inez Denny, the first white woman born in Seattle, grieved for a world that now seemed "like a beautiful dream, wherein people of another world dwelt; the red man with his picturesque garb of blankets and beads; the pioneer in his buckskin hunting blouse and coon skin cap."[42] A few years later, her relative Sophie Frye Bass lamented Seattle's growth and por-trayed herself and her ancestors as a "vanishing race" in their own right, even writing, "I could say with the Indians when they were

driven from their homes, 'chad-quid-del-el' ('Where is my home?'),"
using Whulshootseed to express her sense of dispossession.[43] Such
stories allowed pioneers and their descendants to claim cultural
authority while also evading responsibility for Indigenous dispossession. As the urban scholar Andreas Huyssen has noted, "Inevitably,
every act of memory carries with it a dimension of betrayal, forgetting, and absence," and the place-stories of the pioneers and other
newcomers show this process at work.[44]

Similar patterns also appear in literary representations of Seattle
and its Indigenous residents, in which the city represents the real, the
living, and the modern, while Native people represent the uncanny,
the dead (or undead), and the mystical. In Jack Cady's murder mystery *Street*, for example, his shape-shifting narrator takes on the
form of "an aging Tlingit seduced south from Alaska" who hunkers
down in rain "more gray and ancient than a solitary old Indian."
Tom Robbins's *Still Life with Woodpecker* includes scenes in which
"Indian winos . . . were unhurried by the . . . shamanic rain," while
in the memoir *Hunting Mr. Heartbreak*, Jonathan Raban describes
tiptoeing past sleeping street Indians "as one walks needlessly in
the presence of the dead."[45] Placed alongside Seattle's older ghost
stories, it is clear that the conflation of Indigenous people with
the dead, with nature, and with the past is a persistent narrative
in Seattle's place-story. Even Sherman Alexie, the Spokane–Coeur
d'Alene Indian author and Seattle resident rightly lauded for the
complicated humanity of his Native characters, has evoked the urban
parable of Indians-as-ghosts. During intense debates about public
transportation in Seattle at the beginning of the twenty-first century,
Alexie penned a column in a local alternative weekly about the
ancient monorail of the fictional Kickakickamish Indians, which
had been destroyed along with most of its builders by vengeful
neighbors. "It was genocide," Alexie smirked, noting that the current monorail dating from the 1962 world's fair was still haunted
by Kickakickamish ghosts who would tear to pieces any expansion
of the space-age sky-train's route.[46]

This, then, is the central error of Seattle's imagined past, and
of urban and Indigenous histories more generally. The city's ghost

stories are historical creations, not just because they arise so clearly out of the city's specific past, but because they are also particularly compelling ways to make sense of that past. The danger is that, as place-stories, urban Indian hauntings all too often tell us exactly what we expect to hear, which is this: Indigenous history and urban history—and, indeed, Indians and cities—cannot coexist, and one must necessarily be eclipsed by the other. Nothing could be further from the truth in Seattle, where Indigenous history and urban history created each other. And while such hauntings involve stock characters from the colonial imagination, there is also a kernel of historical truth at the core of each of the city's hauntings—a brothel near the river, an elite Duwamish woman's shanty, the location of ceremonial paint, or, yes, even an Indian burial ground. By examining these ghosts in the context of grounded, specific histories of place, it is possible to resurrect the actual roles Indigenous people and places played in the urban past, and to reclaim the concrete details of a new narrative of urban Indigenous history.

Do places have spirits? And can ghost-hunting, combined with the practices of social and cultural history, be a form of historical methodology? Jacques Derrida once famously noted that "haunting is historical . . . but not dated."[47] Most of Seattle's Indian ghosts may not have dates per se, but they are not so much metaphors drawn from the imaginary of conquest as they are metonyms for the actual material processes by which that conquest took place. While the Chief Seattle Speech, golf-course shaman, and Duwamish burnings for their dead tell us a great deal about the politics of the present, such hauntings are also critical windows into the past. After all, this is what gives ghost stories their resonance for the living; and in complex and dynamic urban environments, the opportunity for haunting is great. As Peter Ackroyd has written, "The ancient city and the modern city literally lie beside each other; one cannot be imagined without the other. That is one of the secrets of the city's power."[48] On Puget Sound, a similar power exists in the dialogue between the past and the present and between the ancient landscapes of the Duwamish and the newer environments of Seattle. The simultaneity of Seattle's urban and Indigenous histories—two stories that seem like they should be mutually exclusive—is what gives the city's ghosts their power. The more intimately Native and newcomer have lived with each other, the more they have each been haunted.

NOTES

Much of the material in this essay, as well as the notion of place-stories, is taken from my book Native Seattle: Histories from the Crossing-Over Place *(Seattle: University of Washington Press, 2007). For their support, enthusiasm, and insights, I would like to thank Colleen Boyd, the coauthor of this volume; William Cronon, the editor of the University of Washington Press's Weyerhaeuser Environmental Books series, in which Native Seattle appeared; and Richard White, John Findlay, and Gail Lee Dubrow, under whose supervision I wrote the dissertation from which the book has evolved.*

1. Keith Basso, *Wisdom Sits in Places: Landscape and Language among the Western Apache* (Albuquerque: University of New Mexico Press, 1996).

2. Julie Cruikshank, *Do Glaciers Listen? Local Knowledge, Colonial Encounters, and Social Imagination* (Vancouver: UBC Press, 2005).

3. Crisca Bierwert, *Brushed by Cedar, Living by the River: Coast Salish Figures of Power* (Tucson: University of Arizona Press, 1999), 44.

4. Peter Nabokov, *A Forest of Time: American Indian Ways of History* (Cambridge: Cambridge University Press, 2002), 132.

5. For an overview of this emerging discipline and its origins, see Merlin Coverley, *Psychogeography* (London: Pocket Essentials, 2006).

6. Peter Ackroyd, *London: The Biography* (London: Chatto & Windus, 2000), 463.

7. Mikhail Bakhtin, *The Dialogic Imagination: Four Essays* (Austin: University of Texas Press, 1981), 7, quoted in Basso, *Wisdom Sits in Places*, 62.

8. This account is based on a version of the story by Jessica Amanda Salmonson in *The Mysterious Doom and Other Ghostly Tales of the Northwest* (Seattle: Sasquatch Books, 1992). Salmonson's version was based on Carol Lind's version, published in *Western Gothic* (Seattle: Lind, 1983), which itself was based on an article by William Arnold in the Halloween 1979 edition of the *Seattle Post–Intelligencer*. All of the ghost stories used as interludes in this article are based on Salmonson, Lind, or personal communications with the author, unless noted otherwise.

9. John Peabody Harrington, *The Papers of John Peabody Harrington in the Smithsonian Institution, 1907–1957*, ed. Elaine L. Miles, frames 409–12; and "Interpretive Essay: Alki Playground," Don Sherwood Collection, University of Washington Manuscripts, Special Collections, and University Archives.

10. For ghosts and the dead in Puget Sound Coast Salish culture, see Mar-

ian W. Smith, *The Puyallup–Nisqually* (New York: Columbia University Press, 1940).

11. Place names in this article are all drawn from Thomas Talbot Waterman's unpublished manuscript, "Puget Sound Geography," a copy of which is held in the University of Washington's Special Collections. English translations are presented here as they appear in the atlas appendix of Thrush, *Native Seattle*, 209–55. For current tribal concerns over the continued development of Foster Island, see "Duwamish Tribe Seeks Protection for Foster Island," *King County Journal*, February 20, 2005.

12. For two examples of such disturbances, see "A Skeleton Found," *Seattle Daily Intelligencer*, August 21, 1876, and "Belltown," *Seattle Daily Intelligencer*, March 22, 1878.

13. Whulshootseed is the southern dialect of Puget Salish; the northern dialect is known as Lushootseed. Together, they are sometimes referred to as Puget Salish.

14. For the journey up the Duwamish, see Arthur A. Denny, *Pioneer Days on Puget Sound* (Seattle: C. B. Bagley, 1888), 10–12.

15. For accounts of life in early Seattle (all by members of the extended Denny family), see A. Denny, *Pioneer Days on Puget Sound*; Emily Inez Denny, *Blazing the Way; or, True Stories, Songs, and Sketches of Puget Sound and Other Pioneers* (Seattle: Rainier Printing, 1909); Sophie Frye Bass, *Pig-Tail Days in Old Seattle* (Portland OR: Metropolitan, 1937); and Roberta Frye Watt, *Four Wagons West: The Story of Seattle* (Portland OR: Metropolitan, 1931).

16. Numinous sites from Waterman; information about Changes-Its-Face (also known as *ayahos*, a rough approximation of its Whulshootseed name) comes from Smith, *Puyallup–Nisqually*, 57, 62.

17. For a comprehensive treatment of epidemics in the region, see Robert Boyd, *The Coming of the Spirit of Pestilence: Introduced Infectious Diseases and Population Decline among Northwest Coast Indians, 1774–1874* (Seattle: University of Washington Press, 1999). For accounts of shaman-killings, see Brad Asher, *Beyond the Reservation: Indians, Settlers, and the Law in Washington Territory, 1853–1889* (Norman: University of Oklahoma Press, 1999). The suicide of Doctor Jim is recounted in J. A. Costello, *The Siwash: Their Life, Legends, and Tales* (Seattle: Calvert, 1895), 86–87.

18. Personal communication with the late John Beal, Hamm Creek Restoration Society.

19. "Story of Alonzo Russell," n.d. (ca. 1910), Museum of History & Industry (MOHAI) Manuscript Collection, folder 116.

20. David Kellogg to Vivian Carkeek, May 20, 1912, MOHAI Manuscript Collection, folder 116.

21. "Ordinances of the Town of Seattle," *Seattle Weekly Gazette*, March 4, 1865.

22. Bass, *Pig-Tail Days in Old Seattle*, 31; Denny, *Pioneer Days on Puget Sound*, 73; and Yvonne Prater, *Snoqualmie Pass: From Indian Trail to Interstate* (Seattle: Mountaineers, 1981), 7–29.

23. This spelling most closely approximates the proper pronunciation of his name within standard English orthography.

24. Rose Simmons, "Old Angeline, the Princess of Seattle," *Overland Monthly* 20 (November 1892): 506.

25. For two examples of editorials demonizing Indigenous women and the settler men connected to them, see "Small-Pox," *Seattle Daily Intelligencer*, December 29, 1876, and "Seattle in Ashes," *Seattle Daily Intelligencer*, July 27, 1879.

26. For coverage of debates over the "vice" question, the best account remains Murray Morgan's beloved study of "history from the bottom up," *Skid Road: An Informal Portrait of Seattle* (New York: Viking, 1951). Seattle's Skid Road is also the source of the term "skid row."

27. Richard Hugo, *The Real West Marginal Way: A Poet's Autobiography*, ed. Ripley S. Hugo, Lois M. Welch, and James Welch (New York: W. W. Norton, 1986), 8, 11; and Donald Francis Roy, "Hooverville: A Study of a Community of Homeless Men in Seattle" (master's thesis, University of Washington, 1935), 12, 25, 83.

28. Paul Burch, "The Story of Licton Springs," *The Westerner* 9, no. 4 (1908): 19, 34.

29. For the single best account of Seattle's environmental history, see Matthew Klingle, *Emerald City: An Environmental History of Seattle* (New Haven CT: Yale University Press, 2007).

30. Schedule of Unenrolled Indians, n.d. (1919), U.S. Department of the Interior, Office of Indian Affairs, National Archives & Records Administration, Seattle; Thomas Talbot Waterman, "The Geographical Names Used by the Indians of the Pacific Coast," *Geographical Review* 12 (1922): 188; and interview with Ollie Wilbur by Lynn Larson, May 26, 1994, Alki/Transfer Combined Sewer Outflow Facilities Project Traditional Cultural Properties, Muckleshoot Indian Tribe Archives, Auburn WA.

31. For examples of articles about these "last" Indians in Seattle, see "Chief Seattle's Nephew Billy Ruined by Gale," *Seattle Post–Intelligencer*, January 6, 1910; "Our Citizens of Yesterday," *Seattle Argus*, December 22, 1900; and "Siwashes Again Seek the Streets," *Seattle Post–Intelligencer*, May 31, 1904.

32. Calhoun, Denny, & Ewing advertisement, *Seattle Post–Intelligencer*, May 23, 1909; "Thousand at Opening of the Licton Plat," *Seattle Post–Intelligencer*, May 23, 1909.

33. Personal communications with Dana Cox, Seattle Underground Tours, and the anthropologist Jay Miller.

34. *Seattle, Her Faults & Her Virtues* (ca. 1925), quoted in Carlos A. Schwantes, *The Pacific Northwest: An Interpretive History* (Lincoln: University of Nebraska Press, 1996), 1.

35. Lynda V. Mapes, "Bones Unearthed; Reburial Carries Hefty Price," *Seattle Times*, October 19, 2002.

36. For the Duwamish Tribe's efforts toward federal recognition, see Thrush, *Native Seattle*, 193–99, and www.duwamishtribe.org. For the Port of Seattle desecration, see Fred Brack, "Port Charged with 'Razing' Unique Site," *Seattle Post–Intelligencer*, July 13, 1976, and Erik Lacitis, "No Single Culprit in Duwamish Probe," *Seattle Times*, July 28, 1976. For a discussion of federally recognized tribes and salmon in the Seattle area, see Thrush, *Native Seattle*, 189–93.

37. Nabokov, *A Forest of Time*, 172–91.

38. For accounts of sesquicentennial events, see Jerry Large, "Interpretation of History Depends on Perspective," *Seattle Times*, November 18, 2001; Paul Shukovsky, "Ballard Locks' Creation Left Tribe High and Dry," *Seattle Post–Intelligencer*, November 24, 2001; and D. Parvaz, "Duwamish Share Lessons of the Water with Others: Canoe Paddle a Tribute to Harmony with White Settlers," *Seattle Post–Intelligencer*, August 29, 2002.

39. Michel de Certeau, Luce Giard, and Pierre Mayol, *The Practice of Everyday Life, Volume 2: Living & Cooking*, trans. Timothy J. Tomasik (Minneapolis: University of Minnesota Press, 1998), 133.

40. For the original printing of the speech attributed to Seeathl, see the October 29, 1887 edition of the *Seattle Star*. For reprintings and embellishments of the speech in local histories, see Frederick James Grant, *History of Seattle, Washington* (New York: American, 1891); Clarence B. Bagley, *History of King County, Washington* (Chicago: S. J. Clarke, 1929); and Watt, *Four Wagons West*. See also Eric Scigliano, "Shaping the City: A New Book Looks Over a Changing Urban Space," *Seattle Times Pacific Northwest Magazine*, November 10, 2002.

41. For discussion of the speech and its various interpretations and uses, see Rudolf Kaiser, "Chief Seattle's Speech(es): American Origins and European Reception," in *Recovering the Word: Essays on Native American Literature*, ed. Brian Swann and Arnold Krupat (Berkeley: University of California Press, 1987), 497–536; Vi Hilbert, "When Chief Seattle Spoke," in *A Time of Gathering: Native Heritage in Washington State*, ed. Robin K. Wright (Seattle: University of Washington Press, 1991), 259–66; Denise Low, "Contemporary Reinventions of Chief Seattle: Variant Texts of Chief Seattle's 1854 Speech," *American Indian Quarterly* 19, no. 3 (1995): 407–22; Albert Furtwangler, *Answering Chief Seattle* (Seattle: University of Washing-

ton Press, 1997); and Crisca Bierwert, "Remembering Chief Seattle: Reversing Cultural Studies of a Vanishing American," *American Indian Quarterly* 22, no. 3 (1998): 280–307.

42. E. I. Denny, *Blazing the Way*, 114–15, 141–42; Emily Inez Denny, "Chapter 13—Miss Denny's Chapter," (n.d.), MOHAI Manuscript Collection, folder 271.

43. Bass, *Pig-Tail Days in Old Seattle*, 46, 84; Sophie Frye Bass, *When Seattle Was a Village* (Seattle: Lowman & Hanford, 1947), 117–18; and Watt, *Four Wagons West*, 377.

44. Andreas Huyssen, *Present Pasts: Urban Palimpsests and the Politics of Memory* (Stanford CA: Stanford University Press, 2003).

45. Jack Cady, *Street: A Novel* (New York: St. Martin's, 1994), 13, 25; Tom Robbins, *Still Life with Woodpecker* (New York: Bantam Books, 1980), 69, 132; Jonathan Raban, *Hunting Mr. Heartbreak: A Discovery of America* (New York: Edward Burlingame Books, 1991), 261–62.

46. Sherman Alexie, "Rapid Transit," *The Stranger*, November 14, 2002, 17.

47. Jacques Derrida, *Specters of Marx* (London: Routledge, 1994), 4, quoted in Diana Taylor, *The Archive and the Repertoire: Performing Cultural Memory in the Americas* (Durham: Duke University Press, 2003), 142.

48. Ackroyd, *London*, 760.

PART 2

HISTORICAL ENCOUNTERS

4

The Anatomy of a Haunting

Black Hawk's Body and the Fabric of History

ADAM JOHN WATERMAN

In January 1863 the members of the State Historical Society of Iowa inaugurated the publication of their journal *Annals of Iowa* with an article they called "The History of Scott County." Serialized over three issues, the article established one of the most basic conceits of midwestern history; namely, its ostensible banality. One of the first counties in the State of Iowa, in 1863 Scott County was most notable as the home of the oldest white settler communities in the state. Anglo-Americans had started to settle land in what would become Scott County by the early nineteenth century; their numbers exploded in the late 1820s, as the regional lead boom and relative abundance of available land drew members of the displaced white working poor whose lives had been upended by the expansion of southern plantation agriculture, the rise of northeastern industry, and the demise of mercantilist trade–labor relations. The first settler town, Valley City, was officially incorporated in 1833, and county status was granted—at the behest of the Wisconsin territorial legislature—with the completion of the federal territorial survey in 1837. Yet, beyond the age and longevity of Scott County relative to other white settler communities, there was very little in its past to recommend it as a site for prolonged historical inquiry. Most Iowa settler communities had been founded fewer than thirty years before, and in each case, the pattern was the same: settlers arrived, men and women worked, mines were sunk, crops were planted, families were raised, and the altogether banal business of social and economic reproduction proceeded at a fairly leisurely pace. Very little, if anything, distinguished Scott County from other counties in Iowa, and from the very general contours of western settlement at large.

In some sense, however, it was the altogether undistinguished course of settlement in Scott County that made it a compelling subject for discussion in the *Annals of Iowa*. One could read the history of the undistinguished Scott County and instantly perceive it as part of a set, one tale in a serialized history of U.S. expansion in which each piece, each element, each story, repeated the patterns of the tale that came before. Establishing the history of Iowa as part of such a set was one of the primary ideological functions of the *Annals of Iowa*, as it carried forth the agenda of the State Historical Society. When founded in 1857, the State Historical Society of Iowa set for its purpose "collecting, embodying, arranging and preserving in an authentic form a library of books, pamphlets, maps, charts, manuscripts, papers, paintings, statuary, and other materials illustrative of the history of Iowa." The end of these efforts was equally straightforward: the founders of the historical society hoped "to rescue from oblivion the memory of [Iowa's] early pioneers; to obtain facts and preserve varieties of their exploits, perils, and hardy adventures; to secure facts and statements relative to the history, genius, and progress or decay of [the] Indian tribes."[1] This agenda reflected the exigencies of the times, and the urgent necessity of forging an affectively charged national culture, forged through a materialist pedagogy of national identity, in the face of the political and economic crisis of federal disunion. Of course, the deliberate development of a national culture had been a topic of some concern since the late 1830s in the United States, the notion that there needed to be a national culture having taken root as executive power within the federal government expanded, and as federal authority over the states expanded. By the late 1850s, however, it was hoped that a common national cultural identity, whereby one could situate one's personal history in relationship to the history and progress of the nation, might offer a psychological bulwark against the rise of sectionalism. By virtue of its ordinariness, the history of Scott County offered an ideal site through which to imagine such a relation. Because it was ordinary, because it was typical, the history of

Scott County could reasonably represent the history of anybody.

Of course, in practical terms, the construction of these historical identities was less about identifying appropriate subjects for historical study than about selectively telling, shading, and ultimately discarding all those details that did not conform to an ideal narrative architecture. The institutional mediation of local history through the archive, the journal, the academy, and the profession, is part of the process by which history—and, thus, the historically constituted and constructed nation—is incorporated into the ideological operations of the capitalist state. Historical institutions, for their part, lent a conspicuously reified half-life to certain details and dimensions of American social history by highlighting the pioneer as the primary agent of national destiny, and rendering the technologies of state function and capital accumulation—the chart, the map, the pamphlet—little more than accessories in his "hardy adventures." In general, the mission and practice of the historical societies abstracted individuals and communities from the material, historical dialectic in which they were embedded, shunting them into an institutionally formulated historical tableau designed to illustrate the continuity of the nation–state in time and over space.[2]

In 1863 the elaboration and repression of certain historical details was a particularly pressing matter for the members of the Iowa State Historical Society, given the relationship among the state, its politicians, and its business leaders, and their relationship to the political crisis that prompted federal disunion. As William Appleman Williams has pointed out, midwestern farmers had long found affinity with southern planters, particularly insofar as both hoped to develop the extensive river system of the Mississippi valley into a southward-tending commercial network that could challenge the rail and canal infrastructure controlled by the Northeast.[3] This economic affinity was compounded by the fact that many of the earliest settlers to the region had come from the states of the upper South. In themselves, such allegiances may not have earned public opprobrium; nonetheless, after Augustus Caesar Dodge, the senator from Iowa, introduced legislation to permit the expansion of slavery into western territories—the infamous Kansas–Nebraska Act of 1854—ties between the Midwest and the South became highly suspect. Voters around the country responded to the act by sweeping antislavery Republicans into office; in turn, proslavery expansionists in the South and the North began seriously contemplating the possibility of secession and implementing different means of expressing their economic concerns through political affiliation. The State Historical Society responded to this public relations crisis by fetishizing and exaggerating the trappings of a less recent history, a history in which the pioneer could be reasonably represented as the master of his fate and, by extension, the fate of the nation; a history in which the political and economic relations that had come to shape—and in some fashion, overdetermine—social life in the river valley were absent, out of frame.

With regard to the history of Scott County, the ideological imperative to present a national history purged of its political and economic entanglements gave rise to certain methodological constraints and narrative constructions, the most significant of which was the articulation of regional settlers' history with local American Indian cultures. As Philip Deloria has argued, the appropriation, theft, or outright fabrication of Native symbols offered mid-nineteenth-century architects of U.S. nationalism a highly effective means both to claim an American identity and to give it some measure of affective resonance. By identifying their history with that of Native peoples—who were perceived by most non-Native Americans as closer to, if not actually part of, nature—nineteenth-century nationalists rooted their nationalisms in the life of the land itself, rendering American national identity as accidental and as inevitable a fact of life as continental topography.[4] In his article, Willard Barrows, the author of "The History of Scott County," effected this identification by linking the immediately sensuous and productive dimensions of his labors as a land surveyor to the remnants of the local Native American past. In a particularly arresting passage, Barrows noted that his measurements, at one point, led him to the grave of the Sauk Indian military leader Black Hawk. Barrows wrote, "One of my section lines ran directly across the wigwam in which this great warrior closed his earthly career, which I marked upon my map, and from his grave took bearings to suitable landmarks; recorded them in my field notes, and transmitted them to the Surveyor General."[5] In this passage, Barrows's representation of his labors effects a functionalist transubstantiation, extracting Black Hawk's grave from the Native cultural heritage and historical dialectics in which it was embedded, and transforming it into a literal point of orientation for a community seeking to confirm its identity in the context of a political and economic crisis within the federal state.

The reference to Black Hawk's grave was by no means arbitrary. For mid-nineteenth-century nationalists, literary invocations of the dead—like fabricated Indian symbols—were a common feature of their historiographic campaigns. The trope of the dead was employed as a means to construct and inculcate a sense of national identity among the greater part of the subject population in any number of nationalizing states.[6] In the United States, to a certain extent, these references merely reflected the preoccupations of the times. The Spiritualism that followed the Second Great Awakening had brought the histrionics of the dead into parlors and dining rooms across the country; by 1860 it was highly likely that the better part of the U.S. population had been to at least one séance, even if they were not believers themselves.[7] In the wartime United States, however, the historiographic trope of the national dead offered an exceedingly effective means to conjure a national community, routing personal mourning over those lost to war into a sense of collective mourning over a sundered national community. Such efforts afforded the literary construct of the nation a measure of personal, affective resonance across a wide spectrum of the population. Elite historiographic constructions of the national dead were complemented, in turn, by popular invocations of figures such as John Brown and, later, Abraham Lincoln. Though extraordinarily dissimilar in most regards, Brown and Lincoln were transfigured in the sphere of popular culture, emptied of their political and intellectual specificities, and read through the metaphysics of the Protestant Millennium to which they, and much of the U.S. citizenry, adhered. Both died as men only to be reborn as American Christs, quasi-messianic figures whose spiritual bodies were constituted by the members of the national community who had dedicated themselves to the eradication of slavery and the reconstruction of the Union. With regard to Lincoln, this affective, ideological process was facilitated by the fact that he had the foresight to be assassinated on Good Friday.[8] In many ways, the reference to Black Hawk's grave in "The History of Scott County" offered a similar sort of affective anchor, a way of tracing the life of the local community and its position within the nation to a collective sense of mourning over a lost hero.

Yet, just as the deliberative construction of nationalist histories and the pedagogical inculcation of nationalist sentiment were meant, in part, to subvert legitimate desires for social communion and to prevent organic modes of political critique, the nationalist invocation of the dead was also meant to prohibit certain modes of memory, and to ensure that mourning found its proper resolution in the attachment to, and perpetual reproduction of, the state.[9] Unrestrained and unanchored, the dead present such a liability for the modern state that many of the historical and historiographic functions of the modern state apparatuses are conscientiously aimed at extirpating the dead from the social milieu of the living.[10] This point is perhaps best illustrated by reference to the postcolonial states of the Caribbean, where the formation of disciplinary knowledge was bound, in a much more immediate fashion, to the development of state apparatuses, and to state sovereignty over geophysical terrain and national populations.[11] In her speculative reconstruction of slave women's lives out of a score of archival phantoms, Jenny Sharpe has suggested that the late nineteenth-century effort to collect ghost stories about the terrain once held by the Maroon leaders Nanny and Cudjoe in the Blue Mountains of Jamaica had as much to do with the effort to open the mountains to commercial coffee production as with any desire to preserve the memory of those Maroon communities for the historical record.[12] In collecting these stories, the Jamaican colonial state hoped to discipline their cultural meaning and, thus, their social effects. By the same token, Fernando Ortiz's earliest sociological work on Afro-Cuban religion was prompted by the Cuban state's attempt to identify the spiritual bases of the witchcraft panic that gripped the country in the wake of the sugar boom and bust of the early 1920s, and to ensure foreign capitalists that Cuba remained a safe bet for investment.[13]

These examples merely scratch the surface of a four-centuries-long campaign to extirpate the spiritual beliefs of African and Indigenous peoples. Although this campaign cannot be reduced to any one motive, as a practical matter the desire to disrupt "traditional" patterns of belief was as much about utilizing Christianity as a mode of social control among Native peoples and enslaved Africans as it was about maintaining order among the indentured servants, peasants, and convicts who comprised the majority of "white" people in the American colonies. As Linebaugh and Rediker have argued, in the early colonial period, one of the most immediate threats to Britain's North American settlements was the relative stability and egalitarianism of Native communities against those established for British religious or commercial interests.[14] In their interactions, displaced and dispossessed peoples of European, African, and American provenance created cultural and spiritual forms that, if not directly at odds with the strident Protestantism of the day, represented a significant threat to the fledgling colonial economies, insofar as they were evidence of unmediated cultural relations among a large laboring population. Consequently, in North America, forms of syncretic Indigenous, African, and European spirituality, akin to vodou in Haiti, were vigorously attacked, to the extent that, where such traditions took root, their African and Indigenous elements are disavowed, if not unknown and unremarked.[15] The wide-ranging extirpation of practices that constitute these cultures comprise one element of the state's attempt at mediating the cultural forms constituted through, and constitutive of, organized dissent.[16]

Given these political stakes, the historiographic reference to Black Hawk's grave in Barrows's article was not necessarily meant to effect the sublimation of his death into the life of the nation but to refuse the relative autonomy of his spirit as a subject of cultural formation. As Dipesh Chakrabarty has argued, "Gods, spirits, [and] the supernatural have agency in the world," as they are registered in and through rituals of history and remembrance, a point that Joseph Roach elaborates in his study of the performative practices that constitute memory-laden space in the circum-Atlantic.[17] The historiographic campaign of the State Historical Society of Iowa must be contextualized against other, contemporaneous social practices through which Black Hawk's death had been sublimated and made culturally meaningful. It is as a response to these other traditions of cultural formation that the State Historical Society, among others, sought to reinscribe Black Hawk within the body of the archive, and to contain the threat posed by his spirit. The remainder of this essay will consider the manifestation of this process as it played out in the burial, theft, dismemberment, and struggle over Black Hawk's dead body.

BLACK HAWK'S GRAVE AND THE REMAINS OF THE MIDDLE GROUND

Black Hawk had died in early October 1838, his body consumed by the political and economic struggles to which he had been party over the course of his long life. Approximately seventy-two years old, Black Hawk had fallen ill with a malarial fever during the first leg of an overland journey from his home in southern Iowa to the Indian agency at Rock Island, where, not coincidentally, he and a group of Sauk and Fox leaders were to collect the semiannual annuity payment from the federal government. Black Hawk's motives for attempting such a journey, considering that he was well advanced in age for a warrior whose last battles had been fought less than a decade before, were highly fraught. No doubt eager to return to the land that he had been forcibly ejected from only eight years earlier and to pay homage to the graves of his fathers, Black Hawk was likely keen to intervene in the backroom politics that were, in his view, impoverishing his people and rendering them increasingly dependent upon the whims of egomaniacal bureaucrats and opportunistic leaders. Black Hawk said he had "put down the tomahawk" at the end of the Black Hawk War, but he was far from submissive. While swearing fidelity to the United States and the new tribal government, Black Hawk did everything in his power to undermine the authority of the man the United States had anointed the leader of the Sauks and Foxes, the civil chief, Keokuck.

Since 1804 Keokuck had brokered almost every bargain the Sauks made with the United States, and Black Hawk held him responsible for all the ills that had befallen their people in the years since. Keokuck, for his part, did not like to let Black Hawk out of his sight, as he was certain that the elder leader was biding his time, waiting for an opportunity to incite the Sauks and Foxes against him. Indeed, in 1837 Keokuck brought Black Hawk with him to New York City and Washington DC rather than leave him alone and unsupervised in the West. A veritable prisoner among his friends, during that trip Black Hawk met with President Martin Van Buren to discuss Native land claims on the Mississippi River. While Keokuck prevented him from speaking, his words were represented to the president by the delegation of Iowa Indians that had traveled to Washington with him and with whom Black Hawk had met in the weeks prior to their journey. Yet, in their long struggle, time and the elements were on Keokuck's side. He lived to see another decade; Black Hawk would not make it to Rock Island. His delegation was to meet with the Indian agent on October 1. Black Hawk set out with the group, but after falling ill, he held back. According to the historian Benjamin Drake, a contemporary of Black Hawk, the stress of the journey and an uncharacteristic spell of fall humidity ended Black Hawk's life. "The weather was both wet and hot, and it is supposed that, on this journey, he imbibed the seeds of the disease which soon after terminated his existence," Drake wrote. Black Hawk died, according to Drake's account, of a malarial fever on October 3, attended by his wife and a Sauk healer.

Black Hawk's physical death carried an enormous symbolic weight. For some seventy years, the events of his life had reflected, in miniature, many of the most significant episodes in the life of the greater Sauk community in its relationship to other Indigenous peoples and Euro-American empires. Born during the latter half of the 1760s, Black Hawk spent the first years of his life in a world changed by the Seven Years' War, and the demise of French colonialism in the upper Great Lakes region. The Sauks had been central players in the life of New France; as a consequence, they had gained many material advantages, and many dangerous enemies. After the French gave up lower Canada, and Pontiac's Rebellion transformed intra-Native politics, the Sauks found themselves without friends, in hostile territory. In response, the Sauk community would make its way southwest along the shores of Lake Michigan, to the Mississippi; they settled in small villages around the Rock River, which would become the hub of their commerce and the site of their most populous town, Saukenuk. When Black Hawk was a little more than ten years old, he would begin leading warriors into battle against the Osages, who lived in small communities across present-day Missouri. In 1778 U.S. forces would destroy Saukenuk during a campaign against British collaborators on the western front of the Revolutionary War. By that time the Sauks had entered into a limited alliance with the British colonial government and the Fox people, a small Native group that had been all but wiped out by the French during the final years of their colony. Saukenuk would be rebuilt, but it would be destroyed twice more: during the War of 1812, and in 1831, as the government sought to implement the relocation of all eastern Native peoples west of the Mississippi along what has become famously known as the Trail of Tears. Black Hawk would respond decisively to each instance of its destruction, fighting on the side of Tecumseh and the British during the Battle of Detroit in 1812, and mounting a guerilla campaign against western settlements and U.S. forts in 1832. This campaign would come to be known as the Black Hawk War; it would mark the end of Black Hawk's overt opposition to U.S. governance, a new era of social and economic instability for the Sauks and Foxes that saw them subjected to intensified political regulation by the government of the United States. After three months, the war came to an end, as Black Hawk surrendered to U.S. forces at Prairie du Chien. His capitulation paved the way for the final removal of the Sauks from the East and the end of Native influence in the commodities networks of the Great Lakes region. With the end of his campaign, the last Native holdouts along the southern shores of Lake Michigan gave up their land; within a year, in 1833, discharged Black Hawk War veterans founded what would become the city of Chicago, just within sight of Fort Dearborn.[18]

Before he died, Black Hawk sought to shape the rituals through which he would be remembered by choosing as a burial place the spot on the north shore of the Des Moines River that had served as the site of his last council with the Iowa Indians in 1837.[19] As a memorial his grave would mark the crossroads of geography and history and establish the point where this past walked into the uncertain present. Long engaged in a social contest over space, by designating this site as his final resting place Black Hawk would, in death, become a part of the social meaning of space.[20] Black Hawk's grave was built to accelerate the process of its decay and to incorporate his physical matter with the matter of the land. Social memory would be shaped by the conditions of nature, which were shaped through the organization of ritual. The decay of the grave, like the decay of Black Hawk's body, was to be witnessed; in being seen over time, the deterioration of the structure and of the body would convey the transience of the physical body, and the slow passage of Black Hawk from corporeal presence to incorporeal principle. Mississippian Native societies had long practiced forms of open-air burial in which the visual presence of the dead was meant to stake a claim upon space. The motivations behind the construction of Black Hawk's grave were no different; yet, unlike the mound builders or platform burials of an earlier era, Black Hawk's burial was meant to claim space not through his presence but through the history his presence implied. From the outside, the structure was covered with rough chunks of bluegrass sod, but on the whole the interior of the grave was left exposed, open to the air and to the gaze. Black Hawk was buried in a seated posture, placed in a shallow hole approximately fifteen inches deep. His torso and head were fastened to a stake that was hammered into the ground, while his body was surrounded by a structure of puncheons that was left open to the gaze and to the air.

If the structure of the grave was built to convey the interplay of nature, ritual, sight, and memory, the interior of the grave was arranged to convey the political struggles to which Black Hawk had been party over the course of his life. In short, the objects arranged in the grave and placed upon Black Hawk's body told the story of the Middle Ground as it met its demise through the militarily enforced Native relocation along the Trail of Tears. Each object was, in itself, part of the elaborate rituals of power through which the Euro-American empires had sought to relate to Native peoples; each object was presented to Black Hawk in order to transform everyday encounters into extraordinary circumstances. According to the account of James Jordan, Black Hawk's friend and neighbor, Black Hawk was outfitted in the U.S. military uniform that was presented to him by Andrew Jackson during Black Hawk's first visit to Washington DC in 1833. The uniform included the traditional officer's sword and golden epaulets; the epaulets graced Black Hawk's shoulders, while the sword was placed in his left hand. In his right hand, Black Hawk grasped the cane that was presented to him by Henry Clay, the Whig presidential candidate who had unsuccessfully challenged Andrew Jackson for the presidency in 1832. Whether deliberate or not, the placement of the objects in relation to Black Hawk's body underscored the political opposition of the Whigs to the Democrats: Jackson and the Democrats were on the left, Clay and the Whigs were on the right, and the social and political interests of Native peoples were caught somewhere in between.[21] The opposition of sword to cane also captured the different approaches each party took toward governance, with Jackson relying upon the federal military to enforce his agenda for the nation, and the Whigs caught up in the exhausting mechanics of parliamentary debate. The uniform itself was meant to illustrate the volition behind Black Hawk's surrender to the U.S. government; during the last years of life, Black Hawk would not allow himself to be painted or otherwise portrayed unless he was wearing the uniform. By choosing to appear in the uniform during public functions and in death, however, Black Hawk no doubt hoped to draw attention to the element of choice in both the construction of his appearance, and his subjection before U.S. power. By choosing to wear the uniform in paintings and as a burial shroud, Black Hawk was taking a subtle jab at the fictions of state power, implying that it was by his choice—and not as an effect of U.S. military might—that he ended his campaign against the United States.

Complementing the histories of U.S. power and politics that were told through the objects on Black Hawk's body, three medals were hung around Black Hawk's neck, one representing the government of France, one the government of Britain, and one the government of the United States. In their entanglement, the three medals distilled the three overlapping and conflicting moments of Euro-American colonialism in the Great Lakes region and the upper Mississippi River valley, and the three international powers that Mississippian Native peoples played off each other in their struggles to maintain political power. The medal from France reflected, in short, the story of Black Hawk's grand-relatives' first encounter with French emissaries, the Sauk power struggles that followed as Black Hawk's family used their relationship with the French to command greater authority within the greater Sauk community, and the centrality of the Sauks to the social and economic life of French colonialism in the upper Lakes region. By contrast, the medal from the British was a memento of Black Hawk's fidelity to the British government in the wake of the Seven Years' War, and of his collaboration with the British during the War of 1812, during which he fought with the British general Isaac Brock at the Battle of Detroit. The American medal was most likely the medal presented to Black Hawk by Lieutenant Zebulon Pike, the military explorer who first encountered the Sauks in 1805, a year after the Sauks had signed their first treaty with the U.S. government.

For those who sought to inscribe Black Hawk's memory into the life of the land, the histories to which these objects referred established their value, as did their relationship to the rituals of memory and mourning. In other words, the value of these objects, as pieces of a ritual claim upon space, was derived from the highly particular circumstances under which they had come to be in Black Hawk's possession, and each object carried in its alienation the trace of its origins. With the destruction of the grave and the theft of Black Hawk's body, however, new rituals and new standards of value would be brought to bear upon the contents of Black Hawk's tomb, as each object within it would become the representation of an abstract measurement of order, knowledge, and value.

BODY-SNATCHING AND THE TRACES IN THE ARCHIVE

Black Hawk's body was stolen from its grave within a year after his death. There is little agreement within archival documents as to when the theft occurred; from the one compelling eyewitness account that exists, we do know, however, that Dr. James Turner was the lead goon, his early nineteenth-century medical training having afforded him many other opportunities to engage in body-snatching. Unlike the conventional grave robbery that supported the expansion of medical knowledge, Turner's appropriation of the body upended the rituals and practices meant to translate Black Hawk into the land and Native memory. In stealing Black Hawk's body, Turner translated its physicality and its memory into the social rituals and activities that were the basis of white settlers' claims upon space, and the domestic labors that made up the substance of the white homestead. According to one eyewitness, Turner spent two weeks watching the grave, waiting for an opportunity to take the body.

In the ritual space constituted by Black Hawk's grave, individuals were meant to mark the visual dissolution of Black Hawk's physicality into memory by witnessing the decay of the grave over time, but Turner cast a covetous glance upon the grave, in which Black Hawk's physicality was dissolved into the exuberant ephemerality of money. Sarah Welch Nossaman, a local pioneer woman, would later recall, "[He] thought if he could only steal Black Hawk's head he could make a fortune out of it by taking it east and putting it on exhibition." After Turner and his accomplices Ed Reed, Warren Cox, and Jefferson Cox finally succeeded in taking the body, they hauled it off to a hiding place on the banks of the Des Moines River and proceeded to dismember it.[22] The carving of the body, in its way, recalled the practices of the surveyors, through which the land upon which they stood had been dismembered, striated, and valued. When he returned to his brother's home shortly thereafter, in the early hours of the morning, he found the household up and waiting, his sister-in-law awake with a fever, and a neighbor woman there to attend her. Nossaman wrote, "He got in with it at four o'clock in the morning, and hid it till the afternoon of the same day, when he cooked the flesh off the skull." Here, the labor involved in cleaning the skull reflects the domestic chores involved with the preparation of food and the sustenance of the pioneer community, who in turn worked the land, and whose labors gave the fictions of property a properly affective dimension.

The metaphorical allusion that I suggest between the theft of Black Hawk's body and the ritual invocation of property lines would be rendered explicit and material in 1843, when the surveying team responsible for completing the national land survey would take bearings from Black Hawk's grave. Published later in his history of Scott County, Iowa, Willard Barrows, the land surveyor, would write, "While performing the public surveys . . . one of my section lines ran directly across the remains of the wigwam in which this great warrior closed his earthly career, which I marked upon my map, and from his grave took bearings to suitable landmarks, recorded them in my regular field notes, and transmitted them to the Surveyor General."[23] Indeed, on the plat of Iowa from 1844, Black Hawk's grave is quite clearly marked with a tiny flag and the crudely drawn figure of a mound. Barrows's measurements were so exacting that James Jordan, Black Hawk's neighbor, could quote them from memory, years later, to designate the location of Black Hawk's burial in relation to his property, and the site of Black Hawk's old home. Jordan wrote, "Black Hawk was buried on the northeast quarter of the southern quarter of section 2, township 70; range 12, Davis County, Iowa, near the northeast corner of the county, on the Des Moines river bottom, about ninety rods from where he lived when he died. . . . I have the ground on which he lived for a door yard, it being between my house and the river." Through the state application of surveying technologies to describe the shape of the land, Black Hawk's grave and its political terms were incorporated into the geometry of expansion, the calculus of property, and the telos of natural history.

The carving of the body and the marking of the land found their purely textual analogy in the phrenological analysis of Black Hawk's skull. Phrenology expressed the claims of science in a strikingly Hegelian language of property, making and exploring racial difference by marking it, forming it, and taking possession of it. Around the same time Black Hawk's analysis was being conducted, Hegel wrote, in *Philosophy of Right*, "We take possession of a thing (a) by directly grasping it, (b) by forming it, and (c) by merely marking it as ours."[24] Drawing its conclusions from the plaster cast crafted by Oswald and Lorenzo Fowler during Black Hawk's visit to New York City in 1837, the analysis appeared in the November 1838 issue of the Fowler brothers' recently launched *American Phrenological Journal*. This was only the second issue of the journal; containing the article that detailed Black Hawk's phrenological profile, it appeared within weeks of his death. After asserting phrenological investigators' superior understanding of the interpretation and characterization of human personality, the article described the three "clusters of organs" that most profoundly and directly shaped Black Hawk's character. As proof of the validity of its findings, the article offered a rendering of Black Hawk's head, drawn from the Fowler brothers' bust, so that "all . . . readers [would] see for themselves these organs, or portions of the head, strikingly exhibited in the cuts."[25] The "cuts" of Black Hawk's head from the journal are striking in so far as they differ from the plaster cast of Black Hawk's visage. In the "cuts" the dimensions of Black Hawk's forehead are greatly exaggerated, and the expression on his face is one of anxious displeasure, discomfort, or strain, as if he were suffering the ministrations of the phrenologists in person. By contrast, the Fowler brothers' bust of Black Hawk—today included in the Luce collection of the New York Historical Society—presents a positively serene portrait, an image of the face and the expression that white Americans stared into, desperately searching for signs of emotion.

Where nineteenth-century crowds failed in their attempts to scan for Black Hawk's psyche, the phrenologists believed they had succeeded, identifying "Combativeness, Destructiveness, Secretiveness, Cautiousness, and Acquisitiveness" as primary determining characteristics, "Self-Esteem, Firmness, and Approbativeness" as second, and "perceptiveness" as third: "Combativeness and Destructiveness . . . would give great propelling power and physical courage, and almost any amount of resistance and severity when necessary.

Secretiveness . . . and Cautiousness . . . would give cunning and induce a resort to stratagems and artful schemes; [and] would also give much forethought and care, with scarcely any dread of danger." That said, whatever forethought that derived from Black Hawk's cautiousness, the phrenologists concluded, would not have been sufficient to counter his altogether moderate degree of causality, which was "too feeble to originate very comprehensive plans, and successfully adapt means to ends," a trait that was common, it was included in a footnote, to Indian peoples generally.[26] Black Hawk's brain, the article concluded, was "so balanced as could scarcely fail to render him distinguished, amid the circumstances and influences which exist in a savage state." As the phrenologists had carved up Black Hawk's skull with calipers, the article carved up Black Hawk's autobiography, offering aspects of a narrative that served to indicate the veracity of the phrenological argument.

The phrenological dissection, as with the measuring and compartmentalization of the land and the vivisection of the body, underscored the links between the state, the law, science, and sensation. Similarly, when the objects from the tomb reappeared, the weight of their historical past were transubstantiated and rendered comparable through an abstract standard of value; their identity was named in dollars, and derived from their strange relation to Black Hawk's body. Underscoring their relationship to money, local newspapers referred to the objects from the grave as "wampum," and in one account of Black Hawk's death, unnamed authorities estimated the approximate monetary value of the objects to be around seventeen hundred dollars; five hundred dollars for the epaulets from Jackson, and twelve hundred dollars for the three medals. Where the monetary reevaluation of the medals suggests only the financial concerns that motivated the body snatchers, their description as "wampum" highlights the connection between the value of the artifacts and an abstract register of Indian racial difference. This interrelation is again suggested by the body snatchers' ultimate ends. Turner, Nossaman reports, hoped to exhibit Black Hawk's skeleton as a sideshow attraction or, at the very least, to sell off his remains to a P. T. Barnum or a Valentine Mott.[27] Barnum, of course, was the infamous purveyor of the nineteenth-century freak show, whose proletarian entertainments peddled visual, physical differences as the substance of racial difference and white superiority, while Mott was the founder of the New York University medical college and a pioneer of the surgical use of anesthesia. He also owned an enormous collection of "medical curiosities," which included body parts that had been harvested from Native peoples across the United States, including, among other gruesome relics, the head of the Seminole leader Osceola.[28] Where Barnum's collection of freaks was a racial education for the white working class, Mott's curiosities were for the elites, who sought to understand and manage racial difference through precise standards of quantification and measurement. In both cases Native peoples were regarded simply as bodies to be gazed at, studied, compared, and sold off.[29]

THE RETRIEVAL OF THE BODY AND THE DISPLACEMENTS OF WHITE MEMORY

No matter how highly symbolic the theft of Black Hawk's body and the destruction of his grave might have been, however, both were material acts, with material consequences, that unavoidably produced material mess. The destruction of the grave and the theft of the body may have temporarily displaced the meanings to which the artifacts in the crypt gestured, but it did not do away with the objects themselves. This was not a medical college or a hospital in New York. Turner performed his vivisection in a frontier community, in which social relations, interactions, and activities, while not necessarily intertwined, were highly, if informally, surveilled. His actions, the theft, the dismemberment, the cleanup, and the transport of the body, were bound to be noticed. In stealing the body, Turner was left with the uniform, the medals, and the headdress, and he would have been forced to consider ways to dispose of those objects without drawing undue attention to his crimes. Similarly, in stealing, dismembering, and cleaning the body, Turner would have been left with a variety of bloodied instruments, his and his accomplices' soiled clothes, and the stinking sacks that he had used to cart the pieces of Black Hawk's body to the various places in which he had hidden and cleaned it. Sarah Nossaman saw only Black Hawk's head enter the Turner kitchen. Drawing on Naseaskuk's account of the theft, most latter accounts suggest that Turner made two trips—months apart—first taking the body, then taking the head. I would like to suggest that Turner stole the body and dismembered it in one night, making at least six, if not more, trips from the Des Moines River to various sites in the small community in order to fully process the remains with the greatest expedience and to avoid detection.[30] Perhaps most gruesome of all, he would have been forced to contend with the cleaning—if not the disposal—of the multiple iron kettles he had used to cook Black Hawk's decaying flesh from his bones.[31] The scope of Turner's crime was such that it could hardly have been covered up without the help of other members of the small frontier community; thus, it should have reverberated in many peoples' memories.

There are, however, no testimonies to this disposal process, no records, no flashbacks; it can be seen only in its consequences. Indeed, within the extant documents from the time, the horror of Turner's act—the horror it invoked for the small community of set-tlers and Native peoples—emerges only between the lines. In Nossa-man's account, her own youthful awe and fear emerges as a sense of disjointed time and self, as if the sight of Black Hawk's severed head disconnected her body from her spirit. In her epistolary reflections on her life, Nossaman writes, "He [Turner] got in with it [the head] at four o'clock in the morning and hid it till the afternoon of the same day, when he cooked the flesh off the skull. So I can say that I am the only one now living that witnessed that sight, for it was surely a sight for me. If Black Hawk's bones were ever removed it was a good many years after his head was stolen."[32] This passage is striking, if only for the utter lack of transitory matter linking the first statement to the second. Her points, in this instance, are not necessarily incor-rect, yet the relationship between these statements is dubious, at best. Nossaman was, at the time of her writing, undoubtedly the only person alive who had witnessed the theft of Black Hawk's body. By her own estimation, the Turner family had been wiped out, within a few years after the theft of the body, by a resurgent bout of cholera that surged through the river valley. Turner's coconspirators in the theft were at least ten to twenty years older than she, and had likely succumbed to the ravages of life in the West. Nonetheless, there is no accounting for the manner in which Nossaman, in the second sentence, travels the distance between objective observation and subjective reflection, no indication of how she knows she is the only person who witnessed the theft, no indication of why it is necessary in this moment to convey this bit of trivia. Sarah Nossaman seems, for a moment, to be more flustered, more concerned, more outside her self than her own prose will allow her to convey. As with Black Hawk's curse against the sound of the cities that had invaded his thoughts and distorted his sense of time and story, in this instance of her narrative, Nossaman seems unhinged by the sight of Black Hawk's head, and the connection between her body, her thoughts, and her senses comes—momentarily—undone. This is indicated, in part, by the proliferation of voices and tenses in the second sentence: "So I can say, that I saw, something that was a sight." Speaking from the present, about an experience in the past, the fact that Black Hawk's dismembered head once occupied her field of vision remains an almost inassimilable moment in her autobiography.

The disconnectedness of Nossaman's observations is underscored by the disjointed recollection of time in her account of the theft of Black Hawk's body, as she recalled the time of the theft at an improbable interval from the time of Black Hawk's death. Nossaman reports that James Turner stole Black Hawk's body within two weeks of his burial and that he returned to William Turner's home at four o'clock in the morning the night he stole the head, while waiting until later that afternoon to clean the flesh from the skull; but she cannot recall if this transpired in 1837 or 1838, adding that only the head was stolen from the body. The pinpoint accuracy with which Nossaman names the hour of Turner's return to the house, and her vague recollection of the year the events occurred, are perhaps understandable; time in the West, as with time before the standardization of industrial measure, was deeply embedded in one's sense of the surrounding world, rather than in chronological devices or contrivances. Four o'clock in the morning would likely have been the hour, in July, when the first birds began to sing and the first hints of light were beginning to dawn in the sky. Likewise, the year was probably of little importance to Nossaman or to any of her neighbors, whose lives were lived in relation to far more local cycles of work and nature. Nossaman's sense of time in its relationship to her witness, however, is deeply unreliable. James Jordan, by contrast, reported that the body was stolen in its entirety almost a year after Black Hawk died, in early July 1839. With regard to the theft of the head, Jordan explained that Black Hawk's widow had come to him, hysterical, because she had visited Black Hawk's grave and his head was missing. Jordan went to investigate and discovered that the head had come untied from the puncheon holding it in place and that it merely seemed as if it had been removed.[33] Jordan's account is, in no small part, born out by what little dated documentation exists: during a council between the government and the Sauk Indians in January 1840, Black Hawk's son Naseaskuk told the governor of Iowa about the theft of his father's body, more or less confirming the timeframe described in Jordan's account. While, as an experience of time, one year is effectively like any other, the difference between two weeks and nine months is not negligible, particularly in an environment where seasonal considerations lend focus to so much of one's experience of time. Here again, Nossaman is undone. Her inability to recollect the timing of events echoes the sound of the city as it unhinges Black Hawk's account of his life, in his narrative.

The disconnection within Nossaman's recollections must be read within the context of events as they unfolded from the time of the destruction of the grave and the theft of Black Hawk's body. As with the events of the Black Hawk War seven years before, for white settlers in southeast Iowa the events that followed from the theft of Black Hawk's body transformed their quiet, familiar frontier settlement into a paranoid landscape awash in the uncanny. The uncanny here should be understood as derived from Freud's later writings on psychoanalysis. As Freud described it, one's sense of the uncanny emerged when an object, words, or circumstances revived a set of childhood beliefs or complexes that had been sublimated but not transcended, rendering the familiar and the routine, the everyday, a realm pregnant with hidden threats, invisible beings, and cold shivers. Crucial to the emergent uncanny was the notion of the double, of repetition, as it summoned a host of repressed complexes related to the historical development of the ego and the instinctual fear of death and the dead.[34] In the wake of Turner's theft, for Nossaman, Black Hawk's physical body would have played the role of the double that disturbed the elemental edifice of the everyday, as the appearance of his head, in the kitchen, echoed the roles that Black Hawk had played in her life, as both an abstract and a particular presence. She and her family, she recalled, moved west to Iowa following the conclusion of the Black Hawk War and the so-called Black Hawk Purchase that ended the war, the purchase that allowed the United States to acquire Native terrain west of the Mississippi.[35] Once Nossaman had settled in Iowa, she recalled, "Black Hawk and his son were frequent visitors and often partook of [her] father's hospitality." The appearance of Black Hawk's dismembered head in her neighbors' kitchen represents the third appearance of Black Hawk in her narrative, but one in which he has been emptied of all particularity and agency, all self and spirit, and rendered pure bone, pure object. Black Hawk's appearance as object rather than subject would have been disturbing for any number of reasons, not the least of which would have been the lingering—if irrational—question about where Black Hawk's subjectivity was, where his presence had gone, and if it would return.

The sense of the uncanny experienced by Nossaman in her narrative was made social and expansive by the atrocities committed against the white settler community at New Lexington by Sauk warriors. After years of relative peace and highly regulated coexistence, the theft of Black Hawk's body again brought the small Sauk community of southeast Iowa to the brink of war. Nossaman recalled, "The second morning after their ruler's head was stolen[,] ten of the best Indian warriors came to William Turner's and asked for his brother, the Doctor. They were painted war style. He told them he did not know where his brother was. They told him they would give him ten days to find his brother, and if he did not find him in that time he would pay the penalty for his brother's crime."[36] In all likelihood, the small group of warriors posed little threat to the settlement, which was larger, and well armed. Indeed, Nossaman makes such a point herself, telling us that "through the influence of their [the Indians'] agent and the citizens [the community of white settlers] together they gave up hostilities for a time." Yet, despite her calm assurance that the situation was well in hand, as far as Nossaman's account of the matter is concerned, the appearance of the Sauk warriors, in full war regalia, prompted a disproportionately fearful reaction from the small settler community, who "expected an outbreak every day." Again, this fear was conditioned by the uncanny appearance of the warriors, and the underlying notion of politico-temporal reversion implied by their presence in the settlement. However minuscule the military threat from these warriors, by appearing in war paint the Native men in question doffed their established social identities for the settler community and assumed a new set of profiles, those of warriors and of subjects of Black Hawk. While Nossaman leaves no record of the men's names, she seems to know of whom she speaks, taking care to note that these are ten of the *best* warriors. The striking sense of familiarity, juxtaposed against the threat implied by the war paint, suggests a willful overturning of the quotidian codes and rituals that governed larger social intercourse between Native peoples and white settlers. At the same time, the threat implied by the paint, and the presence of Sauk warriors in the settler community, suggests that the clock has been turned back on the course of western development, that progress has been bent back upon itself, and that the seemingly absolute claims of settlers to the land are still subject, if in a somewhat casual manner, to the consent of Native power brokers.

No matter how tenuous their claims upon power, though, the presence of the Sauk warriors was enough to send the Turners fleeing their home for Missouri. Upon the first visit of the Sauk warriors to the Turner homestead, William Turner sent word to his brother, who was hiding at the home of a man named Tommy Robb, on the south side of the Des Moines River (he had likely used Robb's home to stash another piece of Black Hawk's body since it would have been close to the grave). He advised his brother to "fly for

Missouri," which he did. Shortly thereafter, William Turner and his family escaped south down the Mississippi in a canoe bound for Missouri as well; there they would be beyond the reach of the Sauks, whose movements—particularly between states—were highly restricted. Again, if Nossaman's account is to be believed, the community at New Lexington was curiously well aware of all these details and silently complicit in the theft of the body and the flight of the Turners. In her account, this complicity extended to and included the agents of the law and the promise of justice. She wrote, "The whites told them they would bring Turner to justice if he could be found." The conditional, in this sentence, reflects the spatial qualifications throughout, with the colloquial invocation of "justice" as a place to which one is brought, and the question of Turner's whereabouts mimicking the vexed spatiality of justice and law. "The sheriff chased Turner around for a while," Nossaman remembered, "which only gave him the more time to get out of the way. The Turner family finally all went to St. Louis, where the Doctor was found again, and to keep the Indians quiet the sheriff went to St. Louis in search of him, but he did not find him. He did not want to find him." Here, again, the spatiality of law and justice is related to the enforcement of law, which is, in turn, related to the volition of the officers of the law. Contingency slides into choice in a manner that confirms the critiques of the law leveled at it by Black Hawk and other Native critics. The complicity of the settlers in the theft of Black Hawk's body perhaps offers one explanation of the depth of their dread: a sense of underlying guilt. In any case, settlers' complicity certainly cuts across Nossaman's tired assertion that Turner's act "made . . . endless trouble . . . [putting] the lives of all settlers in jeopardy for months."

The presence of the Sauk warriors was enough, in any case, to push the Turners to flee their home. For three weeks following the theft of the body, Nossaman reports, the Sauks harassed the small community, and the Turners made plans to cross the border into Missouri. The runaround of the law was the cover under which Black Hawk's bones would circulate through the region, traveling hundreds of miles across three states before finding their way back to Iowa territory. In the aftermath of the theft, James Turner was reported to have made his way first to Saint Louis and then to Quincy, Illinois, where he put Black Hawk's bones in the charge of an anatomist and dentist named Hollowbush. While Turner returned to Saint Louis with his family, the anatomist is reported to have further cleaned, polished, and varnished the bones, in preparation for their re-articulation and display in the East. If Turner had any more-detailed designs about the display of the bones, they have been lost. Which is not to say that he did not have ample time to consider his next steps. Black Hawk's bones were nominally in Turner's possession for well over a year, from July 1839 until their return to the governor of the Iowa territory in December 1840, almost a full year after Naseaskuk first reported their theft to the governor. The local controversies surrounding the theft most likely prevented Turner from furthering his designs for their display, but whatever the reason, Turner was foiled. He remained in Saint Louis for the rest of his life, which was not long. Within three years he and his family had succumbed to cholera. Black Hawk's bones, on the contrary, were returned to Iowa, under an order from Governor Robert Lucas to the mayor of Quincy. The Burlington *Hawk-Eye* reported: "It appears that they were taken to St. Louis and there cleaned; they were then sent to Quincy to a dentist to be put up and wired previous to being sent to the east."[37] As the vivisection of the body recalled the procedures by which the land had been carved into lots, and Native peoples made the racialized bodies as the subjects of scientific knowledge, the circulation of Black Hawk's bones, first to Missouri to be cleaned, then to Illinois to be wired and articulated, suggested the regional connections that were emerging in and through the economic rearrangements of the preceding twenty years.

On December 10, 1840, the *Hawk-Eye* printed a short item on the effort to retrieve Black Hawk's remains from Illinois, noting, "These bones which were stolen from the grave about a year since have been recovered and are now in the Governor's office." The article went on to account for the whereabouts of the objects that had been stolen with the body, and its strange circuitous path through the upper river valley. The article did not, however, comment upon the news items that were positioned immediately adjacent to it in the text: on the one hand, gloating commentaries on Martin Van Buren's unsuccessful reelection bid, General William Henry Harrison's most certain victory, the ascension of the Whigs to the federal administration through the sale of Harrison's long and varied military career, the legislative debate on the border between Iowa and Missouri and its importance to the question of Iowa's admission to the United States as a state; on the other, morbid commentaries on the murder of an infant child who was cast into the Mississippi with a stone tied to its body, and, under the title *"Something New in a New Country,"* the report that another body had turned up in the Mississippi after being stolen from a weeks-old grave in the Fort Madison graveyard.

After successfully requisitioning the body from Quincy, Lucas notified Naseaskuk of the return of the bones, and Black Hawk's family and followers staged an honor retinue to make the ninety miles from their village on the Des Moines River to Burlington. In a strange recalling of the company that approached Burlington to report the theft of the bones to Lucas almost a year earlier, Naseaskuk was accompanied by his mother, Black Hawk's elderly wife. The presentation of the bones was made with the utmost ceremony. On the evening of their arrival in Burlington, the Native delegation called upon the governor, who scheduled an appointment with the group for the following morning. At 10 a.m., the delegates arrived at the governor's office, where Black Hawk's remains had been left packed in a small box. When the company was assembled, "the lid was lifted by the Governor, fully exposing the sacred relics of the renowned chief to the gaze of his sorrowing friends and the very respectable auditors who had ascended to witness the impressive scene."[38] Lucas went on to convey to Black Hawk's widow the circuitous path the remains had taken, and the events attending their disposition, from the grave to Quincy and back to Burlington, as a means of assuring her that they were, indeed, the remains of her husband. Black Hawk's wife was not, it seems, comforted by this assurance. As Lucas described the scene: "The widow then advanced to the lid of the box, and without the least seeming emotion, picked up in her fingers bone after bone, and examined each with the seeming curiosity of a child, and replacing each bone in its proper place, turned to the interpreter, and replied that she fully believed they were Black Hawk's bones." Picking up every bone, testing its weight, looking for marks, Black Hawk's wife was no doubt assessing the veracity of the governor's claim by attempting to re-articulate the bones in her memory, looking for elements of Black Hawk's life in the lifeless tissue. Where the phrenologists and resurrectionists disdained the historicity of the body, preferring to exaggerate its physicality, Black Hawk's wife sought to identify the body by the weight of its history. She was able to identify the remains by the condition of the teeth, and was satisfied in the identification.

The destruction of the grave and the theft of the bones, however, had alerted the Sauks to the insecurity of their lives under the new social conditions of U.S. governmentality. Notwithstanding the effort that had been expended to return the bones to Iowa, Black Hawk's widow decided to leave them in the charge of the governor; he could, at the very least, keep them safe from marauders. The Burlington *Hawk-Eye* would write, "She knew the Governor was a good man, or he would not have taken the great pains he had manifested to oblige her, and, in consideration of the great benevolence and disinterested friendship, she would leave the bones under his care and protection." Perhaps the only recorded words of Black Hawk's widow were that the remains were "in a good dry place." In a world of increasingly constrained options, the Sauks would opt, again, to appropriate the apparatuses and officials of the state to maintain and reproduce a sense—however limited—of their cultural and historical particularity.

Black Hawk's bones, given to the Geological and Historical Institute in Burlington, Iowa, were destroyed in a fire that consumed the building on January 16, 1853. Like his death, some twenty years before, the preservation and eventual destruction of his bones would be colonized by the state, made over as historical events. A history of Des Moines County written in 1879 would describe this moment as the great denouement of Black Hawk's illustrious life, writing, "Thus amid fire and tumult, Black Hawk found a final earthly resting-place in the ashes of the ruined structure, and the last act of his eventful career was not less dramatic than the first public appearance of the Brave." Remaking the circumstances of Black Hawk's life as little more than a theatrical event, here Black Hawk is reduced to a player upon a stage. By so colonizing his life, however, the state becomes the conservator of his spirit. Black Hawk may have lost the war, but to the extent that he continues to orient its historical archive, the state remains haunted by his presence.

NOTES

1. "Introduction," *Annals of the State Historical Society of Iowa* 2 (April 1863): v, Jerome & Duncan, Printers.

2. The institutional professionalization of history, in other words, was bound up in the elaboration of what Walter Benjamin called "historicist" interpretations of the past, where events were conveyed in an empty, homogenous time absent any degree of dialectical negation or critical political response. See Walter Benjamin, "Theses on the Philosophy of History," in *Illuminations*, ed. Hannah Arendt, 253–64 (New York: Schocken Books, 1997); see also Michel Foucault, *Society Must Be Defended*, trans. David Macey (New York: Picador, 2003); on history, nation, and seriality, see Benedict Anderson, *The Spectre of Comparisons* (London: Verso, 1996).

3. William Appleman Williams, *The Roots of the Modern American Empire* (New York: Vintage, 1970); see also William Cronon, *Nature's Metropolis: Chicago and the Great West* (New York: W. W. Norton, 1992), for an examination of the rail infrastructure of northeastern economic hegemony.

4. See Philip J. Deloria, *Playing Indian* (New Haven CT: Yale University Press, 1998).

5. Willard Barrows, "The History of Scott County," in *Annals of Iowa* 3 (April 1863), 50–51.

6. See Michel de Certeau, *The Writing of History*, trans. Tom Conley (New York: Columbia University Press, 1992); see also Benedict Anderson, *Imagined Communities* (London: Verso, 1982), particularly the chapter on the tomb of the unknown soldier; and Eric Hobsbawn, *Nations and Nationalism: Programme, Myth, Reality* (Cambridge: Cambridge University Press, 1990).

7. See Ann Braude, *Radical Spirits: Spiritualism and Women's Rights in Nineteenth-Century America*, 2nd ed. (Bloomington: Indiana University Press, 2001); see also Russ Castronovo, *Necro Citizenship: Death, Eroticism, and the Public Sphere in the Nineteenth-Century United States* (Durham: Duke University Press, 2001).

8. Lincoln's resurrection was abetted by the fact that he was assassinated on Good Friday. See Franny Nudelman, *John Brown's Body: Slavery, Violence, and the Culture of War* (Chapel Hill: University of North Carolina Press, 2004). See also Priscilla Wald, *Constituting Americans: Cultural Anxiety and Narrative Form* (Durham NC: Duke University Press, 1995), and Sarah Vowell, *Assassination Vacation* (New York: Simon & Schuster, 2005).

9. My point here is meant to resonate with Freud's basic distinction between mourning and melancholia. The grief that one experiences after a death, Freud argues, corresponds to the loss of the individual-object and his or her presence as an object of identification. Grief is either healthy (mourning) or pathological (melancholia), depending upon the subject's ability to come to terms with the loss of the individual-object, and to seek out other individual-objects with whom to identify, and in whom to invest a measure of psychic energy. The melancholic, who is incapable of such further identifications, remains locked in his or her ego, cherishing the dead/absent object, and incapable of sublimating grief into any more productive end. Insofar as the state facilitates its construction and occupation of the nation through the harvest of grief in this moment, I want to suggest that the state becomes the object through which grief is resolved, and mourning is transformed into a "more productive" end. The state, in fact, is highly interested in foreclosing other ends for grief, a point that Joseph Roach makes, albeit not in quite this language, in *Cities of the Dead*. See Sigmund Freud, "Mourning and Melancholia," in *The Freud Reader* (New York: W. W. Norton, 1995); see also Joseph Roach, *Cities of the Dead: Circum-Atlantic Performance* (New York: Columbia University, 1996).

10. Walter Benjamin, in his "Theses on the Philosophy of History," argued that the "historical knowledge" that will allow the oppressed classes to complete their revolution is the knowledge of "enslaved ancestors." Benjamin goes on to link the "forward thinking" of Social Democrats with the deliberate negation of this revolutionary potential, a way of concentrating the gaze of the oppressed on the future and its elusive hopes as opposed to the past and its certain horrors. I am suggesting, following recent critics of nationalism, that this negation of revolutionary potential is also accomplished by harnessing the dead to the nation and, thus, to the state.

11. This distinction is overdrawn, although there are certainly very different histories with regard to the institutional formation of the intellectual classes in the United States and the Caribbean. On the Caribbean as a site of disciplinary knowledge formation, see Antonio Benitez-Rojo, *The Repeating Island* (Durham NC: Duke University Press, 1993). Furthermore, as David Scott has indicated in his critical appraisal of Sidney Mintz's life and work, for most of the twentieth century the academy in the United States has produced an intellectual class whose sole purpose was the technocratic

management of Caribbean states. The critical moment in Mintz's life, Scott suggests, was his fieldwork in late-1940s Puerto Rico. Working under the auspices of the Rockefeller Foundation, Mintz and his cohort were in Puerto Rico to conduct studies that could help the colonial government of the United States reorganize the Puerto Rican economy—the infamous Operation Bootstrap. Mintz rejected this colonial intellectual instrumentality. The result of his research from this period, *Worker in the Cane*, is thus a highly personal account of the historical transformation of rural Puerto Rico since the beginning of the U.S. occupation, drawn from Mintz's relationship to the members of the community in which he worked. It is also worth noting that the technocratic use of social science research as a means of disrupting the social and cultural life of the dead contradicts Avery Gordon's argument, in *Ghostly Matters*, that sociology and traditional disciplinary knowledge has ignored ghosts. On the contrary, ghosts have been central to the formation of disciplinary knowledge as it has been put to use by the state. See Avery Gordon, *Haunting and the Sociological Imagination* (Minneapolis: University of Minnesota Press, 1997).

12. Jenny Sharpe, *Ghosts of Slavery: A Literary Archaeology of Black Women's Lives* (Minneapolis: University of Minnesota Press, 2003).

13. See Stephan Palmié, *Wizards and Scientist: Explorations of Afro-Cuban Modernity and Tradition* (Durham NC: Duke University Press, 2002).

14. See Peter Linebaugh and Marcus Rediker, *The Many-Headed Hydra: Sailors, Slaves, and the Revolutionary Atlantic* (Boston: Beacon, 2000).

15. The vigor of these attacks perhaps accounts for the famous, yet ultimately misleading, debate about the dimensions of African "retentions" among black people in the United States versus the Caribbean. See Albert J. Raboteau, *Slave Religion: The "Invisible Institution" in the Antebellum South* (Oxford: Oxford University Press, 1978).

16. Ngugi wa Thiong'o, "Enactment of Power: The Politics of the Performance Space," *Drama Review* 41, no. 3 (Fall 1997), 11–30.

17. See Dipesh Chakrabarty, "The Time of History and the Times of Gods," in *The Politics of Culture in the Shadow of Capital*, ed. Lisa Lowe and David Lloyd, 35–60 (Durham NC: Duke University Press, 1997), 35.

18. Michael Reinschmidt, *Ethnohistory of the Sauk, 1885–1985: A Sociopolitical Study on Continuity and Change* (Gottingen, Germany: Cuvillier, 1993); William Thomas Hagan, *The Sac and Fox Indians* (Norman: University of Oklahoma Press, 1958); Benjamin Drake, *The Life and Adventures of Black Hawk: With Sketches of Keokuck, the Sac and Fox Indians, and the Late Black Hawk War* (Cincinnati: H., S., & J. Applegate, 1851).

19. See Mark Marhus, *Another America: Native American Maps and the History of Our Land* (New York: St. Martin's, 1997).

20. On space and the sacred in Native America, see Peter Nabokov, *Where the Lightning Strikes: The Lives of American Indian Sacred Places* (New York: Viking, 2006); on sacred space in the United States in general, see Belden C. Lane, *Landscapes of the Sacred: Geography and Narrative in American Spirituality* (Baltimore MD: Johns Hopkins University Press, 2002).

21. Kimberly C. Shankman, *Compromise and the Constitution: The Political Thought of Henry Clay* (Lanham MD: Lexington Books, 1999).

22. The names of the perpetrators were recorded by Works Progress Administration (WPA) ethnographers interviewing relatives of the resurrectionists. They was included in the short pamphlet, "Van Buren County," which was written and compiled by the Writers' Program of the WPA. See "Black Hawk: Black Hawk Finds Rest at Old Iowaville," in the clip files of the Burlington Public Library in Burlington, Iowa.

23. Barrows, "History of Scott County," *Annals of Iowa* 3 (April 1863), 50–51.

24. On taking possession, see G. W. F. Hegel, *The Philosophy of Right* (Amherst NY: Prometheus Books, 1996).

25. Author unknown, "Phrenological Developments and Character of the Celebrated Indian Chief and Warrior, Black Hawk: With Cuts," *American Journal of Phrenology and Miscellany* 1, no. 2 (November 1838): 51–61.

26. "Phrenological Developments," 55.

27. See Benjamin Reiss, *The Showman and the Slave: Race, Death, and Memory in Barnum's America* (Cambridge MA: Harvard University Press, 2001); Andrea Stulman Dennett, *Weird and Wonderful: The Dime Museum in America* (New York: New York University Press, 1997); and E *Pluribus Barnum: The Great Showman and the Making of U.S. Popular Culture* (Minneapolis: University of Minnesota Press, 1997).

28. Samuel W. Francis, *Memoir of the Life and Character of Professor Valentine Mott* (New York: W. J. Widdleton, 1865).

29. As suggested, the desecration of Native graves was consistent with the established practices of grave robbery in the nineteenth century, but the theft and preservation of Native graves continued, unabated, through the twentieth century, with many such physical relics remaining on display or in the possession of museums until the 1990s. Only in the 1990s did the federal government—after generations of Native activism—step in to pass the Native American Graves Protection and Repatriation Act, which provided for the return of such remains to Native tribes. See Barbara A. Mann, *Native Americans, Archaeologists, and the Mounds* (New York: P. Lang, 2003); Kathleen S. Fine-Dare, *Grave Injustice: The American Indian Repatriation Movement and NAGPRA* (Lincoln: University of Nebraska Press, 2002); and Tamara L. Bray, *The Future of the Past: Archaeologists, Native Americans, and Repa-*

triation (New York: Garland, 2001). The destruction of Indigenous peoples' graves for the purpose of scientific exploration was not limited to the United States. See Paul Turnbull, "'Outlawed Subjects': The Procurement and Scientific Uses of Australian Aboriginal Heads, ca. 1803–1835," *Eighteenth-Century Life* 22, no. 1 (1998).

30. This is, admittedly, speculative, but it seems to square with what we do know from the various accounts we have. In 1881 James Jordan told an interviewer that Black Hawk's wife told him that Black Hawk's head was missing shortly after his burial; Jordan went to the grave to investigate, only to find that Black Hawk's torso had fallen from the puncheon that was meant to hold it in place. This seems to be the origin of the "two trips, different times" theory. It seems highly unlikely that Turner would have been able to conceal the theft of the head long enough to go back and procure the body without being detected.

31. According to the WPA account of the theft of Black Hawk's body provided by Z. T. and Joseph Cox, relatives of the Cox brothers involved with the theft, at least one of the kettles used to clean Black Hawk's bones found its way to the Black Hawk Historical Site and the museum that were built on Rock Island by the Civilian Conservation Corps in 1939.

32. Sarah Welch Nossaman, "Pioneering at Bonaparte and Near Pella," *Annals of Iowa* 8 (October 1922): 452–62.

33. Author unknown, "The Death of Black Hawk," *History of Des Moines County* (Chicago: Western Historical, 1879), 346; available from the clip files of the Burlington Public Library, Burlington, Iowa.

34. Sigmund Freud, "The Uncanny," in *The Uncanny*, trans. David McLintock (New York: Penguin Books, 2003).

35. Since I am working in a strangely psychoanalytic vein here, I wonder whether the return to Black Hawk in the early part of her narrative is a screen for her family's motivations for leaving the upper South, which were no doubt connected to the expansion of plantation-slave agriculture and the Nat Turner Rebellion in southern Virginia. Nossaman was born in, and her family moved from, a place in North Carolina that was about ten miles from the origin of the Turner Rebellion.

36. Nossaman, "Pioneering at Bonaparte and Near Pella."

37. "Bones of Black Hawk," Burlington *Hawk-Eye*, Thursday, December 10, 1840; available from the Burlington Public Library clip files, Burlington, Iowa.

38. "Death of Black Hawk," 347.

5

The Baldoon Mysteries

LISA PHILIPS AND ALLAN K. MCDOUGALL

Shortly after the British–U.S. border dividing the Great Lakes was established by the 1783 Treaty of Paris, the respective governments began treaty processes with the highly respected and powerful First Nations in the Old Northwest, in an attempt to accommodate the needs of the First Nations in anticipation of an influx of settlers to the regions. Prior to that time, contact with the First Nations in the Great Lakes region was extensive, largely through fur-trading operations and Catholic missions. Priests and traders from Lower Canada and Europe had built close relations with the First Nations. Indeed, many of the traders married into the communities, reaping the benefit of community networks, which allowed access to hunting lands, established trading links with other groups, shared labor, and conferred social capital, especially through marriage to daughters of high-ranking leaders. This was the center for the "middle ground" (White 1990). By the late eighteenth century, many of the children born and socialized into these blended communities were called upon to be liaisons between the state and the First Nations communities, taking positions, such as translator, negotiator, or Indian superintendent, based on the status they held within the First Nations and settler communities. As the border became reified—and it took well over a generation and a war between England and the United States before the border was recognized by those living in the immediate area—the settlers began to reinvent the history of the region to suit themselves. As a result, the place of the First Nations was diminished in the settler landscape.

This paper begins in the period following the American Revolution, when First Nations were still recognized as powerful agents, capable of tipping the balance between U.S. and British interests. At stake was the legal control of the land that was eyed so covetously by would-be speculators and settlers on the eastern seaboard and in European centers. This paper focuses on an area just north and east of Lake St. Clair, between Lake Erie and Lake Huron, on the Upper Canada side of the border of what became Michigan and Ontario. In 1796 the British government, recognizing the importance of maintaining good relations with its First Nations allies when the state border was implemented, set aside a safe haven for those displaced from their lands across the border. The section of land reserved for Britain's allies was chosen for its central location on the St. Clair River and for the abundant locally available hunting, sugaring, and farming resources that would provide the First Nations refugees a reasonable means of subsistence. However, in familiar fashion, the treaty and land settlement were quickly erased from British memory and the reserve that in 1818 had been designated "Shawnese" was changed to "Sombra Township" within the decade.

When the border was drawn in 1796, pressure from potential land speculators to open the area for settlement was intense. The British government was simultaneously struggling to meet the cost of its colonies, given the drain on its treasury caused by the Napoleonic wars. The solution to both sets of pressures was found in opening colonial land for settlement and requiring the colonies to sell and tax that land to meet their expenditures. In 1804 Lord Selkirk attempted to establish one such settlement, Baldoon, just south of the lands reserved for the First Nations in 1796. The Baldoon settlement ultimately failed. Its demise left the colonial government with the opportunity to develop all the land east of Lakes St. Clair and Huron. Treaties were negotiated and the land ceded was divided into townships and lots to be sold. In its haste, the colony ignored their commitment to the First Nations allies in 1796. The 1828 map (see fig. 1) documents the changing focus to European settlement on what had been well established as First Nations' land: Shawnese became Sombra. It was in this period of settler encroachment onto

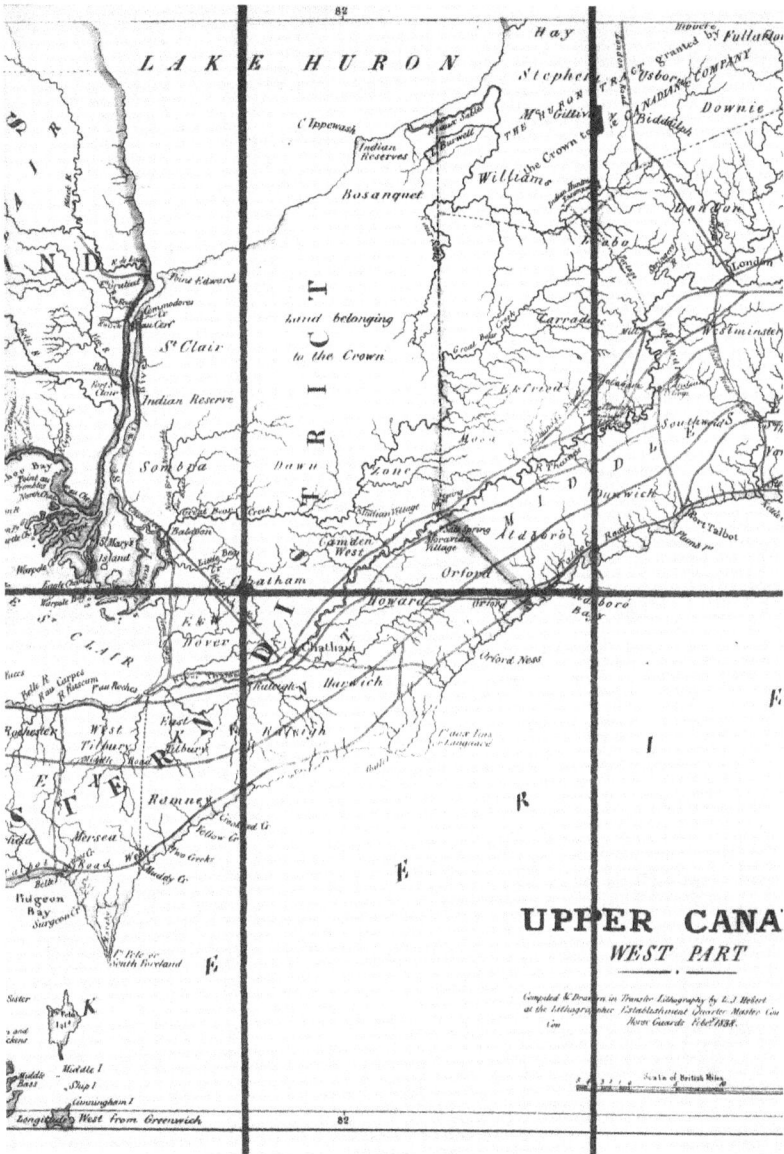

FIGURE 1. Portion of "Map of the Province of Upper Canada" [1838], National Archives of Canada, 2849.

previously occupied land that events dubbed "The Baldoon Mystery" transpired.[1]

This paper first presents the substance of the mystery and then the iterations of the "mysteries" through five periods. The continual re-entextualization of the events that occurred between 1821 and 1823 illustrate how the First Nations connections with the land were eventually erased and replaced with social reconstructions that fit with the contemporary values of each subsequent period.[2] In our analysis of multiple versions of the Baldoon mystery, we begin with the recognition that the recounting of history (and, indeed, any story) tells us as much about the storyteller and audience as it does about the narrative events. Baquedano-López (2001, 429) summarized this quite succinctly: "While narrative focuses on particular protagonists and events, narrative also situates tellers and their audiences within a web of historical and cultural expectations, ideologies, and meanings more broadly. As such, narrative creates shared understandings and community among those participating in narrative activity. Moreover, the narrative process extends beyond the boundaries of the here and now to embrace people and places in a cultural past."

As we traced the Baldoon mystery from era to era, we focused on how each version indexes the social contexts of the "teller" and audience.[3] Folklorists have long addressed the importance of tellings and retellings of a story as a means of structuring experience and as a means of socialization into a community (cf. Benedict[4] and Malinowski as addressed in Duncan 1969, and Bauman 1984). In this paper, we examined more than a dozen versions of the Baldoon mystery, locating the changing epistemologies inherent in each era. Our focus will be on patterns in the explanations of the metaphysical aspects of the stories, which index the social expectations and understandings predominant in the periods examined. This is in keeping with Hymes's observation: "In cultures where the telling of stories was a major way of understanding, explaining and dealing with experience, experience was put into the form of personal or culturally shared narrative. Again and again, instead of a chaos of events, experience was organized into sometimes subtle patterns" (1996, 136).

The initial clue to the "teller" and the (presumed) "audience" is found in the framing of the story (cf. Goffman 1974; Valentine 1995, 1996). Each of these versions has been produced in a given context for an assumed audience. The means of framing indexes the teller's or author's stance, or standpoint, and what are assumed to be shared understandings. For example, the published version written by Rev. Jones in 1861 was part of a larger work, *History of the Ojebway Indians.* Located in his section called "Fairies—Waindegoos, or Giants—Indian Names," Jones began his discussion with the following: "The heathen Indians all believe in the existence of those imaginary little folks called Fairies. The Ojebways call them *mamagwasewug,* the hidden or covered beings. They believe them to be invisible, but possessed of the power of showing themselves. Many old Indians affirm that they have both seen and talked with them" (1861, 156).

Jones's use of the adjective "heathen" to describe those who "believe in the existence of those imaginary little folks" distanced him from that group and their beliefs. His use of the term "believe" (twice) continued to mark him as the skeptical outsider explaining "Indian" knowledge to others more like himself; that is to say, to others who were not heathen. Jones consistently distanced himself from "heathen Indians" and their "beliefs" by his use of evidentials, such as "the (old) Indians say" and "the Indians supposed," and by the use of the passive voice, as in the sentence, "Another tribe of fairies *were said* to have formerly resided on the east bank of the River Credit [Jones's childhood home], about a mile from the lake, where they often showed themselves" (1861, 157). Jones used the passive voice to introduce his story as well: "The following story *is related* of fairies on the River St. Clair" (157). Ojibwe storytellers and authors often directly report their own relationship to their source of information or knowledge; in Jones's case, he explicitly denied personal interaction with *mamagwasewug*—"In all my travels through the wilderness I have never been favoured with a visit from these invisible beings" (157)—further separating his experience as a Christian Ojibwe from that of either older or heathen Indians. Despite his disclaimers, Jones's use of the Ojibwe term and his detailed accounts of the beings that inhabit the Ojibwe world indexed him as an expert—and even insider—in that community. This duality was clear in the title of his book and, indeed, in all of his writings.

Jones's account of the incidents in 1824 focused on the "fairies on the River St. Clair" and their "visitations . . . to a Scotch family living on the St. Clair" (1861, 158). He outlined some of the events that had been reported, including the death of the farmer's poultry, cattle, pigs, and horses, stones and pieces of lead breaking the windows and entering the house, pots and kettles moved from their places, apparently without human agency, and, finally, live coals found "wrapped in tow and rags" throughout the house, which eventually burned it to the ground. In Jones's account, these events were "finally declared to be the work of witchcraft." He continued, "Accordingly, a celebrated witch doctor, by the name of Troyer, residing near Niagara Falls, was sent for, to expel all the witches and wizards from the premises" (158). It appears that in his normal travels as a missionary for the region, Rev. Jones crossed paths with the "celebrated witch doctor" on the road from the St. Clair. Having heard the stories of the odd events on the St. Clair, and having discussed it with the locals, Jones was particularly interested to hear Mr. Troyer's version when they met:

> [Mr. Troyer] then positively stated that he knew the whole affair was witchcraft, and that he would soon make a finish of the witches. I was afterwards informed that he began to expel them by firing off guns loaded with silver bullets, which he stated were the only kind of weapons which could take effect upon a witch. Whilst he was in the midst of his manoeuvring, the neighbouring magistrate, hearing of what was going on, issued a warrant to take him into custody. The great doctor . . . quickly made his escape to his own quiet home. Thus ended the whole affair of the supposed witches and fairies. (159)

The explanation was very different when Jones asked the "noted pow-wow chief, Pashegeeghegwaskum of Walpool [sic] Island," just a few miles southwest of the Baldoon farm, about the "strange occurrences among the white people." Pashegeeghegwaskum responded, "The place on which the white man's house now stands was the former residence of the Mamagwasewug, or fairies. Our forefathers used to see them on the bank of the river. . . . When the white man came and pitched his wigwam on the spot where they lived, they removed back to the poplar grove, where they have been lying for several years. Last spring this white man went and cleared and burnt this grove, and the fairies have again been obliged to remove; . . . they felt indignant at such treatment, and were venting their vengeance at the white man by destroying his property" (1861, 159).

The second story of the series of events on the St. Clair River, published possibly as early as 1871, a mere decade after Jones's book,[5] indexed a very different teller and audience, and a different reason for the telling. While Jones's story about the incident(s) on the River St. Clair was recounted to give evidence—at least in the minds of the "heathen Indians"—about the existence of the little people (*mamagwasewug*), Neil McDonald's version, *The Belledoon Mysteries: An O'er True Story*, focused on the "truth" value of the mysterious happenings, as explicitly indexed in the title. McDonald's version framed the story as a continuation of Lord Selkirk's "establishment of a second Eutopia [*sic*]," the Baldoon settlement at the "Channel Ecarte" in 1804 (1). In McDonald's background statements in his first chapter of *The Belledoon Mysteries*, he included the following evaluation to indicate why this story was worth telling (cf. Labov and Waletzky 1967, Labov 1972): "There are fewer points of history more fraught with interest to the thinking minds than the stories of the first European settlers in this Western World, whether we peruse the adventures of a vast body like the wandering Hugenots [*sic*] or the daily experience of a family of roving emigrants, the tale of human fortitude, endurance and successful encounter of difficulties is ever new to us" (McDonald 1905, 2).

However, by the end of his story, McDonald's ambivalence over the genre was evident, both in the final statement and in the introduction to the appendix. The final two paragraphs of the story, following the story's coda, outline this ambiguity:

In winter time the hearth of many a farm house has seen gathered round it the lads and lasses, telling half in awe and half in jest the strange story we have related.

That such things may point a moral is most true, and that they should not be forgotten as time flies over our heads, we have recorded them in printed form. We make no remarks on the wonders we have recited. We simply tell the tale as it is told to us, and leave all our readers to wrestle with the strange events of the Belledoon Mysteries. (McDonald 1905, 20)

McDonald's appendix, composed of twenty-eight statements by witnesses or relatives of witnesses, presented another clue to his presumptions about his audience. While there was no indication whether McDonald conducted the interviews that comprised the appendix, they all followed a similar format. These statements began with a metanarrative frame that included the speaker or author's entitlement to tell the story, whether through having firsthand knowledge or having heard the story(ies) from close relatives. The opening statements were followed by a recounting of events, which varied greatly in their elaboration from one speaker to the next, and closed with either a testimonial about the character of John T. McDonald or a testimonial about the character of the person from whom the speaker or author received his or her knowledge. Neil McDonald worked very hard to build a space for his audience to accept the truth value of the story, as noted in his introduction to the appendix. McDonald wrote, "The facts already set forth in this work we must admit are liable in this unsuperstitious age to be met with no small amount of incredulity. It would make no difference with the reading public should I assert the truthfulness of the foregoing facts; but, to disbelieve the following statements of some of our best and most reliable citizens would be to entirely revolutionize the popular opinion as regards their moral standing in the communities of which they are respected members" (1905, 21).

This statement presented powerful clues to the temporal and social context. McDonald's remark about "this unsuperstitious age" echoed a statement in the body of the story that spoke of an earlier standard: "Most men's minds were more or less imbued with super-stitious ideas *in those days* before people had become so dreadfully scientific or so properly orthodox as they are now" (1905, 15, italics added). The audience presumed by McDonald needed more than his assertions of "the truthfulness of the foregoing facts"; indeed, that audience needed statements from "the best and most reliable," "respected" citizens who had good "moral standing in the[ir] com-munities." The testimonial assessments of the unfortunate owner of the house at Baldoon almost uniformly described him as "hon-est," "hard-working," "in good standing with the Baptist Church," and/or "respectable," which was consistent with the demands for accepting a source as truthful or reliable at the turn of the twentieth century in southwestern Ontario.

Unlike later versions of the Baldoon mystery, McDonald's rendi-tion was not a retelling or reframing of Jones's earlier narrative. Many elements in his story appear to mirror those in Jones's, but there are significant differences in detail. The similarities in Jones's and McDonald's stories were undoubtedly due to the entextualiza-tion of the same series of events. However, the differences speak to the epistemological shifts between the world Jones addressed and that created by McDonald. McDonald's story indexed a very different teller and audience, and a different reason for the telling.

Throughout Neil McDonald's text, the worldview of the McDon-alds and their ilk was explicitly outlined and discussed. Statements such as "They were strict Baptists of the old Coventish character, determined, steady and little likely to be led away by freaks of the imagination" (1905, 3) and "McDonald [had been] impregnated from childhood by such old world lore that seems part of the Caldo-nian constitution" (15) provide metanarrative cues for understand-ing the worldview of those in the story. These cues point to a certain type of relationship between the events that occurred on the farm and the presumed cause and perpetrator of those events.

The climax to McDonald's story was precipitated by a terrifying visit to Longwoods to seek counsel with the fifteen-year-old daughter of an unnamed doctor who had the "gift of second-sight." Within moments after McDonald and the young woman met, and without any apparent prompting, the young seer asked McDonald about trouble with a piece of land: "Did not some of your neighbors desire to purchase a portion of your land, and did you not refuse them?" (1905, 17). When McDonald confirmed that the statements were true, the young woman responded with "I see . . . a Long, Low, Log House" and then described the inhabitants. After a three-hour session with a moonstone, she emerged from her chamber and declared that a stray goose in McDonald's flock was "the destroyer of [his] peace," adding, "Taking the shape of that bird is your enemy" (17). Immediately after returning home, McDonald, on the advice of the young woman, shot the stray goose with a silver bullet, wounding it in the wing. According to the author, "Whether John McDonald was right in his conjectures or not, it is not the compiler's duty to decide, certain it is that he and all his friends attributed all his troubles to the agency of the woman at the Long, Low, Log house. One thing seemed to corroborate this belief. From the time that the [stray goose] was shot and the woman wounded[,] no spiritual manifestations were ever heard of in the McDonald family, and peace reigned supreme in the woody slopes of Belledoon" (20).

The text of the 1915 version (anonymous) remained identical to the one of 1905, but the title and the illustrations changed dramatically, indexing a further epistemological shift. Illustrations are key to the framing of the 1915 version of the story, as they present yet another channel to guide the interpretation. In the shared text of the stories, the events were described as "mysterious" or "ghostly," or as "a haunting" and as the product of an "unseen hand," "spirits," "an evil agency," and "supernatural agencies," but the term "witchcraft" was never explicitly mentioned. Despite the author's skirting the issue, witchcraft became the obvious culprit behind the events in the 1915 version. A comparison of the title pages of the two versions graphically illustrates this shift in interpretation.

With the changes in the title and the illustrations, the 1915 version moved from one of Scottish fortitude and "old world" beliefs to an obvious case of witchcraft, as attested by the image of the hag emerging from between "The Baldoon" and "Mystery" in the title. The jig-dancing Scotsman of the earlier version was replaced

THE BELLEDOON
MYSTERIES.

An O'er
True Story

By Neil T. McDonald.

CHAPTER I.

"Come roam with me the unsettled forest through,
Where scenes sublime shall meet your wandering view;
The settlers' farm with blazing fires o'er spread;
The hunters' cabin and the Indians' shed;
The log-built hamlet, deep in wilds embraced;
The awful silence of the unpeopled waste.—Ax.

THE broad and beautiful river St. Clair sweeps with majestic force between the great inland seas, lake Huron and lake St. Clair, and at about thirty miles from its source a tributary stream called by the early French settlers Channel Ecarte winds its way into a low-lying tract of country which at the period of which I write was a desolate region of marsh and forest, with here and there a cleared settlement.

In 1803 the philanthropic, but unfortunate Lord Selkirk, racked by home troubles and inspired with visions of the establishment of a second Eutopia, resolved to found a second colony that should be the means of restoring his own shattered fortunes and at the same time be a blessing to his dependants, whose lots as in common in many old English and Scottish families, were bound up in their lord's interests.

Actuated by these motives, he set out on an exploring expedition through Canada, and, after various

FIGURE 2.
Neil T. McDonald's
Belledoon Mysteries
[ca. 1905].

by a child fishing, moving the narrative genre from a story out-lining the strange facts surrounding a Scotsman's misfortunes in Baldoon to a fairytale replete with witches that might be heard in childhood. While the hag of the 1915 version was taken directly from an old-world imagination, it had been incorporated as the prototypical explanation of the "supernatural" events in the New World that defied other interpretations, once again attesting to the absolute change in worldview between Jones's version and the earliest McDonald version.

The shifts in worldview were indexed through the references to First Nations, as well. In the (shared) text of the 1905 and 1915

127

FIGURE 3.
Reprint of Neil T.
McDonald's version
[ca. 1915], updated
by Alan Mann.

versions, First Nations people were introduced only twice, first in the reference to an "Indian knife" with a ten-inch blade, which was dashed against a window frame by an invisible agent, and second, in an episode about an abortive effort by an "Indian Medicine Man" to stop the annoyances. Neil T. McDonald's assessment of this Indian illustrates how divorced the local settler community had become from their First Nations' neighbors: "The Indian, however, never put in an appearance. Perhaps he had lost the secret [to the ceremony], or probably he was not quite prepared to quit the certainties of this humdrum life, even for an eternity of buffalos and innumerable scalps" (1905, 15). The stereotyped Indian of McDonald's story certainly did not match the people in the neighboring community of Walpole Island, described by Jones. However, McDonald did include two testimonials from First Nations' men among the "statements of some of [the] best and most reliable citizens" (21). Those two statements presented very similar explanations of the events.

> The trouble was caused in this way—J. T. McDonald purchased a piece of land which the disturbers wanted to purchase, and these are the steps they took to have revenge on him. . . . We called them wild Indians in our language and we believe they made their abode in the prairies southeast of the house on the same farm. (ReReNahSewa, in McDonald 1905, 24)

> We are satisfied that what you call witchcraft we call wild Indians, and that they had their abode in a small prairie on the same farm, but they could not be seen at any time. . . . We are satisfied that the cause of all this trouble was that John T. McDonald purchased the same farm that the wild Indians wanted, and to have revenge on him they took these steps to destroy his property. (Solomon Par-tar-sung, in McDonald 1905, 25)

Although these testimonials were prominently displayed, in second and third position, the interpretation offered in both, that (New World) aboriginal beings or what "we call wild Indians" were behind the troubles, does not appear to have been incorporated into the broader narrative. ReReNahSewa's comment, "We were aware of their doings and tried to tell him what we knew about them, but we could not understand each other's language," remained accurate some fifty years after the event (McDonald 1905, 24). Here again we see that the events matched referentially, but the interpretations were based on very different worldviews.

In 1900 the "Mystery at Baldoon House" appeared in chapter five of *Baldoon*, a novel by Le Roy Hooker. Because the book was fictional, there was little attempt to locate the historicity of the events at Baldoon, although within the context of the novel there was considerable effort to establish the likelihood of the mystery's being "true," or at least possible. The main character of the larger novel, George M'Garriger, along with his wife and three unmarried daughters, became victims in the now-familiar events when they moved into the "long-abandoned" Baldoon House. As the narrator noted, "Of course we had all heard the ghostly traditions of the house when it was inhabited by the original builder, Mactavish. But that belonged to the distant past" (Hooker 1900, 119–20). Because the purchase of the Baldoon House in the novel was used to illustrate George M'Garriger's turn toward miserliness and his ultimate downfall, the validation of the events at Baldoon fell to Mrs. M'Garriger. According to the narrator of the story, he encouraged Mrs. M'Garriger to detail the "strange happenings," adding, "I want to put it on record, just here, that I believe any statement made by Mary M'Garriger as I believe the verities of the multiplication table. I record this because I could not accept the views of some who were inclined to discount her understandings of the things she described on grounds of her supposed leaning toward old-world superstitions, and the influence of fear upon her mind" (123–24).

The events in this fictional version mirrored those found in McDonald and Jones: strange lights at night, the sound of a flail on the floor, bullets thrown through the window, beds being lifted and dropped, a kettle upending then righting itself, dishes rattling and breaking and, finally, spontaneous fires throughout the house. The focus, again, was on the interpretation of those events. In Hooker, there were two possible interpretations: one was supernatural and the other was "material," involving smugglers working the border between the United States and Canada: "The house is no more accursed than you are, Tom. . . . I believe that smuggling has been carried on in this quarter since before Mactavish and his clansmen built their first house" (Hooker 1900, 141). This explanation was proposed by two young men in the novel who were trying to aid the M'Garrigers. The supernatural interpretation was attributed to Mrs. M'Garriger, whose strong Scottish accent in the book indexed her connections with the "old world" and the "Caledonian constitution" McDonald referred to.

Hooker's novel, like the stories related by Rev. Jones and Neil T. McDonald, was set in a very specific, identifiable location. Hooker wove local references throughout his story, melding facts of the original stories of the farm with the activities of the fictional M'Garrigers. In many respects, Hooker was more attentive to the Baldoon setting than McDonald had been, inserting references to features of the landscape such as the "little lagoon that connects at one end with the North Branch, and at the other with Channel E'Carte and the St. Clair River" (1900, 142) and to the scant six-mile distance between Baldoon and Walpole Island. When the young customs collector proposed his material solution—that is, that all the problems were caused by smugglers—the descriptions were couched in terms that would have been instantly recognizable to a contemporary audience of southwestern Ontario readers, who shared stereotypes of the local populations. According to the young man, the smugglers were "four men of shady reputation—Peewee, the Potawatomie Indian, of Walpole Island, Black Dick Douglas, Tonc Le Roux, and an American supposed to be confederate with these, named Julius Heyward, whose home was on the Michigan side of the St. Clair River, near Algonac" (144). This declaration presented a remarkably detailed look into the regional delineation of established—and potentially dangerous—groups (e.g., Potawatomies from the Walpole Island Reserve, Black Scots, French, and Americans). The change from a narrative to a fictional "detective" genre further highlights the changing epistemologies from one focused on the response of aboriginal beings to settler incursions to one rooted wholly in either a Scottish woman's superstitions or in local criminal activities.

The next version appeared two generations later, in 1952, as a chapter in Victor Lauriston's larger work, *Romantic Kent: More Than Three Centuries of History, 1626–1952*. The metanarrative framework of this volume positioned it as a part of a settler history of Kent County that had been contracted by the county council in 1949. Lauriston's book began:

> The year 1950 marked the completion of a century of municipal self-government for Kent. Yet this was not all the county's history. Before our municipal system was established under the Baldwin Act there had been, in Kent, more than six decades of white pioneering.

To understand the condition those pioneers confronted, it is needful to go yet farther back, to the more remote era when the powerful Attawandarons [Iroquoian people] occupied the fertile lands of what later became the southwestern Ontario peninsula. (1952, 11)

In his version of the history of the region, Lauriston attempted to establish that the region was, as Neil McDonald had asserted some fifty years earlier, a "vast waste land," and even went so far as to declare that "after the downfall of the Attawandarons, their country became a land without a history" (1952, 20). Lauriston admitted that there were some Algonquian people in the area, but cast doubts on their claim to the area throughout his first two chapters: "In time, wandering Ojibway tribes, particularly the Mississaugas, drifted in from the north; and *though they never settled the land* to any great extent, by the time of the American Revolutionary War they had established some sort of title to the territory between the Ottawa and Detroit which the British authorities, for purposes of purchase, recognized as valid" (19).

Given the explicit task of writing a pioneer history, it is no surprise that First Nations peoples (such as Potawatomie and Ojibwe) or beings were entirely excluded from Lauriston's account, which otherwise so closely followed Neil McDonald's story that it shared the distinctive spelling of Belledoon in its title, *The Belledoon Mystery*. The focus on pioneer history, replete with toil and building, was evident in the introduction to the story, which began: "A mile or more west of the nearest Baldoon settler, the sturdy Daniel McDonald about 1828 built a large frame house on the Chenal Ecarte. After years of toil and tribulation, he found himself head of a prosperous family. A son, John T. McDonald, married, and built himself a frame house nearby. This house was to be the scene of the Belledoon mystery" (Lauriston 1952, 464).

Lauriston concluded his—or more accurately, Neil McDonald's—version of the Belledoon story with an overt evaluation that relied on mid-twentieth-century standards of evidence: "The narrative itself is supplemented by detailed statements of numerous eye-witnesses; giving the impression that the material had been gathered at first hand from old people who had witnessed the episodes. The preliminary narrative dealing with Lord Selkirk and the founding of the settlement, *the only portion that can be checked with independent authorities*, is in many respects inaccurate, due possibly to the compiler depending on local word-of-mouth tradition rather than on contemporary records" (1952, 470). This version, then, removed the story from "history" and turned it into a "tale" that was "inaccurately" presented as based in fact. In keeping with the rest of his volume, this history erased all evidence of First Nations in southwestern Ontario.

A quarter century later, C. H. Gervais and James Reaney transformed the story into a play. Attendant with the shift in genre from story to play were changes in the participants, the events, and the story's rationale or moral. Such changes were acknowledged in passing by Gervais and Reaney when they wrote, "The story has been changed slightly and given a more complicated interpretation." The published version of the play was followed by an "Appendix Incorporating Scholarly Apparatus for the use of Educators." The appendix began with Gervais and Reaney's version of the basic story, again based on Neil McDonald's version, including the statements in the appendix, although they cited Hugh Colwell as the author.[6] Taking a tack entirely opposite that of Lauriston, Gervais and Reaney framed the story on which their play was based within a historical and, hence, "fact-based" context: "The events portrayed in Baldoon are based on fact—on actual occurrences that took place in the 19th century settlement of Baldoon near Wallaceburg, Ontario" (1976, 105).

Apparently, unlike that of McDonald, the reputations of Gervais and Reaney (a "Governor-General award winning author") were sufficient to allow them to declare the events as factual without their providing documentation from the "contemporary record." Or perhaps the publication of McDonald's ("Cowell") pamphlet at the turn of the twentieth century was, by 1976, considered an exemplar of authenticity because of its age, making it indeed another type of contemporary record. Gervais and Reaney further established the story as part of the historical record in their presentation of a settler history that, again, began with Selkirk: "Baldoon was settled in 1804 by a collection of families from Scotland brought to the New World by the philanthropic Lord Selkirk. According to Lord Selkirk's arrangements, each family was given a homestead of fifty acres. Through the years this colony prospered and eventually the community of Wallaceburg was incorporated and grew" (1976, 105).

By invoking Lord Selkirk and the "Baldoon settlement," Gervais and Reaney placed the story into a recognizable context—many people have heard of the Baldoon settlement even if they know little else about the history of Upper Canada. The direct path from the Baldoon settlement to the incorporation of Wallaceburg presented by Gervais and Reaney linked a documented event (the Baldoon settlement) with a fixed, contemporary location (Wallaceburg), evoking an on-the-ground reality for both the settlement effort and the established town. They did this despite historians' almost universal declaration that the Baldoon settlement was a failure; the Anglo-Canadian settlement of the area happened despite Lord Selkirk's schemes. However, Gervais's and Reaney's individually authored notes "incorporating scholarly apparatus" presented a very different framing of their play, one that echoes Hymes's statement, cited earlier, that "experience [is] put into the form of personal or culturally shared narrative" (1996, 136). Gervais wrote, "Baldoon was like looking into a genealogical mirror—it was a similar story ["to my mother's stories of poltergeists at Pointe-aux-Roches"], but one more fascinating and legendary. The crux of it for me however was the fact that something had taken place, no matter how mysterious or weird. *It was the feeling of authenticity coupled with my own personal family poltergeists that sent me in search. That to me is the background to the play*" (Gervais and Reaney 1976, 117).

Their fascination with mysticism, "witchcraft," religious dogmatism, and "beliefs" motivated many of the artistic choices made in translating this particular series of historical events into a play. Gervais and Reaney's focus on experiential and spiritual mystery marked broader shifts from a focus on "progress and materialism" to a focus in the mid-1970s on an emerging sense of spiritual "authenticity." As Reaney wrote:

We couldn't get all the marvelous events of this old story into the play . . . but what we hope to have left in is the sense that out of the past comes a world where the laws of atheism, progress and materialism suddenly break down. Surely it is a good thing that they do break down occasionally to let in some terror and some mystery. This is a story from our deep past and our own Lake St. Clair fen country[,] which should add a feeling of there being more depths and heights to existence than our present day usually discovers. (Reaney, in Gervais and Reaney 1976, 119)

In Reaney's personal notes, he recounted how locals skeptically asked him if he believed in the events that they mockingly called the "Baboon Mystery." His response had been to laugh the question off, but in his personal notes in the appendix, Reaney presented his own statement of belief:

I believe that there was an old house here besieged by demonic phenomena. . . . I refuse to believe all materialist explanations: i.e., jealous Indians, neighbouring pranksters and smugglers in need of an empty house etc. I particularly favour the Indian explanation that since the owners of the house had built on the dancing ground of Indian fairies (and when these fairies—2 feet high with hairy faces—moved to a nearby grove) cut this last down as well. I believe the Mama Quesswukke struck back with all their magic powers until the Macdonalds (McTavishes in the play) fled. I believe too that no doubt there was a feud with a neighbouring family, one of whose members had learned magic in the Highlands before arrival in this Selkirk settlement, and no doubt when the silver bullet was fired at the mysterious strange goose always listening about at the Macdonald yard, no doubt this caused the apparitions to vanish and broke the left arm of Mrs Buchanan (Pharland in the play). (1976, 119)

Reaney prefaced his next paragraph with the words "I want to believe too" before addressing Dr. Troyer's "magic beneficent powers" and the "witches" that pursued McTavish and Mr McDorman, an elder of the Methodist church as they traveled to meet Dr. Troyer.

Reaney concluded his litany of beliefs with the statement, "I believe principally because it's a great deal more interesting to, than not," graphically documenting the authors' concerns to experiment with or try on alternative epistemologies (119).

The text of the play hinted at many of the theories of causation available in the earlier versions by Jones, McDonald, Cowell, and Hooker, but the ultimate cause of the disturbances was laid at the feet of McTavish, who had left his pregnant betrothed to marry a wealthy widow. After giving birth, the wronged woman had hung herself and the child had gone to live with McTavish and his wife as a servant. Mrs. Pharland, the mother of the cast-off love, was found to be a shape-shifting witch seeking vengeance for her lost daughter and grandchild. Many of the specific incidents in the house were traced to the dead daughter's ghost after Mrs. McTavish had refused Mr. McTavish's attempt to lay his deceased love's body to rest at their homestead. The play revolved around McTavish's hypocrisy and denials of having done anything that warranted confession or atonement. Throughout, the heavily Christian themes were interspersed with Northern European understandings of witchcraft.

In 1999 the story was published as "The Baldoon Goose," a song that was written and performed by Al Parrish and Joe Grant, of the group Tanglefoot, on the album *Full Throated Abandon*. This was but one of many original Tanglefoot songs fashioned from stories, legends, and events associated with Canadian history. One of the most remarkable transformations from the Baldoon mystery story to the song was the erasure of place. Outside of the reference to Baldoon in the title, there was no other indication that this was a retelling of the Baldoon mystery. Similarly, the characters in the song were made generic; except for "Young Moira Black, it's said she has the Second Sight," no other character was named. This was a fascinating permutation, as each of the other nine versions addressed in this paper named John T. McDonald (changed to McTavish by Gervais and Reaney), most named a (Dr.) Troyer, and many named various other intercessors and witnesses. The Parrish-Grant song was the only version that included the name of "Moira Black." The song was written in the tradition of an old Celtic ballad or folksong rather than in the tradition of tellings of the Baldoon mystery. Another device shared only by these two staged versions, the play and the song, was the suggestion that the primary perpetrator of the strange events at the farm was a scorned woman. By the turn of the twenty-first century, the story had become disassociated with a specific temporal period, location, and family—that is, disassociated from history; it had instead become a generic Celtic-style ballad. Its tie to Canadian history was found only in its inclusion on an album with other historic Canadian legends and stories. With these changes, questions of historicity of any kind were rendered entirely moot, and issues of spiritual activities ("the spirit of a witch," "spells," "second sight," and "sixth sense") were relegated to the realm of the unspecified, legendary past, as was typical of Northern European fairytales. The final three stanzas of the song, reproduced below, illustrate the themes of revenge, witchcraft, and the "pioneer spirit" as equivalent to spiritual purity.

> Within your flock is a wild goose; inside the goose there
>   dwells a witch
> A witch, when young, who fancied she would have your
>   father to herself
> But cast aside, she swore revenge. In recompense she wants
>   your land
> Your farm it is, or silver, that will pay the debt and lift this
>   curse!
>
> That witch shall never have this land where my father built
>   our home!
> This debt I thus must call my own, and pay I shall, with my
>   own hand!
> Three silver coins are just the thing, formed within the
>   forge's fire
> Into a bullet which now flies—and hits the goose in her left
>   wing!
>
> Gone the goose. and the spells, but ever since that day
> The witch's wounded left arm will not heal

The debt has been repaid
With silver it has been repaid. (Parrish 1999)

After memorializing the incident in song, yet more versions of the Baldoon mystery appeared. In September 2004 we located four brief narratives and an encyclopedia entry of the Baldoon mystery on the Internet. By early 2007 these had expanded to include entries on Wikipedia, a seven-minute podcast of the events, and a geocaching site that listed a waymarker for the site of the Baldoon mystery. The question of the genre of the Baldoon mystery (i.e., whether it was a historical event or a local folktale) that was evident in the earlier tellings became even more pronounced in the more recent presentations. For example, Kristeena Natili's story, repeated on two Web sites (wallaceburg.ca and mysteriesofcanada.com), began with the statement, "The events recorded in this strange mystery occurred between 1830 and 1840. This all happened within a few kilometers of WALLACEBURG, Ontario." By giving a specific time and place for the events, Natili placed the "strange mystery" within the realm of the historical. Following Natili's coda ("From the time that the bird was shot and the old woman was wounded, no spiritual manifestations were ever heard of at the McDonald farm and peace again fell on the Baldoon"), two notes were included. The first was that "Kristeena lives about 2 kilometers from where this mystery was said to have taken place." This repeated the tone of "authenticity" and connection that were found in the notes following the Gervais and Reaney play. The second note read: "Special note: Mysteries of Canada does not normally accept 'ghost stories.' However, a quick look through the files finds that the Baldoon story is part of the heritage of the Wallaceburg area. And that makes it part of the History of Canadians" (Natili 2004, 2). This note further blurred the line between folktale and history. In this metanarrative statement framing the story, a tie between the tradition of telling this story and the heritage "of the Wallaceburg area" allowed its construction as history rather than as a "ghost story"!

Another posting with an even more extensive metanarrative framing was "Poltergeist of Baldoon" by Sue Darroch (with a somewhat confusing copyright of 1997–2005). This version was framed in two ways, first by its inclusion under the heading, "Ontario Ghosts and Hauntings Research Society," and then by the use of "poltergeist" in the title, which put it directly into the realm of the (Northern European) supernatural. Second, Darroch presented an introduction and final note, which functioned to retain the story's ambiguous position between folktale and historical event. Darroch began, "I have long been interested in the events known as the Baldoon Mystery. And whilst I admit that elements of the story definitely have the ring of a good folktale, I cannot dismiss the sheer number of witnesses and the volume of good documentation, which suggests that something perhaps not of this world did occur in this tiny Scottish settlement through the years of 1829 to 1831" (2004, 1).

As was standard in all the tellings framed as historical, Darroch's began with Lord Selkirk's settlement, although she included a statement that the only thing left of the failed settlement was a plaque that made "no mention of the seemingly supernatural events that would make it infamous amongst Canadian paranormalists."[7] Darroch's sources included Gervais and Reaney, one version of the McDonald story, and three of the "statements" from the McDonald interviews supplied by the Wallaceburg and District Museum. Darroch had several variations not found elsewhere; for example, her use of "Dr. John F. Troyner," with its unique spelling. She included a date for a pardon granted to Robert Baker by the lieutenant governor on May 6, 1830, cited in Hamil's history of the Lower Thames Valley (1951, 185). With each such addition of specific information, she built her case for "the volume of good documentation" and the "sheer number of witnesses." Darroch finished her story with a second version of her initial frame, which repeated the essence of the ambiguity:

> As I stated in the opening paragraph[,] some of the elements of this story sound much like folklore[,] particularly in how the poltergeist events were eventually resolved. However, all the folks involved in these events were actual people, including the would-be "house clearer" [Barker] and the witch hunter. Events were

documented at the time they were occurring and not (as is often the case with myths and legends) presumably many years after the fact.

So the question remains—[who] or what was haunting the Macdonalds and their farm? In all probability[,] we will never know. (Darroch 2004, 3)

The other 2004 Internet postings were similar in several respects: both were titled "The Baldoon Mystery," neither was attributed to an author, and both were on Web sites tied to the histories of the Chatham–Kent and Wallaceburg areas, with an eye toward attracting tourists. The first was on kent.net, under the subhead "wallaceburg-museum," and the second was on baldoon.com, under "1804–2004 Baldoon Bicentennial." The story on the museum site gave a single-paragraph synopsis followed by a statement that framed the story as a tourist attraction, both historically and in the present: "The Baldoon Mystery has brought much attention to Wallaceburg. The Globe newspaper of Toronto published the events as they occurred & the story was republished in 1896. Deckhands of a passenger excursion vessel, the Thousand Islander, point out the site to passengers during the 1920's. Testimonials of prominent local figures who lived through and were involved in the Mystery add credibility to the tale" ("The Baldoon Mystery," 2004, 1).

The same three statements from McDonald's 1905 book that were found on the Ontario Ghost and Hauntings Research Society Web site were presented on this site. The museum's posting closed with the following line, which again privileged published documentation: "On display here at the Wallaceburg & District Museum you will see actual newspaper clippings documenting the Baldoon Mystery as well as artefacts from the time period and a model of the witch herself. And don't forget to stop at the Beledoon [*sic*] Gift Shop where you will be able to find a book outlining the Mystery at Baldoon" ("The Baldoon Mystery," 2004, 2).

On the baldoon.com site,[8] the focus was on the 1804–2004 Baldoon Bicentennial, which marked the beginning of Selkirk's ill-fated Baldoon settlement. The direct tie between Selkirk and the mystery at Baldoon was maintained in the introduction to the story, which was located in its own subdirectory ("The Baldoon Mystery") under "Bicentennial":

> Taking place nearly 200 years ago, The Baldoon Mystery is a strange story of mystery and disaster that suddenly overtook a family living near the Snye. It began with a Scotsman named Lord Selkirk, a philanthropist, racked by home troubles, who sets out on an exploring expedition and settles in the Channel Ecarte area. After the arrival of his Scottish clan, Lord Selkirk arranges homesteads of fifty acres to each family. [A member of] [o]ne such clan, a Mr. Daniel McDonald, head of a prosperous family, settles near Lord Selkirk. Many years later, one of Daniel McDonald's son, John, built his own house. This infamous house becomes the scene of one, The Baldoon Mystery. ("Bicentennial," 2004, 1)

This anonymously written tale (which, especially in its discussion of Selkirk, borrowed heavily from McDonald 1905), closed in standard fashion with the words "after this incident no spiritual manifestation ever occurred," but it included a final clause that linked it to the Baldoon Centennial project ("and peace reigned in the Baldoon"). The final comment in the posting repeated the difficulties of "understanding" the story, but in a manner that clearly marked it as a folktale: "For many years this strange story has been told and readers left to wrestle with the unusual and extraordinary events of The Baldoon Mystery."

All versions, but particularly those published after the beginning of the twentieth century, took two, divergent, epistemological tacks, depending on their perceived audience. The first attempted to explain the events by matching them to contemporary paranormal activities, including especially witchcraft by older women, ghostly hauntings, and poltergeist activity precipitated by troubled young women. The second focused on "material" explanations, including trickery, smuggling, jealous misdeeds, and criminal acts. The material explanations were far more apparent in versions directed toward the local southwestern Ontario (settler) audience. The more "spiritual" explanations, and those in genres that deviated from a strictly narrative structure, such as plays and songs, tended to be more generic in form and less tied to a specific location and time period. While many versions contained evidence consistent with both epistemologies, those versions written after 1900 clearly dismissed the paranormal explanations in favor of those more consistent with an empiricist perspective.

By tracing the "perpetrators" of the events in each of the stories, one can easily spot the diverging epistemologies. Through time, the potential perpetrators changed, indexing changing social and environmental contexts. Even the gender of the perpetrators speaks to the expectations of each subsequent period. Members of the "supernatural"—fairies, ghosts, and poltergeists—tended to be ungendered, although Reaney's spelling of *mamagwasewug* as "Mama Quesswukke" evoked a feminine association. Witches went from being cast as either male or female in 1861 to being always cast as female by the turn of the twentieth century. By the time of McDonald's 1871 version, the unneighborly old witch woman became the prototypical antagonist. A scorned woman was transformed into a witch or ghost in the song and in the play a century later. Male perpetrators were predominantly associated with First Nations or criminal activity, or both, as with the Potawatomie smuggler accused in Hooker's 1900 novel. In Gervais and Reaney's 1976 play, *ParTar-Sung and Renahsewa*, the eponymous authors of McDonald's second and third testimonials were included in the background-murmured list of potential suspects. (See Table 1: Chart of Perpetrators, below.)

Alternatively, it was interesting to find that in no version of the mystery was an *English (Anglo)*-Canadian man viewed as anything other than a victim, an ineffectual helper, or a guide to a woman who ultimately provided the key to end the terrifying events. Mr. Troyer was an ineffective witch doctor in Jones's account. Although the first statement in McDonald's appendix gave credit directly to Dr. Troyer as the seer who solved McDonald's problem, Neil McDonald's narrative gave the role of efficacious seer to Dr. Troyer's *daughter*. In 1976 Gervais and Reaney further distanced Troyer from the role of seer by transforming the person with "second sight" (also "far sight") from his daughter to his granddaughter, although the

Chart of Perpetrators

Notes:

F = female
U = gender unknown (supernatural)
N = gender unspecified (supernatural)
M = male

	Smugglers (French, Scottish, American)	Indian(s) from Walpole Island	Re-re-nah-sewa and Par-tar-sung	"Wild Indians"	Neighbor, Buchanan	McTavish's (McDonald's) illegitimate daughter	Daughter of old woman	Old woman ("Buchanan" or "Mrs. Pharlan" at "Long, low Log House")	Witch or witches	Ghosts	Poltergeists	Mamagwasewug/Fairies/"Hidden ones"	Notes
1861 Jones										N		U	
1871, 1905, 1915 (anon) McDonald			N*						F	U F			*ReRe NahSewa in appendix
1900 Hooker	M	M											
1952 Lauriston									F				
1976 Gervais & Reaney			M	N	F[2]	F[1]	F[1]	F[2]	F	U	U*	N / F^	^Spelling indicates female *From Gervais's notes [1]/[2] same person
1999 Parrish									F				
2004 Natili									F*				*"covetous others, headed by an old woman"
2004 Baldoon Bicentennial			N*						F				*ReNah Sewa's Testimonial
2004 Anon.									F				
2005 Darroch									F+	F+		U	+These refer to the same person
2006 OVHP		M			F+ / M				F+	F			+These refer to the same person

play retained Troyer's status as a "witch hunter." By 2004, poltergeists, attracted to the presence of troubled young women, and
female witches—who were simultaneously positioned as covetous
neighbors—were the only potential "nonmaterial," supernatural,
explanation that the audience could imagine.

THE TRANSFORMATIONS CONTINUE

In July 2006 the Ontario Visual Heritage Project (OVHP) launched
the Chatham–Kent: A Place of Refuge Web site promoting local
historical narratives.[9] Narratives were collected from interviews from
"local historians" and reenacted by local volunteers. The reenact-
ments were then videotaped and posted as podcasts for community
use on the project's Web sites and offered for resale in local museums
and libraries. The Chatham–Kent project was the second completed
of some ten planned for regions in southern Ontario. According
to promotional statements, "We [the OVHP] create sets of modern, entertaining media meant to teach, preserve and promote *our
past*" (visualheritage.ca/about.php, italics added), which positioned
the project's version of the Baldoon mystery as one linked to the
local community. However, like Lauriston's 1951 version, set in the
context of a larger settler history, this Web site's broader historical
context reaches back to 1793 and *settler* land surveys and occupation. The "Baldoon Mystery" podcast on the site is more than seven
minutes long, although the basic narrative is less than half that. In
it, after a relatively sketchy synopsis of the story, including some
of McDonald's 1871 interviews, a local historian proposes local
"theories" about what happened. This is followed by a three- to
four-minute discussion of the "virgin timberlands" on which the
economy of the emerging town of Wallaceburg, "Canada's inland
deep-water port," had been based.

With each different telling of the Baldoon mystery, we learn more
about the (story)teller and her or his social context than we do about
the mystery, consistent with Hymes's insight that "the telling of stories was a major way of understanding, explaining and dealing with
experience" and that "experience was put into the form of personal
or culturally shared narrative" (1996, 136). Not unexpectedly, the

OVHP explicitly acknowledges this connection between story and socialization into the local community:

THE POWER TO CONNECT

Local history has the power to enable connections between people and the places they live, work and visit. *In order for people to care about these places, they must know the ingenuity, hard-work and determination that created their community, their way of life, or their business.* They must know the forces of nature that for millions of years carved the lake, grew the forest, or created the natural resource that they use daily. *The best way to do this is through the personal narrative—through stories.* (Melnick n.d., 4, italics added)

The OHVP podcast of the Baldoon mystery is accompanied by a twenty-three-page course guide, geared to students in grades seven to twelve. The course guide provides "chapter summaries" for each podcast, complete with "related questions" and "activities." The penultimate paragraph[10] of the truncated, one-page text version of the Baldoon mystery in the course guide presents the following "theories" about the events: "Once the goose was killed, the problems stopped, just as the girl said they would. It has been theorized that because the neighboring Buchanan family had squabbled with the McDonalds over the land for years, they were the ones responsible for the happenings. Other theories posit the natives of Walpole Island as the culprits.[11] It is said that the Buchanans desecrated a native burial ground and blamed this act on the McDonalds. There is no definitive evidence as to who was to blame" (Course guide, n.d., 10–11).

The discourse blaming the local First Nations band—the same Walpole Islanders interviewed by Jones in the 1820s—was a new variation in 2006, reflecting the community backlash against aboriginal land claims since the 1980s. The "wild Indians" held responsible by ParTarSung and ReReNahSewa in McDonald's testimonials of 1871 continued to be cited—without explanation or elaboration—in later versions of the mystery, including those on the contemporary Wallaceburg museum site, keeping open the potential for an "Indian" perpetrator. While the beings that ParTarSung and ReReNahSewa called "wild Indians" ("what you call witchcraft") could easily have been the *mamagwasewug* of Jones's 1861 account, that connection was apparently incomprehensible to—and perhaps more accurately, unhearable by—the settler community. Witches, covetous neighbors, scorned women, neighboring First Nations, or criminals could be conceived as perpetrators, but not so the original occupants, the "little people" whose land had been appropriated. Instead, the "wild Indians" became the local First Nations, and, in reaction to their well-substantiated land claims, their presence has been constructed in local politics as a threat to regional economic growth.

The questions in the course guide further illustrate the importance of determining the perpetrator of the events and the relationship of the story to pioneer life and future economic prosperity, socializing the students into a world populated with innocent, industrious settlers forced to fight malicious others who would thwart their settlement efforts:

Related Questions

(a) Name five strange occurrences that the McDonald family experienced on their farm.

(b) What did Troyer's daughter advise the McDonalds to do to rid themselves of their problem?

(c) Who was responsible for the hauntings?

(d) What was the primary industry in Wallaceburg? (Course guide, n.d., 11)

The suggested activity continues the lesson on differentiating between "mystical" and "logical" epistemologies: "Students are to create their own short story using elements of the mystical. The strange events in their stories can be supernatural at the root or can be explained by logic, as they were in the story of the Baldoon Mystery" (Course guide, n.d., 11).

CONCLUSION

This paper began with an examination of the building of a refuge for First Nations dislocated by the imposition of the U.S.–British border. It is deeply ironic that we found the final transformation of the Baldoon mystery on the site entitled Chatham–Kent: A Place of Refuge, where the refuge was described as being for European settlers and Moravians, and for African Americans fleeing slavery in the United States. The encroachment of settlers onto land occupied by the *mamagwasewug* and the First Nations was quickly elided from the story, rendering it a tale of the triumph of the hardworking "pioneer" over all forms of adversity.

Although the Baldoon mystery continues to be told, the story has been transformed over time to fit the contemporary social context. The story has erased First Nations' connection to the land and its (supernatural) inhabitants and substituted stories of pioneer fortitude or, alternatively, of historical paranormal activity to encourage the tourist trade. In some cases the story lost its connection to the land entirely, as in the song. Also lost were the narratives of the 1796 treaty negotiated by Alexander McKee reserving the land of the Chenail Ecarte for otherwise displaced First Nations, and of the subsequent nonrecognition of that treaty when the land was reclaimed for "acceptable" settlers. This disjunction between land and people was echoed in Lauriston, who rewrote the history entirely so as to allow the settlers to move into his imagined ahistorical, unpopulated "wilderness." The shape-shifters so familiar to the Ojibwe people were documented in all renditions of this story (as a dark-headed goose, a black dog, or both), but they were always associated with the old, unneighborly woman who took on the characteristics of a witch one might meet in British Isles lore. That this might be someone (*mamagwaasi* or other being) resisting the encroachment of the settlers was unthinkable in versions by non-Natives. Once again, the narratives situated the tellers and the audience, reinforcing whatever social expectations and norms characterized a given era. We end with the question: Who does the story haunt now?

NOTES

1. See also McDougall and Philips Valentine (2003) for a discussion about how the Moore Reserve, the area mapped as being just north of the Sombra Township, lost its status as "land reserved for the Indians."

2. The authors wish to thank Social Sciences and Humanities Research Council of Canada for its support of our 2003–2006 grant documenting the impact of the imposition of the U.S. and British–Canadian border in the period 1763–1830, which enabled us to compile the data and background research on the Shawanese and Baldoon areas. In Philips and McDougall (2008), we present some of the earlier versions of the Baldoon mystery analyzed here, those published from 1861 through 1951, although with a different focus.

3. White's book on metahistory (1973) highlighted similar concerns for the historian and historiography in an excellent discussion of entextualization and genre, although not using those terms. White wrote, "What one history may emplot as a tragedy, another may emplot as a comedy or romance. . . . [T]he historian must draw upon a fund of culturally provided 'mythoi' in order to constitute the facts as figuring a story of a particular kind, just as he must appeal to that same fund of 'mythoi' in the minds of his readers to endow his account of the past with the odor of meaning or significance" (294).

4. "[Ruth] Benedict argued that symbolic form 'reflected' the 'context of situation.' . . . In her discussion of folklore, she wrote: 'Peoples' folk tales . . . are their autobiography and the clearest mirror on their life. . . . Behavior and attitudes became more articulate in folklore than in any other cultural trait, and folklore then tends to crystallize and perpetuate the forms of culture that it has made articulate'" (entry on folklore in *Encyclopedia of Social Sciences* 6:291, quoted in Duncan 1969, 169).

5. In a 2001 article the *London Free Press* reported that the McDonald version of the story was first published in 1871. We have not located a version with that date; the earliest version we have found, published circa 1905, had its origins in a serial published around 1895 by Rev. Cowan (or Colwell), in a new newspaper published in Wallaceburg, a sizable town near the Baldoon site. The serial probably formed the basis for both the 1905 and 1915 version of the pamphlet.

6. Rev. Colwell (or Cowan Colwell) was apparently the publisher rather than the author of McDonald's 1905 (and other) version(s).

7. That same plaque, however, has become a waymark for geocaching enthusiasts. A brief version of the mystery is presented alongside the instructions for finding the site using GPS.

8. This site is no longer active, having been superseded by the Chatham–Kent Ontario Visual Heritage Project site.

9. According to their Web site, the Ontario Visual Heritage Project is funded by the "Ontario Trillium Foundation, with supporting funding from municipal governments, corporate donors, community organizations, and, in some cases, individuals" (Melnick n.d., 13).

10. The final paragraph focused on the establishment of Wallaceburg by others from the original Baldoon site, and the importance of the "excess of trees" in the area to future economic development.

11. The Buchanans were historical enemies of the McDonald clan in Highland Scotland. The fact that the appropriate clan antagonisms were retained in the versions from 1900 through 2007 is evidence that this piece of cultural knowledge remains embedded in the region.

WORKS CITED

"The Baldoon Mystery." 2004. Posted at www.kent.net/wallaceburg-museum/Exhibits/mystery.html.

Baquedano-López, P. 2001. "Narrating Community in Doctrina Classes." *Narrative Inquiry* 10, no. 2 (May): 429–52.

Bauman, Richard. 1984. *Verbal Art as Performance*. Long Grove IL: Waveland.

"Bicentennial." 2004. Posted at baldoon.com/baldoon-mystery.php (no longer active); archived site at http://web.archive.org/web/*/http://baldoon.com/baldoon-mystery.php.

Darroch, Sue. 1997–2005. "*Poltergeist of Baldoon*." Ontario Ghosts and Hauntings Research Society. Posted at torontoghosts.org/chathamkent/baldoon1.htm.

Duncan, Hugh Dalziel. 1969. *Symbols and Social Theory*. New York: Oxford University Press.

Gervais, C. H., and James Reaney. 1976. *Baldoon*. [A play] Erin ON: Porcupine's Quill.

Goffman, Erving. 1974. *Frame Analysis: An Essay on the Organization of Experience*. New York: Harper & Row.

Hamil, Fred Coyne. 1951. *The Valley of the Lower Thames: 1640 to 1850*. Toronto: University of Toronto Press.

Hooker, Le Roy. 190. *Baldoon*. Toronto: Poole Publishing.

Hymes, Dell. 1996. *Ethnography, Linguistics, Narrative Inequality*. London: Taylor & Francis.

Jones, Rev. Peter (Kahkewaquonaby). 1861. *History of the Ojebway Indians*. London: Houlston & Wright.

Labov, William. 1972. "Transformation of Experience in Narrative Syntax." In *Language in the Inner City*, ed. William Labov, 354–96. Philadelphia: University of Pennsylvania Press.

———, and J. Waletzky. 1967. "Narrative Analysis." In *Essays on the Verbal and Visual Arts*, ed. J. Helm, 12–44. Seattle: University of Washington Press.

Lauriston, Victor. 1952. "The Belledoon Mystery," ch. 41 of *Romantic Kent:*

More than Three Centuries of History, 1626–1952. Chatham ON: Shepherd Printing.

McDonald, Neil T. [ca. 1905]. *The Belledoon Mysteries: An O'er True Story*. Wallaceburg ON: Wallaceburg News Book.

McDougall, Allan K., and Lisa Philips Valentine. 2003. "Treaty 29: Why Moore Became Less." In *Papers of the Thirty-Fourth Algonquian Conference*, ed. H. C. Wolfart, 393–400. Winnipeg: University of Manitoba.

Melnick, Zach. n.d. *Ontario Visual Heritage Project Overview*. pixeldust studios.com/OVHP_Info.pdf (accessed February 2007).

Natili, Kristeena. 2004. The Baldoon Mystery. mysteriesofcanada.com and wallaceburg.ca (accessed February 2007).

Ontario Visual Heritage Project (OVHP). 2006. Chatham–Kent: A Place of Refuge. The Living History Multimedia Association. visualheritage.ca/kent/baldoonmystery.htm.

Parrish, Al, and Joe Grant (Tanglefoot). ℗1999. "The Baldoon Goose," on *Full Throated Abandon*, compact disc, Borealis.

Philips, Lisa, and Allan K. McDougall. 2008. "Shifting Boundaries and the Baldoon Mysteries." In *Lines Drawn upon the Water: The First Nations Experience with the Great Lakes Borderlands and Borders*, ed. Karl Hele, 131–50. Waterloo ON: Wilfrid Laurier Press.

Valentine, Lisa Philips. 1995. *Making It Their Own: Severn Ojibwe Communicative Practices*. Toronto: University of Toronto Press.

———. 1996. Metanarration. *Festschrift for H. Christoph Wolfart*, ed. J. Nichols, 429–59. Winnipeg: University of Manitoba.

White, H. 1973. *Metahistory: The Historical Imagination in Nineteenth-century Europe*. Baltimore MD: Johns Hopkins Press.

White, Richard. 1990. *The Middle Ground*. Palo Alto CA: Stanford University Press.

6

Haunting Remains

Educating a New American Citizenry
at Indian Hill Cemetery

SARAH SCHNEIDER KAVANAGH

On the morning of September 30, 1850, a crowd of Middletown, Connecticut, residents, including the mayor, city authorities, several full choirs, and "citizens generally" gathered at a local church and began a march through their small city.[1] The march concluded at the crest of a nearby hill known to the marchers as "Indian Hill." The name "Indian Hill" was given to the site by local whites because of the hill's history as a community and government center for the Wangunk, the first people of central Connecticut.[2] The Wangunk, however, knew the hill by a different name: "Wune Wahjet," meaning "at the place of the good mountain," or "on the beautiful hill."[3] After the march to the hilltop, several speeches, the delivery of original poetry, and a handful of hymns, Wune Wahjet was officially declared "Indian Hill Cemetery," a name and purpose still applied to the site today.[4]

According to Rev. Frederick J. Goodwin, who spoke atop the hill at the conclusion of the 1850 march, the location of this new cemetery was by no means a random one. In fact, Goodwin believed that the history of the hill as a center of Wangunk life was of central importance to its new purpose as a cemetery.

> Long has it been a favorite spot. It is a spot, moreover, which from the very name applied to it, and the associations connected with it, is seen to be suited for its destined purpose. Forcibly must it remind us, that passing away is written on the world, and all that the world contains. Where now is the red man of the forest, who

here was wont to roam—who here found so much to attract his interest, who here chose for himself a home. Long since could it be said of them, as it will one day be said of us, they have passed away.[5]

For Goodwin, the myth of Indigenous extinction is embedded in the very ground at Indian Hill. These extinction myths teach lessons about mortality that fertilize the soil, creating perfect conditions for an almost predestined cemetery. However, as many nineteenth-century New England historians have noted, in 1850, Native peoples in New England were far from extinct. The fact that Native people were living and working within New England communities did not stop Goodwin, and many other nineteenth-century New Englanders, from claiming that Native peoples had "long since passed away."[6] Jean M. O'Brien illustrates how the abundance of fictitious histories of Indigenous extinction produced in New England enabled European settlers and their descendants, who had little or no connection to American bloodlines, to "justify colonialism, absolve themselves of wrongdoing and guilt, and place Indians firmly and safely in the past."[7] Thus, extinction myths allowed Europeans and their descendants to claim and adopt an American identity that, without these myths, belonged to Native peoples.

Another speaker at the ceremony's dedication, Rev. Stephen Olin, believed that the new cemetery would be "the centre of elevating sentiments and hallowing emotions, the nursery of domestic and civic virtues, and in some measure, at least, the hand-maid of civilization."[8] Olin's speech illustrates that the cemetery's founders firmly believed that their creation would be more than just a graveyard. It would educate the American citizenry about their nascent American republic and instruct them in the duties and virtues of citizenship. The centuries of civic education delivered by Indian Hill Cemetery would be enabled through the fertilization of Native lands, exhumed of their histories and bodies, with European American bodies, histories, and ideologies.

In this chapter I will discuss the extinction claims embedded in the speeches given at the dedication of Indian Hill Cemetery and how these claims have been implanted into the architecture of the cemetery. I will argue that the creation of Indian Hill Cemetery was a project aimed at planting an Indigenous extinction narrative into the American land itself. Further, I will argue that this implantation of white bodies and histories, paired with an exhumation of Native ones, transformed the land into a text that would forever convey Euro-American ideologies about land, ownership, and "Indian-ness" serving to legitimize and edify white American nationhood. Next, I will extend my argument to examine how the cemetery plants not only extinction claims but also the Frontier Myth itself into New England soil. I will argue that the cemetery can be read as a vertically penetrative frontier that, instead of moving westward across American land, moves into the soil itself, thus rendering the frontier permanent. I will argue that Indian Hill Cemetery's founders meant the site to be read as a Frontier Myth text and that their hope was that the spatially stationary place of Indian Hill Cemetery would ground the moral lessons of the Frontier Myth in American soil and American minds for time immemorial. I will end with an analysis of how hauntings by "Indian" ghosts are integral to the maintenance of white American citizenship and how the ghosts of Indian Hill are themselves haunted by ideologies of nationalism.

The construction of Indian Hill Cemetery falls within the larger national context of the Rural Cemetery Movement, which aimed to transform rural sites into cemeteries that used monuments and graves to create and claim a unique American history and identity.[9] Because the Rural Cemetery Movement swept across the eastern United States with such strong force, there were many cemeteries built in the decades preceding Indian Hill Cemetery's construction that were created with nation-building aims. The construction of Indian Hill Cemetery, while firmly planted within this movement, is distinct from that of its neighbors. Whereas most rural cemeteries used symbols from antiquity to construct a white American history for the relatively nascent United States,[10] the architects of Indian Hill Cemetery broke the mold by using representations of "Indian-ness" in place of symbols from antiquity. This shift in symbolism allowed Middletown residents to lay claim to a national identity and culture rooted in the American land as opposed to one inexorably tied to the Old World.

Although I am focused specifically on one cemetery in Middletown, Connecticut, on a broader level my project is an exploration of how places wield power and enact history. I am particularly interested in how our constructions and experiences of the physical world are reproduced out of historical relationships of power. This examination of Indian Hill Cemetery as a place that (re)produces race and nation is founded upon theories of how places themselves continuously reconstruct existing relationships of power. In this analysis I use D. W. Meinig's definition of place as outlined in Richard White and John M. Findlay's *Power and Place in the North American West.* Meinig defines place as "a mental imposition of order, a parcelization of the earth's surface, a transformation of space—an abstraction—into something more specific and limited." Richard White and John M. Findlay dissect Meinig's definition, arguing that if place is involved in "imposing order" it must represent "the exercise of power." White and Findlay go on to say that power "is never evenly distributed, but it is also probably never monopolized," adding, "Among people, power implies a relationship between persons."[11] Thus, any discussion of place is also, at its heart, a discussion of persons in relationships of power. My analysis of Indian Hill Cemetery is an attempt to dissect how a specific place (re)presents a national mythology and is defined through relationships of power, specifically between Natives and whites.

INDIAN HILL CEMETERY AND THE RURAL CEMETERY MOVEMENT

Although the American Revolution marked the birth of the new nation–state, it was not until several decades later that U.S. citizens realized that their experimental government could transform into a lasting republic. American victories in the War of 1812 revealed that a unified national culture and history could help the United States become a "nation among nations."[12] In his discussion of the cultural roots of nationalism, Benedict Anderson writes that "nation–states ... always loom out of an immemorial past, and, still more important, glide into a limitless future."[13] And so as American citizens realized that their experiment in republican government had the potential for a "limitless future," they were faced with the daunting task of constructing for themselves an "immemorial past."

Since accomplishing this task would be no small feat, it is not surprising that the end of the War of 1812 marked the beginning of what Blanche Linden-Ward has termed the "American monument-building era"—how better to construct the immemorial than with monuments and memorials? This era was defined by an explosion of cultural and artistic production in support of the men and principles that had founded the nation: a carving of a new U.S. history into old American stone.[14] In 1836 Ralph Waldo Emerson wrote, "Our age is retrospective. It builds the sepulchers of the fathers. It writes biographies, history, criticism. The foregoing generation beheld God and nature face to face; we, through their eyes."[15] Although American history was being consciously constructed through many forms, including literature, painting, and oratory, it is no surprise that Emerson highlights the building of "sepulchers of the fathers" as the primary project of his era. Early-nineteenth-century scholars were quite aware of the implications of the fixation on tomb building. This fixation was made most visible through the Rural Cemetery Movement,[16] an integral development in the conscious construction of U.S. history.[17]

In 1850 the creation of Indian Hill Cemetery marked the spread of the mid-nineteenth-century monument-building fever into Middletown, Connecticut. The cemetery project, much like rural cemetery projects all along the east coast, was at its heart a patriotic enterprise.[18] In his speech at the Indian Hill Cemetery dedication, Olin discussed how the site would instill patriotism in its visitors: "I trust I am no visionary, but I also give credit, in advance, to this enterprise for contributing something towards erecting a *past* for posterity—towards establishing a common centre for edifying remembrances and holy associations—a common ground where we of the present may wait to greet the men of the future, to commune with them and impart such lessons of wisdom as we have in store. I venture, also, to rely upon this improvement to strengthen, or even to create in some individuals and families much-needed local attachments, so essential an element of real patriotism."[19] Olin's focus on the patriotic purpose of the new cemetery echoes the sentiments of speakers at cemetery dedication ceremonies across the country during the nineteenth century.[20] The rural-cemetery movement as a whole was informed by the needs of the monument-building era: the goal was to create a national identity through the construction of an American past rooted in American soil.

Such attempts at U.S. cultural production were often critiqued by European artists and scholars who argued that architecture and art would be unsuccessful in creating a national culture and inciting true patriotism if the aesthetics used were borrowed and not developed "Indigenously."[21] In spite of these critiques, the decades following the War of 1812 saw countless artistic attempts aimed at the construction of a national past. Linden-Ward claims that the "creation of public monuments and pastoral cemetery landscapes revealed Americans' ability to adapt borrowed aesthetic forms to create their own usable past through self commemoration."[22] However, nineteenth-century Americans must have agreed, at least in part, with European critiques. Even a brief glimpse into the relationship of the United States to both European and Native American populations makes clear that Euro-Americans "borrowed" much more than "aesthetic forms" to create a distinctly American past. They borrowed, appropriated, and abstracted Native American identities in order to create a U.S. national identity and lay claim to American land.

Without a claim to land upon which to anchor their nascent nation, Euro-Americans' claim to nationhood was unsustainable. Richard Grusin argues, "The construction of American identity has always been inseparable from nature. Unlike European nations, whose identity derived from a common language, ethnic or racial heritage, religion, or cultural history, the identity of the United States of America as 'nature's nation' was grounded in large part in the land itself."[23] Because of this connection between land and nation, non-Natives have attempted to claim Indigenous identities to validate their own constructions of national identity.[24] The first claim is that Indigenous peoples belong to whites as a child belongs to a parent. Second, Indigenous identities have been claimed through the appropriation of Indigenous symbols, actions, and histories. These Euro-American claims to Indigenous identity manifest themselves in the histories and mythologies that Euro-Americans have created to stabilize their nation.[25]

From the American Revolution to the present day, examples abound of whites donning faux-Indian attire, yelping ultra-stereo-typed war whoops, or engaging in stereotyped "Indian" rituals in moments of national crisis. In *Playing Indian*, Philip Deloria argues that these actions are associated with the white American need to dissociate with Europe and claim a different national heritage. He argues that whites covet what they have historically viewed as the Native connection to the land and its spirit.[26] This is in part because a sense of place and an attachment to the land were prerequisites for the creation of a U.S. national identity. The Boston mayor Josiah Quincy stated in 1813 that "loyalty to place" was the nineteenth-century U.S. citizen's primary connection with the nation.[27]

Ideas about the relationship between "loyalty to place" and national identity were not foreign to Middletown residents in the mid-nineteenth century. In fact, Stephen Olin spoke to the need for a loyalty to place in his speech at the 1850 opening of Indian Hill Cemetery. Discussing the creation of the cemetery, he expressed his "strong hope that [it] and similar improvements [that had] become so common in [the United States], [would] contribute, in some small measure, towards providing for one of the most urgent, though little appreciated wants of our great republic . . . the want of local attachments, and in so far as this essential element is concerned of love of country."[28] Olin, like many nineteenth-century whites, was dedicated to the task of connecting his vision for the nation to the American landscape.

In order to implant a national vision into the land itself, whites needed to grapple not only with the history of American citizens and their forefathers but also with the Native peoples Indigenous to the land. In order for the United States to become a legitimate nation, it had to become, as one unknown writer said in 1828 "a perfect union of the past and present; the rigor of a nation just born walk-ing over the hallowed ashes of a race whose history is too early for a record, and surrounded by the living forms of a people hovering between the two."[29] The drive for this perfect union of Native past with white present led whites toward two courses of action in their relation with Native peoples. First, if white Americans were to posit any claim over the land, they had to adopt the history, identity, and "spirit of the land" that belonged to the Native peoples Indigenous to the continent and glorify it, since it held such a central position in any sense of American nation.[30] Second, through attempts at the ethnocide of Native American populations, whites tried to transform living societies into "the hallowed ashes of a race." As I will explore in the next section, this ethnocide was carried out both in the flesh and by the pen.

INDIAN HILL CEMETERY'S SPECTRAL INDIAN

The literary figure of the "Vanishing American" manifests itself as a ghostly American presence in nineteenth-century literature, history, art, and performance.[31] According to the logic of the Vanishing American theory, "Indians were doomed to 'utter extinction' because they belonged to 'an inferior race of men . . . [who were] neither qualified to rise higher in the scale of being, nor to enjoy the benefits and blessings of the civilized and Christian state.'"[32] Nowhere in the writings on Indian Hill Cemetery is the connection between Native peoples and death as clear as in a poem written by Rev. J. Pierpont for the occasion of the opening of the cemetery.

> On this high place, that swells so fair,
> O'er town and river, grove and lea,
> We stand, O God, with song and prayer,
> To give these grounds to Death and Thee.
>
> To Death, thy servant, who, of old,
> With tomahawk and arrowy spear,
> As by our fathers we are told,
> Hath reaped a bloody harvest here.[33]

Through Pierpont's poetry, death is personified in Indian form. It is unclear whether Pierpont is alluding to the death of Wangunk people or the death of whites at the hands of Indian foes. The fact that there is no record of white Middletown residents being killed by Wangunk people may not have been an issue for Pierpont, a Bostonian who, most likely, knew little Middletown history and was simply calling upon a tradition of warlike representations of Native peoples.

This supposed inevitable death of Native peoples and the vision of death *as* an "Indian" carried with it the implied birth of a white civilization. For whites, Native death was necessary death, natural death; it was an evolution from savagery to civilization. As a nation was built in the late eighteenth and early nineteenth centuries, gaining ideological control over American land meant claiming ownership over Native histories and legacies, and over Native peoples themselves. Despite whites' attempts at the ethnocide and forced migration of Indigenous people, early nineteenth-century New England was still home to many Native peoples. But because of its prominence in literature, art, and performance (and, in the case of Indian Hill, in the land itself), the "Vanishing American" was vastly more visible to New England whites than were actual Native peoples. In this way, living Native peoples were made invisible by the manufactured stereotype of an Indian ghost purposefully rendered to haunt the newly born American civilization.

This ghostly presence was not a remnant of a time past but a necessary creation for the construction of an American national future. In *The National Uncanny: Indian Ghosts and American Subjects*, Renée Bergland argues that American nationalism is maintained by the reproduction of the Indian ghost in literature.[34] However, these ghosts are found not only in books but also in the actions of American citizens[35] and on the historical markers scattered across the American landscape. The spectral Indian, forever present and forever ancient, is a conscious creation essential to American nationalism. Often, it serves to mask the fact that living Native people still exist and helps justify white claims to U.S. land.

It is on the American land itself that we find Indian ghosts in Middletown. Stephen Olin's dedication speech focuses on how Indian Hill Cemetery will promote patriotism in Middletown residents of the present and future and how the site will become an archive of national historical memory. His words portray U.S. citizens as possessing a violent patriotism, but he suggests that a love for the land itself is markedly absent from citizens of the youthful country. Olin writes, "With all of this fiery patriotism, however, no people on earth, civilized and well- to-do are so nearly destitute of love for their Native land. There is amongst us almost no attachment to the soil—to the spot where our ancestors lived and died, and were entombed."[36] Olin does not note that perhaps the majority of the ancestors of most white Middletown citizens in the mid-nineteenth century did not live, or die, or become entombed in or on American soil. In 1654, two hundred years earlier, there were only thirty white families living in Middletown.[37] Thus, in 1850 there may have been a few New Englanders, mostly of the upper classes, who had genealogies that extended back several generations. However, in 1850 it was primarily European immigrants who inhabited Middletown.[38] Because of this, Olin's call for patriotism and a celebration of a timeless American nation is in actuality a project in illusion. The cemetery, he hoped, would present the illusion of an "immemorial [American] past" upon which to build a "limitless future."[39]

Interestingly, Olin pairs his longing for an American "attachment to the soil," with an assertion of the importance of the ahistorical nature of 1850s America, writing, "We are a new people without radication in the past; without prescription, and without traditions; and yet it is of the very genius of our nation, to turn its back upon all history, and work out social and political problems for itself."[40] These two seemingly contradictory statements, one focusing on the national need for historical memory and the other on the benefits of the American lack of historical national precedent, illustrate the central paradox in the creation of a lasting American nation. The ethnocide and appropriation of Native American lands is unquestionably linked to the white American struggle to construct a national identity separate from that of Europe.

Olin's speech provides more insight into this appropriation of Native history and land as he moves on to address the naming of the new cemetery and what it will add to his proposed patriotic project.

He wrote, "I like the name [Indian Hill] also, and trust it will be retained, despite the fastidiousness of tasteful and fashionable, or of classical innovators. . . . I will consent . . . that their hoary chief, now present in spirit, stretches out both his invisible hands, rejoicing to be the link of connexion between the once rival, now peaceful races, and the medium of communicating venerable traditions that shall anticipate the lapse of coming ages in enriching the Indian Hill Cemetery, with a legendary sanctity."[41] Here Olin provides a clear solution to the history/a-history paradox presented earlier in his speech. Because Americans were struggling to dissociate with Europe, they could no longer be haunted by their own ancestors. The haunting necessary for national survival required a new figure that could haunt the literature, architecture, people, and land of a new nation.

Olin's spectral Indian rears his head, arms extended, welcoming the quite literal implantation of white history and white bodies into his land. This ghost of the "hoary chief" embodies both the land itself and the historic claim to the land that Olin sees missing from American patriotism. In Olin's hands, the Native history of the land becomes "legend" and not fact. As he speaks to the importance of including "the Indian" in the structure of the cemetery, he mentions that there is "slender historical evidence that a tribe of aboriginal men pre-occupied"[42] the hill. This uniquely American ghost loomed over all attempts to construct an American identity separate from citizens' European heritage. For white Americans, the Indian ghost became a familiar figure haunting the ground they stood on, the books they read, and their everyday practices. Since before the republic was founded, white Americans have been adopting Native symbols, items, and stereotyped mannerisms for their own purposes. There have been myriad incidences since Europeans began settling North America of white Americans performing "Indian-ness" in moments of American identity crises. "Savage" Indians became figures against which whites could construct a civilized American subject.[43] This unique American self is contingent upon the existence of an Indian ghost: an Indian who is at once forever present and forever past.

FRONTIER MYTH-MAKING AT INDIAN HILL CEMETERY

The frontier is often understood in two dimensions. It is drawn across the American imagination as a line always at the toes of early pioneers. Histories have negotiated this fine line as if it were an impermeable separation of past and present, of primitive and modern. And the "closing of the frontier" in 1890, famously expounded upon by Frederick Jackson Turner, has long been hailed the end of an era and the birth of a modern nation.[44] For decades now, historians have attempted to change how Americans imagine the frontier. In *The Legacy of Conquest: The Unbroken Past of the American West*, Patricia Nelson Limerick attempts to demythologize western history of its preoccupation with the closing of the frontier as the ending of an era. She argues that past and present do not define themselves along the line of the frontier or its 1890 "closure." Comparing the history of the American West to the forgotten mines left behind by nineteenth-century Colorado miners, Limerick writes, "The conquest of Western America shapes the present as dramatically—and sometimes as perilously—as the old mines shape the mountainsides." She examines how the history of conquest marks the landscape and blurs the lines between past and present in unexpected places. The land itself is evidence that the past is inexorably connected to the present and informs the paths Americans choose to tread even today. She writes, "Americans are left to stumble over—and sometimes into—those connections, caught off guard by the continued vitality of issues widely believed to be dead."[45] Although Limerick is writing explicitly about the American West, we cannot forget that conquest was not confined to the West. The history of New England, although markedly different, can boast similar historical mine shafts. And often it is precisely in the places where issues, peoples, and histories are presumed dead that the connections between past and present are most apparent.

Even if the traditional line of the Turnerian frontier drowned in the Pacific in 1890, it certainly did not die quietly. When one looks closely at any American town today, the mythology of the frontier litters the landscape. This modern mythology is a ghost of the original perhaps, both here and not here (perhaps the frontier has always been spectral), but it functions today just as effectively as it did before 1890. Modern places of myth-making exist in every American town. They house active apparitions pulling the past into the present through mine shafts built long ago.

In his speech at Indian Hill, Stephen Olin provides a glimpse of just how pervasive and influential frontier myths were in nineteenth-century Middletown, Connecticut. This glimpse comes not in the form of the laudatory remarks on American exceptionalism and the surging wave of democracy that contemporary readers are so accustomed to seeing in any discussion of the Frontier Myth in the nineteenth century. Instead, Olin's audience and readers are warned of the "evils" of the frontier "which deteriorate our national character and depress our civilization."[46] Olin's objections to the pervasive nature of the Frontier Myth in the construction of "character" and "civilization" stemmed from specifically local concerns. Olin expresses frustration that the lure of the frontier drew Middletown youth, who he calls "our life-blood," westward "to animate and fructify crude frontier settlements."[47] For Olin, the frontier and mythic frontier narratives had so much influence on the character of Middletown youth that the city was drained of its potential for growth "in fine arts, in education, in refinement, in morals, in piety—in all that adorns and enriches human society."[48] For Olin, the lure of the West was so great because, among white Americans, there was "almost no attachment to the soil—to the spot where our ancestors lived and died, and were entombed."[49] Olin wholeheartedly believed that an attachment to the soil was an "essential . . . element of real patriotism."[50]

Olin's solution, however, was not the abandonment of "crude frontier settlements"; he does not go on to plead for an end to "eternal pioneering."[51] In fact, his most poignant illustration of the pervasive nature of the Frontier Myth is that he, too, believes in it. He writes, "This preternatural alacrity to emigrate . . . may not be wholly unconnected with our destiny as a nation, appointed to assimilate such crude masses of foreign population, and to subdue to the purposes of civilization and liberty, a vast continent still mostly in forest."[52] Although he is frustrated that Middletown youth are abandoning their city, lured by the romance of the frontier, he believes that the frontier's lure is a natural, destined force. Richard Slotkin has argued that an "essential illusion fostered by all mythology" is the belief that "Nature or God composed the story and assigned its meanings, rather than men."[53] In Olin's discussion of the lure of the frontier, he displays a clear belief in Slotkin's "essential illusion" by equating westward migration with the destiny of the American nation.

Olin and his Middletown audience's attachment to the Frontier Myth were so strong that it structured the very landscape of their city. Indeed, the frontier mythology's influence on the Middletown landscape was just as strong as its influence on the creation of western American landscapes. For despite Olin's intense frustrations with the frontier mentality of the American character, his proposed "antidote or palliation of [these] tendencies"[54] was not the overthrow of the frontier as a foundational American mythology. Instead, his solution was the extension of the mythic space of the frontier into the city of Middletown itself through the creation of Indian Hill Cemetery. Therefore, in Olin's eyes, Indian Hill Cemetery was a landscape created both in opposition to, and in imitation of, a mythic western frontier.

Strangely enough, the problem of the Frontier Myth for Olin, and perhaps his audience, was not its presence but its absence. Olin did not want the frontier and frontier mythology to disappear; he wanted Middletown to lay claim to it. Therefore, Indian Hill Cemetery, as a place-/myth-making project aimed at instilling American patriotism through cultivating local attachment, is devoted instilling the Frontier Myth into a stationary place. The cemetery re-presents the Frontier Myth, plotting it into the land. However, unlike the western frontier, which was represented as a phenomenon that penetrated space horizontally (moving westward), the cemetery was instead vertically penetrative (moving into the soil itself). It is also temporally penetrative, presenting the movement of history not as a spatial wave from east to west, but as a temporal wave from past to present. This enables the spatially stationary place of Indian

Hill Cemetery to ground the moral lessons of the Frontier Myth in both American soil and American minds. In the next sections, I will examine how Indian Hill Cemetery adopts three specific progress narratives of the Frontier Myth: turning rural savagery into urban civilization, filling ahistorical land with history, and replacing chaos with order.

FROM RURAL SAVAGERY TO URBAN CIVILIZATION

The first progress narrative of the Frontier Myth at Indian Hill Cemetery is the tale of how the conquest and transformation of "empty" and "savage" space exerts an Americanizing influence on "productive," urban places. The cemeteries constructed during the Rural Cemetery Movement were the first American parks; they were places within urban areas slated to remain "rural" and natural. Thus, these cemeteries were constructed as a peripheral other to urban spaces, existing for two central purposes: enriching and civilizing urban places and quarantining the "diseased other," the dead.

Rural cemeteries were constructed as "didactic landscapes"[55] in a frontier-like relationship with the cities they complemented. They were created to impart the wisdom of nature to colonized, urban areas. In 1850 Stephen Olin spoke of how Indian Hill Cemetery "look[ed] down from its serene elevation like a guardian angel upon [the] rural city, and [was] yet so near, it [might] breathe out in gentle whispers the lessons of wisdom it [had] to deliver."[56] These words resonate with a speech that was presented two decades earlier, in 1831, when Mount Auburn, the first rural cemetery in the United States, opened outside of Boston. Supreme Court Justice Joseph Story gave a consecration address outlining some of the ideological foundations for the institution of a rural cemetery.

"All around us," he observed, "there breathes a solemn calm, as if we were in the bosom of a wilderness." Yet, "ascend but a few steps, and what a change of scenery to surprise and delight us. . . . In the distance, the City—at once the object of our admiration and our love—rears its proud eminences, its glittering spires, its lofty towers, its graceful mansions, its curling smoke, its crowded haunts of business and pleasure. . . . There is, therefore, within our reach, every variety of natural and artificial scenery. . . . We stand, as it were, upon the borders of two worlds; and as the mood of our minds may be, we may father lessons of profound wisdom by contrasting the one with the other."[57]

The rural cemetery is thus a "border" between "two worlds": "the wilderness" and "the City." Through the rural cemetery, wilderness is (re)created within the city and for the purposes of city dwellers. A central tenant of the Frontier Myth is that the wilderness of the North American continent existed for the purposes to which European immigrants would put it. Within this myth, the Indigenous lands and peoples of the North American continent were blank slates upon which Europeans could write their own history. Using the logic of this myth, the natural, "primitive" state of Indigenous American lands and peoples were texts created only for the purpose of European observation and learning.

This Frontier Myth approach to Indigenous lands and peoples is the same approach that U.S. citizens were encouraged to take with respect to the rural cemetery. The cemetery is presented as a natural, ahistoric place that becomes implanted with Euro-American history.[58] The western frontier and the rural cemetery are parallel "borders of two worlds." While the frontier fills with civilization and urbanity, the rural cemetery fills with Euro-American memorials and bodies that quickly become the landscape itself. Through the implantation of bodies and their memorials, the site of the rural cemetery remains natural and rural, even as it becomes embedded with Euro-American history. Thus, the cemetery can always act as a text of nature for urban, "civilized" populations.

FROM A-HISTORY TO HISTORY

A pervasive part of the Frontier Myth was that, as European civilization extended across the continent, the ahistorical land would be filled with history. This progressive sequence from timelessness to history is another narrative embedded into Indian Hill Cemetery. This progress narrative is rooted in Indian Hill Cemetery through several avenues, not the least of which is the history of the hill itself. Indian Hill was the last reserved Wangunk land in Middletown, Connecticut, and had long before been put aside for "the heirs of Sowheag [a Wangunk chief] forever."[59] We know that within the cemetery founders' lifetime the hill was still being used for ceremonial purposes by Wangunk people.[60] And the name applied to the site, "Indian Hill," divulges that it was situated in the landscape of Middletown as a savage space within a civilized society. The construction of the cemetery drew on the history of the land, and on local mythologies of Native presence in Middletown. The land was purchased in 1850 by the Indian Hill Cemetery Association, an organization created by and for the city, yet the name "Indian Hill or Wune Wahjet"[61] was retained even though the site was no longer legally under Native control. Thus the name "Indian Hill" no longer indicated that the hill *belonged* to Indians, but that the hill itself *was* Indian: Indian space under the control of white proprietors. The name of the hill, combined with the fact of its ownership by non-Natives, positions the site as a controlled frontier space, a "border between two worlds."

Much effort has gone into erasing documented histories and corporeal evidence of actual Native peoples. This erasure is, however, paired with an insistent memorializing of "the Indian" who is constantly institutionalized as an American legend—a replacement of actual people with imagined constructions. The gates of Indian Hill Cemetery are topped by a plaque depicting a stereotyped Indian adorned in feathers resembling the attire not of Native peoples of New England but of those living thousands of miles to the west in the American plains. Although this stereotyped Indian figure adorns the gates to the cemetery, no remnant remains of the Wangunk people whose dead once rested in the same soil, because these remains have been exhumed and removed.[62] Therefore, the "Indian" of Indian Hill Cemetery is not a representative of the Wangunk people, but is instead a representative of the figure that Robert Berkhofer has termed the "White Man's Indian." This Indian represents white fears and desires while simultaneously erasing actual Native histories and land claims.[63]

As early as 1850, scholars were presenting the Native history of Middletown as legend rather than as historical fact. This is an important distinction because "the Indian" as legend or myth can serve as a national American symbol, whereas actual histories of Native people, which often include contested land claims and ethnocide, cannot serve as a buttress to the creation of white American identity. Indian Hill Cemetery was primary ground for this abstracting of "Indian-ness" away from Wangunk peoples. When addressing the Native history of Indian Hill, Stephen Olin said, "I gladly accept whatever venerable legends do, by favor of the popular tradition, linger about these summits. I will consent, on slender historical evidence, that a tribe of aboriginal men pre-occupied this chosen site with their ancient dust."[64] In this passage, Olin presents "the Indian" as "legend" and as "ancient." He denies the corporeal evidence of Wangunk people and appeals instead to a sort of ghostly evidence. He discounts "historical evidence" of Wangunk people in the area but consents to the "lingering legends." Olin's choice to appeal to a spiritual source of authority rather than a historical one is quite informative. By so appealing, he makes clear to his listeners that he is not speaking of real, embodied Native peoples, but of legend, of illusion, of the spectral.

FROM CHAOS TO ORDER

The Frontier Myth provides an easily conceptualized spatial boundary between the civilized self and the primitive other. For nineteenth-century believers in the Frontier Myth, the primitive, Indian other was conceptualized always on the other side of the imaginary line of the frontier; the other always occupied *other spaces*. The myth was so pervasive that White Middletown residents began thinking of the Indian as beyond the frontier line even while Native peoples remained living and working in their city.[65] All cemeteries take on the task of quarantining non-normative others, the dead, on the other side of real spatial boundaries. In the case of Indian Hill Cemetery, the Indian is quarantined alongside, and thus equated with, the dead. Through the drawing of boundaries to keep out "other peoples," both cemeteries and the frontier clearly illustrate the relationships of power that are the foundations of place. The cemetery and the frontier are intentionally constructed as physical manifestations of power.

In "Of Other Spaces," Michel Foucault outlines a theory of heterotopias. Foucault's theory of heterotopias approaches places themselves (and particularly the cemetery, which he uses as a primary example of a heterotopia) as social texts. Although Foucault does not mention the Frontier Myth in his analysis of heterotopic spaces, his heterotopia and the frontier have much in common. Understanding the commonalities between these two spaces is useful in understanding the relationship between frontier mythology and Indian Hill Cemetery. In his theory of heterotopias, Foucault analyzes how a space created to house the deviant constructs space for the "normal." A heterotopia is a place that incites thought about what society is, by portraying what it is not, a place that sparks imagination about what should be, by displaying that which deviates from the norm.[66] It is, in effect, a boundary between two worlds that contains and orders deviance, presenting an idealized version of normative society.

Foucault's heterotopia and the frontier both exist as abstracted spaces of interaction not only between the normative and the deviant, but also between the past and the present. As discussed earlier, both the Frontier Myth and Indian Hill Cemetery are built on a progress narrative that outlines the move from a-history to history. The space of the mythic frontier is the boundary between primitive and modern. Just like the cemetery, the frontier functions as a site of interaction between past and present. Similar to the frontier, heterotopias are "often linked to slices in time . . . [and] begin to function at full capacity when men arrive at a sort of absolute break with their traditional time."[67] To inhabit a cemetery, permanent residents (the dead) must break with real time. Visitors, through viewing the living quarters of the long-since dead, experience a break in traditional time as well. Through these temporal breakages, the cemetery fulfills "the idea of constituting a place of all times that is itself outside of time and inaccessible to its ravages, the project of organizing in this way a sort of perpetual and indefinite accumulation of time in an immobile place."[68] The cemetery becomes the timeless reflection of the city it stands outside of, reflecting a universalized and timeless society back onto itself in idealized, yet inverted form: a "city of the dead" to promote life in a city of the living.

Foucault describes the role of a heterotopia as creating "a space that is other, another real space, as perfect, as meticulous, as well arranged as ours is messy, ill constructed, and jumbled."[69] The heterotopic cemetery here becomes an idealized version of the city, displacing the city itself and ordering its complications into an organized form. Blanche Linden-Ward argues that Mount Auburn Cemetery was constructed as a complementary and idealized "city on a hill" that would "offer lessons to the entire nation."[70] In both Mount Auburn Cemetery and Indian Hill Cemetery, the "messy, ill constructed, and jumbled" nature of real life is idealized through the easily organized dead. History, struggle, controversy, societal structure, family, and race relations are displayed through the structure of the rural cemetery as timeless and structured, meticulously arranged and seemingly inevitable.

Indian Hill Cemetery presents an idealized mirror image of a particular social structure in several specific ways. As can be seen on the 1850 map of the original Indian Hill Cemetery, almost all of the trails that meander across the hill have faux-Indian names. There are a few paths that are named after actual Wangunk people who had been proprietors of the site prior to 1850. For example, "Sowheage Ave." can be found on the southeastern corner of the hill. Some evidence indicates that this particular path marks the spot where the remains of Sowheage, a Wangunk leader, were found and exhumed, although this cannot be verified.[71] Evidence indicates that the exhumation of Native bodies at Wune Wahjet was commonplace in the years preceding the creation of the cemetery.[72] While the corporeal evidence of Wangunk people has been erased, evidence of what Robert Berkhofer has termed "the white man's Indian"[73] have been systematically moved into the site through faux-Indian path names, plaques at the entry to the cemetery that depict Noble Savage–like profiles, and the words of the Revs. Olin and Goodwin.

Indian Hill Cemetery is bounded by its outermost path, which is called "Mattebeseck Ave." Mattebeseck, the Wangunk name for the city of Middletown, becomes the outer boundary of this mirror city, this city of the dead. In an ironic twist of fate, the Wangunk are given full ownership of Wune Wahjet, but this ownership comes with the price of forever being understood as the definition of death itself. The Wangunk city of Mattebeseck is remembered only by its own death and is re-created as an embodiment of inevitable death.

This idealized societal mirroring can also be seen in the actual structure of the cemetery plots and organization. Patriarchal familial structures are created, organized, and idealized through family plots and grave placement. Just as the patriarchal family is the foundation of Euro-American societal structure, so, too, does it provide the structure for the cemetery's organization. However, in the cemetery, this family structure is portrayed exactly as Foucault's description of heterotopic structure outlines, "as perfect, as meticulous, [and] as well arranged," whereas in the greater society, this structure "is messy, ill constructed, and jumbled."[74] The "messiness" of structures such as gender, family, race, and nation are perfectly blueprinted and organized in the cemetery. Family plots are organized around phallic stone monuments; each grave indicates the familial position occupied by the body it marks. In some cases the only indication of who occupies the grave is the person's kin terms, such as "mother," "father," or "daughter." Through the title, "Indian Hill," and the stoic Indian profiles that adorn the gates, the memorial site of local history extends its backward reach into time immemorial. Through the cemetery, "messy" racial and national histories are portrayed with simplicity and provide to living, non-Native, American visitors an opportunity for identification and historical memory—a memory that is perhaps most profoundly a forgetting.

HAUNTING METAPHORS

According to Jacques Derrida "haunting belongs to the structure of every hegemony."[75] Renée Bergland, in *The National Uncanny: Indian Ghosts and American Subjects*, has unpacked Derrida's statement thusly: "Power is unreal, insubstantial, somehow imaginary. At the same time, of course, it is undeniably real. When we describe hegemonies as socially constructed, we mean that they are built on history, memory, fear, and desire. They are made from the same things that ghosts are made from. Because the politics of the national, the racial, the classed, and the gendered are the politics of memory and false memory, they are also, necessarily, the politics of spectrality."[76] Pairing Derrida and Bergland's analysis of haunting with Richard White's analysis of place (which states that places enact power and are constructed within hegemonic systems)[77] leads me to claim that *all* places are haunted.

Perhaps Indian Hill Cemetery is a revealing site for an analysis of place as a haunting and haunted actor not because it is extraordinary, but because it is so ordinary, so commonplace. Through the haunting of Indian ghosts, through the construction of mythic Indian tropes, and through the presentation of national narrative mythologies, Indian Hill Cemetery haunts the city it serves. The place (re)presents power structures that are at once real and imaginary, tangible and insubstantial, here and not here. These tropes, mythologies, and power structures have been constructed locally, nationally, and internationally for hundreds of years, "built on history, memory, fear, and desire." "They are made," Bergland observes, "from the same things that ghosts are made from."[78] And, in turn, ghosts have been made from them.

The names and structures at Indian Hill Cemetery are physical metaphors that transmit ideological narratives. Tombstones, landscape design, and the name of the site itself are all tangible structures that stand in for and arrange into a meticulous order the "messy, ill constructed, and jumbled"[79] concepts of nation and race. These structural metaphors are haunted by the messages they were created to impart. At Indian Hill, hauntings are complicated by the fact that the Indian ghost (that Olin suggests haunts the site)[80] is itself a constructed structural metaphor. As discussed above, the Indian ghost is introduced into the discourse surrounding Indian Hill Cemetery as a metaphor for the inevitable death of Native peoples; it is a tool of Indigenous erasure. If the Indian ghost itself is a structural metaphor, and metaphors are haunted by the messages that they impart, then, at Indian Hill, haunting ghosts are themselves haunted. The verb "to haunt" is defined in the *Oxford English Dictionary* as "of unseen or immaterial visitants."[81] Thus, the creation of a metaphor[82] is in fact the creation of a haunted symbol. If a metaphor is defined by the simultaneous absence and presence of the "something else" that it is suggestive of, a metaphor then is a symbol that is constantly accompanied by that which is unseen or immaterial. Metaphors, symbols, and representations are all inherently haunted.

What does the haunted nature of metaphor mean for a structure such as Indian Hill Cemetery, whose central metaphor is an Indian ghost? Could it be that the metaphoric ghost of Indian Hill is haunted not by "imaginary or spiritual beings"[83] but by narrative ideologies of nation, race, ethnocide, and removal? Could it be that at Indian Hill Cemetery even the ephemeral is haunted? In the speeches presented at the dedication ceremony, physical realities of history are treated as legend, and legends of lingering ghosts are treated as fact.[84] The physical fact of Native existence is denied, while the ephemeral Indian ghost is ensconced.

Indian Hill Cemetery was created to instill haunting citizenship into Middletown residents. In Olin's words, the cemetery exerts "a real and powerful, though silent influence, in molding the character, and in exalting and purifying the sentiments of a people."[85] This "silent influence" is attained through a manipulation of "Indianness" in an attempt to construct non-Native American history and identity and also through an expansion of spatial frontier mythology in Middletown. The cemetery was a project aimed at expanding patriotism and active citizenship. The site's founders approached this project by creating Indian ghosts and erasing Native bodies. Indian Hill Cemetery was established in an attempt to ensure that, even as the visible remains of Native people were removed, the spectral Indian, ghosted and forever haunting white citizenry, remains.

NOTES

1. Steven Olin, *The Addresses Delivered at the Dedication of the Indian Hill Cemetery; with the Articles of Association, by Laws.* (Middletown CT: Charles H. Pelton, Printer, 1850), 34.

2. J. B. Beers, *History of Middlesex County, Connecticut* (New York NY: J. B. Beers, 1884), 62.

3. John C. Huden, ed., *Indian Place Names of New England* (New York NY: Museum of the American Indian, Heye Foundation, 1962), 295.

4. Olin, *Addresses Delivered*.

5. Frederick J. Goodwin, *Addresses Delivered at the Dedication of the Indian Hill Cemetery*, 14.

6. Jean M. O'Brien, "'Vanishing' Indians in Nineteenth-Century New England: Local Historians' Erasure of Still-Present Indian Peoples," in *New Perspectives on Native North America: Cultures, Histories, and Representations*, ed. Sergei Kan, Pauline Turner Strong, and Raymond Fogelson (Lincoln NE: 2006), 414–32. O'Brien examines seventeen historical accounts from the nineteenth century, most from Massachusetts, that make extinction claims, including Frederick Freeman, *The History of Cape Cod: The Annals of Barnstable County, Including the District of Mashpee* (Boston: Printed for the Author, 1860), vol. 1; Charles Brooks, *History of the Town of Medford, Middlesex County, Massachusetts, from Its First Settlement, in 1630 to the Present Time, 1855* (Boston: James M. Usher, 1855); *Woburn Records of Births, Deaths, Marriages, and Marriage Intentions, from 1640 to 1900* (Woburn MA: Andrews & Cutler, 1890–1919); Charles Brooks, *History of the Town of Medford, Middlesex County, Massachusetts, from Its First Settlement, in 1630 to 1855, Revised, Enlarged, and Brought Down to 1885, by James M. Usher* (Boston: Rand, Avery, 1886); John Greenleaf Whittier, *Legends of New England* (Gainesville FL: Scholars' Facsimilies & Reprints, 1965; Daniel Ricketson, *The History of New Bedford, Bristol County, Massachusetts* (New Bedford MA: Published by the Author, 1858); Samuel F. Haven, *An Historical Address, Delivered before the Citizens of the Town of Dedham* (Dedham MA: Printed by Herman Mann, 1837); *Old Dartmouth Historical Sketches, No. 51* (1921); Emory Washburn, *Historical Sketches of the Town of Leicester, Massachusetts, during the First Century from Its Settlement* (Boston: John Wilson & Son, 1860); Jane Van Norman Turano, "Taken from Life: Early Photographic Portraits of New England Algonkians, ca. 1844–1865," in *Algonkians of New England: Past and Present*, Peter Benes and Jane Montague Benes and Dublin Seminar for New England Folklife, 121–43 (Boston: Boston University, 1993).

7. O'Brien, "'Vanishing' Indians in Nineteenth-Century New England," 415.

8. Olin, *Addresses Delivered*, 34.

9. The role of the cemetery as a purveyor of history is discussed in Demond Shondell Miller and Jason David Rivera, "Hallowed Ground, Place, and Culture: The Cemetery and the Creation of Place," in *Space and Culture* 9 (2006): 349.

10. Stanley French, "The Cemetery as Cultural Institution: The Establish-

ment of Mount Auburn and the 'Rural Cemetery' Movement," *American Quarterly* 26, no. 1 (March 1974): 46.

11. John M. Findlay and Richard White, "Introduction," in *Power and Place in the North American West*, ed. Richard White and John M. Findlay, x (Seattle: University of Washington Press, 1999).

12. Blanche Linden-Ward, *Silent City on a Hill: Landscapes of Memory and Boston's Mount Auburn Cemetery* (Columbus: Ohio State University Press, 1989), 105.

13. Benedict Anderson, *Imagined Communities: Reflections on the Origin and Spread of Nationalism* (London: Verso, 1983), 19.

14. Linden-Ward, *Silent City on a Hill*, 115.

15. Ralph Waldo Emerson, *Nature* (1836), in *Ralph Waldo Emerson: Essays and Lectures* (New York: Library of America, 1983), 7. Cited in Linden-Ward, *Silent City on a Hill*, 118.

16. Histories of the Rural Cemetery Movement can be found in Linden-Ward, *Silent City on a Hill*; French, "Cemetery as Cultural Institution"; Jacob Bigelow, *A History of the Cemetery of Mount Auburn* (J. Munroe, 1860); David Schuyler, *The New Urban Landscape: The Redefinition of City Form in Nineteenth-Century America* (Baltimore MD: Johns Hopkins University Press, 1986); David Charles Sloane, *The Last Great Necessity: Cemeteries in American History* (Baltimore MD: Johns Hopkins University Press, 1995); Gary Laderman, *The Sacred Remains: American Attitudes towards Death, 1799–1883* (New Haven CT: Yale University Press, 1999).

17. Neil Harris, *The Artist in American Society: The Formative Years, 1790–1860* (Chicago: University of Chicago Press: 1982), 205.

18. Colleen McDannell, *Material Christianity: Religion and Popular Culture in America* (New Haven CT: Yale University Press, 1998), 107.

19. Olin, *Addresses Delivered*, 31–32.

20. Joseph Story, *An Address Delivered on the Dedication of the Cemetery at Mount Auburn, September 24, 1831* (Joseph & Edwin Buckingham: 1831), 14; John Russell Bartlett, *The Soldiers' National Cemetery at Gettysburg: With the Proceedings at Its Consecration, at the Laying of the Cornerstone of the Monument, and at Its Dedication* (Providence Press Co. for the Board of Commissioners of the Soldiers' National Cemetery, 1874), 4; *Dedication of the Confederate Monument, at Greenwood Cemetery, on Friday, April 10th, 1874* (New Orleans LA: J. A. Gresham: 1874), 23.

21. [William Tudor,] "Instruction for the Fine Arts," *North American Review* 2 (January 1816): 161; *Monthly Anthology* 4 (May 1807): 230; cited in Linden-Ward, *Silent City on a Hill*, 115.

22. Linden-Ward, *Silent City on a Hill*, 106.

23. Richard Grusin, *The Reproduction of Nature: Cultural Origins of America's National Parks* (Vanderbilt University Publications and Design,

2000 [cited March 14, 2004]); available from www.vanderbilt.edu/rpw
_center/lsooc.htm.

24. Philip J. Deloria, *Playing Indian* (New Haven CT: Yale University
Press, 1998), 4.

25. Daniel K. Richter, *Facing East from Indian Country: A Native History
of Early America* (Cambridge MA: Harvard University Press, 2001), 252.

26. Deloria, *Playing Indian*, 3.

27. Linden-Ward, *Silent City on a Hill*, 119.

28. Olin, *Addresses Delivered*, 27.

29. "American Antiquities," *Western Monthly Rev.* 1 (March 1828): 656.
Cited in Brian W. Dippie, *The Vanishing American: White Attitudes and U.S.
Indian* Policy (Middletown CT: Wesleyan University Press, 1982), 17.

30. D. H. Lawrence wrote, "There has been all the time, in the White
American soul, a dual feeling about the Indian. The desire to extirpate [him].
And the contradictory desire to glorify him" (*Studies in Classic American
Literature* [1924], cited in Deloria, *Playing Indian*, 4).

31. Dippie, *Vanishing American*.

32. "Indians Removing Westward" (January 7, 1828), *House Rep. No.
56*, 20th Cong., 1st sess. p. 2, cited in Dippie, *Vanishing American*, 10–11.

33. Rev. J. Pierpont, *Addresses Delivered at the Dedication of the Indian
Hill Cemetery*, 1.

34. Reneé L. Bergland, *The National Uncanny: Indian Ghosts and American Subjects* (Hanover NH: University Press of New England, 2000), 4.

35. Deloria, *Playing Indian*, 3.

36. Olin, *Addresses Delivered*, 27–28.

37. Barber, *Our Whole Country*, 351.

38. The year 1850 marked the first time that industry in Connecticut
could boast more workers than agriculture, and Middletown was an important industrial center. The state's population increased by almost 10 percent
between 1840 and 1850 alone. Most of the state's new inhabitants were
immigrants who arrived between 1845 and 1850. John F. Sutherland, *Immigration to Connecticut* (Connecticut Heritage Gateway, 2003 [cited March
31, 2004]) available from http://www.ctheritage.org/encyclopedia/topicalsur
veys/immegration.htm.

39. Anderson, *Imagined Communities*, 19.

40. Olin, *Addresses Delivered*, 30.

41. Olin, *Addresses Delivered*, 32.

42. Olin, *Addresses Delivered*, 32.

43. Deloria, *Playing Indian*, 3.

44. Frederick Jackson Turner, *The Significance of the Frontier in American History, The Early Writings of Frederick Jackson Turner* (Madison: University of Wisconsin Press, 1938).

45. Patricia Nelson Limerick, *The Legacy of Conquest: The Unbroken Past of the American West* (New York: W. W. Norton, 1987), 18.

46. Olin, *Addresses Delivered*, 28.

47. Olin, *Addresses Delivered*, 29.

48. Olin, *Addresses Delivered*, 29.

49. Olin, *Addresses Delivered*, 27–28.

50. Olin, *Addresses Delivered*, 32.

51. Olin, *Addresses Delivered*, 29.

52. Olin, *Addresses Delivered*, 28.

53. Slotkin, *The Fatal Environment: The Myth of the Frontier in the Age of Industrialization, 1800–1890* (Norman: University of Oklahoma Press, 1994), 11.

54. Olin, *Addressed Delivered*, 29.

55. David Schuyler, *The New Urban Landscape: The Redefinition of City Form in Nineteenth-Century America* (Baltimore MD: The Johns Hopkins University Press, 1986), 37.

56. Olin, *Addresses Delivered*, 32–33.

57. Joseph Story quoted in Thomas Bender, "The 'Rural' Cemetery Movement: Urban Travail and the Appeal of Nature," *New England Quarterly: A Historical Review of New England Life and Letters* 47, no. 2 (June 1974): 163.

58. In *God Is Red* (New York: Grosset & Dunlap, 1973), Vine Deloria discusses how nonwhite people have been habitually barred from internment in Christian cemeteries (185).

59. Beers, *History of Middlesex County*.

60. Doris Sherrow, "What Happened to the Wangunk?" (Portland Historical Society, 1999 [cited May 1, 2003]).

61. This is the heading on the first map of Indian Hill Cemetery (1850) in *Addresses Delivered at the Dedication of the Indian Hill Cemetery*.

62. Beers, *History of Middlesex County*.

63. Robert Berkhofer, *The White Man's Indian: Images of the American Indian From Columbus to the Present* (New York: Alfred A. Knopf, 1978), 3.

64. Olin, *Addresses Delivered*, 32.

65. Census data shows that Indians still inhabited Middlesex County as late as 1920. However, Rev. Frederick J. Goodwin says of Indians in the *Addresses Delivered at the Opening of Indian Hill Cemetery* seventy years earlier: "Long since could it be said of them . . . they have passed away" (14).

66. Michel Foucault, "Of Other Spaces," *Diacritics* 16, no. 1 (Spring 1986): 26.

67. Foucault, "Of Other Spaces," 25.

68. Foucault, "Of Other Spaces," 26.

69. Foucault, "Of Other Spaces," 27.

70. Linden-Ward, *Silent City on a Hill*, 130.

71. Beers, *History of Middlesex County*, 495.

72. Beers, *History of Middlesex County*, 495.

73. Berkhofer states that "since the original inhabitants of the Western Hemisphere neither called themselves by a single term nor understood themselves as a collectivity, the idea and the image of "the Indian" must be a White conception." Thus, he argues, "the Indian" has historically been a signifier primarily of specific European and white American fears and has not been representative of the peoples he supposedly stands for. In Berkhofer, *White Man's Indian*, 3, 27.

74. Foucault, "Of Other Spaces," 27.

75. Jacques Derrida, *Spectres of Marx* (New York: Routledge, 1994), 37.

76. Bergland, *National Uncanny*, 6.

77. Findlay and White, "Introduction," *Power and Place*, x.

78. Bergland, *National Uncanny*, 6.

79. Foucault, on the function of heterotopias, in Foucault, "Of Other Spaces," *Diacritics* 16, no. 1 (Spring 1986): 25.

80. Olin, *Addresses Delivered*, 32.

81. This definition even precedes "of imaginary or spiritual beings, ghosts" (*Oxford English Dictionary Online* [cited December 30, 2008]).

82. Defined as "something regarded as representative or suggestive of something else, esp. as a material emblem of an abstract quality, condition, notion, etc.; a symbol, a token" (*Oxford English Dictionary Online* [cited December 30, 2008]).

83. Under "metaphor" in *Oxford English Dictionary Online* (cited December 30, 2008).

84. Olin, *Addresses Delivered*, 32.

85. Olin, *Addresses Delivered*, 31.

PART 3

THE PAST IN THE PRESENT

7

"We Are Standing in My Ancestor's Longhouse"

Learning the Language of Spirits and Ghosts

COLLEEN E. BOYD

The "metaphor" model is everywhere to be found in anthropology, but it is rarely found in the real world where events of the psyche are regarded as common place.
EDITH TURNER, "A Visible Spirit Form in Zambia" (1994, 93)

You don't have anything if you don't have stories.
LESLIE MARMON SILKO, *Ceremony* (2006, 2)

"IT'S OUR FRIEND — HE'S HERE": Learning to Speak among Spirits

One early evening in June, I stood with my husband, John, and one
of his maternal uncles, near a small patch of woods on the edges
of the Lower Elwha Klallam Reservation. We encountered Uncle
while walking after dinner. He was excited to tell us about the little
mowitch[1] with tiny spikes he had spotted earlier that afternoon at
the very spot where we now stood. As we talked, my nose slowly
became aware of a foul odor—a smell halfway between rotting fish
and feces. The small patch of woods is a few feet from "the end of
the road," a place where reservation fishermen have snagged salmon
and steelhead for generations. Possibly, the rotten smell was nothing
more than the remains left by people who had cleaned their catch.
I have cleaned salmon and processed wild game enough to not be
overly sensitive to the rich smell of animal remains. It was hardly
worth a second thought, so I returned to the conversation, but not
before Uncle noticed my nose wrinkle in mild distaste. "You smell

that?" he asked, with a meaningful look. I nodded. "It's our friend. *He's* here."

Reviewing my field notes a few years later it is easy to dismiss this exchange as nothing more than rotting fish entrails and the kind of teasing that is common within large extended families. However, the careful reference to "him"—the "wild man"/Sasquatch/ *čičəy'íqwtən*[2]—is not uncommon or casual in most instances, and encounters with him are often reported to include strong smells reminiscent of feces or dead animals. Uncle may have been joking—or not. Spirits are everywhere in this small Coast Salish community. They permeate the land and people's consciousness. The terms spirit and ghost are misleading, as each suggests a certain homogeneity that does not really exist.

Although social scientists have frequently recorded stories that might be termed "supernatural," scholars have recently begun to more seriously consider the complex meanings behind such claims (Goulet and Miller 2007, Nabokov 2002, Young and Goulet 1994). The question is where stories of ghosts, spirits, and the like belong in our contemporary representations or reconstructions of culture, community, the environment and the past. Yi-Fu Tuan wrote, "The United States of America would seem to be the country in the world least hospitable to ghosts. It does not believe in the sanctity of the past" (1979, 127). Yet North America *is* a haunted land, and many of its wandering spirits are those associated with Indigenous peoples, cultures, and histories (cf. Thrush 2007). The sheer number of tales regarding the restless dead or inhuman spirits that are linked to urban, rural, and tribal development projects is startling. How often are Americans cautioned, through stories, films, and books, to beware disturbing the proverbial "Indian burial ground?" At the same time, anthropologists who focus on how cultures and communities change may, in turn, find themselves transformed when they conduct research within societies where "ghosts and spirits are as 'real' as merchants and clients" (Goulet 1994, 16). What might seem "extraordinary" to Western anthropologists, however, may be merely commonplace for the people with whom they work. Furthermore, even as anthropologists are moved to question why people hold "unusual or extreme beliefs" (cf. Zimmerman 2008, 55–86), it is just as worthwhile to question why the fear of "going native"—or losing one's objectivity—makes it so difficult to seriously consider the stories, beliefs, and evidence on which consultants and collaborators base these truth claims.

In 2003, construction workers unearthed human remains and artifacts at a site along the waterfront in downtown Port Angeles, a city of some eighteen thousand people in the shadow of the Olympic Mountains. North of the city is the Strait of Juan de Fuca and the Canada–U.S border. For most of Clallam County's existence, its citizens have labored in natural resources industries such as fishing and logging. In recent years, however, there has been a downturn in these industries, so the people of Port Angeles have looked to other forms of development. The project that inadvertently resulted in the excavation of Tse-whit-zen village had promised increased tourism, new jobs, and further economic development in the region. Unearthing the Olympic Peninsula's American Indian history and heritage was therefore viewed as a threat to the region's economic future. In many ways, disturbing what remained of the village and its cemetery proved threatening to tribal citizens as well, although for very different reasons. As archaeologists and tribal employees of the project removed hundreds of human remains, grave goods, and other artifacts, some experienced disturbing encounters with spirits. The purpose of this chapter is to explore the significance of these stories and the ensuing traumatic events for citizens of the Lower Elwha Klallam tribe, a small reservation community nine miles east of Port Angeles. To do so, we must consider the complex ways that Indigenous people frame encounters with spirits and how such stories influence the entwined projects of anthropology, ethnohistory, archaeology, and environmental studies. As well, we must consider what kinds of cultural teachings, experiences, and assumptions anthropologists and archaeologists bring to bear on their interpretations of aboriginal "ghosts." Lastly, how might "ghostly matters" help identify a more collaborative "middle path" for American Indian and nonnative researchers?

In 1990 Michael Michlovic published an essay titled "Folk

Archaeology in Anthropological Perspective." His intent was to challenge the defensive posturing of archaeologists in their responses to "folk" interpretations of the past. Archaeologists, he argued, have "abandoned the anthropological tradition, which instead of denouncing folk beliefs seeks to understand both the cultural context from which they emerge and the cultural needs to which they respond" (104). Furthermore, the folk beliefs of descendant communities challenge "archaeology's monopoly on interpretation of the past" (103; see also Zimmerman 2008). Similarly, the story of the Tse-whit-zen dig underscores that sites of aboriginal historicity are freighted with multiple answers to the question "what happened here?" Likewise, present-day stakeholders possess multiple ideas about how knowledge can best be obtained, how data should be interpreted, and what actually satisfies tests for reliability and validity. For example, a tribal member sifting for artifacts at the Tse-whit-zen site came across an unusually large olive shell (Olividae). She was frustrated when archaeologists did not share her opinion that this was an artifact and not just a random shell found at the site. She reasoned that an olive shell of this size was out of the ordinary and therefore would have been valued and used by her ancestors (John Boyd, pers. comm.). It goes without saying that conflicting views about research methods and historic interpretations are more contentious and complicated when human remains and grave goods are disturbed. In these circumstances, Indigenous stakeholders will generally argue that disturbing ancestral remains is tantamount to disturbing the ancestors themselves.

Among Coast Salish peoples, such as the Lower Elwha Klallam, human remains are sacrosanct, regardless of their age or provenance. At Tse-whit-zen the "discovery" and unearthing of human remains demanded a certain protocol on the part of Indigenous participants in archaeological recovery work. Tribal citizens hired to work at the site were instructed by elders and cultural consultants to follow a strict protocol in the event human remains and associated grave items were found. These instructions served the dual purpose of demonstrating respect for ancestors and their remains and keeping workers safe from the kinds of harm the dead might still inflict on the living.

Such problems included the possibility of being "followed" home by ghosts. Spirits within the contemporary Lower Elwha Klallam Reservation are not tattered remnants of primordial "tradition." Rather, they are powerful signifiers that depict contemporary Indigenous relationships to culture, spirituality, places, colonialism, and modernity. In the twenty-first century, hauntings continue to provide dimension to unseen, unvoiced, and marginalized emotions, experiences, and imaginings that nonetheless contribute to the "realness" of social life and the memories of people. Tales of ghostly encounters told by Coast Salish people cross boundaries of space, time, and culture, and, along the way, give historical breadth and depth to memories. They are alternatives for laying claim to place and the past.

Haunting, Avery Gordon notes, "is a constituent element of modern social life," explaining, "It is neither pre-modern superstition nor individual psychosis; it is a . . . social phenomenon of great import" (1997, 7). Like magic and witchcraft, hauntings critique modernity and at the same time "belong" to it (Pels 2003, 5). The Klallam word for ghost, *snúʔnəkw*, for instance, is also used, according to members of the Port Gamble Klallam, for "movie [and] T.V." because "the old-timers thought the moving pictures looked like ghosts."[3] In the 1930s a Coast Salish elder named Frank Allen told the young anthropologist William Elmendorf that an Indian doctor had revealed to him how ghosts dwelling in the land of the dead have "automobiles now, stores now, just like we have here" (Elmendorf 1993, 227). With this statement, the Indian doctor challenges modernity's power to banish ancestral ghosts by demonstrating how spirits embrace selected aspects of modernity and therefore survive—paralleling Native people's resilience, as shown by their ability to resist, transform, and ultimately survive. "Embracing the subjectivity of death," Sharon Patricia Holland argues, enables oppressed peoples to speak from "familiar sites" about that which has been unspoken or left for dead (2000, 4–5).

WHAT IS HAUNTING THE COAST SALISH PRESENT?

In his provocative article "Traditions of Disbelief," David Hufford asks why it is that "most" academics view "supernatural beliefs" as arising from "various kinds of obvious error" (1982, 47–55). He states, "What *I* know, I *know*; what you know, you only *believe*" (47). Similarly, Antonia Mills, in her ethnographic study of reincarnation, asks why it is that anthropologists are unwilling to examine their "reluctance to look at the evidence, presented by the people [they] study, with an open mind" (1994, 238). Hufford and Mills speak to the heart of the issue here. As anthropologists and scientists, we are trained in the Western "tradition of disbelief," automatically dismissing as false any claims that cannot be proven through observable facts. Clearly, this is a familiar divide. In August 2005, at a healing ceremony for the Tse-whit-zen village site hosted by the Lower Elwha Klallam tribe, a visitor from the Tulalip tribes echoed Hufford's premise:

> Sometimes people do not recognize what is dear to us
> They never say it *is* a sacred site to the Klallam people
> They say "the Klallam people *believe* it is a sacred site"
> —not that it just *is*.[4]

More than a decade ago, the Haitian scholar Michel-Rolph Trouillot argued that "history has many hearths" (1995, 20). In other words, humans fashion their own unique versions of history and sense of place. Which vision of history or place eventually triumphs is dependent on numerous factors. For this reason, Trouillot cautions all to be aware of silence—its causes and reasons for existing—especially when it concerns relationships of inequality that serve to reproduce themselves in the present, as through the "legacies of past horrors" such as slavery and colonialism. Trouillot notes, "Only in the present can we be true or false to the past we choose to acknowledge" (151). In this regard, present-day Klallam stories of spirits disturbed by the horrific legacies of imperialism and colonialism clarify or "authenticate" the past for Native peoples in ways that Western visions cannot (C. Boyd 2009). When issues pertaining to land development and environmental, historic, or cultural preservation cut across political, social, and economic boundaries, stakeholders within descendant communities may define what matters in very different ways—each drawing from their own traditions of belief or disbelief. Everyone has an opinion and a stake in such highly charged debates. Vine Deloria Jr., in the film *In the Light of Reverence* (2001), identified the basic issue as one of rights versus responsibilities. American society, he argued, is based on people claiming to have "rights" to land and resources. Native societies, on the other hand, teach that people have "responsibilities" to the land itself and to all that dwell within, including spirits. When Klallam people claim that a place is haunted by the spirits of dead ancestors, they are speaking from a position of responsibility: they are the principle caretakers for the land and their ancestors.

My interests in the interplay of spirits, the environment, and the past began when I heard stories about hauntings associated with the Tse-whit-zen village and cemetery, an archaeological site dating back twenty-five hundred years that is located near the base of Ediz Hook in Port Angeles, Washington. One of my husband's cousins, Mark, found employment as an archaeological technician for the site. The stories he shared motivated me to secure funding for summer fieldwork in 2005. Mark said he was not the only tribal member to experience strange occurrences at the site. Indeed, concern for restless ancestors illustrated the difficulties many tribal citizens experienced when ancestral remains were inadvertently unearthed.

Mark has maternal and paternal kin ties to several Northwest Coast Indigenous communities in the United States and Canada. As a member of a large and well-established family on the reservation, he is respected. He is also an avid fisherman and hunter well known for his subsistence skills and generosity. I have spent a great deal of time with Mark and other family members over the years, learning about contemporary subsistence practices. Generally, we talk about the conditions of the salmon and shell fisheries, not specifically about spirits. However, in the summer of 2005, Mark's attention, like that of most community members, turned to recent events surrounding Tse-whit-zen—the ancient Klallam village and cemetery that had been unearthed by construction workers at the base of Ediz Hook two years earlier, in August 2003. And it quickly became evident that by the summer of 2005, for many people, the subjects of land development, spirits, and the Tse-whit-zen site had become thoroughly intertwined.

For the first time ever, in the summer of 2005 the Lower Elwha Klallam tribe was scheduled to host the Paddle to Elwha, the annual Tribal Journeys canoe festival, an event that has occurred each summer for the last twenty years and involves thousands of Native peoples in the United States and Canada from as far away as the Aleutian Islands. The host community is responsible for housing, feeding, entertaining, and potlatching thousands of visitors, many of whom arrive via traditional dugout canoes, over a five-day period. Tribal Journeys is an event steeped in the Northwest Coast traditions of canoe travel, oratory, feasting, singing, dancing, and gift-giving. For many children and their families, it is an important source of cultural education and community pride. Therefore, it came as no surprise that in 2005 the Elwha Klallam had selected as the theme of their event "Reflections on Our Past: Tse-whit-zen Village"—a commemoration meant to draw attention to the village site dig, which had become a hotly contested political and cultural issue. Tribal Journeys thus became not just a forum for celebrating the vibrancy of Northwest canoe culture but an opportunity to engage people near and far in a political debate about land use, cultural resource management, and Indigenous human rights. It was clear that the people of Lower Elwha were seeking—and finding—allies from among the thousands of Northwest Coast villagers participating in the festivities.

The primary conflict involved the Lower Elwha Klallam tribe's relationship to their ancestral village of Tse-whit-zen and its cemetery and the State of Washington's and City of Port Angeles's desire to develop the site, which they regard as prime waterfront property. Development took the form of a graving yard, a marine construction facility where bridge pontoons would be created. Along with ferry boats, bridges are important elements of modern-day survival for the year-round residents of the Olympic Peninsula. Indeed, the Hood Canal Bridge is a main artery connecting Washington State's westernmost corner region to Bainbridge Island and, more importantly, to the Puget Sound Basin. In the late 1990s the State of Washington announced that the aging "floating" bridge required repairs. Port Angeles leaders were delighted that the town was selected from among several small cities in the region to win the bid for the new graving-yard site, where the large pontoons necessary for the repairs would be constructed. The graving-yard site meant economic revival and jobs for people left unemployed in the sagging post-timber economy. Shortly after construction began in August 2003, human remains were unearthed.

Conflicts between state and tribal governments over control of the Pacific Northwest's abundant natural resources are common in the region. In this instance, town residents told people from the reservation to "Stop Grieving and Start Graving," out of genuine frustration over job losses in an extremely depressed regional economy. Tribal citizens responded by referring to the graving-site-turned-archaeological-dig as an "open grave," out of sincere and desperate fear over the consequences of irrevocable actions. In both cases, each only scratched the surface of what is at stake for the entire community—Natives and non-Natives alike. In this chapter I will examine the underpinnings of the stories I was told by Mark and other tribe members in 2005 and situate these in the larger context of graving and grieving by exploring how studies of the spectral lay the theoretical groundwork for complex multicultural back stories about human relationships to space, time, and place on the Olympic Peninsula and beyond.

LOCATING GHOSTS: ADDRESSING THE PRESENT

In her sociological study *Ghostly Matters*, Avery Gordon ponders the "lost subjects of history" and argues that "perceiving . . . the missing and lost ones and the blind fields they inhabit . . . makes all the difference to any project trying to find the address of the present" (1997, 195), while Michel-Rolph Trouillot suggests that "dead Indians [have returned] to haunt professional and amateur historians" locked in battle over how different cultural perspectives might be incorporated into historic sites and presented for public consumption (1995, 9). Trouillot's critique about who should control the means and modes of historical production intersects with

Gordon's struggle to identify "what cannot be seen" yet nonetheless belongs to modernity and the present. How will the living locate these histories and stories?

Native peoples, as members of descendant communities, should play a central role in controlling the means and modes of historical production and in interpreting the multiple meanings and significance of archaeological and historical evidence from the past. Anthropology, like archaeology, "is inseparably entwined with the past policies and programs of colonialism, the appropriation and exploitation of one people's resources to enrich another[,] more powerful people" (Colwell-Chanthaphonh and Ferguson 2008, 3). In the twenty-first century, professional anthropologists, who specialize in the business of cultural and community heritage, have the opportunity and obligation to confront the errors of the past through collaborative engagement with communities. This includes striving to understand how knowledge of place and the past is internally evaluated and understood. What can we learn from spirits?

Avery Gordon challenges scholars to consider the role of haunting in the construction of social knowledge. Those that question the significance or intent of Gordon's argument have never faced a "seething presence of absence" in their own research. In short, they have not seriously contemplated the form and function of ghosts in contemporary life. While Gordon's book is an indispensable aid for investigating the role of cultural haunting in the production of memory, knowledge, and the historical past, scholars from diverse fields are engaging what Andrew Weinstock calls "spectral studies" within literary criticism (Bergland 2000, Brogan 1998, Richardson 2003, Weinstock 2004), geography and architecture (Tuan 1979, Vidler 1999), and postcolonial interpretations of folklore and history (Nabokov 2002, 146–48; Simmons 1986; Thrush 2007; Trouillot 1995), through examination of the relationship among performance, memory, and the past (Holland 2000, Roach 1996) and the relationship of the spectral to nation-building and modernity (Ivy 1995). Places inhabited by the ancestral dead, Peter Nabokov argues, are foundational to Native perceptions of history and claims to the past: "When Indian claimants [lose their lands], our shared cultural folklore grants their history one last ace up its sleeve. It slips into the earth to haunt our dreams. Both white and Indian literatures remind us how memories of the Native American's recriminating shadows and uncompensated losses still inhabit America's dark forests, bottomless lakes, mountain mists and midnight crossroads" (2002, 147–48). Furthermore, Nabokov argues, ancestral bones possess inordinate power to mobilize politics and emotions while "Indian history continues to hinder and haunt the doctrine of progress by placing human remains in its path" (2002, 148). The "contours and boundaries" of space as "sites of struggle" in contemporary discourse "are called upon to stand in for contested realms" of national and ethnic identities (Vidler 1999, 167).

Gordon asserts that "to study social life one must confront the ghostly aspects of it" (1997, 7). Haunting is not merely superstition somehow left over from premodern times; rather, it actually *constitutes* modern life. Stories of ghosts provide resistance to the "hypervisibility" that is characteristic of this era in which "we are led to believe not only that everything can be seen, but also that everything is available and accessible for consumption." Ghosts remind us of who came before us and of the limits to our vision. Through spirits we ask the hard questions about what becomes of those stories edited from "official" accounts of the past.

On the Olympic Peninsula in Washington State, Native peoples tell stories of human remains and hauntings. The stories included here exemplify how space is called upon to mark the "contested realms of identity" and demonstrate that ancestral remains, located in places defined as sacred and historic, mobilize political action and emotions, alter the trajectory of economic development, and proclaim Indigenous points of view. The value of these stories is not to be found in their power to prove or disprove the validity of the spectral. Rather, such stories are valuable because they create doubt and even fear in the minds of individuals who may be overly certain about the reliability and validity of their own truth claims regarding landscape, memory, and place. Haunted stories pertaining to the Tse-whit-zen site center on the place where developers of the graving site, armed with the doctrines of progress, are forced to reevaluate the contested meanings of dirt, stones, and bones. The site has become, in every sense, a "site of struggle" (Vidler 1999, 165–75).

More than one hundred tribal citizens worked at the Tse-whit-zen village site during the fifteen-month dig. Most but not all of the Native people hired were of the Lower Elwha Klallam tribe. Mark was hired with tribal emergency funds to work the security detail in April 2004. He spent less than a week providing security on the night shift. Mark switched jobs rather quickly, even though he possessed no skills or formal training in archaeological recovery work. Like most of the tribal employees, he received on-the-job training from contract field archaeologists hired for the dig. Mark came to enjoy the challenges of his new job and the thrill of discovering evidence of his ancestral past. He continued to work as an archaeological technician until the site shut down.

From the beginning, Mark, who is passionate about his cultural heritage, took the teachings of his elders "very seriously" with regard to how he conducted himself while at the cemetery and village site. Employees, for instance, were instructed to wash with water infused with snowberries[5] (*Symphoricarpos albus*) before entering or leaving the site and to smear dabs of *tumas*[6] near their eyes as protection against spirits. Snowberries are white, waxy-looking berries considered poisonous by Indigenous peoples. Interestingly, in some languages, they are given a name meaning "corpse berry," and for at least one group they were called "the Saskatoon berries of the people of the land of the dead" (Pojar and MacKinnon 1994, 70). *Tumas*, or red ochre, has been widely used for ceremonial and practical purposes by Coast Salish peoples.

Workers also participated in prayer circles. Sometimes, non-Native employees at the site joined them. When I attended a 2005 healing ceremony at the site, which had by then closed, I noticed members of the original crew in attendance; Natives and non-Natives alike used red ochre during the ceremony.

Mark accepted the presence of spirits at the village site. He stated, for instance, "I had to pray about what I was doing out there, and I asked [the ancestors] to show me what they wanted me to show the world. After that, I started to find some awesome artifacts. Around that time I ended up finding my first human remains; it was kind of disturbing." He explained the first strange experience he had while on the dig. He had been given the choice to dig in various areas. While standing in a location he had selected, he heard a very loud, sharp knocking sound. Mark hammered the coffee table in front of him with his balled fist to emphasize how loud it had sounded to him: he described it as a sharp rapping sound that seemed to come up through his feet. He decided to dig on that exact spot and soon unearthed a human pelvic bone—"I was probably standing on the chest of our ancestors, it was like they were in a box saying, 'You're standing on me, step aside!'"

The remains Mark found that day were male. "[I've been a] fisherman all my life," he explained, "this guy I found had hooks and harpoons buried with him." Mark's own status as a fisherman caused him to identify strongly with the decedent. The kinds of objects found in association with this individual indicated that he was highly respected for what he did, just as Mark himself is respected within the community for his subsistence skills.

Mark did not choose to share with anyone immediately that he had heard the knocking sound or how he came to dig at that spot. But these experiences referenced his own ancestral ties to the site in powerful ways: "People just told me that I'm blessed to be doing what [we] are doing . . . [when] we uncovered a longhouse in that same [area]. I told the archaeologists, we are standing in my ancestor's longhouse."

In summer 2005 Mark remained conflicted about his experiences. Months after the dig site had been closed, he found there was no simple way to explain what he had experienced. He knew that his familiarity with spirits set him apart from at least some people, particularly the scientists working on the dig. That did not prevent him from accepting these experiences as "real." For many of the Native people associated with the dig, spirits have agency to influence the living and are a part of everyday life. On the other hand, Mark and others were also being trained in scientific methodology, which gave some credence to Western points of view.

Besides Mark, other people had similar experiences and feelings about the site. A young mother who was pregnant at the time had been instructed to avoid the dig altogether because she was in a sacred state and it could be "dangerous" for her and the baby (LEKT August 2, 2005). Another woman explained that her boyfriend's house had to be "brushed out" with cedar boughs after a sibling working on the site brought spirits home from the dig (LEKT August 4, 2005). During the excavation, the entire community gathered with relations from Vancouver Island for a ceremonial "burning" of food and clothing—offerings to appease the ancestors. Each person who participated was someone with direct ancestral ties to the village.

Other community members felt agitated about the site and bothered by spirits. One woman hired to dig and screen artifacts was also available throughout the workday to smudge workers with the smoke of burning sage if they felt uncomfortable for any reason. She described the terrible nightmares about death she endured prior to joining the crew. Eventually, the nightmares compelled her to visit a family allotment site on a quiet beach where she stayed all day until she found five sacred items, including eagle fluffs and olive shells. It took all day to identify these items, and when she was done, she was protected and the nightmares stopped. This woman is a mother and believes that is why she found so many remains of children while working at the site. Besides having nightmares, she had not, in 2003, suffered any ill effects from working at the dig; consequently, because of the power objects she collected, she was asked to help people who did not follow instructions for brushing off spirits when leaving the site and whose homes were subsequently plagued by ghosts (LEKT August 5, 2005).

Stories of spirits and ghosts were not uniformly respected by all members of the archaeology crew. In summer 2005 a story repeated with great frequency illustrated how a lack of understanding might disrupt collaborative efforts. Allegedly, while driving home in the van, some of the archaeologists would burst into refrains of "There's something strange in the neighborhood, who ya gonna call? Ghostbusters!" (LEKT August 5, 2005). For Klallam people, hearing such stories affirmed their worst suspicions about non-Natives and university-trained anthropologists. Bad jokes created more tension in a workplace already marred by stress and grief. Perhaps this was a young and inexperienced crew, but people were angry to hear these stories. This was especially the case since tribal citizens already felt under fire from the greater Port Angeles community as city council members' "private" emails, which had now become public, were found to outline "concerns" that the tribe was "taking over." Other non-Natives called for the reexamination of treaty rights, and angry residents erected handmade signs in their yards in support of the graving yard. Clearly, as with natural resources, cultural and historical resources significant to local tribes, no matter how scientifically "worthy" they may be, are sometimes cited as reasons to mobilize against assertions of tribal sovereignty at the local level.[7]

"WE ARE NOT ALONE TODAY": Spirits and the Wavering Present

A healing ceremony held on August 2, 2005, during the Paddle to Elwha, drew about 250 people to the Tse-whit-zen site. Some twenty-five canoes, representing as many Indigenous nations, gathered on the water near the beach, where participants engaged in song, prayer, dances, and speech-making. The group included members of the original archaeology crew and members of the regional media, in addition to private documentary filmmakers there to witness as people acknowledged Tse-whit-zen's spirits. One hereditary chief from Canada stated:

> We are not alone today
> Your beaches are full of all the ancestors
> Who have come from different places.

Another individual from the Esquimault community on Vancouver Island stated:

> I want the young Elwha people to remember who stood
>   with you.
> It is truly a testimony to Indian people that we are caring
>   for the land, the water

> You can't give up because things are standing in your way
> The old people want you to be together
> It was the old people who pulled you together
> You see your culture coming out of the ground like a power.

And finally from Lower Elwha:

> They cannot continue to desecrate this sacred site,
> The ground that you walk on is very sacred to the Klallam
>   people . . .
> It is an honor to speak to them
> For I know they are smiling . . .
> Take care as you leave
> The ancestors are among us
> They walk among us.

Each speaker emphasized that the land is home to the past and that ancestral memories reside in these physical locations. The word "palimpsest" comes from the Greek *palimpsēstos*—"to scrape." It refers specifically to writing parchments or tablets that were scraped clean so they could be reused. Ediz Hook and the surrounding lands, which include Tse-whit-zen village and cemetery, is also a palimpsest—a place that had been buried in layers and whose purposes and meanings have been scraped away and replaced by newer ones. The reality of the colonial displacement of Coast Salish people was covered up by industrial progress even though, in 1920, "hundreds of Indian bones [had been] disturbed" when the pilings were driven into the earth to begin construction on the new timber mill (Crown-Z News 1940). Less than one hundred years later, hundreds of human remains were disturbed once again when workers broke ground on another development project. The city's residents had forgotten that Indians once lived on Ediz Hook and at its base.

Like Avery Gordon, we ask, "Does it matter who controls the shape of the story?" Does it matter, for instance, that the story of Tse-whit-zen lies "sandwiched" between layers of other stories—epidemic diseases, dispossession, ill-gotten wealth, industrial waste, archaeological retrieval? How can the rich textures and deeply rooted meanings contained within the palimpsest be revealed and appreciated? For one thing, the story could be shaped by what tribal citizens have to say of their experiences. It is the work of anthropologists and other social scientists to follow them down unfamiliar paths and to strive to discern the parameters of the story.

Eloquent words influence and reflect a community's belief in the power of both place and ancestral spirits to inspire, educate, and transform. Klallam people maintain that spirits will protect them and their unique way of life, or, out of anger and betrayal, lash out. Regardless, the figure of the ancestral ghost encourages a sense of propriety and cultural identity with respect to a place. The graving-yard project promised to bring jobs and prosperity to a beleaguered town that does not have enough of either. While the discovery of graves postponed this economic-recovery plan, it also reminded everyone that the future of the town, for better or worse, is linked to its past; and Klallam people belong not only to the past, but to the present and future of the Olympic Peninsula. Avery Gordon has said that "to be haunted is to be tied to historical and social effects . . .[that imbue places with] re-memories that you can bump into, even if they do not happen to you personally, they are waiting for you, even if you think they are finished and gone" (in Nabokov 2002, 147). Similarly, Klallam people, like Indigenous people in far-flung locales, are affirming their role in the present by re-membering their links to landscape and history through stories of haunting encounters with their ancestral dead.

FINDING A "MIDDLE PATH": Unlocking the Door
between Spirits, Stories, and Science

On the Olympic Peninsula the descendants of Indigenous villagers and white pioneers interact on ground they each view as central to their sense of personal history, purpose, culture, and place. Developers and municipal and tribal governments spar over whose vision will best serve the social and economic needs of the greater community. As well, tourists and other visitors bring their own "Muir-like expectations" to the region (Thornton 2008, 26). To further complicate matters, Indigenous communities sometimes hold competing claims to the same places, telling competing stories about them. For example, friction between the Klallam and the Makah has emerged in recent years over boundary disputes regarding the Hoko River fisheries (*Makah Indian Tribe v. Lower Elwha Tribe*, No. 79-4066, U.S. Court of Appeals, 9th Circuit). It can be difficult to determine the primacy of competing claims.[8] It is not a simple task to ask people to explain what a place means to them or why, or what has happened there. Whose stories will be validated, and whose will go unheard, dismissed or forgotten or buried in footnotes? How do we know when or where to strike a balance? What sorts of maps exist to tell us where and how to forge a middle ground?

"What do you think about ghosts and spirits?" I asked my husband. After years of patiently fielding questions about a subject that makes him uncomfortable, my husband turned these questions around one day. I thought about it. What did I think? As an environmental anthropologist and ethnohistorian with undergraduate training in archaeology and geology, I am a strong proponent of science education. Each semester I clarify to undergraduates, most of whom were born in the U.S. heartland and practice some version of Christianity, that evolutionary theory is not a "belief." Rather, it is a powerful explanatory framework one either accepts as valid or does not. For me, Western science remains a valid and significant enterprise.

Yet humans are as multilayered as landscapes and just as complex. I was not raised on stories of Darwin. I begged for books and a toy microscope and conducted archaeological digs in the backyard, which my parents patiently indulged. However, each Sunday I went to Mass with my family, and every breathing moment I inhaled what it means to be Irish and Roman Catholic in America. This was my cultural foundation, and I would be dishonest if I did not acknowledge it as a location from which I have come to understand Klallam culture and history.

Spirits, ghosts, and all the other "unusual beliefs" people hold, for lack of more-inclusive terms, were *not* first introduced to me by Indian people. As an Irish Catholic I was raised in an "ethnic" family and parish enclave. When I took Communion I was taught that the Host was not a metaphor for the body of Christ but was the actual body and blood of Christ, transformed each Sunday through the "mystery" of faith by the parish priest. The rhythm of the liturgical year was marked by various holy days of obligation, such as All Saints' Day and All Souls' Day and the Feast of Saint Mary (May Day), that at times seemed to parallel more ancient rhythms. This is in no way an endorsement of Margaret Alice Murray's claim (1921) that a pagan "witch-cult" managed to survive in modern Europe.[9] Few contemporary scholars accept Murray's conclusions as valid. Yet there is some evidence to suggest that pre-Christian superstitions died hard in many places, particularly within peasant agrarian societies (cf. Ginzburg 1992). And there is additional evidence that documents the transfer of Irish culture and folklore from "the old country" to Irish immigrants' new home in America.

Heaven, I was told as a child, was a place where everyone was young—forever—which is also the story of *Tir Na Nog*, the mythical land west of Ireland where no one grows old. "The Irish view of death and the afterworld is beautiful," my father told me one morning at the breakfast table when I was a child. He shared stories of wild Irish wakes he attended when he was a boy that were still held in private homes to celebrate and honor the recently deceased and send them on their journey to the afterworld. Death was not to be feared but to be greeted with laughter, stories, songs, food, and Jameson's. Death, I learned, was less the creepy figure from a Dickens's story and more an old friend who finds us when we least expect him to turn up. And when small items went missing—shoes or keys, mittens or library books—my mother blamed the fairies while admonishing us to "pray to Saint Anthony"—the patron saint of lost or stolen items.

The fairies or the *síde* (the "good people," as they are also known in Ireland)[10]—are the frequently troublesome and occasionally helpful otherworldly creatures deeply rooted in Gaelic landscapes (Evans-Wentz 2002). Apparently, they also traveled to America in ships carrying the immigrating or exiled. My father was raised in the small city of Butte, Montana, a place built by Irish immigrants who came mostly from County Cork. They and their American-born descendants worked in Butte's copper mines. Spirits of dead miners and "pixies" haunted the mines, just as they had in the old country (Emmons 1989, 42). Miners crumbled bits of "Cornish pasty" (meat pie) leftover from their lunches to appease them. If these are not precisely the same as the "little people" about whom Native people in the Northwest and throughout Indian Country share stories, they dwell in similar locales.

People do not ask for saintly intercessions, bribe the little people, or sing someone to their place in the afterworld because they believe in these practices. Quite the opposite, people practice and believe such things *because they work* and produce tangible results. This is a "truth" accepted but not easily explained with the tools of Western science. Therefore *how* I have come to understand unusual events and stories shared among Coast Salish peoples is refracted through an already clouded lens that includes a strong commitment to science *and* a deep foundation in ethnic heritage. When I hear accounts of Sasquatch, I understand why people hold "unusual or extreme beliefs" (see Zimmerman 2008). Indeed, I have some of my own.

When Native people in the Pacific Northwest share stories about the "wild man," such encounters are not framed as beliefs or metaphors. My husband told me about the night čičəy'íqwtən threw rocks at him and his two frightened dogs from the opposite bank as he set a fishing net near the mouth of the Elwha River. Another young tribal member recounted a time when the same being chased him along the trails that parallel the river—in the dark. An elder told a story about driving with her husband at night in a storm and glimpsing "him" in the headlights as he made his way across a rain-swept highway. Perhaps the most dramatic accounts of čičəy'íqwtən I ever heard occurred one summer in the early 1990s, when I was doing predoctoral fieldwork. It began when a young teenager saw Sasquatch in the woods that parallel the Elwha River and frame the reservation. Uncertain about what to do, he left fruit he had picked in the road as an offering. The experience disturbed him so deeply that elders from the Indian Shaker Church held a shake for him.

After that, children began reporting frequent sightings along reservation trails and in the woods. The fact that it was children encountering him, coupled with the sheer number of reports, was cause for alarm. The Lower Elwha community responded swiftly by organizing a meeting led by tribal elders who gathered families together and offered teachings and stories from a variety of perspectives that anchored the young people's experiences in culturally appropriate contexts. As members of the community, we attended the event with our sons. We clustered in a small public room in the tribal center, the children sitting on the carpeted floor and parents standing against the walls. The elders sat in front of the children in chairs and took turns speaking about how they understood the meaning of these visitations from the wild man.

The purpose of the community gathering was to comfort frightened children and provide them with the different possible meanings of Sasquatch. In the community there are Christians, members of the Indian Shaker Church, and people who have joined, or support, the Smokehouse religion. Some people participate in more than one religious tradition. The gathering enabled elders to provide a variety of teachings so that no one was left out. For some, the random appearance of Sasquatch is a kind of blessing since he is a powerful spirit guardian. For others, it is an ominous warning, as he is seen as dangerous and even evil. Following the initial sighting, I witnessed a disagreement between two tribal members about whether or not the teenage boy who initially saw him should have offered him food. One individual thought it was the "wrong" action to take, given the dangerous circumstances; the other thought the small gift of food was a proper effort at honoring the wild man. Interestingly, neither individual disputed the basic facts of the story but only how the boy should have behaved. It is clear to me after years of hearing such stories that people accept sightings and encounters with *čičəy'íqwtən* and other spirit beings not as articles of faith but as fact. These things happen and *that* is why people believe and respond.

So, why write about this subject at all? Would it not be better to stuff these experiences into a folder labeled "Coast Salish beliefs" and leave it at that? How should anthropologists and other researchers respond to assertions that what science considers "supernatural" and fictive is actually an accepted part of everyday life? If recent and past anthropological research is any indicator, anthropologists do, in fact, struggle with how best to respond to and represent such claims. This is even more the case when anthropologists themselves experience encounters they cannot easily dismiss or explain. The folklorist and anthropologist Frank Speck wrote about a frightful encounter he had in the Connecticut woods with a ghost named the "old Indian stonecutter." After enjoying dinner with a Mohegan couple, Speck decided to walk home, against their advice (Simmons 1986, 144). They warned him about walking alone near a certain quarry, for fear he would hear the stonecutter at work. Sure enough:

> As [Speck] came close to the quarry, he felt strange and stopped for a moment. The chink, chink sound of someone cutting stone was coming from the quarry. Dr. Speck said to himself, "Oh that is just my imagination playing tricks upon me." He started to walk again and the closer he came to the quarry, the louder the sound of stone cutting became. . . . Finally[,] as he walked closer to the sound, and as it became louder[,] he could see no one in sight though the moon was nice and clear. Suddenly the sound stopped and . . . he breathed a sigh of relief, but suddenly the sound commenced again, and this time it was directly in back of him. He wheeled around and saw no one, and then he decided to move. He ran through the woods and the sound followed him and he never stopped until he reached the Cooper home. (145–46)

In 1962, in as venerable a journal as the *American Anthropologist*, John Messenger wrote an essay about "Brendan"—a *leipreachán* that followed him home after he and his wife had completed field-work on Inis Beag, an island off the coast of Ireland. He noted, "Brendan has always shown a predilection for opening doors and windows, but after settling down [in the United States] he soon took to switching on the basement lights and manipulating the thermo-stat. . . . [O]ne evening I went to bed suffering from a severe head-ache and[,] once comfortably settled under the covers, recalled that I had neglected to take an aspirin. . . . As my feet touched the floor I heard the sound of running water in the bathroom" (367–73).

Messenger and his wife enjoyed Brendan's antics, and when for a few days they believed he had moved out were "crestfallen." When it seemed he had returned and resumed his activities, they were delighted and relieved.

Edith Turner wrote candidly about the exorcism in which she participated in 1985 during her first visit among the Ndembu of Zambia following the death of her husband, Victor Turner (1992, 1994). Longtime friends and consultants with whom the Turners had worked over the years urged her to assist them with the removal of a spirit from a possessed individual. As the ceremony proceeded, she witnessed the spirit "leaving" its unwilling host. She recalled, "It was a large gray blob about six inches across, opaque and something between solid and smoke. I was amazed, delighted. I still laugh with glee at the realization of having seen it" (1994, 83).

The experience transformed Turner and altered how she viewed the anthropological project: "How does acceptance of the informant's world view affect anthropology? It leaves a door unlocked" (1994, 93). In other words, Turner cautioned against viewing the experiences people report as only "metaphoric." She asks, "Is this faithful reportage of the people's experience? The people would deny it. The 'metaphor' model is everywhere to be found in anthropology, but it is rarely found in the real world where events of the psyche are regarded as common place, where different cultures have for long been exploring the intangible in terms of their everyday experience" (93).

What of anthropologists with personal and family ties to "traditional" or "ethnic" communities, where such truths are more readily accepted? A graduate teaching assistant assigned to an introductory course I taught remarked one day after class, "I get to have a culture, too!" I understand her frustration. It is as though we are expected to abandon entire cultural frameworks when we enter academia. This is a difficult and painful expectation for people tied to communities, cultures, and traditions. It probably should not be assumed that many or all are seeking to be rescued from their previous belief systems or that Western science always provides a welcome antidote to "superstitions." It is like sailing on rough seas without a rudder with which to turn away from one's foundation and ignore familiar teachings. "There is nothing I learned at university that I did not learn first from my grandparents," my husband emphatically maintains to this day. He is a Native American man with two bachelor's degrees and a master of fine arts, and one of the first people from his community to attend university. Yet he was raised at Lower Elwha by his maternal grandparents, for whom English was a second language and who were deeply knowledgeable about the Coast Salish culture they shared with their descendants. Although he could easily have survived without the academy, he could never survive without the teachings of his grandparents.

How can we approach unusual stories and experiences—those alter-*Native* truths—in the true spirit of inquiry and in ways that do not condescend? What do we owe the people with whom we work—or our own ancestors, for that matter—when we acknowledge that sometimes the little people follow us home? And last, how do we frame the inexplicable in our work with community consultants and students in an evenhanded and reasoned way that encourages scholarly and scientific debate without dismissing the "realness" of such events for the consultants with whom we work? Models for collaborative research (cf. Lassiter 2005) and theoretical orientations that emphasize multilocality and multivocality (cf. Colwell-Chanthaphonh and Ferguson 2006, 2008; Rodman 1992) go a long way toward addressing these concerns and, in the process, further assist in decolonizing the anthropological project. As one Hopi consultant underscored for archaeologists, "I thank the archaeologists because these are our ancestor's sites. The only thing I ask for is protection because this place is like our history books and it's for us, not for the archaeologists" (Dalton Taylor in Colwell-Chanthaphonh and Ferguson 2006, 159). Anthropologists, archaeologists, and ethnohistorians routinely consider sensitive subjects that engage people intellectually, spiritually, and emotionally. The collaborative model strives to give all stakeholders a voice in the research process. Although this model may not always be appropriate, it suggests new possibilities, especially in developing research projects with Indigenous descendant communities (Colwell-Chanthaphonh and

Ferguson 2008, 11–17). To embrace a collaborative model is to let go of the power to claim authority over the research process itself. Perhaps moving away from the binaries that guided anthropology in the past—right versus wrong, us versus them, and superstitions versus reality—will instead point the way toward a "middle path" for bridging science, ethics, beliefs, values, *and* cross-cultural understanding.

NOTES

The research for this paper was made possible by generous grants from the Melville Jacobs Research Fund and the International Studies Program at Ball State University.

1. *Mowitch* is the Chinook jargon word for "deer."

2. This is the Klallam word for *Sasquatch* (see http://www.ling.unt.edu/~montler/Klallam/WordList/index.htm, accessed March 1, 2007).

3. See Klallam Word of the Day, http://www.facebook.com/pages/Klallam-Word-of-the-Day/190354267028?v=wall#!/pages/Klallam-Word-of-the-Day/190354267028?ref=mf, accessed February 25, 2010.

4. This brief speech was delivered by an elder from the Tulalip tribes during the Healing Ceremony held August 2, 2005, at the *Tse-whit-zen* site (C. Boyd 2005, unpublished field notes).

5. Timothy Montler lists *snúʔnəkʷ sčayíqʷɬ* as Klallam words for "snowberry" (see http://www.lingtechcomm.unt.edu//~montler/Klallam/WordList/plants.htm, accessed February 27, 2010). Erna Gunther, in *Ethnobotany of Western Washington* (1995/1973), lists the Klallam word for "snowberry" as *p'astciɬxtc.*

6. Red ochre is a red-tinted soft clay used for pigment the world over.

7. How local residents responded to the decision to protect Tse-whit-zen calls to mind the anti-Indian rhetoric rampant during the Makah whale hunt in 1999 and the destruction of ancient Hopi petroglyphs by developers detailed in the film *In the Light of Reverence.*

8. There are interesting stories on the Olympic Peninsula regarding tribal claims that could be explored in greater detail and more productively in a separate publication.

9. I am grateful to my friend and colleague Dr. Abel Alves, from Ball State's Department of History, for our many stimulating conversations about magic, witchcraft, science, and the unknown. His ideas inform my own here.

10. In Ireland, people refer to these beings using terms such as this, preferring not to speak directly of them. Similarly, Native peoples in the Northwest avoid saying "wild man's" name out loud or reserve the right to do so in prescribed settings.

WORKS CITED

Bergland, Reneé. 2000. *The National Uncanny: Indian Ghosts and American Subjects.* Hanover NH: University Press of New England.

Boyd, Colleen. 2009. "'You See Your Culture Coming out of the Ground Like a Power': Uncanny Narratives in Time and Space on the Northwest Coast." *Ethnohistory* 56 (4): 699–732.

Brogan, Kathleen. 1998. *Cultural Haunting: Ghosts and Ethnicity in Recent American Literature.* Charlottesville: University Press of Virginia.

Castile, George Pierre, ed. 1985. *The Indians of Puget Sound: The Notebooks of Myron Eells.* Seattle: University of Washington Press.

Colwell-Chanthaphonh, Chip, and T. J. Ferguson. 2006. "Memory Pieces and Footprints: Multivocality and the Meanings of Ancient Times and Ancestral Places among the Zuni and Hopi." *American Anthropologist* 108(1): 148–62.

————. 2008. *Collaboration in Archaeological Practice: Engaging Descendant Communities.* Lanham MD: Alta Mira.

Crown-Z News. 1940. "Squatters and Bones of Indians Bother Builders." November 5. Crown-Zellerbach company newsletter, Port Angeles local history collection, North Olympic Library System, Port Angeles WA.

Derrida, Jacques. 1994. *Specters of Marx: The State of the Debt, the Work of Mourning and the New International.* New York: Routledge.

Elmendorf, William. 1993. *Twana Narratives: Native Historical Accounts of a Coast Salish Culture.* Seattle: University of Washington Press.

Emmons, David M. 1989. *The Butte Irish: Class and Ethnicity in an American Mining Town, 1875–1925.* Champaign: University of Illinois Press.

Evans-Wentz, W. Y. 2002. *The Fairy Faith in Celtic Countries.* London: Citadel. (Orig. pub. 1911.)

Foucault, Michel. 1980. *Power/Knowledge: Selected Interviews and Other Writings, 1972–1977.* New York: Pantheon Books. (Orig. pub. 1972.)

Ginzburg, Carlo. 1992. *The Night Battles: Witchcraft and Agrarian Cults in the 16th and 17th Centuries.* Baltimore MD: Johns Hopkins University Press.

Gordon, Avery. 1997. *Ghostly Matters: Haunting and the Sociological Imagination.* Minneapolis: University of Minnesota Press.

Goulet, Jean-Guy. 1994. "Dreams and Visions in Other Lifeworlds." In Young and Goulet, *Being Changed by Cross-Cultural Encounters*, 16–38.

————, and Bruce Miller, eds. 2007. *Extraordinary Anthropology: Transformations in the Field.* Lincoln: University of Nebraska Press.

Gunther, Erna. 1995. *Ethnobotany of Western Washington: The Knowledge and Use of Indigenous Plants by Native Americans.* Seattle: University of Washington Press. (Orig. pub. 1973.)

Holland, Sharon Patricia. 2000. *Raising the Dead: Readings of Death and (Black) Subjectivity*. Durham NC: Duke University Press.

Hufford, David. 1982. Traditions of Disbelief. *New York Quarterly* 8:47–55.

Ivy, Marilyn. 1995. *Discourses of the Vanishing: Modernity, Phantasm, Japan*. Chicago: University of Chicago Press.

Lassiter, Luke Eric. 2005. *The Chicago Guide to Collaborative Ethnography*. Chicago: University of Chicago Press.

LEKT (Lower Elwha Klallam Tribe). 2005. Interviews collected by Colleen Boyd in July and August 2005, Port Angeles WA.

Lien, Carsten, ed. 2000. *Exploring the Olympic Mountains: Accounts of the Earliest Expeditions, 1878–1890*. Seattle: Mountaineers Books.

Messenger, John. 1962. "A Critical Reexamination of the Concept of Spirits: With Special Reference to Traditional Irish Folklore and Contemporary Irish Folk Culture." *American Anthropologist* 64 (2): 367–73.

Michlovic, Michael G. 1990. Folk Archaeology in Anthropological Perspective. *Current Anthropology* 31 (1): 103–7.

Mills, Antonia. 1994. "Making a Scientific Investigation of Ethnographic Cases Suggestive of Reincarnation." In Young and Goulet, *Being Changed by Cross-Cultural Encounters*, 237–72.

Murray, Margaret Alice. 1921. The Witch-Cult in Western Europe: A Study in Anthropology. Oxford UK: Clarendon.

Nabokov, Peter. 2002. *A Forest of Time: American Indian Ways of History*. Los Angeles: Cambridge University Press.

Pels, Peter. 2003. "Introduction: Magic and Modernity." In *Magic and Modernity: Interfaces of Revelation and Concealment*, ed. Brigit Meyer and Peter Pels, 1–38. Stanford: University of California Press.

Pojar, Jim, and Andy MacKinnon. 1994. *Plants of the Pacific Northwest Coast: Washington, Oregon, British Columbia and Alaska*. Vancouver: Lone Pine.

Richardson, Judith. 2003. *Possessions: The History and Uses of Haunting in the Hudson Valley*. Cambridge MA: Harvard University Press.

Roach, Joseph. 1996. *Cities of the Dead: Circum-Atlantic Performance*. New York: Columbia University Press.

Rodman, Margaret. 1992. "Empowering Place: Multilocality and Multivocality." *American Anthropologist* 94 (3): 640–56.

Silko, Leslie Marmon. 2006. *Ceremony*. New York: Penguin.

Simmons, William. 1986. *Spirit of the New England Tribes: Indian History and Folklore, 1620–1984*. Hanover NH: University Press of New England.

Thornton, Thomas. 2008. *Being and Place among the Tlingit*. Seattle: University of Washington Press.

Thrush, Coll. 2007. *Native Seattle: Stories from the Little Crossing-Over Place*. Seattle: University of Washington Press.

Trouillot, Michel-Rolph. 1995. *Silencing the Past: Power and the Production of History*. Boston: Beacon.

Tuan, Yi-Fu. 1979. *Landscapes of Fear*. Minneapolis: University of Minnesota Press.

Turner, Edith. 1994. "A Visible Spirit Form in Zambia." In Young and Goulet, *Being Changed by Cross-Cultural Encounters*, 71–98.

———, with William Blodgett, Singleton Kahona, and Fideli Benwa. 1992. *Experiencing Ritual: An Interpretation of African Healing*. Philadelphia: University of Pennsylvania Press.

Vidler, Anthony. 1999. *The Architectural Uncanny: Essays in the Modern Unhomely*. Cambridge MA: MIT Press.

Weinstock, Jeffrey Andrew. 2003. *Spectral America: Phantoms and the National Imagination*. Madison: University of Wisconsin Press.

———. 2004. *Spectral America: Phantoms and the National Imagination*. Madison: University of Wisconsin Press/Popular Press.

Young, David E., and Jean-Guy Goulet, eds. 1994. *Being Changed by Cross-Cultural Encounters: The Anthropology of Extraordinary Experience*. Peterborough ON: Broadview.

Zimmerman, Larry. 2008. Unusual or Extreme Beliefs about the Past, Community Identity, and Dealing With the Fringe. In Colwell-Chanthaphonh and Ferguson, *Collaboration in Archaeological Practice*, 55–86.

8

Indigenous Hauntings in Settler–Colonial Spaces

The Activism of Indigenous Ancestors
in the City of Toronto

VICTORIA FREEMAN

At a multi-faith event in the fall of 2005, a group of Indigenous and non-Indigenous activists reclaimed one of the Toronto Islands as "Spirit Island," reconsecrating and reactivating the land as a sacred site for healing ceremonies and teachings by elders. During that ceremony, an Indigenous elder from Greenland sang a healing song passed down from his great-great-grandmother. He sang it for the sculptor who hoped to create a healing garden for children on the site, which he envisioned as a medicine wheel of sculptures by Indigenous artists. The sculptor spoke of being raised white and only later in life realizing that his family's multigenerational history of physical, sexual, and emotional abuse were the result of the catastrophic effect of the Trail of Tears on the Cherokee–Choctaw lineage running through his grandmother. That was a history and geography far removed from Toronto—and the medicine wheel also came from elsewhere[1]—yet he and others present seemed to draw strength from connecting their own particular histories and concerns with the Mississaugas' historic use of that land for healing[2] and to the First Nation's assertion that the islands remained unceded territory.[3] In many of the speeches and prayers that day, there was a palpable sense of return.

The gathering certainly exemplified the diverse ways that various Indigeneities, histories, and other cultural influences mix, meld, and mutate in this global city. A white pine was planted, both recalling and making manifest the Great Tree of Peace planted long ago by the Iroquoian prophet known as the Peacemaker. Although he is said to have been born near Belleville, his people, the Huron-Wendats, were also Indigenous to the Toronto area, and he brought peace to the Haudenosaunee, one of the largest groups of Aboriginal people now living in the city. Also present was an Anglo-Canadian woman who practiced a form of ancestral healing and understood herself as a shaman; her healing practice drew on New Age conceptions of Indigenous spiritual traditions, although she was not strongly connected to Indigenous people herself. Later, an Anglo-Canadian man arrived who proudly traced his lineage back to the brother of Augustus Jones, the eighteenth-century surveyor of the fledgling settlement of York that later became the City of Toronto. Augustus Jones was also the Welsh father of the nineteenth-century Mississauga missionary Kahkewaquonaby (Rev. Peter Jones), perhaps the most famous and influential Mississauga of his time.[4] This descendant brought with him the physical manifestations of his connection to Peter Jones: an old photograph of the missionary and a mid-nineteenth-century Christian hymn book Jones had translated into Ojibway, which were examined reverently by the group. Some Anishinaabeg who worked in the healing professions were also there, people related by ethnicity to the Mississaugas who had lived in the area until 1847.

What was interesting about this event was that all of these people believed in one way or another in the potency of ancestors as forces or influences from the past on present-day Toronto. Whether their progenitors were buried in the vicinity or in unknown graves thousands of miles away, their ancestry and the ancestry of others mattered. What was also notable was that they all wanted to forge new connections to the Indigenous history of the place, and in some sense to reactivate, or even reanimate, the site as Indigenous space.

On another day in Toronto, on the Great Indian Bus Tour of the city sponsored by the Native Canadian Centre of Toronto, a tour guide presented an alternative history of the city, challenging the tour participants to imaginatively "strip back the layers of concrete" to learn the true history of what had happened to the Indigenous peoples of the area, a history that she spoke of as being hidden and suppressed. Referring to the Bering Strait theory as "voodoo science," she spoke of the widespread Indigenous belief that Native

Americans had originated in North America, that Indigenous people had always been here. She described how, in the traditional Anishinaabe migration story, the ancestors followed the megis shell from the east coast of North America to Madeleine Island, Wisconsin; some Anishinaabeg had been left at points along the way, she said, including on the peninsula that later became the Toronto Islands.[5] Her point, reinforced by her references to the hundreds of Indigenous archaeological sites along the shores of the region's rivers, was that Indigenous people, including the Anishinaabeg, who academic historians generally describe as moving into the area only after about 1700 CE, had always been present in the city and its environs and were still there. In spite of the layers of concrete, the footprints of the ancestors were everywhere, a spiritual presence that proved both Indigenous continuity and persistence and demonstrated true ownership of the land.

At one point, the bus tour participants disembarked at an unusual grassy mound that looked like a good tobogganing hill in a Scarborough suburban neighborhood, the top of which was marked with a cairn and a plaque describing the mound as the site of a Wendat ossuary dating from the fourteenth or fifteenth century.[6] There the remains of 475 Iroquoian people were buried communally, in manner ritually consistent with the Huron-Wendat Feast of Souls (also known as the Feast of the Dead) now known largely through a description by Jean Brébeuf in the Jesuit Relations of 1636.[7] The modern visitors, who were mainly but not exclusively of Aboriginal heritage, made offerings of tobacco and prayed for the spirits of the ancestors, who were referred to as such regardless of the particular tribal ancestry of the tour participants. The tour guide remarked that in the past the site had not been properly cared for; houses in the area had often been put up for sale because they were haunted. Since then, she said, the non-Aboriginal neighbors had learned to watch over Tabor Hill, protect its sanctity, and even honor the spirits with tobacco.[8]

These two anecdotes are suggestive of a pattern I want to explore in this paper, which is how and why the Indigenous past of the Toronto area is being reinscribed on the modern city through the

medium of Indigenous ancestral spiritual presence. What was striking in both examples was that the Aboriginal past and the Aboriginal
sacred were one and the same, still existing at very specific sites but
also experienced as being everywhere in the city in a largely invisible but unbounded way. In my research on the historical memory
of the Indigenous and colonial past of Toronto, I have encountered
many such narratives of Indigenous ancestral spiritual presence in
Toronto, a city where Indigenous people are a tiny minority, where
there is no Indigenous reserved land, and where detailed knowledge
of the city's history, Indigenous or otherwise, is rare. In my interviews with current residents of the city, or those whose ancestors
lived there,[9] many of the Indigenous interviewees have spoken of
ancestors, ghosts, spirits, the energy of sacred sites, and other forms
of haunting or spiritual presence from the past actively and invisibly
at work in the present-day city, often for Indigenous ends, always
producing Indigenous difference.

For a non-Indigenous Toronto citizen such as myself, stories relat-
ing the historic Indigenous and especially the historic Indigenous
sacred to familiar Toronto places had a curious effect. They rendered
my hometown unfamiliar and strange—*unheimlich*, to use the termi-
nology of Sigmund Freud[10]—leaving me as a settler with a curious
double vision where I was both in place and out of place, living in
the present yet haunted by an Indigenous past. This was an interesting turnaround, given that being both in place and out of place is an
everyday experience for most Indigenous people in Canada, living as
they do in a land that is and is no longer their own land, where they
are often haunted by the past and particularly the suffering of their
ancestors. Such experiences are examples of what Ken Gelder and
Jane M. Jacobs, in *Uncanny Australia: Sacredness and Identity in a
Postcolonial Nation*, describe as manifestations of the Indigenous
"uncanny" (again, following Freud). In a settler–colonial context,
this experience of unsettlement is a potentially decolonizing force,
where "what is 'ours' as settlers is also recognized as potentially, or
even always already 'theirs.'"[11]

As a historian, I am curious about how such discourses of Indigenous ancestral spiritual presence relate to questions of histori-

cal memory and historical consciousness and how and why they have become a mode of empowerment for Aboriginal people in the city. For Toronto is a place where the colonial past and the people affected by it often appear to be completely absent, as if colonialism never happened[12]—or perhaps as if it had been completely accomplished. If reconciliation is, at least in part, a process of "bringing the nation into contact with the ghosts of its past,"[13] reworking the nation's sense of itself to make possible the development of just and equitable relations between Indigenous and non-Indigenous peoples, what role do these local Indigenous ghosts and ancestors play in this process?

One of the first things that becomes apparent in exploring the links between narratives about Indigenous ancestors and ghosts and historical memory in Toronto is that most contemporary Torontonians do not appear to be very interested in the city's past, Indigenous or otherwise, and they certainly do not have much opportunity to explore what interest they do have. The city currently defines itself largely in terms of its present ethnic diversity rather than its history, in contrast to some other North American cities of comparable size, such as Boston and Montreal.[14] History does not form a large part of the city's urban mythology or tourism promotion, and Toronto is anomalous in that there is currently no museum or large-scale institution that is devoted to the whole span of the city's history or that situates the history of Toronto in a larger context, though there have been recent calls for one.[15] In many respects, it seems, Toronto is a city without public consciousness of its roots.

Toronto's Indigenous history appears to be particularly invisible and unknown to most Torontonians.[16] Its ten existing city-run museums are mostly small historic houses, focused on nineteenth-century Anglo–Celtic Toronto. Most of the hundred thousand artifacts and one million archaeological objects in the city's collection date from the 1790–1920 period and are quite limited in terms of representing First Nations history.[17] The Royal Ontario Museum, a provincial institution also in Toronto, has large Aboriginal collections from all over Canada, including artifacts from the Toronto area, but its geographically broad mandate means that local or regional history is rarely a focus.[18] Only since 2006 has the city's own Web site offered a historical overview of Toronto's past, which includes a sizable Indigenous component,[19] perhaps signaling a shift in historical consciousness—but the people I interviewed were generally unaware of it.

The invisibility of local Indigenous history is a common North American settler–colonial phenomenon. In published town histories across North America, "Indians" usually appear only in the first chapter and then "exit stage left after treaty or battle."[20] Popular books on Toronto history that sit on local library shelves largely follow this pattern, with a few interesting exceptions—most notably a volume published by the Native Canadian Centre of Toronto in 1997.[21] In the most common version of the Toronto "creation" story, history really begins in 1793 with Lieutenant-Governor John Graves Simcoe founding the settlement of York in a "trackless wilderness" devoid of Indigenous people except for two Mississauga families camped on the peninsula that is now the Toronto Islands[22] (though there is usually also some mention of the ancient Indigenous portage route along the Humber River to Lake Simcoe as a significant local feature, instantly belying the region's "tracklessness"). Usually, once such histories describe the founding of the city, Indigenous peoples disappear from the story.

Perhaps not surprisingly, few of these works discuss the fact that the so-called Toronto Purchase of 1787 was known to be invalid by 1794, a year after York's founding, or that when the treaty was finally "confirmed" eleven years later in 1805, government negotiators increased the amount of land surrendered without the Mississaugas' knowledge and, according to the Mississaugas of New Credit, paid them only ten shillings for 250,880 acres.[23] In fact, several of the early historians of the city saw no need to mention the Toronto Purchase at all.[24] Yet the confirmed treaty is the foundation for Toronto's legal existence, and since 1986 that treaty has been subject to a land claim. Like other treaties, it is fundamental to the historic relationship created between Indigenous and non-Indigenous peoples in Canada. Most of the non-Indigenous Torontonians I interviewed were completely unaware of it.

Perhaps the Indigenous past has also been disconnected from the history of Toronto because of outdated distinctions between the urban history of the city and its non-urban antecedents, or between history and so-called prehistory, to which the Indigenous past is usually relegated.[25] As Coll Thrush pointed out in *Native Seattle: Histories from the Crossing-Over Place*, connections between urban and Indigenous history are only beginning to be made; in fact, "Indian" and "urban" are often seen as antonyms, at opposite ends of a national past and imagined future.[26] Cities, he says, are seen as the "ultimate avatars of progress," representing "the pinnacle of technology, commerce, and cultural sophistication"; at the same time, cities obliterate the Indigenous landscape of the past. Yet the Toronto area's human, if not urban, history goes back at least eleven thousand years.

If the public culture of Toronto has been largely silent about the history of Indigenous people in the region, we might ask ourselves, as Elizabeth Furniss does in relation to the history of Queensland, Australia, "What is in the history of Aboriginal—settler relations in [this area] that has created the contemporary situation in which silence is perpetuated?"[27] Is there any ethical obligation to remember this history? Is this settler–colonial silence a factor in the phenomenon of Indigenous haunting?

In the more than forty interviews I have conducted for my research on historical memory in Toronto, both Indigenous and non-Indigenous residents of Toronto sometimes described instances of Indigenous haunting in the city, either in the sense of disaffected spirits returning or sometimes in the more metaphoric sense of a returning or haunting memory or image, or a slight trace or vestige of something lost. Indigenous and non-Indigenous uses of such stories differed: for most of the non-Indigenous people I interviewed, stories of haunting expressed what was once and is no longer, hence a kind of absence, whereas for Indigenous interviewees and some of their allies, ghost and spirit stories articulated what had been and is still present, if invisible, in the city, and what could become more visibly manifest in the future.[28]

Haunting as Indigenous absence has an old pedigree in the settler trope of the "vanishing Indian." In 1855, for example, Johann Georg Kohl, a German visitor to Toronto, noted that Native people "were numerous when the English founded here the town of York, and there are still people in Toronto who remember the fleets of bark canoes and little skiffs, in which the Indians used to bring fish and other things to sell to the inhabitants—mostly encamping on that long sandy peninsula [now the Toronto islands]." He continued, "But the Indians have now vanished like the morning mist, and nothing remains to recall even their memory, but the well sounding name they invented for this locality—the sonorous Toronto."[29]

Kohl's nostalgic description itself reenacts that ghostly vanishing, with only the word "Toronto" lingering as a haunting vestige of that history. Indeed, from Kohl's time to the present, Toronto's name has been one of the few remaining links with its Indigenous past, though even its exact meaning is uncertain.[30] While virtually all my non-Indigenous interviewees were aware that the city had an Indigenous name, and some were aware of at least one possible meaning, that Indigenous name was alive in a completely different way for some Indigenous interviewees. As one person explained, the word "Toronto" carried spirit energy from the past into the present because the language itself was alive. Created by the ancestors, it continued to do their spiritual work.[31] Such ancestral energy brought both the Indigenous past and a current Indigenous presence into the consciousness of the city through its very name. It always accompanied current Indigenous residents so they would never be alone, so they would never be only in a settler–colonial place. Such perceptions are illustrative of the way some of the people I interviewed spoke of the activism of their ancestors; either in spirit or by example the ancestors invisibly helped their descendants in their personal lives and also influenced the development of the city. Such activity by the ancestors inspired activism in their descendants in turn, strengthening their commitment to Indigeneity[32] in their own lives and to the passing on of Indigenous culture to future generations of descendants.

In some interviews, particularly with non-Indigenous Torontonians, Indigeneity itself was often experienced as a kind of ghostly absence in the modern multicultural city,[33] somewhat akin to the city's "lost rivers."[34] Indeed, Toronto is known globally for its cosmopolitanism and not for its Indigeneity; the city exemplifies what Marshall Berman has described as "that immense demographic upheaval, severing millions of people from their ancestral habitats, hurtling them halfway across the world into new lives,"[35] a condition that is a fundamental characteristic of (post)modernity. Fully 50 percent of Toronto's almost 2.5 million citizens were born outside of Canada, and half of all immigrants to Toronto have been in Canada for less than fifteen years.[36] While the Aboriginal population of the City of Toronto was 13,605, according to the 2006 census, and was 31,910 in the Greater Toronto Area (GTA), Aboriginal organizations in the city estimate as many as 70,000 Aboriginal residents.[37] While this constitutes one of the largest Aboriginal populations of any Canadian city, it is a tiny, if increasingly vibrant, proportion of the city's multicultural mix. To many of the non-Indigenous people I interviewed, Toronto appeared to be a place where Indigenous historical presence, and especially the Indigenous sacred, appeared to be wholly absent or to have been destroyed by modernity, something that had been "lost," and that existed only as a residue, if it existed at all.[38]

Questions of who is Indigenous to Toronto are complex, and it is worth reviewing the outlines of the history of the region to understand the relationship between the current Indigenous population and narratives of Indigenous spiritual presence or haunting in the modern city. Whose ancestors' bones are buried in the earth? Whose ancestors' spirits haunt the land? Huron-Wendats and the related Petun (Tionnontati),[39] Haudenosaunee, and Anishinaabe peoples have all lived in the Toronto area at various times, but creation and migration stories in oral tradition, archaeological evidence, and linguistic analysis do not cohere to provide easy universally accepted answers to the question of their origins or movements, or the length of their occupation. While the creation stories of all these groups speak to their long residency in the Great Lakes region, the earliest archaeological evidence (c. 9000 BCE) in the immediate Toronto area is of hunter–gatherers, likely the ancestors of Algonquian speakers (though the Anishinaabeg have an oral tradition of migration from the east). Corn growers, the ancestors of the Iroquoian Haudenosaunee, Neutral,[40] and Huron-Wendat peoples, were in the region by at least five hundred CE, but whether they developed in situ from hunter–gatherers who embraced a new corn technology from the south or arrived from the south with an existing corn culture and displaced the hunter–gatherers is unclear.[41] Certainly, by 1100 CE, there were numerous Iroquoian villages along the rivers of the Toronto area. Over the next several centuries, cosmopolitan Wendat and Tionnontati villages flourished in the area (and changed location about every fifty years), while from the fourteenth to the sixteenth century, there was a gradual relocation of these villages to the Georgian Bay area, for reasons unknown but variously theorized.[42]

Even after their relocation, these peoples continued to use the Toronto area as hunting territory until 1649, when they were defeated and dispersed by the Haudenosaunee (whose ancestral homeland is considered to be south of Lake Ontario). While some of the defeated Huron-Wendats followed the Jesuits back to Lorette, in Quebec, and others escaped to Michigan and beyond to become the Wyandots, a substantial number of the survivors were adopted and absorbed into the Haudenosaunee; Joseph Brant, for example, had Wendat ancestry.[43] Thus, although historically the Haudenosaunee originated south of Lake Ontario, an unknown number of people now living at Six Nations or in the city have very deep historical roots in the Toronto region through their Wendat or Tionnontati ancestry.[44]

By the 1660s the Haudenosaunee, and particularly the Seneca, were using the Toronto area for hunting, fishing, and fur trading. The mainly Seneca villages of Teiaiagon and Ganetsakwyagon appeared on French maps of the Humber and Rouge rivers from the mid-1600s to at least 1687 when they seem to have been abandoned in the wake of a devastating and far-reaching French campaign against the Seneca.

The Toronto area continued to be Haudenosaunee hunting territory until about 1695, but by 1701 a branch of the Anishinaabeg known to the French as the Mississaugas had moved into the area, and in the Great Peace of Montreal their right to hunt there was recognized by the Haudenosaunee delegates. How the Mississaugas came to be in the region and who retained ultimate jurisdiction over the land remains to this day a source of controversy among both Indigenous peoples and historians. Anishinaabe oral traditions published in the mid-nineteenth century[45] described Anishinaabeg driving the Haudenosaunee out of southern Ontario in a series of fierce battles believed to have occurred in the late 1600s; according to the Mississaugas of New Credit, one battle is said to have been fought at the mouth of the Humber River.[46] In this version the Anishinaabeg gained title to the Toronto region through conquest; the Anishinaabeg and Haudenosaunee then made peace, and Anishinaabe control over the lands north of Lake Ontario was recognized in the Great Peace of Montreal in 1701.[47] Haudenosaunee perspectives, articulated by the Confederacy and scholars of Iroquoian history, such as J. A. Brandao and William Starna, maintain that in 1701, the Haudenosaunee agreed to make peace with the Mississaugas and share the territory for hunting only as part of their deal with France, while the British agreed to guarantee their continued use of their "Beaver Hunting Grounds" (which extended to the Toronto area) through the Nanfan Treaty of the same year.[48] In any event, by the time a French trading fort was established at Toronto in the mid-eighteenth century, the Mississaugas were in de facto possession of the north shore of Lake Ontario; in this area, they were particularly associated with the Credit River because of its very productive salmon fishery.[49] They were in situ when the British gained control of the area in 1760 and founded York, later Toronto, in 1793, and it was they who signed the land surrenders with the British.

Contrary to Kohl's narrative, the Mississaugas did not subsequently "vanish" from the growing city like mist in some inevitable natural process—they were forced out of the Toronto area. Indeed, the story of the dispossession of the Mississaugas is one that perhaps should haunt Torontonians, but which they and their popular historians rarely seem to know or tell, although academic historians such as Donald B. Smith, Leo Johnson, and Alan Taylor have over the last twenty years minutely detailed that process.[50] After signing the

1805 "confirmation" of the Toronto Purchase and simultaneously agreeing under considerable pressure to a surrender of the adjacent "Mississauga Tract" for 2.5 percent of its market value,[51] the Mississaugas retained only minimal lands in the area, while Toronto's population increased rapidly following the end of the Napoleonic wars in 1815, rising from 2,500 in 1815 to 9,256 in 1834 to 30,775 in 1851.[52] Settlers transformed the land, clearing the forest and sowing crops all along the north shore of Lake Ontario, including near the Credit River, west of the city as then constituted. The Mississaugas suffered the destruction of their hunting and fishing grounds, and their numbers dropped by two-thirds within one generation as many died from disease or alcohol abuse, falling from more than five hundred in 1778 to fewer than two hundred by 1818.[53] "Thin and miserable" and obviously suffering from trauma, they agreed in 1818 and 1820 to sell all the remainder of their lands, save for two hundred acres along the Credit River, in order to receive "goods yearly to cover . . . [their] Women and Children," a supplement to their regular annual presents that was clearly a desperate attempt at self-preservation.[54] Rather than agreeing to an outright sale, the Mississaugas thought they had agreed that the Crown would protect their land from greedy settlers, because members of the band "wanted to keep it for [their] children forever."[55]

On their last two hundred acres, the Mississaugas then made a radical attempt to save themselves from physical extinction. They began in 1826 to convert to Methodism, renounce alcohol, and become Christian farmers under Kahkewaquonaby, the Mississauga missionary Peter Jones. Yet, despite their rapid "civilization," which was widely touted by the Methodists, they were unable to gain secure legal title to even this small patch of land. In despair, the Mississaugas left the Credit River in 1847 and were finally given refuge by the Six Nations of Grand River. They moved to a corner of the territory that they had earlier ceded to the British colonizers in 1784 for use by the Six Nations loyalist refugees forced from their homelands during the American Revolution.[56]

Following the forced departure of the Mississaugas, Indigenous people became invisible to Torontonians except as exotic visitors such as performers in Wild West and other shows or as sellers of crafts at the Ontario Industrial Exhibition.[57] A few high-profile individuals remained visible in the city,[58] but most remaining Indigenous residents were banished from the consciousness of Torontonians, who, like other Canadians, increasingly conceptualized "Indians" as living in the North or West, far from urbanized spaces.[59] Increasing racism and the rejection of intermarriage also led to the shunning of Native relatives and the concealment of Native ancestry.[60]

If those mostly unknown and invisible Indigenous individuals living in the city between 1850 and 1950 seem a bit ghostly to us now, there is also a sense in which Indigenous peoples now living in the city, though very much alive and thriving, can also be said to haunt it. Just as peoples formerly colonized by the British and French have flocked to the European metropoles of their former colonizers, so Toronto's current Aboriginal inhabitants, the vast majority of whom arrived after World War II, are part of a postcolonial phenomenon arising from a history of oppression and dispossession in which Toronto businesses, government, churches, and residents played an active if rarely acknowledged role.[61] Indeed, Toronto's current Indigenous population largely represents, in Bonita Lawrence's words, "the children and grandchildren of people removed, dispersed, and continuously bled off from Native communities"[62] across Canada through such instruments of oppression as the Indian Act, residential schools, colonial land policies, and reserve poverty. While many Indigenous residents of Toronto continue to maintain their connection to their "home" territories or First Nations, others lack official Indian status, are of mixed heritage, and have lost their formal attachment to a band or territory and to other bonds of identity, such as language or clan. As Lawrence says, their identity cannot be adequately understood except as shaped by a legacy of genocide.[63]

While few Indigenous families currently living in Toronto can claim ancestral residency in the city, the majority of Aboriginal residents are of Anishinaabe and Haudenosaunee heritage and are thus Indigenous to the broader Great Lakes region, which includes the Toronto area. However, because of globalization, the Toronto

Native community now includes Indigenous people from all over the Americas. Thus, the current Indigenous population of Toronto, like much of the non-Indigenous population, is multicultural, cosmopolitan, and diasporic. In fact, some interviewees expressed a Native version of "placelessness," where their sense of home was a more generalized or idealized Indigenous space or even an idealized Indigenous past, rather than a specific reserve or territory.[64] For some Indigenous interviewees, contemporary Toronto was that idealized space where divisive or painful histories could be superseded and a pan-Indigenous urban territory could be created. Discourses of Indigenous spiritual presence thus occurred in a context of Indigenous dispossession and alternative place-making.

As Gelder and Jacobs argue in *Uncanny Australia*, however, Indigenous cultures are adaptable and mobile: one is never simply dispossessed, nor can dispossession be completely equated with disempowerment. Rather, they argue, to be out of place provides new ways of being in place. In fact, they argue, "new forms of authority may come into being through the very structures of dispossession."[65] In Toronto, ghosts, ancestors, and historical discourses of spirit and sacredness are integral to these new forms. As in Gelder and Jacobs's Australia, the Aboriginal sacred becomes more than a relic of the past; it becomes a new form of authority, facilitating a return of Indigeneity, in the context of dispossession.[66]

Today, with more Native people arriving in the city every day, Toronto's "Indians" are no longer vanishing. Rather, their past has disappeared—often both their familial past and the Indigenous past of Toronto. Not just "lost," these are pasts from which Indigenous peoples have been actively dispossessed, both in terms of who controls the actual physical remains and artifacts from that history and who controls the content and form of historical narratives about this past. It is in this context that Indigenous discourses about haunting and ancestral spiritual presence are especially salient, a context in which, among other things, they do symbolic and ideological "work" in the political struggle to reclaim the city's Indigenous past on Indigenous terms and to reclaim the city as Indigenous territory.

Many of the stories I heard of Indigenous spiritual presence in the

Toronto area related to archaeological sites where Indigenous people had lived, were buried, or had used the land in the past. Indigenous haunting, which above all is the *ephemeral* presence of beings from the past, occurs in Toronto in a context where local Indigenous peoples have little or no access to the material remains left by their ancestors. Although roughly 135 Indigenous archaeological sites are known to exist in the City of Toronto, and there are more than 185 in the GTA, many of these known sites are poorly documented and are under threat.[67] Many more are likely to be discovered during ongoing suburban expansion into relatively undisturbed farmlands. Several of the Indigenous people I interviewed were actively involved in political struggles to protect these sites, which were seen as sacred sites even more than as repositories of evidence of an Indigenous past. In fact, Indigenous bones were markers for important connections to land, cultural traditions, and, ultimately, sovereignty.

Interviewees told me that "bones come up for a reason"; the uncovering of human and other remains in the GTA, such as the accidental uncovering of ancient bones during road widening on Teston Road in Vaughan (just north of Toronto) in August 2005, was interpreted by some as a direct communication from the ancestors and a form of strategic action and manifestation of solidarity with Indigenous peoples in the present. The ancestors' reappearance obstructed wanton and environmentally harmful "development," asserted Indigenous presence, reclaimed the land, and called for respect, return, and recognition. Certainly, their manifestation directly engaged the settler–colonial state in a complex chain of interactions, claims, and counterclaims that cut to the core of settler–colonial and postcolonial dynamics between Indigenous and non-Indigenous residents in the GTA.

Settler disturbance of Indigenous burial sites is a problem with a long history in the Toronto area. Four years after the founding of York in 1793, the colonial authorities issued a Proclamation to Protect the Fishing Places and Burial Grounds of the Mississaugas in response to "many heavy and grievous complaints . . . made by the Mississauga Indians of depredations committed by some of His Majesty's subjects and others upon their . . . burial places . . . in violation of decency and good order."[68] Later, nine-teenth-century Toronto archaeological investigators such as David Boyle and Andrew F. Hunter removed skeletons and crania from the region's Indigenous burial sites, and academics such as Daniel Wilson displayed them or studied them in local museums.[69] These actions reinforced the widespread North American settler perception that the Indigenous past consisted of "a long chronological period known as prehistory . . . that was inhabited by anonymous ancestors with no particular connection to the aboriginal people of today."[70] Even where archaeologists did make connections between ancient bones and contemporary Indigenous peoples, they still sanctioned a double standard in the treatment of human remains where acciden-tally uncovered Euro-Canadian remains were immediately reburied but Indigenous ones were retained for scientific study without the consent of descendant groups. This differential treatment was justi-fied on the grounds that scientific knowledge about "Indians" was essential for the public good.[71]

Cultural differences with respect to death and ancestors have been an important aspect of local conflicts over ancestral remains. The Anishinaabe historical scholar Darlene Johnston, an expert witness on Anishinaabe history for the Ipperwash Inquiry into the death of Dudley George (who was shot by the Ontario Provincial Police while nonviolently protecting an Indigenous burial site), noted that both Iroquoian and Anishinaabe spiritual beliefs documented since the seventeenth century and still powerful today accord at least two souls to the dead. One of these souls remains with the bones unless reborn in a child, while another leaves the body after death but remains close by until properly honored through ceremony and feast, after which it travels to the Village of Souls.[72] Thus, for many local Indigenous people today, and perhaps even increasingly as cultural traditions are revived, the remains of the dead are believed to retain a spiritual essence that requires ongoing respect. Further-more, it is the responsibility of the living to care for the dead through visiting, feasting, and prayer; failure to perform these duties harms not only the dead but also the living. If human remains or spiritual objects such as grave goods are handled inappropriately, bad things may happen to the people and communities involved. Historically, the loss of ancestral lands was especially traumatic because it also entailed separation from the graves of ancestors and thus prevented descendants from carrying out these essential spiritual duties.

In the Jesuit Relation of 1639, Father Paul LeJeune recorded that the Montagnais, another Algonkian-speaking people with similar cultural traits to the Anishinaabeg, referred to the soul that remained with the bones as "the soul of their Nation," a concept that Johnston reported was still resonant among Anishinaabeg today.[73] This conception of death and the ongoing spirit nature of ancestors gives modern local Indigenous peoples who are traditionalists, or even unconscious inheritors of these cultural understandings, a very different orientation to their past and its relation to the present than mainstream Euro-Canadian culture does. The First Nations archaeologist Eldon Yellowhorn speaks of "the perception of the past as a spirit nation" that brings "the mythic era into the daily lives of aboriginal people"[74] (though Yellowhorn describes this as a premodern belief system to be superseded, a position with which many of the people I interviewed would disagree). In an Anishinaabe context, Johnston explained, "the remains of the First Animals [founders of the ancestral clans in the Anishinaabe creation story] contained a powerful spiritual essence that gave birth to the First Humans." She added, "Human remains return to the earth with their spiritual essence intact, continuing the spiritual cycle of birth and rebirth." Indigenous bones, Indigenous ghosts, and ancestral spirits, then, signify much more than individual ancestors; they embody the continuity of the people as a whole.

If "bones come up for a reason," surely the most striking result of such ancestor activism in the Toronto area has been the resurgence of a Huron-Wendat presence in Toronto. Until recently, Toronto archaeologists and administrators, like the general public, had assumed that for all practical purposes the Wendats were an extinct people, whose wishes no longer needed to be taken into account. But in 1997 the Wendat scholar and activist Michel Gros-Louis of Wendake, Quebec, convinced the Royal Ontario Museum to repatriate Wendat bones excavated in the 1930s from the 1636 Feast of Souls at Ossassane (near Midland, Ontario). The scattered descendants of the Huron-Wendats in Quebec, Michigan, Oklahoma, and elsewhere gathered in Huronia for the first time since their dispersal in 1649. There they ceremonially reburied their ancestors' remains at the site of the original ossuary as part of the first Wendat Feast of Souls held in more than 350 years.[75] Many of the Wendats who attended the ceremony experienced an intense spiritual reconnection with their ancestors, their Ontario homeland, and their living relations,[76] and as a result the Wendats have become an increasingly vocal political force for heritage preservation in southern Ontario, including the Toronto area. For them, the repatriation of the ancestors activated the descendants.

Until recently, the Huron-Wendat people were "completely oblivious to what has been happening to their ancestral habitat," according to David Donnelly, a Toronto lawyer who has represented the Wendake First Nation in relation to Toronto archaeological sites.[77] A precedent was set in 2004, when a court ruled that the Huron-Wendat people should have been consulted before a local Wendat village site (which may also have contained remains) was sold to the Catholic Archdiocese of Toronto for use as a cemetery. In May 2006 the Wendats asked the province to revoke archaeological licenses permitting excavation at a fifteenth-century village site known as Skandatut in Vaughan, because they had not been properly consulted. Other bands joined the Wendats in demanding a province-wide moratorium on village-site excavations at that time and threatened to occupy the Skandatut site to support the Wendat protest. In October 2006 the Wendats called for a moratorium on all excavations on Toronto and Region Conservation Authority (TRCA) lands to ensure that scientific, cultural, and legal principles were being respected, and demanded to know why the Huron-Wendat nation "[had] not been contacted by TRCA for consultation, participation, accommodation, monitoring, ceremony, etc., in any of its archaeological projects."[78]

With the increasing politicization of the Wendats with regard to their ancestors, there has been a shift in local historical consciousness. It is now recognized in the public sphere of Toronto that the Wendats are a contemporary polity with ancestral ties to the region.[79] There has also been a resurgence of recognition of Wendat ancestry among some Haudenosaunee in the Six Nations territory, where many Wendats were adopted after their defeat by the Iroquois in 1649–50 but gradually lost their distinctive identity over the generations.[80]

The archaeological activism of the Wendats and other groups, such as the Haudenosaunee, is a response to the rampant destruction of Indigenous archaeological sites in the region, where thousands of sites have already been destroyed because of weak provincial legislation.[81] While the Cemeteries Act provides some protection for burial sites, other legislation covers nonhuman remains, such as village sites and the thousands of artifacts recovered from them. First Nations have no legal control over those items, nor is there a legal requirement to consult with them regarding such artifacts, which serves the interests of developers and governments intent on quickly clearing land for new construction. The Eurocentric legal separation of the "sacred" and "non-sacred" does not reflect First Nations cultural understandings of an interconnected "living cosmos" in constant flux, where all aspects of the world manifest spirit, and humans, animals, objects, and other spirits may influence or be transformations of each other. For example, as the archaeologist Ron Williamson has noted, "a flint spearhead is a prosaic hunting tool to archaeologists, but in both Iroquoian and Anishinaabe creation stories, flint represents the blood or bodies of culture heroes."[82] Thus, all artifacts of the ancestors contribute to the sacredness of a place. While many sites are destroyed without ever being excavated, even those sites that are excavated in the GTA employ "salvage" archaeology conducted by private archaeologists hired by developers, and these sites are usually permanently destroyed once excavation is completed.

Because of legislative ambiguity over the question of ownership of archaeological remains, whether they are village or hunting sites or individual artifacts, virtually all excavated items remain completely out of the reach of the descendants of the peoples who created the artifacts in the first place. By law, archaeologists are required to hold all objects in trust for the people of Ontario until such artifacts can be placed in a public institution, but since there is no public money provided for their preservation or curation, hundreds of thousands of artifacts are inappropriately stored wherever archaeologists can find the space, and have sometimes been inadvertently discarded, such as when four hundred thousand Wendat artifacts at the University of Toronto were mistakenly sent to a garbage dump in Michigan.[83] Meanwhile, the Wendats of Wendake, Quebec, whose ancestors lived in the Toronto area, are attempting to create their own museum of Wendat history on their own territory in Quebec but have virtually no artifacts of their ancestors that they can call their own.[84]

In her comments to the Ipperwash inquiry, Prof. Johnston articulated an important distinction between the two souls of Indigenous ancestors: "the fear of the disembodied soul vs. tenderness toward the soul that remains with the body."[85] Commentators such as Paul LeJeune in the seventeenth century and Peter Jones in the nineteenth commented on the fear of the living toward souls that have left the body to travel with dead relatives and on the efforts of the living to get ghosts to leave.[86] These beliefs, mixed with elements from European traditions, underlay my interviewees' representations of ghosts as unhappy spirit beings from the past who remained in the human world to remind the living of what was unfinished or lost or because they were unable to move on to the spirit world. They were unsettled, not properly put to rest or accorded appropriate respect, often because of colonialism. Such ghosts haunted both people and places, making places unlivable or uncomfortable, and were dangerous to people in the present. For example, haunting was cited as the reason for a cave-in during the demolition of the Uptown Theatre on Yonge Street that caused the death of an innocent bystander in 2003; the theatre was disrespectfully built over an ancient Indigenous burial ground.[87]

Such haunting did not necessarily involve visual apparitions of dead people, though a couple of people showed me photographs of what they perceived to be Indigenous spirits hovering over historic Toronto lands such as village sites. Some interviewees spoke instead of experiencing historical trauma, especially of one's own ancestors or of Indigenous ancestors generally, either as a haunting energy in the Toronto environment or as physical or emotional pain in the body or psyche, where one was literally possessed by the pain of previous generations.[88] A man of Seneca heritage told me that he knew his own ancestor had been murdered by the French at Teiaiagon, the seventeenth-century Seneca village on the Humber River in western Toronto, because of the terrible pain in his shoulder that assailed him one day while he was walking along the Humber River not far from the village site. He spoke of sensing the souls of the dead, who he said still haunted the area because so many had been killed in an attack by the French in 1687 that they had not been properly feasted.[89]

The connections between historical trauma and ancestors were also highlighted in a remarkable series of commentaries by the Mohawk traditionalist and city resident William Woodworth on four lectures on the Indigenous history of the Toronto area given by the City of Toronto's chief curator Carl Benn, a noted historian of Iroquois history and of the city's Fort York. These lectures, given in May and June 2006, were part of the Humanitas Festival, an attempt by the City of Toronto to kickstart its initiative to create a new civic institution that would "tell Toronto's stories" to the world. Benn had suggested in his scholarly account that the Seneca villages on the Humber and Rouge rivers may have already been abandoned by the time the French governor Denonville sailed past Toronto on his way back to New France after ransacking Seneca villages south of Lake Ontario in 1687, since Denonville did not mention them in his journal but boasted of attacking other Seneca villages. Contesting Benn's remarks, Woodworth said there was an oral tradition that Teiaiagon had been destroyed by fire, the people massacred by the French, and the whole area around Toronto deforested. Woodworth spoke further of how he had formerly hated being in Toronto because of the "dark energy" he felt in the city, which he described as a deep sense of abandonment, because the souls of the dead had not been properly addressed and cared for. He recalled, "I used to hate it here; it hurt me [because] of the history. . . . I feel genocide in Toronto." He spoke of Baby Point (the site of Teiaiagon) as a sacred place, sanctified by the horror of what happened there, and described the English houses built over the site as the epitome of colonization.[90]

Evaluating such comments is a difficult task for a historian trained in the Western academic discipline of history, which generally privileges textual records over oral traditions (though historians of Indigenous history are increasingly grappling with the latter); secular accounts over those that draw on other-than-human spiritual forces; material or oral evidence over intuitive knowledge; and critical distance over emotional connection and identification, all of which are elements of the historical consciousness and worldview of many contemporary Indigenous peoples (and also of many non-Indigenous people, especially those who are religious). But from Indigenous perspectives, the distanced, "neutral" tone of academic historical narratives can be equally problematic. Woodworth spoke of how horrifying it was to hear his ancestors' painful experience "objectified" by an academic historian. He spoke of how Native people were inside the history and the feeling of the history—they did not just think about this history in their heads but experienced it bodily, even in the DNA their ancestors had passed on to them—a view shared by a number of interviewees. For them, the more "objective" accounts of history were empty, because they did not address the way they were haunted by the historical experience passed on to them or the spiritual connection they felt with their ancestors.

Such emotional, bodily, or "energetic" haunting can be interpreted in various ways. Regardless of one's beliefs regarding the existence of ancestral souls, ghosts, spiritual energy, or blood memory, at the very least one can consider such experiences a form of "postmemory," which Marianne Hirsch defines as the memory of later generations not directly involved in the original traumatic event, whose own lives are "dominated by narratives that preceded their birth," by "events that can be neither [fully] understood nor recreated."[91] Indigenous healers often describe the same phenomena as intergenerational trauma. According to Indigenous psychologists, intergenerational trauma is itself a form of memory, truer than anything written in the history books about Indigenous experience, which can often be passed on wordlessly, as in the familial dysfunction caused by the experience of the Trail of Tears mentioned earlier in this paper. According to the Native American psychologists Eduardo and Bonnie Duran, many Indigenous people are possessed or haunted by the past.[92] Traumatic memory, characterized by flashbacks, nightmares, and anxiety attacks, occurs when the past is uncontrollably relived, when the distance between past and present collapses.[93] In the case of Indigenous people, there is not one trauma but many, over a long time period, not just their own personal experience, but that of their ancestors over generations. A common feature of such traumas is that those who survive feel they must not betray those who were overwhelmed by the trauma (such as ancestors), and reliving the past becomes a necessary commemoration, though it may also be re-traumatizing.[94]

The healing of traumatic memory, according to Dominick LaCapra, begins when the past becomes accessible to recall in memory and language, providing some conscious control, distance, and perspective, so that those who are haunted begin working through the trauma, laying ghosts to rest—but, as Duran and Duran emphasize, there are very culturally specific ways to propitiate such ghosts.[95] Indigenous forms of expression are critical to such healing. On the other hand, historical narratives imposed by outsiders can be experienced as re-traumatizing.

While the painful experience of ancestors affected many Indigenous interviewees directly, their connection to their ancestors was by no means only negative. The distinction articulated by Johnston in responses to the two souls of the Indigenous dead was echoed in the difference in how people spoke of Indigenous ghosts haunting the city and of the beneficial spiritual presence of Indigenous ancestors in their own lives. Many of the people I interviewed had had positive experiences of the spiritual presence of their ancestors, who admonished them, guided them, or helped them heal.[96] While some of the non-Indigenous Torontonians I interviewed were also very interested in their ancestors and imagined them vividly, and a few sensed them as spiritual presences even if they had lived on other continents, almost all my Aboriginal interviewees felt deeply connected to history through their ancestors. As one audience member at the Humanitas talks put it, "[Woodworth] is not a historian but he feels very personally connected to the history in a way that I don't think generally people in the Western tradition feel. . . . I don't feel it and I don't think [Benn] feels that connection. . . . I don't feel that connection with my European ancestors of 400 years ago."[97]

But for many of the Indigenous people I interviewed, their ancestors were, in some sense, still alive; although they had "passed on," they continued to work for present and future generations in another medium, from another level of reality, and to be aware of how their descendants treated them in turn. The relationship between ancestors and descendants could best be described as based on reciprocity, one of the most fundamental Indigenous values, and one that promotes strength and continuance.[98] Reciprocity and relationship with ancestors helped Indigenous interviewees find the persistence necessary to endure in a colonial context, despite the legacy of cultural genocide.

For a number of the Indigenous interviewees, their awareness of the presence of their ancestors in their lives produced a sense of doubleness, in which past and present coexisted; thus, their sense of the present included a sense of repetition and return. For example, some interviewees identified with their ancestors when colonial patterns were repeated, such as when they experienced a lack of power in negotiations over land. "I can understand now what happened to our ancestors because we're in the same boat," a Mississauga interviewee who had taken part in land-claims negotiations recounted.[99] Others connected with the spirits of ancestors through treaties, ceremonies, and traditional practices because of their consciousness that these were how the ancestors had provided for future generations. For some, there was even a sense of becoming one with the ancestors, a communion of spirit. As one person I interviewed said, there is "this tremendous interweaving of tradition and personal life." He explained, "My personal life is a lot more than a personal life. It is actually a repetition of ancestral ways and I'm carrying it. These aren't my decisions, it's just my nature and I'm actually streaming it."[100] Whether or not Indigenous historical consciousness was primarily cyclical in the past—a matter of considerable debate among historians of Indigenous history[101]—paradigms of historical return or historical cycles were articulated by many of my interviewees. These were employed not only as a sign of Indigenous difference, but also because if the future is a return to the past, there is hope for an end to colonialism and a return of Indigenous sovereignty.

In contrast to most of the non-Indigenous people I interviewed, Indigenous interviewees felt a deep sense of responsibility toward their ancestors, to protect their physical remains, to survive as a people, and to teach future generations their history and the cultural practices they created (though some members of immigrant groups also felt a very strong commitment to preserve language, culture, and the continuous identity of their ethnic group). As Woodworth commented during the Humanitas lectures, this sense of duty is highlighted by the fact that local Indigenous cultures exist only here; they are localized, particular, and unique. Indigenous North Americans, he said, are the only ones who have not crossed the oceans and gone to live elsewhere; they may have been displaced through forced removal and other effects of colonialism, but they have not disappeared. Many Indigenous interviewees insisted on a strong sense of Indigenous continuity in Toronto: it was "a place infused by [their] energy," "very much alive and very much imbued with the spirit of its history," "covered with the footprints of ancestors."[102]

While unfeasted or ill-treated spirits may make places uninhabitable, it is ancestors who make a place sacred. A form of the past experienced in the present by many of the Indigenous people I interviewed was the accumulated energy or spirit of places in Toronto, such as the site of Teiaiagon or Spirit Island, an energy they perceived as coming from the traces of all the beings that had inhabited that place before, the events that had occurred there, the emotions and words expressed, prayers said, offerings left, the bones and remains of the dead in the earth, the blood spilt or tears shed. The feeling and energy of places in Toronto reflected how the land itself had been treated—whether it had been treated with respect in the past, was appropriately honored and nourished through ceremony, and thus was a healthy place, or whether it had become a place of desecration and pain. The spiritual energy of a place also reflected the influence of non-human spirit beings on that place. Some of the Indigenous people I spoke to conceived of invisible lines of power that linked places to other places in a web or grid of spirit energy; to them, Toronto was a place linked to others in a vast web of spirit. It was the role of human beings to try to maintain this web by ensuring balance, the good energy of a place, which would then actively influence what transpired there. It was this energy—an energy that contained within it all the historical experience of the place—that the people attending the Spirit Island ceremony sought to connect to.

With similar understandings, Woodworth spoke to the Humanitas Festival audience about his vision to create a new sacred site for condolence ceremonies on the original Toronto waterfront to bring arriving immigrants to the city into spiritual relationship with the Indigenous ancestors of the land. He called on the Indigenous peoples of the area to resume their ancient hosting duties and to adopt newcomers into their clans. In a brochure for his Beacon to the Ancestors Foundation, he wrote that through seventeen specific ceremonies over a twelve-month period Toronto would be "reinvigorated and recontextualized in the spirit of the Ancestors," with "reconciliation and healing between peoples, with the ancestors, and with the created world itself."

In his historical understanding, the city's famous CN Tower was the modern realization of the Great Tree of Peace, envisioned thousands of years ago in the prophecy of the Peacemaker:

> The Hotinonshon:ni prophecy of gathering the peoples from the four directions under the Great White Pine Tree of Peace is now coming to fruition. In a place still named in the language of the Ancestors, peoples from virtually every part of the world find refuge in Toronto. The original Hotinonshon:ni teachings instruct us to share with all peoples who visit our lands. In an understanding held in the Two Row Wampum, our many Ancestors agreed to share this place in our separate yet collateral streams. The time has come to recover and refresh these old responsibilities in this special place which is nurturing a powerful form of global community.[103]

Woodworth's interpretations of history and the Peacemaker's prophesies may be idiosyncratic, and are specifically Haudeno-saunee-based in a way that Anishinaabe commentators might not relate to, but his general orientation to the past is broadly discernible among the many Indigenous people I have talked to in my research and in numerous other circumstances. In interpreting the past and present through Indigenous prophecy, Woodworth was not alone in seeing the words of the ancestors become manifest. Others I spoke to viewed Toronto history through the interpretative framework of the Seven Fires prophecy of the Anishinaabeg. This, I believe, is an orientation to the past that deeply affects how many Indigenous people interact with the Western discipline of history (particularly those who self-identify as traditional) and how they understand their history and present life in Toronto.

Indigenous assertions about the spiritual presence and activities of ancestors in Toronto are, among other things, claims to the validity of Indigenous knowledge practices and point to the fundamental question of authority in the construction of historical narratives. People of Indigenous heritage who I interviewed for my research were far more likely to give primacy to oral tradition, literally the words of the ancestors, which they sought from elders and trusted over professional historians' information and interpretations and the documentary records produced by colonizers. For example, while historians' narratives have often focused on conflict between Haudenosaunee, Huron-Wendat, and Anishinaabe peoples, Indigenous interviewees stressed that archivally documented historical conflicts represent a short period of post-contact turmoil, whereas oral tradition speaks of millennia of regional interaction and mainly peaceful coexistence.

As noted earlier, several Indigenous interviewees spoke of knowing aspects of Toronto history through feeling and intuition and through direct, often bodily experience[104] rather than through intellectual knowledge of official historical narratives focused on events and chronologies, although many people I interviewed were also well versed in these. Some spoke of encountering ancestral spirits through direct communication in a vision or a dream.[105] Even when the past was narrated in stories in the oral tradition, the story itself, even apart from its content, was experienced as carrying spiritual life energy from the past, medicine from the ancestors, that would help sustain the spirit of the people.[106] In such instances the past was experienced as a presence as much as and perhaps even more than as historical narrative, and as continuity more than as a sequence of discrete events.

In the Humanitas lectures, Woodworth spoke of the fact that much Indigenous knowledge was not shared with outsiders, that many stories were told only among Native people and were not shared. They were "protected by the ancestral energy—they're not in history."[107] The Mohawk historical scholar Susan Hill (among many others) has also spoken of the spiritual repercussions of disrespectful relations to sacred knowledge.[108] Thus, Indigenous knowledge can be for others a kind of absence, something concealed from the gaze of the "marauding" and secular non-Indigenous world.[109]

Because of this secrecy, claims about Toronto's history based on Indigenous knowledge may sometimes be associated by others with the possibility of deception. The suspicion or fear that some Indigenous people are "inventing" history for their own purposes relates specifically and especially to Indigenous claims made about historical events or historical places based on non-rational, spiritual or sacred knowledge, including communication with ancestors, which is essentially unverifiable through Western historical practices.[110] But, perhaps, as Gelder and Jacobs suggest, rather than focusing solely on the issue of verification in the Western sense, it is more fruitful to consider that the Indigenous sacred, and in this case, the historical Indigenous sacred, represents what Western historical practices cannot describe or explain." Perhaps, as they suggest, this is a case of Lyotard's differand, "a case of conflict . . . that cannot be equitably resolved for lack of a rule of judgment applicable to both arguments," where "one side's legitimacy does not imply the other's lack of legitimacy," a condition of incommensurability.[111] The Canadian historian Toby Morantz suggested a similar incommensurability in her consideration of the blending of oral history with Western approaches to the history of the Swampy Cree;[112]

other Canadian historians of Indigenous history, such as Keith Thor Carlson, are grappling with similar questions.[113] Among Indigenous scholars, there is also critical discussion about the nature and role of various forms of Indigenous knowledge in the construction of historical narratives.[114]

In addition to presenting problems of verification, Indigenous knowledge claims about ancestral spiritual presence in Toronto may also cause settlers anxiety because of their inherent unboundedness; from a non-Indigenous perspective, such knowledge is unpredictable and beyond colonial control.[115] It thus at least potentially institutes new forms of authority and power for Indigenous people. Perhaps for these reasons—and because of increased Indigenous confidence and the need to speak publicly of the sacred when it is increasingly under threat—there is, according to Gelder and Jacobs, an "amplification of the sacred" in Australia,[116] an assertion that more and more previously unknown sites are sacred, for example. This phenomenon is also observable in Toronto. For example, one Indigenous activist in Toronto has claimed that a large mound on the floodplain of the Humber River near the site of Teiaiagon is an ancient "thunderbird" mound; he told me he discovered this knowledge not only through investigation of the shape of the mound and other physical characteristics but also through visionary contact with an ancient leader buried there. The activist posted signs on the mound identifying it as an Indigenous sacred site and warning others to stay away, creating a new geography of Indigenous significance in the city.[117]

Yet the marshaling of discourses of Indigenous ghosts and ancestors can also prove uncontrollable to Indigenous residents. Unlike the situation in a reserve community, where the community is bounded and is itself the ultimate verifier of Indigenous knowledge and a check on spurious claims, in the free-floating more openended Indigenous communities of the city, where new people are constantly arriving and others leaving, individuals who do not have strong connections with Indigenous communities or a solid grounding in Indigenous culture can attach themselves to the Indigenous sacred, make claims regarding their knowledge of an unverifiable oral tradition through unknown Indigenous ancestors, and attract a following, especially of less culturally knowledgeable Indigenous or non-Indigenous city dwellers. Such people may have little or no support from knowledgeable elders in the city's Indigenous community or from leaders at Wendake, New Credit, or Six Nations, or be only cautiously tolerated when the result is good (such as the preservation of archaeological sites), even if the means are questionable. In Toronto this phenomenon is remarked on by various Indigenous and non-Indigenous commentators, and their most damning criticisms of such people are not only that they may use questionable historical evidence or speak for communities they do not actually represent, but that they do not have the ancestry they claim, that the Indigenous ancestors and cultural heritage they claim are guiding their actions are bogus.[118] This was the single most common criticism I heard of activists involved in Indigenous heritage preservation in the city, and one that various activists made about each other in disputes over heritage, identity, and cultural knowledge, disputes that are themselves the legacy of colonialism.

For many Indigenous people in Toronto, as elsewhere in the world, Indigeneity is, of necessity, both heritage and project.[119] Ancestral spirit energy was perceived by many of my interviewees as actively reasserting an Indigenous historical and spiritual presence both on the landscape and on the dreamscape of the city, acting simultaneously on multiple levels of reality, only some of them visible in everyday life. Ancestral spirits assured and represented Indigenous continuity and remade the city as Indigenous sacred space, creating or recreating geographies of meaning and spirit that on the one hand could be used to assert difference, including the validity of a particular kind of knowledge, and on the other hand could unsettle non-Indigenous residents in a way that promoted greater recognition of an Indigenous historical presence and opened up the possibility of healing and reconciliation between Indigenous and settler–immigrant peoples. Thus, ancestors were not perceived as dead relics of a premodern past but as active and dialogic, influencing modernity in Toronto, though Toronto's modernity also reshaped the narratives of ancestors in turn, by reformulating the context in which they were active.[120] Because narratives of Indigenous ancestors and ghosts in Toronto represent many things that Western historical practices cannot or do not describe or account for in relation to the region's Indigenous past, these spirit beings can be understood ultimately as expressing Indigenous historical consciousness in the city.

NOTES

Some interviewees referenced in the text and in the notes below are identified by pseudonyms.

1. Popular conceptions of "medicine wheels" are largely an invented Plains tradition, according to the Piikani (Peigan) archaeologist Eldon Yellowhorn, "Awakening of Internalist Archaeology in the Aboriginal World," 200–1.

2. Simcoe, *Diary of Mrs. John Graves Simcoe*, 184.

3. See Mississaugas of the New Credit First Nation, *Toronto Purchase Specific Claim*.

4. See Smith, *Sacred Feathers*.

5. This claim of pre-1700 Anishinaabe occupation of the Toronto Islands was made by the Great Indian Bus Tour originator Rodney Bobiwash, in his chapter "A History of Native People in the Toronto Area: An Overview" in *Meeting Place*, ed. Sanderson and Howard-Bobiwash, 8. According to Bobiwash, "There is no doubt that the Toronto Islands were a stopping place along the migration route," but his source or reasons for saying this are not clear. In his discussion of the Great Migration, he quotes from the Anishinaabe elder Eddie Benton-Benai's rendition of the oral tradition in *The Mishomis Book*, but the latter depicts the migrating Anishinaabeg as traveling along the southern rather than northern shore of Lake Ontario. However, there are a number of versions of the routes taken by various subgroups of the Anishinaabeg.

6. Kenyon, "Prehistoric Cemetery," and Emerson, "The Village and the Cemetery," 181–83.

7. Thwaites, *Jesuit Relations and Allied Documents*, 10:375ff.

8. Alanis King, tour guide, Great Indian Bus Tour, October 29, 2005.

9. I have interviewed forty-five Toronto residents to date, almost half of them of Indigenous heritages. My data is suggestive rather than a statistically accurate representative sample of the Toronto population.

10. See Sigmund Freud's influential essay "The 'Uncanny'."

11. Gelder and Jacobs, *Uncanny Australia*, 23.

12. Cf. Jennifer Cole, quoted in Shaw, *Memories of the Slave Trade*, 49.

13. Gelder and Jacobs, *Uncanny Australia*, 30.

14. The city's current motto is "diversity our strength."

15. City of Toronto, *Humanitas*, 18, 27; "Toronto's Hidden History: Why

Doesn't the City Have a Proper Museum to Showcase Its Past?" *Toronto Star*, January 21, 2007, A1; Pier Giorgio De Cicco, "How to Showcase Toronto," *Toronto Star*, February 19, 2007, A13; "More Than One Plan in Place for T.O. City Museum," *Toronto Star*, January 28, 2007, A7.

16. Archaeological Services, *Master Plan*, 12. The authors note "little widespread awareness of the depth of this pre-contact settlement history, or general knowledge of the societies that inhabited Ontario prior to the onset of Euro-Canadian settlement." This assessment is born out in the interviews I conducted for my research on historical memory in Toronto.

17. City of Toronto, *Humanitas*, 20–23.

18. However, in 2002, in partnership with the Native-run Woodland Cultural Centre of Brantford, the ROM hosted an exhibit on the nineteenth-century Mohawk doctor and Toronto resident, Oronhyatekha (Dr. Peter Martin), a significant Aboriginal historical figure from the city's past.

19. See the City of Toronto's Web site at www.toronto.ca.

20. Thrush, *Native Seattle*, 12.

21. Sanderson and Howard-Bobiwash, *Meeting Place*. See also Robinson, *Toronto during the French Regime*, and, more recently, Dieterman, *Mississauga*, and Williamson, *Toronto*.

22. The two families were observed in 1793 by Joseph Bouchette, as he recounted in *British Dominions in North America*, 1:89. Most popular authors have shown little comprehension of the depth of Indigenous history in the region or the fact that the Mississaugas had been decimated by small-pox by the time the British arrived. They also show little comprehension of Mississauga land-use patterns, involving seasonal resource collection in various locations, so the fact that two families were on site when the British arrived was not necessarily a measure of the "emptiness" of the land.

23. An incomplete deed to the land found several years after the negotiations of 1787 was blank where the description of the area ceded should have been, and the marks of three chiefs from the Toronto area were on separate papers attached to it. It is unclear if presents distributed to the Mississaugas at the 1787 meeting at the Bay of Quinte or during the surveying of the land in 1788 were intended as specific payment for the purchase of Toronto lands. For details of the current claim, see Mississaugas of New Credit, *Toronto Purchase Specific Claim*, and Indian Claims Commission, *Mississaugas of the New Credit First Nation Inquiry: Toronto Purchase Claim*, June 2003.

24. Early major histories of Toronto, such as Scadding and Dent, *Toronto, Past and Present*; Mulvany, Adam, and Blackett Robinson, *History of Toronto and County of York*; Adam, *Toronto: Old and New*; and Middleton, *Municipality of Toronto*, make little or no reference to the Toronto Purchase. More recent works generally do, but they rarely address its problematic nature.

25. In fact, the term "prehistory" appears to have been coined in 1851 by the University of Toronto's first professor of history and English, Sir Daniel Wilson, according to Killan, *David Boyle*, 85. The term was coined before Wilson's arrival in Toronto. See also Ash et al., *Thinking with Both Hands*. North American writers immediately latched on to "prehistory" as a "categorical catch-basin into which Indians were put" (Cohn, *History's Shadow*, 211).

26. Thrush, *Native Seattle*, 11.

27. Furniss, "Challenging the Myth," 188.

28. Settler hauntologies have a long genealogy and political significance in Canada and have been examined by Cameron, "Indigenous Spectrality and the Politics of Postcolonial Ghost Stories," 383–93; and in many of the essays of the *University of Toronto Quarterly* 75, no. 2 (Spring 2006), a special issue with the theme of haunting in Canadian cultural production, especially Bentley's "Shadows in the Soul," and Carriou's "Haunted Prairie." Carriou distinguishes between the very different deployment of ghosts and spectral/spiritual presence in literature by Indigenous and settler writers.

29. Kohl, *Travels in Canada*, 2:14.

30. The debate about the meaning of the name is sometimes vociferous. Henry Scadding, Toronto's first historian, was of the view that the word meant "meeting place," which became the most common translation and was used, for example, in the *Meeting Place: Aboriginal Life in Toronto*, ed. Sanderson and Howard-Bobiwash, and published by the Native Canadian Centre of Toronto in 1997. John Steckley, the foremost linguist of the Huron-Wendat language, has proposed "sticks in the water" or "fish weir" as more accurate translations of Mohawk "Tkaronto," and suggests that it was first applied to the ancient fish weir at The Narrows between Lake Simcoe and Lake Couchiching ("'Toronto' Meaning Lost in Translation," *Toronto Star*, December 24, 2007, sidebar at http://www.thestar.com/News/Ontario/article/288382). According to Michel Gros-Louis, a Wendat linguist, the word also has a sense of "abundant life" (private communication, July 23, 2006). Peter Jones, in *History of the Ojebway Indians*, said the word meant "a looming of trees," while Mohawk interviewee William Woodworth was told by Haudenosaunee elders that the word comes from *delondo*, a Mohawk word for a log, or fallen white pine. The anthropologist Heather Howard argued in her doctoral dissertation, "Dreamcatchers in the City," that the multiple meanings should not be seen as mutually exclusive. Percy J. Robinson, in *Toronto during the French Regime*, referred to early French maps showing the word "Toronto" or "Taranto" attached to Lake Simcoe, the general region of Lake Simcoe, or rivers or portage routes leading to it, including, eventually the Humber River. From the evidence of French maps, it does not appear to have been originally applied to the Toronto area,

though some Haundenosaunee people contest this. The City of Toronto Web site says it means "fish weir."

31. William Woodworth, Interview with author, July 19, 2006. This comment reflects the general conception of language in the Indigenous oral tradition: "Native people view words as living, breathing, dynamic beings. . . . Uttered sound vibrations possess physical and spiritual energies that find their expression in the voices and visions of all sentient beings. . . . Words carry one's physical totality or state of being and become part of one's being. . . . To Native people, then, words affirm existence" (Einhorn, *Native American Oral Tradition*, 3.

32. "Indigeneity" has a number of definitions. It does not refer only to being in a given territory first. The Acoma Pueblo writer Simon Ortiz speaks of Indigeneity as "Indigenous land, culture and community that is a way of life for Indigenous American people because of the connection or bond that is primarily articulated as a sharing of responsibilities or sacred trust (spiritual law or principles) between Indigenous human culture and the land that is native and aboriginal to them" (pers. comm., November 27, 2007). The Seminole historian Susan Miller defines "indigenousness" as a pattern of characteristics shared by polities that are not organized as nation–states but conceive of their peoples as communities within a living and sacred cosmos (Miller, "Native America Writes Back: The Origin of the Indigenous Paradigm," 25–45). Jeffrey Sissons defines Indigenous cultures as those "that have been transformed through the struggles of colonized peoples to resist and redirect projects of settler nationhood" (*First Peoples*, 15).

33. Sneja Marina Gunew, also commented on this phenomenon in *Haunted Nations*, 128.

34. By the beginning of the twentieth century these rivers were buried underground and had combined with sewers.

35. Berman, *All That Is Solid Melts into Air*, quoted in Soja, *Postmodern Geographies*, 28.

36. According to Statistics Canada 2006 Census figures, there are 5.47 million people in the Greater Toronto Area ("Release of the 2006 Census on Language, Immigration, Citizenship, Mobility/Migration," http://www.toronto.ca/demographics/pdf/2006_lang_imm_citizenship_mobility_backgrounder.pdf).

37. Lawrence gives a figure of seventy thousand, including mixed-blood, non-status people (*"Real" Indians and Others*, 17). The City of Toronto posts a figure of 13,605 "reported" Aboriginal people, but many Indigenous people do not participate in censuses. See "Release of the 2006 Census on Persons of Aboriginal Identity," http://www.toronto.ca/demographics/pdf/2006_aboriginal_identity_backgrounder.pdf.

38. Gelder and Jacobs describe a similar phenomenon in *Uncanny Australia*, 1.

39. The Petun or Tionnontati were politically distinct but culturally very similar to and related to the Huron-Wendats; the two peoples lived in proximity both in the Toronto area and later in Huronia. For simplicity I will refer subsequently to the Huron-Wendats only, but this is understood to mean both groups.

40. The Neutrals lived just west of Toronto; the Niagara Escarpment marked the border region between these groups. Warrick, "Population History of the Huron-Petun," 362; Sioui, *Huron/Wendat*, 56, 83.

41. Archaeology records the presence of Paleo-Indian big-game hunters from 9000 to 7000 BC, and Archaic hunter–gatherers to 1000 BC, of whom very little is known but who may have been ancestral to both Algonquian (Anishinaabeg) and Iroquoian groups. While some scholars and some Iroquoian oral traditions suggest Iroquoian migration from elsewhere, likely the south, Trigger and others argue that local Woodland cultures appear to have evolved after 500 AD into corn-growing cultures that gradually developed the classic form of Iroquoian culture, with longhouse villages, corn-beans-squash horticulture, and matrilineal descent (Trigger, *Children of Aataentsic*, 105–48). See also Sioui, *Huron/Wendat*, and Wright, *History of the Native People of Canada*.

42. It has been suggested that the Huron-Wendats moved north to distance themselves from Iroquois enemies and/or to be closer to major trading routes and Algonquians who provided them with meat, fur, and other trade items. Trigger, *Children of Aataentsic*, 164–68, and Sioui, *Huron/Wendat*, 72.

43. Kelsay, *Joseph Brant*, 43.

44. David Redwolf, in a March 19, 2006, interview with the author, spoke of at least two thousand people at Six Nations as having Wendat ancestry, but I have no confirmation of this figure.

45. George Copway, Peter Jones, and William Warren all published Anishinaabeg oral tradition of this conquest, and this version of the history is accepted as fact by many historians, including Peter Schmalz, Donald B. Smith, and Leroy V. Eid. See Eid, "Ojibwa–Iroquois War"; Schmalz, *Ojibwa of Southern Ontario*; and Smith, "Who Are the Mississauga?"

46. Mississaugas of New Credit, *Toronto Purchase Specific Claim*. Peter Schmalz, working from Anishinaabe, Wyandot, and Haudenosaunee oral traditions and French records, suggested that Teiaiagon may have been one of ten Iroquois villages destroyed by the Mississaugas in their conquest of southern Ontario ("Role of the Ojibwa in the Conquest of Southern Ontario," 340). According to Peter Jones in *History of the Ojebway Indians*, the beach of Burlington Bay was the site of the last battle.

47. Schmalz, *Ojibwa of Southern Ontario*, 26–33; Jones, *History of the Ojebway Indians*, also related the proceedings of a council on the Credit River in 1840 renewing the peace and friendship treaty between the Anishinaabeg and Haudenosaunee, 114–22. See also Smith, "Who Are the Mississauga?," 215–17.

48. See Brandao and Starna, "Treaties of 1701."

49. William Claus to Lieutenant-Governor Maitland, York, May 1, 1819, Library and Archives Canada, Colonial Office 42, 362:203, referenced in Smith, *Sacred Feathers*, 39.

50. See Smith, "Dispossession of the Mississauga Indians."

51. Johnson, "Mississauga–Lake Ontario Land Surrender of 1805," 249.

52. Masters, *Rise of Toronto*, 8, 11.

53. Return of the Missesayey, September 23, 1787, Library and Archives Canada (hereafter LAC), Record Group (hereafter RG) 10, 1834:197; W. Claus to Lieutenant-Governor Maitland, York, May 1, 1819, Colonial Office 42, 362:203, referenced in Smith, *Sacred Feathers*, 39.

54. William Claus, "Minutes of the Proceedings of a Council at the River au Credit on the 27th, 28th and 29th October, 1818," LAC, Claus Papers, Vol. 11, 110–12.

55. Joseph Sawyer, John Jones to Sir John Colborne, River Credit, April 3, 1829, LAC, RG 10, 5:47.

56. Their removal to New Credit is described in Smith, *Sacred Feathers*, 212.

57. For example, in December 1856, Mr. Ma-zaw-keyaw-se-gay and Mr. and Mrs. Mah-koonce performed at St. Lawrence Hall. The latter was described in the program as a "grand-daughter of the famous, brave and warlike, yet generous and hospitable Captain Brant," while in March 1858, Kawshawgance and his troupe gave a performance "illustrating the manners and customs of the Rocky Mountain Indians" at St. Lawrence Hall (Guillet, *Toronto*, 409, 411). Later Indigenous performers included Pauline Johnson and Frances Nickawa.

58. For example, Oronhyatekha (Dr. Peter Martin), Alex Johnson, Ellen Hill, James Ross, Dr. Peter Edmund Jones (the son of Peter Jones), George Henry Jr., Francis Assignack, Frederick Loft, Ethel Monture, Fioretta Katherine Maracle, and John Sero-Brant, as well as Pauline Johnson and her siblings Evelyn and Allen Wawanosh Johnson, were all Toronto residents at various times. Other "civilized Indians" involved with Christian missionary and educational efforts, such as Peter Jones, Alan Salt, and others, visited Toronto regularly to meet with members of missionary societies and attend missionary conferences. That less well-known Indigenous people still lived in or frequented the city is suggested by an 1859 painting of the first Union Station in Toronto, which clearly shows an Aboriginal woman with a basket

waiting for a train heading west (William Armstrong, "First Union Station" [1859], Watercolour, Toronto Public Library, Acc. John Ross Robertson Collection 291).

59. Amelia Kalant, *National Identity and the Conflict at Oka*, 81.

60. Sanderson and Howard-Bobiwash, *Meeting Place*, 20–22. See also Van Kirk, "What If Mama Is an Indian?" 207–15, and the stories of Pauline Johnson for a discussion of the social pressure to assimilate that was prevalent in Canada at the time.

61. As the developing metropolitan center dominated its southern Ontario hinterlands economically and politically, Torontonians were at the forefront of calls for the annexation of northern Ontario and the Red River Colony, both of which had significant Aboriginal populations. Toronto political commentators also called for harsh treatment of the leaders of Métis resistance movements in the west in 1869–70 and 1885; six hundred of the twelve hundred men in General Middleton's expeditionary force to quell the 1885 resistance came from Toronto. Toronto churches and their national offices (also located in Toronto) played a large part in supporting Indian residential schools in the west.

62. Lawrence, *"Real" Indians and Others*, xv.

63. Lawrence, *"Real" Indians and Others*, 6.

64. Ellen Wise, Interview with author, February 26, 2006; Roger Obansawin, Interview with author, March 13, 2006.

65. Gelder and Jacobs, *Uncanny Australia*, 43, 51.

66. Gelder and Jacobs, *Uncanny Australia*, 46.

67. Preserving historic sites has not been a priority in Toronto, and many important Aboriginal sites have been destroyed, according to Archaeological Services, *Master Plan*, 28.

68. Cruikshank, *Correspondence of the Honourable Peter Russell*, 2:41.

69. See Bennet McCardle, "'Heart of Heart': Daniel Wilson's Human Biology," in Ash et al., *Thinking with Both Hands*, 101–13, and Teather, *Royal Ontario Museum*, for discussions of collections of the museum of the Canadian Institute, the Provincial Archeological Museum, and various museums of the University of Toronto. A photograph of "Indian" exhibits at the Provincial Museum show an entire wall of cases filled with crania (Teather, *Royal Ontario Museum*, 188). Andrew F. Hunter catalogued village and ossuary sites in Simcoe, York, and Ontario counties, counting thirty-three village sites in York and five ossuaries ("French Relics from Village Sites of the Hurons," *Archaeological Reports of Ontario 1888–89*, 42–44). In 1889 Boyle and others opened a village site at Maple village site and the Keffer ossuary in York and Vaughan townships, north of Toronto.

70. Yellowhorn, "Awakening of Internalist Archaeology," 198.

71. Ferris, "Between Colonial and Indigenous Archaeologies," 160.

72. Ron Williamson, "Remarks," December 8, 2005; D. Johnston, "Connecting People to Place," 28; Jean Brébeuf, Jesuit Relations, 10:141–43, 287; Paul LeJeune, Jesuit Relations, Volume 16:191–93.

73. Jesuit Relations, 16:191–93, cited in D. Johnston, "Connecting People," 28.

74. Yellowhorn, "Awakening of Internalist Archaeology," 207.

75. Gros Louis, "Reburial of the Human Remains."

76. Gros Louis, "Reburial of the Human Remains." This was confirmed by two Wendat interviewees.

77. "Huron oppose digs on ancestral lands," *Toronto Star*, October 5, 2006, R5.

78. "Huron oppose digs on ancestral lands," *Toronto Star*, October 5, 2006, R5.

79. This shift is noticeable not only in terms of archaeological consultation, but also in terms of ceremonial acknowledgments of the Indigenous peoples of the area at the beginning of some public meetings.

80. Redwolf, March 19, 2006. While there is increasing inter-First Nations cooperation between archaeologists and some Wendat, Mississauga, and Haudenosaunee representatives concerning the disposition of uncovered remains, in the complex and ever-shifting political struggle between various Indigenous groups trying to protect archaeological sites and by extension make claims of Indigeneity in the Toronto area, one group of Haudenosaunee activists has claimed that most Toronto sites are Erie–Neutral rather than Wendat sites, and thus fall under the jurisdiction of the Haudenosaunee Confederacy rather than the Wendats (David Redwolf, pers. comm. with author, December 4, 2007).

81. According to the archaeologist Ron Williamson, an estimated eight thousand sites in the regional municipalities of Halton, Durham, Peel, and York were destroyed between 1951 and 1991, and 25 percent of them "should have been protected or at the very least excavated before their destruction by development." Between 2000 and 2005, more than twenty-five ancestral Huron-Wendat and Neutral Iroquoian villages were excavated in Ontario, and although archaeologists recommended preservation in situ in every case, all were destroyed. Williamson, "Remarks," 3–4.

82. Williamson, "Remarks," 2–3. See also B. Johnston, *Manitous*, xx–xxii. Furthermore, in Native understandings of imagery, the tool does not just represent the blood or hero; it becomes one with it, and the viewer, in perceiving the relationship, also becomes one with it (Einhorn, *Native American Oral Tradition*, 28).

83. Ron Williamson, Interview with author, May 18, 2006.

84. Marie Georges, Interview with author, April 22, 2007.

85. D. Johnston, "Connecting People," 29.

86. Jesuit Relations, 16:195–97; Jones, *History of the Ojebway Indians*, 99–100.

87. Alanis King, October 29, 2005. Henry Scadding referred to a Native warrior killed during the siege of Toronto in 1813 as being buried at Sandhill, a very ancient burial ground believed to have been located just west of Yonge and south of Bloor (Scadding, *Toronto of Old*, 399).

88. In the Toronto Native community and among Indigenous peoples in settler countries generally, there is considerable discussion of the transgenerational effects of trauma created by the historical experience of colonialism and particularly of residential boarding schools. Indigenous psychologists and healers are exploring techniques of ancestral and intergenerational healing. See Duran and Duran, *Native American Postcolonial Psychology*; Atkinson, *Trauma Trails*; and Wesley-Esquimaux and Smolewski, *Historic Trauma and Aboriginal Healing*.

89. Redwolf, March 19, 2006.

90. William Woodworth speaking at the Humanitas Festival First Nations history lecture series, Toronto, June 21, 2006.

91. Hirsch, *Family Frames*, 22, quoted in LaCapra, *Writing History*, 112–13.

92. Duran and Duran, *Native American Postcolonial Psychology*.

93. LaCapra, *Writing History*, 70, 89.

94. "One's bond with the dead, especially with dead intimates, may invest trauma with value and make its reliving a painful but necessary commemoration or memorial to which one remains dedicated or at least bound" (LaCapra, *Writing History*, 22).

95. LaCapra's notion of "working through" trauma crucially involves distinguishing past and present, self and other. This paradigm may be problematic for Indigenous peoples and others whose worldviews involve less rigid distinctions between such categories.

96. I also interviewed two non-Aboriginal spiritual healers (one of them a New Age healer, the other a traditional South African *sangoma*) who also said they had frequent contact with ancestral spirits, but they did not know any Toronto history and did not have relationships with Indigenous people or Indigenous spirits here (Sibongile Nene, Interview with author, May 22, 2006, and Marlayna Lynne Marks, Interview with author, January 6, 2006).

97. Margo Dunn, Interview with author, July 5, 2006. This point is arguable, as ancestral grievances have fanned ethnic hatred in various countries, including the former Yugoslavia, for example, but it may be generally true of non-Indigenous Torontonians.

98. Ortiz, "Towards a National Indian Literature," 254.

99. Carolyn King, Interview with author, July 30, 2006.

100. Woodworth, July 19, 2006.

101. See for example Martin, *The American Indian and the Problem of History*; Fixico, *American Indian Mind in a Linear World*; Krech, "Bringing Linear Time Back In."

102. Woodworth, July 19, 2006; Redwolf, March 19, 2006; David Grey Eagle Sanford, Interview with author, March 5, 2006. I am also indebted to Jon Johnson, whose unpublished dissertation chapter on the Great Indian Bus Tour offered by the Native Canadian Centre of Toronto emphasizes the importance of this sense of continuity of Indigenous presence in the city as expressed in that guided tour.

103. Woodworth, "Toronto Beacon to the Ancestors: The Return of Native Peoples to their Hosting Duties."

104. "Knowledge is gathered through the body, mind and heart in altered states of being, in songs and dance, in meditation and reflection, and in dreams and visions" (Cajete, "Philosophy of Native Science," 52).

105. Redwolf, March 19, 2006; Sanford, March 5, 2006; Woodworth, July 19, 2006; Daniel Justice, Interview with author, February 23, 2006; Helen Thundercloud, Interview with author, February 4, 2006. This intuitive sensing was most pronounced in people working on the preservation of local Indigenous archaeological sites. A few non-Aboriginal people also said they sensed energy or spirit but generally not in relation to Toronto's Indigenous history, though a couple of allies of Native people did (Mark Warner, Interview with author, January 31, 2006, and Anna Petrov, Interview with author, January 25, 2006).

106. For example, Ortiz writes, "Story, whether in oral or written form, substantiates life, continues it, and creates it" ("Toward a National Indian Literature," 258).

107. William Woodworth, Humanitas Festival First Nations History lecture series, June 21, 2006.

108. Hill, "Ethics and the Use of Indigenous Knowledge in Academic Research."

109. Gelder and Jacobs, *Uncanny Australia*, 106–7.

110. Gelder and Jacobs, *Uncanny Australia*, 26.

111. Jean-François Lyotard, quoted in Gelder and Jacobs, *Uncanny Australia*, 17–18.

112. Toby Morantz, "Plunder or Harmony?"

113. Carlson, "Making Sense of Memory," Paper given at Canadian Historical Association Annual Meeting, Saskatoon, May 29, 2007.

114. For example, the Piikani (Peigan) archaeologist Eldon Yellowhorn, who has called for a rational, secular practice of "internalist" archaeology informed by Indigenous oral traditions, speaks of the need for Indigenous peoples to recognize that "a secular antiquity exists that is independent of the sacred versions related in traditional narratives." He decries "the ten-

dency to revere a putative aboriginal utopia," and to uncritically accept largely invented traditions, such as the medicine wheel (Yellowhorn, "Awakening of Internalist Archaeology," 194, 199–200). Susan Miller, on the other hand, insists on the sacred as an integral part of Indigenous historiography writing: "Within the Indigenous paradigm, the cosmos is alive. Spirits recognized in Indigenous worldviews are real and have power within the material world" ("Native America Writes Back: The Origin of the Indigenous Paradigm in Historiography," 10).

115. Gelder and Jacobs, *Uncanny Australia*, 106–7.

116. Gelder and Jacobs, *Uncanny Australia*, 26.

117. Gelder and Jacobs, *Uncanny Australia*, 118; Redwolf, March 19, 2006. The site was also registered with the Ontario Ministry of Culture; Ontario Ministry of Culture Archaeological Site Record, Borden Number Aj Gu 44, November 4, 2003. Similarly, protesters led by David Grey Eagle Sanford set up camp on "sacred land" to push the city to save an old bridge over the Rouge River, "Natives Aim to Save Bridge," *Toronto Star*, October 14, 2007, A3. He was quoted as saying, "My ancestors are buried all through here. It is sacred land to me."

118. Redwolf, March 19, 2006; Sanford, March 5, 2006; Woodworth, July 19, 2006; Ron Williamson, May 18, 2006; Petrov, January 25, 2006; Susan Hill, personal communication with author, July 24, 2007.

119. Sissons, *First Peoples*, 13.

120. Gelder and Jacobs, *Uncanny Australia*, 22.

BIBLIOGRAPHY

Adam, G. Mercer. *Toronto: Old and New*. Toronto: Mail Print, 1905. (Orig. pub. 1891.)

Archaeological Services, Inc. *A Master Plan of Archaeological Resources for the City of Toronto: Interim Report*. Submitted to Heritage Preservation Services, Culture Division, City of Toronto, August 2004.

Ash, Marinell, et al. *Thinking with Both Hands: Sir Daniel Wilson in the Old World and the New*. Ed. Elizabeth Hulse. Toronto: University of Toronto Press, 1999.

Atkinson, Judy. *Trauma Trails, Recreating Song Lines: The Transgenerational Effects of Trauma in Indigenous Australia*. North Melbourne, Australia: Spinifex, 2002.

Bentley, D. M. R. "Shadows in the Soul: Racial Haunting in the Poetry of Duncan Campbell Scott." *University of Toronto Quarterly* 75, no. 2 (Spring 2006): 752–70.

Benton-Benai, Edward. *The Mishomis Book*. Hayward WI: Indian Country Communications, 1988.

Berman, Marshall. *All That Is Solid Melts into Air: The Experience of Modernity*. New York : Simon & Schuster, 1982.

Bouchette, Joseph. *The British Dominions in North America*. London: H. Colburn and R. Bentley, 1831.

Brandao, J. A., and William A. Starna, "The Treaties of 1701: A Triumph of Iroquois Diplomacy," *Ethnohistory* 43, no. 2 (1996): 209–44.

Cajete, Gregory. "Philosophy of Native Science." In *American Indian Thought*, ed. Anne Waters, 45–57. Malden MA: Blackwell, 2004.

Cameron, Emilie. "Indigenous Spectrality and the Politics of Postcolonial Ghost Stories." *Cultural Geographies* 15 (2008), 383–93.

Carriou, Warren. "Haunted Prairie: Aboriginal 'Ghosts' and the Spectres of Settlement." *University of Toronto Quarterly* 75, no. 2 (Spring 2006):727–34.

City of Toronto, Culture Division, Economic Development, Culture and Tourism Department. *Humanitas: Feasibility Study for a New Cultural Attraction on Toronto's Waterfront*, September 2004.

Cohn, Steven. *History's Shadow: Native Americans and Historical Consciousness in the Nineteenth Century*. Chicago: University of Chicago Press, 2004.

Cruikshank, E. A., ed. *The Correspondence of the Honourable Peter Russell*. 3 vols. Toronto: Historical Society, 1932–36.

Dieterman, Frank A., ed. *Mississauga: The First 10,000 Years*. Toronto: Mississauga Heritage Foundation, 2002.

Duran, Eduardo, and Bonnie Duran. *Native American Postcolonial Psychology*. Albany: State University of New York Press, 1995.

Eid, Leroy V. "The Ojibwa–Iroquois War: The War the Five Nations Did Not Win." *Ethnohistory* 26 (1979): 297–324.

Einhorn, Lois J. *The Native American Oral Tradition: Voices of the Spirit and Soul*. Westport CT: Praeger, 2000.

Emerson, J. N. "The Village and the Cemetery [Iroquois, ossuary, site, Tabor Hill]." *Ontario History* 48, no. 4 (1956): 181–83.

Ferris, Neal. "Between Colonial and Indigenous Archaeologies: Legal and Extra-Legal Ownership of the Archaeological Past in North America." *Canadian Journal of Archaeology* 27, no. 2 (2003): 154–90.

Fixico, Donald. *The American Indian Mind in a Linear World: American Indian Studies and Traditional Knowledge*. New York: Routledge, 2003.

Freud, Sigmund. "The 'Uncanny'" [Das Unheimliche] (1919). *Standard Edition of the Complete Psychological Works*. Vol. 17. Trans. James Strachey. London: Hogarth, 1955.

Furniss, Elizabeth. "Challenging the Myth of Indigenous Peoples' 'Last Stand' in Canada and Australia: Public Discourse and the Condition of Silence." In *Rethinking Settler Colonialism: History and Memory in Aus-

tralia, Canada, Aotearoa New Zealand and South Africa, ed. Annie E. Coombes, 172–92. Manchester UK: Manchester University Press, 2006.

Gelder, Ken, and Jane M. Jacobs. *Uncanny Australia: Sacredness and Identity in a Postcolonial Nation*. Melbourne: Melbourne University Press, 1998.

Gros Louis, Francis. "The Reburial of the Human Remains of My 350-Year-Old Ancestors." www.ossossane.org/cemetery.html.

Guillet, Edwin C. *Toronto: From Trading Post to Great City*. Toronto: Ontario Publishing, 1934.

Gunew, Sneja Marina. *Haunted Nations: The Colonial Dimensions of Multiculturalisms*. London: Routledge, 2004.

Hill, Susan. "Ethics and the Use of Indigenous Knowledge in Academic Research," lecture, University of Toronto, January 17, 2006.

Hirsch, Marianne. *Family Frames: Photography, Narrative and Postmemory*. Cambridge MA: Harvard University Press, 1997.

Howard, Heather A. "Dreamcatchers in the City: An Ethnohistory of Social Action, Gender and Class in Native Community Production in Toronto." PhD diss., University of Toronto, 2005.

Indian Claims Commission, Canada. *Mississaugas of the New Credit First Nation Inquiry: Toronto Purchase Claim*. June 2003.

Johnson, Leo A. "The Mississauga–Lake Ontario Land Surrender of 1805." Ontario History 83, no. 3 (1990): 233–53.

Johnston, Basil. *The Manitous: The Spiritual World of the Ojibway*. New York: HarperCollins, 1995.

Johnston, Darlene. "Connecting People to Place: Great Lakes Aboriginal History in Cultural Context." Research paper prepared for the Ipperwash Commission of Inquiry, 2004.

Jones, Peter (Kahkewaquonaby). *History of the Ojebway Indians*. London: A. W. Bennett, 1861.

Kalant, Amelia. *National Identity and the Conflict at Oka: Native Belonging and Myths of Postcolonial Nationhood in Canada*. New York: Routledge, 2004.

Kelsay, Isabel Thompson. *Joseph Brant, 1743–1807: Man of Two Worlds*. Syracuse NY: Syracuse University Press, 1984.

Kenyon, W. A. "A Prehistoric Cemetery [Highland Creek, Scarborough, site, Tabor Hill]." *Ontario History* 48, no. 4 (1956): 181–82.

Killan, Gerald. *David Boyle: From Artisan to Archaeologist*. Toronto: University of Toronto Press, 1983.

Kohl, J. G. *Travels in Canada and through the States of New York and Pennsylvania*. Trans. Mrs. Percy Siinnett. 2 vols. London: George Manwaring, 1861.

Krech III, Shepard. "Bringing Linear Time Back In." *Ethnohistory* 53, no. 3 (Summer 2006): 567–93.

LaCapra, Dominick. *Writing History, Writing Trauma.* Baltimore MD: Johns Hopkins University Press, 2001.

Lawrence, Bonita. *"Real" Indians and Others: Mixed-Blood Urban Native Peoples and Indigenous Nationhood.* Lincoln: University of Nebraska Press, 2004.

Martin, Calvin, ed. *The American Indian and the Problem of History.* New York: Oxford University Press, 1987.

Masters, D. C. *The Rise of Toronto: 1850–1890.* Toronto: University of Toronto Press, 1947.

Middleton, Jesse Edgar. *The Municipality of Toronto: A History.* 3 vols. Toronto: Dominion, 1923.

Miller, Susan A. "Native Historians Write Back: The Indigenous Paradigm in American Indian Historiography." *Wicazo Sa Review* 24, no. 1 (Spring 2009): 25–45.

———. "Native America Writes Back: The Origin of the Indigenous Paradigm in Historiography." *Wicazo Sa Review* 23, no. 2 (Fall 2008): 9–28.

Mississaugas of the New Credit First Nation. *Toronto Purchase Specific Claim: Arriving at an Agreement.* Hagersville ON: Mississaugas of New Credit First Nation, n.d.

Morantz, Toby. "Plunder or Harmony? On Merging European and Native Views of Early Contact." In *Decentering the Renaissance: Canada and Europe in Multidisciplinary Perspective, 1500–1700,* ed. Germaine Warkentin and Carolyn Podruchny, 48–67. Toronto: University of Toronto Press, 2001.

Mulvany, Charles Pelham, G. Mercer Adam, and Christopher Blackett Robinson. *History of Toronto and County of York.* Toronto: C. B. Robinson, 1885.

Ortiz, Simon J. "Towards a National Indian Literature: Cultural Authenticity in Nationalism." In *American Indian Literary Nationalism,* ed. Jace Weaver, Craig S. Womack, and Robert Warrior, 253–60. Albuquerque: New Mexico Press, 2006.

Robinson, Percy. *Toronto during the French Regime, 1615–1793.* 2nd ed. Toronto: University of Toronto Press, 1965 [1933].

Sanderson, Frances, and Heather Howard-Bobiwash, eds. *The Meeting Place: Aboriginal Life in Toronto.* Toronto: Native Canadian Centre of Toronto, 1997.

Scadding, Henry. *Toronto of Old: Collections and Recollections, Illustrative of the Early Settlement and Social Life of the Capital of Ontario.* Toronto: Adam Stevenson, 1873.

————, and John Dent, eds. *Toronto, Past and Present, Historical and Descriptive: A Memorial Volume for the Semi-Centennial of 1884.* Toronto: Hunter, Rose, 1884.

Schmalz, Peter. *The Ojibwa of Southern Ontario.* Toronto: University of Toronto Press, 1991.

————. "The Role of the Ojibwa in the Conquest of Southern Ontario, 1650–1701." *Ontario History* 76, no. 4 (1984): 326–52.

Shaw, Rosalind. *Memories of the Slave Trade: Ritual and the Historical Imagination in Sierra Leone.* Chicago: University of Chicago Press, 2002.

Simcoe, Elizabeth. *The Diary of Mrs. John Graves Simcoe.* Notes by John Ross Robertson. Toronto: William Briggs, 1911.

Sioui, Georges E. *Huron/Wendat: The Heritage of the Circle.* Trans. Jane Brierley. Vancouver: University of British Columbia Press, 1999.

Sissons, Jeffrey. *First Peoples: Indigenous Cultures and their Futures.* London: Reaktion Books, 2005.

Smith, Donald B. "The Dispossession of the Mississauga Indians: A Missing Chapter in the Early History of Upper Canada." *Ontario History* 73 (1981): 67–87.

————. *Sacred Feathers: The Reverend Peter Jones (Kahkewaquonaby) and the Mississauga Indians.* Toronto: University of Toronto Press, 1991.

————. "Who Are the Mississauga?" *Ontario History* 7, no. 4 (1975): 211–22.

Soja, Edward W. *Postmodern Geographies: The Reassertion of Space in Critical Social Theory.* London: Verso, 1989.

Teather, J. Lynne. *The Royal Ontario Museum: A Prehistory, 1830–1914.* Toronto: Canada University Press, 2005.

Thrush, Coll. *Native Seattle: Histories from the Crossing-Over Place.* Seattle: University of Washington Press, 2007.

Thwaites, R. G. *The Jesuit Relations and Allied Documents: Travels and Explorations of the Jesuit Missionaries in New France, 1610–1791.* Cleveland: Burrows Brothers, 1898.

Trigger, Bruce. *The Children of Aataentsic: A History of the Huron People to 1660.* Montreal: McGill-Queen's University Press, 1976.

Van Kirk, Sylvia. "'What If Mama Is an Indian?': The Cultural Ambivalence of the Alexander Ross Family." In *The New Peoples: Being and Becoming Metis in North America*, ed. Jacqueline Peterson and Jennifer S. H Brown, 207–20. Winnipeg: University of Manitoba Press, 1985.

Warrick, Gary A. "A Population History of the Huron-Petun." PhD diss., McGill University, 1990.

Wesley-Esquimaux, Cynthia C., and Magdalena Smolewski. *Historic Trauma and Aboriginal Healing.* Aboriginal Healing Foundation Research Series. Ottawa: Aboriginal Healing Foundation, 2004.

Williamson, Ron. "Remarks." Panel Discussion, Ipperwash Commission of Inquiry, December 8, 2005.

———, ed. *Toronto: A Short Illustrated History of Its First 12,000 Years.* Toronto: James Lorimer, 2008.

Woodworth, William. "Toronto Beacon to the Ancestors: The Return of Native Peoples to Their Hosting Duties," brochure of the Beacon to the Ancestors Foundation, n.d.

Wright, J. V. *A History of the Native People of Canada.* 3 vols. Hull QC: Canadian Museum of Civilization, 1995.

Yellowhorn, Eldon. "The Awakening of Internalist Archaeology in the Aboriginal World." In *The Archaeology of Bruce Trigger: Theoretical Empiricism*, ed. Ronald F. Williamson and Michael W. Bisson, 194–209. Montreal: McGill-Queens University Press, 2006.

9

Shape-shifters, Ghosts, and Residual Power

An Examination of Northern Plains Spiritual Beliefs, Location, Objects, and Spiritual Colonialism

CYNTHIA LANDRUM

In the summer of 1991, a Hunkpapa Lakota Sioux tribal member, Don Tenoso, was scheduled to provide a routine demonstration of traditional doll-making techniques in the Native American exhibition hall at the National Museum of Natural History of the Smithsonian Institution in Washington DC. At the time, I was a museum technician with the Department of Anthropology and was working in the Natural History building. Since we were about to begin the work of conserving and moving the Plains Indian collection that was in storage, I was curious to see what he had to say about the cultural significance of the dolls.

When I approached the demonstration area, the hall was nearly empty, with the exception of a few tourists, the exhibit mannequins, myself, and Don Tenoso, with his long black braids and modern Sioux Indian garb. As he quietly worked on his project just around the corner from the life-size mannequin of the Sioux warrior Kicking Bear, I wondered if he found it unnerving to be amid an exhibition that honored only the troubled "ghosts" of the Plains tribes' cultural and historical past—trophies of the Indian wars—and the collections of the anthropological expeditions.

While I watched from afar and contemplated the obvious irony of the situation, a woman with the spectral remnants of a 1960s bee-hive appeared, stood directly in front of Tenoso, and stated, "Are you an Indian? I thought you people were all dead. Why are you still here? Why haven't you done what my relatives did and blended in with the rest of the American melting pot? It's time for you to move on and live in the present." Don Tenoso shrugged his shoulders and said, "I am here to demonstrate traditional doll-making techniques from my tribe." Dumbfounded, I wondered how he could withstand this diatribe, as the only living and breathing exhibit in an exhibition hall that housed the physical manifestations of his own and others' ancestral ghosts. How could this woman, descended from European immigrants, really understand all that the Sioux had encountered in the face of physical and cultural genocide?

Stories of ghosts and hauntings are present in every society.[1] The traditional conviction among most American Indian people is that ghosts can be malignant forces or act as guardian spirits. In particular, the Lakota believe that spirits or ghosts seen in daylight or at dusk can be dangerous *and* benevolent, depending on the context in which they are encountered. It is believed that benevolent ghosts can provide protection or guidance, or even become part of the landscape where a traumatic or powerful event occurred. Malevolent spirits, however, can cause spiritual, physical, and/or emotional harm to the living.[2] Stories of the uncanny or supernatural are actively reinforced by the oral historical narratives that emanate directly from tribal communities despite generations of assimilation, territorial conquest, spiritual colonialism, and academic and religious bigotry toward Northern Plains beliefs. Likewise, for many Lakota people, material objects that have been collected by museums still resonate with "power" despite the fact that they have been removed from their original context. As a result, such objects—and the new places they inhabit—may also become haunted. In this essay I will examine and compare Northern Plains beliefs about haunted locations, spirits, and objects in three contexts: the ghosts of victims massacred in 1890 at the Wounded Knee site in South Dakota; stories about the Deer People, shape-shifters that are half-deer and half-human; and hauntings that allegedly occurred around material objects displayed in the Great Plains exhibition hall and storage areas at the National Museum of Natural History. Further, I will show that Indigenous belief systems have survived despite cultural genocide, will demonstrate the hybridity of everyday beliefs as American Indians contribute to American popular culture, will show that Native beliefs are not hermetically sealed but rather engage the stories of colonial society as well, and, finally, discuss how these everyday/everywhere ghost stories are grounded in actual histories of colonialism.

Traditional sacred sites, stories, and/or museum objects act as vessels for "power"—both temporary and permanent—that connect the everyday world with the supernatural. The Northern Plains stories recorded here were told to me by individual consultants from various tribes, and museum employees and professionals who choose to remain anonymous. Some of the interviews are from as early as the fall of 1991, while others took place in the fall of 2008. However, I have worked with tribal members in the Northern Plains since 1991. My work as a historian has focused primarily on American Indian government-sponsored boarding schools and the effect of the educational system upon the Northern Plains tribes. In addition to performing scholarly research, I have worked as a museum professional and have specifically dealt with the care of Native American museum objects. Over the years, individuals, Native and non-Native alike, have shared with me stories of the uncanny—as these relate to the experience of boarding schools and policies of assimilation or as they relate to the frustration and anger many have felt concerning the removal of human remains and material objects from their original cultural settings. In both settings, many Indigenous people have experienced trauma, oppression, and uncertainty, the kinds of conditions that seem to elicit hauntings. This essay is the result of stories told to me while I worked in museums or was in the process of conducting research on other topics. And whether it was a conversation in passing or a formal interview, the information was shared with me in order to further illuminate how the dynamics among "power," sacred sites, traditional folklore, and/or material objects operate.

Power, for many American Indians, including the Lakota, is fixed in place. For Lakota people, sacred sites include the Black Hills, Bear Butte, Harney Peak, the Badlands, and Pipestone.[3] Bear Butte has been a site for vision quests for the Lakota Sioux and Cheyenne for thousands of years. The eastern edge of the Black Hills in

South Dakota, the area where the first peoples emerged, has been a focal point for religious activity involving sun dances, prayers, and fasting and prophecies. Pipestone also serves as an important religious site for many tribes, but in particular for the Dakota Sioux. For centuries, people have mined the red stone in western Minnesota in order to make the sacred pipe, pipe bowls, and other objects. Again, these sites serve as access points between the physical world and the realm of the spirits. Dreams, visions, and aberrations are a part of the lived reality of many Indian people, as are ghosts, spirits, and witches. Indian traditionalists believe that those spiritual powers have control over their lives, and they use protective medicines and take precautions to keep themselves safe. It is a life where the metaphysical is more powerful than the physical world, and where certain ceremonies and important rites, performed at specific sacred sites, such as Bear Butte, are necessary for protection or blessings for individuals and communities as people seek deeper communion with those powers greater than themselves.[4]

Thus, interactions with spirits and ghosts are viewed by many Native Americans as a normal component of life. All things, animate or inanimate, possess spirit. For Lakota people, contact with the spirit realm is the basis of most of their rituals. It is believed that the thin veil between this temporary world and the lasting world of the spirits may be penetrated for a variety of reasons—either a holy person travels to that world, or the spirit must come forth on its own.[5] Among the Lakota, a person who calls and speaks with spirits is referred to as a Wana'gi Wapiye, or Ghost Conjurer. In this capacity the person serves to unite two communities, or Tiyo'spaye—that of the living relatives and that of the dead, and, in that sense, those people who are alive actively retain knowledge of the past and present.[6]

The enduring relationship between these two worlds is best described by the Sioux activist and artist Rosalie Little Thunder when she states, "The Lakota have a prayer emphasis, Mitakuye Oyas'in, which refers to the interrelationship of all beings. It is difficult to explain this concept to a people who have a tendency to want everything validated and explained by science. It is even harder to explain to English speakers that Mitakuye Oyas'in also encompasses the energy fields that hum with timelessness and the connectedness of déjà vu and premonitions of aya and ayaptan, and the multitude of unseen, unexplainable things that are carelessly tossed into the superstitious heap by observers who do not understand."[7]

Gail Small, head chief of the Northern Cheyenne tribe of Montana, corroborates this view when she states that she can feel spirits of the ancestors within the Cheyenne homeland and that they guide the people every day. Small also believes in water spirits and has seen and felt their power.[8]

Such views contrast sharply with those expressed by the anthropologist Robert Lowie, when he described "plains superstition" in the mid-1950s as a means to an end. Lowie, and others of his generation of anthropologists, believed it was useful to have a single term for an entire system of beliefs and practices involving power beyond that of mortal beings.[9] Lowie further argued, "Of course, the Native cannot conceive of nature as the modern scientist does, and accordingly he cannot oppose to such a concept another that transcends what are called natural laws. But he can and does react vehemently to perceptions that are wholly out of the normal range of his experience. American Indians have a variety of words to express the cause of such reactions, i.e., to describe what strikes them as mysterious, weird, or miraculous, thrilling or awe-inspiring."[10]

In recent years, scholars have moved away from this narrow interpretation of traditional American Indian beliefs with respect to the supernatural by producing publications that reflect a more enlightened view of how the cosmological belief system and paranormal operate with respect to ghosts and hauntings. More recently, scholars are prioritizing Indigenous concepts of place and time,[11] the relationship of dreams and visions to perceptions of power,[12] and the intersection of ceremony, cosmology, and belief.[13]

Lee Irwin introduces the concept that topological structures in the Northern Plains function to organize communal perceptions and meaning that provides stability in the physical world for visionary experience. Further, he posits that the topological description is a description of received ideas, social interactions, and personal encounters. The ecology of visionary perception represents a particular way of "seeing" or "knowing" the lived world. The topology is not determined by the physical structure of that world, in the Western scientific sense, but by the way in which that world incorporates a variety of mysterious powers, beings, and realms. Physical boundaries are not rigidly distinct, nor are they classified according to any predetermined analytical schema. Among Plains Indian visionaries, there is a strong sense of the continuum of human perception, the natural world, and the mysterious appearance of visionary events. This continuum allows features of the lived world to blend, transform, or suddenly reveal new dimensions of meaning and power. A stone might speak, an animal can transform into another creature, a star falls to the earth as a beautiful woman. The individual's experiences of the world are not limited to ordinary motor action or to the five physical senses. Much more is possible.[14]

Donald Fixico continues in this same philosophical vein when he describes how the true reality of Indian people is a tandem of physical and metaphysical realities and that Native Americans encounter visions and spirits on a regular basis as a part of life.[15]

Within this metaphysical framework, Oglala Lakota ceremonial life is based upon the quest for power. Wakan is the awesome, the unknowable, the ineffable, the expansive universal, and can become conditionally manifest in persons, creatures, and things, but it is fundamentally an attribute of the supernatural. Wakan is the space occupied by the dead and by their condensations into named benevolent and evil beings. Everything within life is interconnected to a power system that is rooted in the supernatural.[16]

Thus, Lakota epistemology is a complex approach to the beliefs that connect the past to the present, rooting these in geography and revealing them through ritual and traditional storytelling. Ceremonies such as the Sun Dance, sweat lodges, or vision quests provide access points that connect traditional stories to sacred sites so that the past and the present are one and continue to be rooted in the context from which this epistemological structure emerged. This illuminates how Northern Plains people still place their faith in the supernatural world on a daily basis, without abstracting it to the point that this belief system is simply cast aside as unfounded superstition.

As other disciplines grapple with the definition of hauntings and ghostly phenomena, they have tried to extend their interpretations to be inclusive of American Indian cosmologies and rituals. Ironically, Native American cosmological systems seem to have a life of their own, regardless of how many times they are poked, prodded, and deconstructed on paper by generations of scholars. I will begin by examining the Wounded Knee Massacre site and how the location is believed to be haunted because of the traumatic event of 1890.

WOUNDED KNEE MASSACRE SITE: CULTURAL LOSS
AND ANCESTRAL HAUNTINGS

In the 1992 film *Thunderheart*, a young man of Sioux ancestry, Ray Levoi, returns to his homeland as an FBI agent to help solve a string of murders of Indian activists. He learns that his ancestor Thunderheart was among those murdered by U.S. soldiers during the 1890 massacre at Wounded Knee. After a while Ray begins to have fitful dreams and visions of the event. In the dream he is "running with the Old Ones" and is shot in the back. The film implies that his biological ties to the community are enough to trigger a series of metaphysical events. His ancestors return to haunt him and to help provide knowledge that will aid him in his quest for truth.

Thunderheart is not the first film in which Hollywood has attempted to tell the story of one of the worst incidents of genocide in the history of U.S.–Indigenous relations, the Wounded Knee Massacre. However, the filmmaker takes a different approach as he blends history and familiar uncanny motifs in an effort to move the story toward its inevitable conclusion. For instance, it is implied that Jimmy Looks Twice, a fictional activist played by the real-life American Indian Movement (AIM) member John Trudell, has the power to shape-shift into a deer. An elderly medicine man, Grandpa Reaches, has mystical connections to the ancestral past—he simply "knows" things. When Ray Levoi wistfully wishes that Maggie (a character reminiscent of the real-life Anna Mae Aquash), a female activist murdered during the course of the film, could be there in person to see the triumph of good over evil, Walter Crow Horse (played by Graham Greene) gently reminds him: "She was, Ray, she was." The film blends fact and fiction in a way that underscores that, for modern-day Lakota people, Wounded Knee is a haunted location.

On December 29, 1890, the Minneconjou Sioux Chief Big Foot and his "bedraggled band of starving Ghost Dancers" were camped along the Wounded Knee Creek, where they were slain by members of the U.S. Calvary on the Pine Ridge Indian Reservation in South Dakota.[17] Big Foot and his band were pursued by the U.S. Cavalry soldiers, who feared a localized outbreak of the Ghost Dance religion.[18]

In the aftermath of the massacre, the ethnologist James Mooney acquired objects and personal belongings, including the Ghost Dance shirts worn by the deceased, and shipped them east to the Smithsonian Institution. Under the auspices of the Bureau of Ethnology, Mooney was commissioned to acquire and curate an ethnographic collection for the World's Columbian Exposition and to continue his work among the Cherokee of Oklahoma, which initially involved several trips west between 1891 and 1894.[19]

In the aftermath of the Wounded Knee Massacre,[20] the Northern Plains people were both militarily and spiritually disarmed. And as their lands were occupied, they were corralled onto reservations and their secular and religious objects were placed in storage units in large metropolitan museums. According to the AIM activist, modern Ghost Dancer, and adopted Lakota Sioux tribal member Robert Van Pelt (Siletz/Umatilla), the people parted with their objects only when forced to by economic hardship and constant duress from outside forces.[21]

In a sense, the Ghost Dance religion[22] succeeded, because the dead did return, but not in the fashion in which the followers of the religion had anticipated.[23] According to Sioux tribal members today, the Wounded Knee site is haunted by those who were gunned down in the snow on December 29, 1890. The activist Mary Crow Dog, in her memoir, references the spirits of the site as she describes the birth of her first child during AIM's occupancy at Wounded Knee:

Monday, just as the morning star came out, my water broke and I went down to the sweat lodge to pray. I wanted to go into the sweat but Black Elk would not let me. Maybe there was a taboo against my participating, just as a menstruating woman is not allowed to take part in a ceremony. I was disappointed. I did not feel that the fact that my water burst had made me ritually unclean. As I walked away from the vapor hut, for the third time, I heard that ghostly cry and lamenting of a woman and child coming out of the massacre ravine. Others had heard it too. I felt that the spirits were all around me. I was later told that some of the marshals inside their sandbagged positions had also heard it, and some could not stand it and had themselves transferred.[24]

More than thirty years after the AIM occupation, tribal members are still processing the 1890 massacre as if it just happened. They remain respectful and wary of the site, as I learned in 2001 when I prepared to marry. I called one of my bridesmaids on her cell phone to make flight arrangements. She happened to be a Sioux tribal member, and as we spoke she indicated that she was at the Wounded Knee Massacre site with a flat tire. We did not speak for very long, because she said that she wanted to get off the phone to repair the tire. Her main concern was that it was dusk, and she did not want to be caught at the location much after dark. She feared that if she were there for any length of time, she would hear the cries of those who had been massacred more than one hundred years earlier, which is a common concern among tribal members today and a reason cited for avoiding the place after dusk.[25]

Other Lakota commemorate the Wounded Knee site more formally as they trace the route of Big Foot's people on horseback from Sitting Bull's assassination site on the Standing Rock Reservation to Wounded Knee in a ceremony held on the anniversary of the massacre called the "Wiping Away of the Tears." Direct descendants of the victims publicly mourn the dead and simultaneously honor the future generations. Since 1986 the ride has become an annual event. In more recent years most of the riders have been replaced by children, who are referred to as the Future Generation Riders.

One such rider, named Melanie Kuts, states, "They told me our ancestors were watching as we rode—and, you know, I truly felt it."[26] One ten-year-old girl that I met while I was living in South Dakota said that almost every time she drove by the massacre site she would see the spirit of her ancestor on horseback, dressed in full traditional regalia. It is common knowledge among the Sioux that the dead walk at night, particularly at that location, because of the emotional trauma that was imprinted upon the land. They also believe that the land is timeless and that the lines between the past and the present, the day-to-day and the supernatural, are skewed, rather than neatly drawn. Unlike Deer People, the returning dead at Wounded Knee cannot harm you, because they are like a film loop or a photograph of the past that is caught between the two worlds as a reminder and a memorial, yet traditional Sioux Indians still avoid the site at night out of respect for the dead. Deer People, however, operate on another "plane" altogether in that they are wielders of magic and enchantment who are simply part of the terrain yet are considered dangerous and are feared.

When places are actively sensed, the physical landscape becomes wedded to the landscape of the mind as these places animate the ideas and feelings of persons who attend to them.[27] And this animation of place, ideas, and feelings can also be applied to material objects and traditional folklore, in reference to "power" dynamics. I will next examine the phenomena of Deer People and shape-shifters in Northern Plains culture and how these half-human and half-deer beings are still an integral part of traditional storytelling and the landscape.

DEER PEOPLE: SPIRIT TRANSFORMATION

The prevalence of shape-shifters in American Indian folk traditions reflects a commonly held belief that an individual can change his or her external form at will. The individuals that wield this much power are usually people who are witches, shamans, or mythological beings.[28] The most powerful story of transformation among the Lakota is that of the White Buffalo Calf Woman, which is also synonymous with the Sacred Pipe religion.[29] In the story, a beautiful woman appears before two Lakota warriors with a bundle on her back. One man has impure thoughts and is killed on the spot. Meanwhile, the other warrior, with good intentions, is allowed to lead the White Buffalo Calf Woman to his village in order for her to present spiritual instruction and the sacred pipe to the tribal elders. After the mysterious woman leaves, she walks a short distance, looks back toward the people, and sits down. When she rises, she has become a young red and brown calf. The calf walks farther, lays down, rolls, and looks back at the people, and when she rises she is a white buffalo. She walks a bit farther, repeats the ritual, and turns black. In her transformed state, White Buffalo Calf Woman walks farther away, stops, bows to the four directions, and disappears over the hill.[30]

Today, the story of White Buffalo Calf Woman is played out through formal and everyday rituals and beliefs. In 1994 a white buffalo calf was born in Janesville, Wisconsin, on the ranch of a non-Indian named Dave Heider. Thousands of people of many faiths visited the calf, named Miracle, testifying that her birth was a call for all races to come together to heal the earth and solve our mutual problems.[31]

In the spring of 1996, two other white buffalo calves were born to an Oglala Lakota Sioux tribal member and rancher, Joe Merrival, on the Pine Ridge Indian Reservation in South Dakota. The first one, Rainbow, died shortly after birth, but the second one, Medicine Wheel, lived long enough for people, including myself, to visit the calf in the summer of 1996.[32] I was working at the SuAnne Big Crow Boys and Girls Club in the town of Pine Ridge at the time and was led to the calf by Melissa Red Cloud in a Winnebago piloted by a white couple from Kansas. When we arrived at Merrival's ranch, he loaded us into pickups and delivered we "pilgrims" to the buffalo herd from as far away as tribal nations in New Mexico and Arizona.

The buffalo were scattered about the field as we dug our hands into the feedbag in the back of the pickup and lay our palms flat so that the buffalo could feast with their rough leathery tongues. Medicine Wheel did not at all resemble a "prophecy come true" so much as a vulnerable newborn calf that could barely stand on its legs as the other buffalo, American Indian, and non-Indian people from across the nation gathered around to pay homage. And, like Miracle, this calf eventually transformed into the four prescribed colors associated with the myth, symbolizing the dawning of a new era.

Deer People are messengers of a different kind. As much as the White Buffalo Calf Woman represents transformation and is central to the religion, Deer People are both a temptation and a threat. Among the tribes of the Northern Plains, Deer People are viewed as tangible phenomena in the same way that the White Buffalo Calf Woman is simultaneously part of the supernatural and the day-to-day world. Each brings a story of transformation and a warning, acting as a potential harbinger of life or death. In particular, the phenomenon of Deer People could easily fall into the larger category of "urban legend" and American popular culture. An urban legend or urban myth is a form of modern folklore consisting of stories thought to be factual by those circulating them. The term is often used to mean something akin to an "apocryphal story." Like all folklore, urban legends are not necessarily fake but are often distorted or exaggerated. Despite its name, a typical urban legend does not necessarily originate in an urban setting; the term is simply used to differentiate a modern legend from traditional folklore. Therefore, sociologists and folklorists such as Jan Harold Brunvand prefer the term "contemporary legend."

The compelling appeal of a typical urban legend is its elements of mystery, horror, fear, or humor. Many urban legends are presented as warnings or cautionary tales, which is the service that traditional Deer People stories continue to provide for Northern Plains people, regardless of whether they have been grafted onto other urban legends, such as the phantom hitchhiker, and so on, that are usually associated with the larger American popular culture.

Whether it is the fabled "Deer Woman" of Ponca City, Oklahoma, who traveled south when the Ponca were removed in the 1870s,[33] or a lone hitchhiker in a remote area of Pine Ridge Indian Reservation in South Dakota, these beings are to be feared. Deer People are purported to be half-human and half-deer and have the power to harm humans, but only if they are foolish enough to pick them up in their vehicle from the side of the road or take them home from a powwow. In *Walking in the Sacred Manner*, the Sioux tribal member Tilda Long Soldier warns, "Some deer can transform themselves into people. If you like a person or have a secret crush on someone, the Deer People can know your thoughts and appear as that person and lead you astray. They can make your mind go crazy. You should be fearful and respectful of all these kind."[34]

The Deer Woman of Ponca City is said to appear only at night and at powwows in human form. She is known for luring unsuspecting young men away from the crowd, and when alone she reveals that she is half-deer by lifting her skirt to reveal her deer legs. The Deer Woman is considered to be both beautiful and dangerous, and it is believed that close contact with her can result only in death.[35]

Among the Sioux Indians of North and South Dakota, it is common knowledge that you never pick up strangers late at night, and in particular in desolate and remote areas of the reservation. There is a shared fear among tribal members that if you do allow such a hitchhiker into your car, you are inviting a Deer Person into your life. Like the tribes of the Southern Plains, the Sioux believe Deer People can cause serious injury or even death to the people with whom they come into contact.[36]

A typical story involves a person driving along a reservation road late at night and coming across a person who is walking alone in the middle of nowhere. For whatever reason, the driver picks the person up. Sometimes it is clear from the moment that the person gets in the car that it is a Deer Person, because the deer legs are exposed. At other times, it is only after the person has been let out that the driver does a double-take and sees him or her turned into a half or full deer. Death or harm usually follows shortly after contact. Sometimes, however, the Deer Person is merely trying to startle the driver of the car.[37]

In the mid-1980s, a tribal police officer on the Pine Ridge Indian Reservation was driving along the highway, doing his usual late-night patrol of the area.[38] He spotted a young man by the side of the road and decided to stop and give him a ride. He let the young man sit in the back of the squad car, and they talked at length. At one point, the young man in the back lit a cigarette and the police officer asked him to put his cigarette out, because it was illegal to smoke in police vehicles. He not only smelled the smoke but could see the cigarette glowing in the rear-view mirror. When the person refused to comply, the officer let him out of the car.[39]

A few minutes later, the police officer again smelled the cigarette burning in the back. He tried to remain calm; as he looked in the rear-view mirror, he saw both the red glow of the cigarette and the young man he had just let out of the car several miles back. He once again asked the young man to put out his cigarette and said that he would stop the car and let him out if he did not comply. This time the young man did not respond, and the officer simply let him out. Quickly pulling away, within minutes the officer spotted the same young man, but this time he was running alongside the car at the same speed as the vehicle. It was then that he realized that his passenger had been a Deer Person, because he could now see his exposed deer legs from the waist down. In this particular instance, the officer lived to tell his story.[40]

The phenomenon of Deer People on the Northern Plains existed even before contact with the dominant society. In some instances, these stories traveled with the tribes as they were removed to Indian Territory in the South. To the people of the plains, these stories educate, dictate morals, and reinforce a strict code of ethics. Yet, at the same time, they are considered tangible and real and cannot be easily cast aside by Western rationalism. Further, the story holds an important place in Native cultures and has multiple purposes for learning and sharing traditional knowledge. A story possesses power, energy, and a life of its own and transcends time and place as the story comes alive again in the minds and ears of the listeners when the storytelling touches the emotions.[41]

SMITHSONIAN INSTITUTION: OBJECTS, POWER, AND PLACE

Among American Indians, another shared belief is that material objects, particularly those objects tied to religion or warfare, resonate with power in the same way that a geographic location can. It is also believed that objects contain stored energy and that, upon release, the spirit of that object is manifested such that the object has a life of its own. This concept is supported by the Native belief that sacred sites exist, trees are living entities, and rivers are alive.[42]

The historian Gregory Evans Dowd further supports this position when he directly links the "power" of objects to warfare. The American Indian concept of war was no simple matter, because it involved a complex series of ritual acts that constituted a ceremony that rectified the spiritual order of Native people. American Indian warriors danced, purified themselves, and relied on charms in order to divine their chances for success, supplicate the chthonic forces for assistance, handle safely the deadly powers in a hostile environment, satisfy the anguished souls of their slain kinsmen, and send their enemies to death and a miserable afterlife. In all these actions Native Americans passed through or communicated across the categorical frontiers that organized their world.[43] Further, ritual ties and ties to objects or "charms" loomed so large in the culture of Indian people because ritual delivered the assistance of sacred powers through these objects or "charms."[44]

Robert Van Pelt corroborates this belief, as he describes how he acquired the "power" of an eagle feather headdress that was given to him by an Umatilla elder:

I can recall my first experience from an early age (seven or eight) learning how to dance in the style of native tradition. There was a celebration in the township of Siletz, Oregon, located in the coastal mountain range of Lincoln County, Oregon. It was in the summer months and it was hot. The native peoples of the region were terminated in 1954. This never stopped the people from coming together and dancing. The regalia would flow in to the Siletz valley, the drums and drummers, the gathering of the people to celebrate the life we lived. It was at this celebration that I was offered a chance to dance. There was a native man from the Umatilla Agency. He had a beautiful eagle feather headdress adorned with a beaded headband. I was admiring it as any curios eight-year-old would do. The man asked if I would like to wear it to dance. I can recall how excited I was to be respected and honored by this man to dance in the eagle feather headdress. I knew nothing of the history of my people, all the trials and tribulations they had endured. Those trials and tribulations, for that moment in time, allowed me to be the evidence to the spiritual triumph of my ancestors. At this age I was never instructed on the way of dance, or any of its meaning. I just put the headdress on and went on my merry way out into the crowd. It all came natural and the heartbeat of the nation lived within the pulsating of blood that surged through my veins.[45]

In this particular situation, the object that acted as the "vessel" for power was transferred to the individual who was meant to inherit the "power." This was not the case, however, for the objects of "power" removed from their homelands and placed in museum collections, far away from the people that were meant to inherit their gifts.

The Pawnee tribal member and historian James Riding In further discusses this dilemma as it relates to the repatriation of objects and human remains:

The Acts committed against deceased Indians have had profound, even harmful, effects on the living. Therefore, as an activist and historian, I have had to develop a conceptual framework for giving meaning and order to conflict. The foundation of my perspective concerning repatriation is derived from a combination of cultural, personal, and academic experiences. An understanding of Pawnee religion and philosophical beliefs about death, gained through oral traditions, dreams, and research, inform my view that repatriation is a social justice movement, supported by Native spirituality and sovereignty, committed to the amelioration of the twin evils of oppression and scientific racism.[46]

According to Pawnee belief, when a grave is disturbed, the spirit becomes restless and cannot be at peace. Wandering spirits often beset the living with both psychological and physical health problems. Traditionally, Pawnee remains would be disinterred only for a compelling religious reason, and not for scientific investigation.

Scientific racism, stemming from several centuries of contact and conflict, and the conditioning of white society to view American Indians as intellectually inferior and even subhuman, contributed to the wide-scale practice of collecting human remains, funerary objects, and other items of cultural patrimony.[47]

As a result, graves were looted without remorse. After the Pawnee were removed from Nebraska to Oklahoma in the 1870s, local settlers, alongside amateur and professional archaeologists, looted Pawnee cemeteries, taking remains and burial offerings. Over time, many of these objects were placed in an array of institutions, including the Nebraska Historical Society, and the Smithsonian Institution.[48]

Thus, for generations Indian country has been "looted" by collectors, scientists, tourists, and soldiers. The 1979 Archaeological Resource Protection Act, passed as an update to the 1906 American Antiquities Act, declared that all Indian bones and objects found on federal land were the property of the United States. This meant that between six hundred thousand and two million skeletal remains were taken to museums, laboratories, historical societies, and universities across the United States. The Smithsonian Institution alone held the remains of 18,500 people. These remains and material objects were arbitrarily displayed or indefinitely held in storage, without consulting the individual tribes or descendants to whom the objects originally belonged. For decades, anthropologists and archaeologists went unchallenged in their pursuit of knowledge about diet, mortuary customs, levels of health, and causes of death.[49]

In the 1970s American Indian activists began to challenge the right of government and private museums to hold the religious objects and other artifacts and skeletal remains of American Indian people. Finally, in 1990, President George H. W. Bush signed into law the Native American Graves Protection and Repatriation Act, requiring all institutions receiving federal funds to inventory their American Indian collections, share the list with Indian tribes, and return requested items to the tribes.[50]

Many American Indian communities are still involved in the ongoing campaign to have skeletal remains and sacred objects returned to them.[51] Outside of cultural patrimony, human respect, and access to knowledge, for many Native Americans it is also a question of health. It is believed by most American Indians that the wrenching of human remains and sacred objects from their proper place may have jeopardized the spiritual well-being and the physical health of communities, and even of the universe.[52] At the October 11, 2008, Gathering of the Eagle Staffs of the Great Lakes Tribes, the guest speaker Dorothea Botimer (a Saginaw Chippewa) of the Ziibiwing Center of Anishinabe Culture and Lifeways of Mount Pleasant, Michigan, specifically referred to the skeletal remains and funerary objects of her ancestors that remained in storage at museums and universities across North America as being "held hostage"[53] under the widespread system of institutionalized spiritual colonialism.

When I worked at the National Museum of Natural History, the Native American collections were in transition because of the inception of the Repatriation Office. The objective that year was to remove all ethnological and archaeological Southwest pottery and Plains Indian objects from the attics of the Natural History building to the Museum Support Center in Suitland, Maryland. This was the first time in roughly one hundred years that these objects had been moved from storage in the upper levels of the museum.

Each unit housed some great "anthropological find" that had been shipped to the museum at the end of the nineteenth century by James Mooney, Franz Boas, or John Wesley Powell. These were the collections of the founders of the field of anthropology, who had worked under the direction of the War Department, the Geological Survey, the Bureau of American Ethnology, or the Smithsonian Institution when anthropology was in its infancy.

As the collections emerged from the attics, so did the stories of haunted halls and the sightings of individual apparitions. These stories were candidly discussed among the security guards and hinted at by the American Indian staff. At the time, there was a consensus among the guards and the American Indian staff that the collections still carried the spirits of the dead, who were either the creators or former owners of the objects.

Traditional tribal members such as James Riding In, Robert Van Pelt, and Dorothea Botimer believe that the "trophies of the Indian wars" retained a spiritual power that may or may not have been dormant for many decades. The power that should have been transferred to a direct descendant of the original owner or creator of the object had never been passed on. Instead, in a sense, the energy was "held hostage" along with the object that acted as the "vessel" for the power. And in turn, these "vessels" of power carried the energy of the land and the people that they represented. Therefore, even though an object, such as the Ghost Dance shirts collected by Mooney in the 1890s, had been removed from the Northern Plains, it still retained the power of the person who created it and the geographic location from whence it came. And just as the power was "held hostage" in museums and private collections, so, too, were Lakota men, women, and children, as they were simultaneously corralled onto reservations, sent to prisons, or shipped off to boarding schools to be educated and assimilated in the wake of the Indian Wars of the post–Civil War era. According to Robert Van Pelt, the objective of the conquerors was to separate the mind from the spirit in order to break the body so that the federal government could systematically seize control of the minds, hearts, and lands of the Indigenous peoples.[54] Part of that equation of total conquest was seizing the sacred and secular objects of the American Indians in order to cripple them spiritually under this new system of spiritual colonialism.

Some of the objects, such as medicine bundles, were religious in nature, while others had more of a secular purpose (children's toys and cradle boards). Regardless of whether the object was used for ceremony or in daily life, from the perspective of traditional tribal people—and some of the guards and museum staff—the objects still "resonated" with power.

According to the guards I spoke to in the fall of 1991, it was quite common to hear the footsteps and voices of the dead while they made their rounds in both the storage areas and in the Native American exhibition halls. In particular, the Plains exhibition area near the statue of Kicking Bear (labeled simply as a "Sioux warrior" even though he was the apostle of the Ghost Dance religion) was considered to be "charged" with activity. One guard was so unnerved by the ghosts that she refused to walk that stretch of the museum alone at night. She said that once she entered the area, she could clearly hear someone "walking in moccasins" behind her, yet when she turned to look, no one was there.

Essentially, what these tales do is corroborate the traditional tribal beliefs posited by individuals such as James Riding In, Robert Van Pelt, and Dorothea Botimer, who believe that the dead do return to haunt the living. Most American Indians believe that these museum objects still resonate with power. Until the physical remains and material objects are returned to the tribes and properly cared for through ceremony—so that those who were meant to inherit the power of the objects will be able to "complete the cycle"—the objects, the people, and the land will not be in balance or at rest.

The controversy and issue of control continue over Indian artifacts being housed in museums or given back to tribes. It is important to remember to respect Indigenous artifacts for they hold the key to understanding traditional knowledge.[55] This issue falls into the larger category of cultural patrimony, spiritual colonialism, and who ultimately controls the "filter" between the American Indian communities and the dominant society in reference to sacred sites, traditional folklore, and material objects. The tribal member Joshua Smith (Paiute/Modoc) from the Warms Springs Indian Reservation in Oregon takes this dialogue one step further by expanding it to include the larger issues of sovereignty and the empowerment of American Indian people:

> Many reservations are like other countries that rely on tourism as a source of income. The place that visitors see is one that will comfort the guests into thinking that they are in paradise while just across the fence many are struggling with very poor living conditions. . . . It is atrocious that we as a nation are able to force people into live or die situations and then fault them for their choices or lack thereof. There are many "chains" that keep Native Americans scrounging for table scraps. It is not until we break this chain and make our spot at the table [that we] as a people [will] truly be free.[56]

Tribal peoples of the Northern Plains perpetually perform a balancing act between two parallel and paradoxical worlds: that of the day-to-day and the supernatural, and that of the Indian and the non-Indian. The spirit world is tangibly reflected in the land and is reinforced through oral traditions, beliefs, objects, and ceremonies within the tribal communities. Ritual provides access to the otherworld and is maintained by songs, sacred objects, order, and ceremonial communications that are at the basis of the manifestation of power. Shape-shifters or Deer People, ghosts, and material objects can provide that point of contact between the two worlds when the "door" swings open in either direction.

Judith Richardson, in her study of place and cultural hauntings, defines the supernatural as the relationship between ghosts and language, ghosts and memory, and ghosts and history. Further, she states that ghosts often represent the things that words have not expressed—or cannot express. They emanate from and embody the blank spaces between words in historical narratives.[57] The Creek Indian poet Joy Harjo expresses this relationship between land, memory, blood, and belief in her poem "New Orleans." Typical of most Native American literature, art, music, and traditional storytelling, the supernatural is addressed indirectly, and what is implied is as important as what is stated. She writes:

I have a memory.
It swims deep in blood,
a delta in the skin. It swims out of Oklahoma,
deep the Mississippi River. It carries my
feet to these places: the French Quarter,
stale rooms, the sun behind thick and moist
clouds, and I hear boats hauling themselves up
and down the river

My spirit comes here to drink
My spirit comes here to drink
Blood is the undercurrent.

There are voices buried in the Mississippi
mud. There are ancestors and future children
buried beneath the currents stirred up by
pleasure boats going up and down.
There are stories here made of memory.[58]

NOTES

1. Hirschfelder and Molin, *Encyclopedia of Native American Religions*, 97.
2. Hirschfelder and Molin, *Encyclopedia of Native American Religions*, 97.
3. Fixico, *American Indian Mind in a Linear World*, 71.
4. Fixico, *American Indian Mind in a Linear World*, 92.
5. St. Pierre and Long Soldier, *Walking in the Sacred Manner*, 108–9.
6. St. Pierre and Long Soldier, *Walking in the Sacred Manner*, 104.
7. Mankiller, *Every Day Is a Good Day*, 165.
8. Mankiller, *Every Day Is a Good Day*, 55.
9. Lowie, *Indians of the Plains*, 154.
10. Lowie, *Indians of the Plains*, 154.
11. Basso, *Wisdom Sits in Place*, 107.
12. Irwin, *Dream Seekers*, 26–27.
13. Irwin, *Dream Seekers*, 26–27.
14. Irwin, *Dream Seekers*, 26–27.
15. Fixico, *American Indian Mind in a Linear World*, 70.
16. Lewis, *Medicine Men*, 43.
17. Nabokov, *Native American Testimony*, 253.
18. Nabokov, *Native American Testimony*, 253.
19. This commission further gave him an opportunity to study the "Messiah Craze," which led him to interview individuals and collect items from any tribe associated with the Ghost Dance Religion (Paiute, Sioux, Cheyenne, Arapaho, etc.) from Indian Territory, to South Dakota, and eventually the Far West.
20. Mooney, *Ghost Dance Religion and Wounded Knee*, 653–54.
21. Van Pelt, Interviewer Cynthia L. Landrum, Portland OR, Fall 2008.
22. Ruby and Brown, *Dreamer Prophets*, 9.
23. The Ghost Dance originated in Nevada among the Paiute Indians in the late 1880s, with Wovoka as the central prophet. His beliefs, however, had ties to earlier more regional movements under the leadership of the Dreamer Prophets such as Smohalla (Wanapum) with the Washat religion of the Columbia River People. At the end of 1888, Wovoka became ill with fever, and on January 1, 1889, an eclipse of the sun occurred. During that time Wovoka had a religious experience, where he was taken to the spirit

world and was told that the earth would be renewed, the Indian dead would
return to life, and misery and death would end if they followed the revelations he received. He further stated that the people should be industrious,
at peace with the whites, not engage in stealing and lying, and to perform a
ritual dance for five days and nights. By 1890 it had spread to almost every
tribe in the West and it was the Sioux warrior Kicking Bear who became the
apostle of the religion among his people in the Dakotas.

24. Crow Dog, *Lakota Woman*, 161.

25. Big Crow, Interviewer Cynthia L. Landrum, Pine Ridge SD, Spring
2001.

26. "Why We Must Return to Wounded Knee," *Oregonian*, 16 May
2004.

27. Basso, *Wisdom Sits in Place*, 107.

28. Kluckhon and Leighton, *The Navajo*, 128.

29. Brown, *Sacred Pipe*, 3–9.

30. Brown, *Sacred Pipe*, 9.

31. www.merceronline.com/native/native05htm.

32. www.merceronline.com/native/native05htm.

33. Wright, *Guide to the Tribes of Oklahoma*, 1951.

34. St. Pierre and Long Soldier, *Walking in the Sacred Manner*, 70.

35. Holly and Landon Young, Interviewer Cynthia L. Landrum, Stillwater
OK, Spring 1996.

36. Big Crow, Interviewer Cynthia L. Landrum, Vermillion SD, Spring
1994.

37. Big Crow, Spring 1994.

38. Big Crow, Spring 1994.

39. Big Crow, Spring 1994.

40. Big Crow, Spring 1994.

41. Fixico, *American Indian Mind in a Linear World*, 36.

42. Fixico, *American Indian Mind in a Linear World*, 73.

43. Dowd, *Spirited Resistance*, 11.

44. Dowd, *Spirited Resistance*, 11.

45. Van Pelt, Fall 2008.

46. Hurtado and Iverson, *Major Problems in American Indian History*,
490–91.

47. Hurtado and Iverson, *Major Problems in American Indian History*,
490–91.

48. Hurtado and Iverson, *Major Problems in American Indian History*,
490–91.

49. Calloway, *First Peoples*, 502.

50. Calloway, *First Peoples*, 503.

51. Outside of the Pawnee, two other tribes challenged the museum com-

munity for the return of their objects, the Zunis and the Iroquois. The Zunis of New Mexico demanded the return of carved wooden gods from museums and private collections. They pointed out that since the war gods were communally owned and could not be sold or given away, that any god that had been removed from their proper shrines were considered stolen property. The Zuni considered them the spiritual guardians of their people, and when they were removed from their shrines the Zuni religious leaders could not pray to them. As a result, their cast powers caused fires, wars, storms, and wanton destruction of the world. Once recovered, the gods could be placed in the desert and continue the cycle of decay back to earth. The Iroquois also demanded the return of twelve belts from the New York State Museum to be held on Onondaga, where other Iroquois Confederacy records were kept. The twelve belts were finally restored to Onondaga chiefs in a ceremony in Albany, New York, in 1989.

52. Calloway, *First Peoples*, 502.
53. www.nationtalk.com/modules/news/article.
54. Van Pelt, Fall 2008.
55. Fixico, *American Indian Mind in a Linear World*, 139.
56. Smith, Interviewer Cynthia L. Landrum, Portland OR, 2008.
57. Richardson, *Possessions*, 26.
58. Harjo, "New Orleans," 212.

BIBLIOGRAPHY

Basso, Keith H. *Wisdom Sits in Place: Landscape and Language among the Western Apache*. Albuquerque: University of New Mexico Press, 1996.

Brown, Joseph Epes. *The Sacred Pipe: Black Elk's Account of the Seven Sacred Rites of the Oglala Sioux*. Norman: University of Oklahoma Press, 1953.

Calloway, Colin. *First Peoples: A Documentary Survey of American Indian People*. Boston: Bedford/St. Martins, 2004.

Crow Dog, Mary. *Lakota Woman*. New York: Harper Collins, 1990.

Dowd, Gregory Evans. *A Spirited Resistance: The North American Indian Struggle For Unity, 1745–1815*. Baltimore MD: John Hopkins University Press, 1992.

Fixico, Donald L. *The American Indian Mind in a Linear World*. New York: Routledge, 2003.

Harjo, Joy. "New Orleans," *Words in the Blood*. New York: Meridian Books, 1984.

Hirschfelder, Arlene, and Paulette Molin, eds. *The Encyclopedia of Native American Religions: A Comprehensive Guide to the Spiritual Traditions and Practices of North American Indians*. New York: MJF Books, 1992.

Hurtado, Albert, and Peter Iverson, eds. *Major Problems in American Indian History*. Boston: Houghton Mifflin, 2001.

Irwin, Lee. *The Dream Seekers: Native American Visionary Traditions of the Great Plains*. Norman: University of Oklahoma Press, 1994.

Kluckhon, Clyde, and Dorothea Leighton. *The Navajo*. London: Oxford University Press, 1958.

Lewis, Thomas H. *The Medicine Men: Oglala Sioux Ceremony and Healing*. Lincoln: University of Nebraska Press, 1990.

Lowie, Robert H. *Indians of the Plains*. Lincoln: University of Nebraska Press, 1954.

Mankiller, Wilma. *Every Day Is a Good Day: Reflections by Contemporary Indigenous Women*. Golden CO: Fulcrum, 2004.

Mooney, James. *The Ghost Dance Religion and Wounded Knee*. Mineola NY: Dover Publications, 1973.

Nabokov, Peter. *Native American Testimony*. New York: Penguin Books, 1991.

Richardson, Judith. *Possessions: The History of Hauntings in the Hudson River Valley*. Cambridge MA: Harvard University Press, 2003.

Ruby, Robert H., and John A. Brown. *Dreamer Prophets of the Columbia River Plateau: Smohalla and Skolaskin*. Norman: University of Oklahoma Press, 1989.

St. Pierre, Mark, and Tilda Long Soldier. *Walking in the Sacred Manner*. New York: Simon & Schuster, 1995.

"Why We Must Return to Wounded Knee," *Oregonian*, May 16, 2004.

Wright, Muriel H. *A Guide to the Tribes of Oklahoma*. Norman: University of Oklahoma Press, 1951.

10

Ancestors, Ethnohistorical Practice, and the Authentication of Native Place and Past

C. JILL GRADY

At the turn of the twenty-first century, scholars produced a series of analyses that addressed the literary works written about Native American ghosts (Brogan 1998, Bergland 2000, Richardson 2003). These critics constructed the analyses by relying primarily upon the Euro-Western philosophical and social theories of Freud and Marx, with scant attention given to the extant ethnohistorical and anthropological analyses that pertain to cross-cultural and multicultural studies. Anthropologists and ethnohistorians have long recognized the significant roles played by ghosts in Native American social organizations and belief systems, though they hesitate to apply analytical theories to those roles. It is my intent here to introduce and inject several anthropological principles of cultural relevance and relativity into the recent literary criticisms of Native ghosts, by contrasting and comparing some of the cultural constructions or realities offered within both disciplines.

MARX AND FREUD IN NATIVE AMERICA

Within literary disciplines, the Native American ghosts described in novels, historic documents, and storytelling have been studied (Richardson 2003), analyzed (Bergland 2000), and psychoanalyzed and defined (Brogan 1998) using Western social theories. The analyses provide rich resources for anthropological investigations of the subject and an enhanced perspective on a somewhat silent anthropological stance surrounding analyses of Native American ghosts. Infusing these analyses with anthropological data may also expand perspectives on the analytical bounds of Marxist and Freudian theories.

Renée L. Bergland (2000) traces a Native American ghost discourse through American literature from 1620 into the early nineteenth century. It was in Bergland's *National Uncanny: Indian Ghosts and American Subjects* that I read and learned about the writing of William Apess, a mixed-blood white, Pequot Indian, and African American minister whose "autobiographical writings . . . [and] sermons . . . countered the discourse of disappearance and spectralization" of Native Americans so prevalent in the imagination of American readers during the early 1800s (122). Apess asserted his existence as a living Pequot writer and practicing Christian believer, thereby challenging the oppressive contemporary ideas of "vanishing Indians" and extinct Pequots. Bergland invokes a Foucauldian–Marxist model of language as a culturally hegemonic agent of social control, arguing that the literary discourse of Native Americans' spectralization, popular during Apess's lifetime, worked to enforce the uneven power relations between "Indians" and whites. Bergland assumes that Apess had psychologically repressed the ghostly discourse of "Indians" in his early writings, then later inverted it in order to resist and reverse its effectiveness (121).

Apess's final published work, "Eulogy on King Philip" (1836), provides insight specifically useful for anthropological studies. Apess eulogized the long-dead Mashpee warrior, Philip, by bringing him back to life and bestowing immortality on him, calling him a better person than the Puritan colonizers against whom he rebelled in 1676. According to Bergland, Apess's writing controverted the "Indian" spectralization of the early 1800s by refusing to portray "Indians" as evanescent or extinct (2000, 143). Instead, Apess insisted that the authentic original possessors of the land remained in these places and had not died out. They may have been burned out of their homes and cheated out of their lands, but they had not disappeared.

Little has changed in the dominant discourse since the 1800s, when Apess struggled to define his Native American identity against this discourse of the "vanishing Indian." The same discourse continues to juxtaposition itself within U.S. "Indian" policies and Native Americans' cultural identities. Today, as during Apess's time, the dominant discourse on Native Americans endures as a discourse of the dead. Those who no longer speak their native languages, practice their traditional arts, maintain their ancestral political structures, or wear traditional clothes are considered to be inauthentic "Indians." Moreover, the dominant discourse further requires that when Native Americans have official dealings with outside, non-Native entities, the measures of evidence for valid "Indianness" should be provided from the dead.

Accurate, reliable, and valid substantiations of "Indian" existence must be obtained through archaeological assessments of vanished communities; the historical accounts and maps created by people who are long dead; the oral histories, genealogies and court testimonies of deceased Native peoples; and records created by governmental entities and/or officials that no longer exist. In contrast, most Native peoples today, like Apess in the 1800s, rely upon evidence of vital living people who are in contact with the ongoing living spirits of their ancestors. This living counter-evidence, though perceived as spectral and unempirical by the dominant culture, actually lives on, thriving and affirming numerous tribal identities in perpetuity within their traditional practices and places. For Native people, such vitality verifies and authenticates "Indianness."

Moreover, for Coast Salish peoples, the group with whom I work, imposing the dominant discourse of the dead requires an additional unreliable measurement of validity, written documents. Not only do archival documents contain words written by dead people, most Native American groups on the Northwest Coast have not had positive historical experiences with written documents. As Crisca Bierwert found, "Coast people have experienced fixed texts—legal agreements, survey boundaries, fishing allocations, and ethnographic documentation—as being applied firmly to them and flexibly to others" (1999, 112). Instead, they prefer orality, and this is demonstrated throughout their religious ceremonies, wherein no speeches or stories are written in advance. It is "speaking from the heart alone" (112) that has value. Written accounts are judged to be comparatively lifeless and suspicious. Northwest Coast people question the measurements of reliability, accuracy, and validity that are so commonly associated with the written documents used to validate the dominant discourse. Such documents have a shared history of betrayal, of rescinding rights and silencing ancestral speakers (121).

GHOSTS IN THE FIELD

Reading about William Apess's resistance to the discourse of the dead assisted me with fieldwork and the analysis of data in my consulting work for the Stillaguamish Tribe in Washington State. After decades of struggling with the loss of their original lands, members of this tribe are now working with consultants to gather the tribe's cultural resources and construct a tribal cultural center.[1] Most of the tribal consultants are hired from area universities and come to the project offering the usual volumes of historical documents, archaeological reports, cartographies, and ethnohistorical journals relevant to the scope of historical research. Over a period of eighteen months, I worked as an anthropological consultant, along with other consultants to the tribe. Together, the consultants and tribal personnel organized and surveyed written documentation for its cultural resource significance in the reorganization of the Stillaguamish peoples' history. Historic sites revealed in the archival data were visited by the consultants with cultural resource personnel, plotted on a map, then coalesced within an interactive computer GIS ArcView archival-mapping program.[2]

During the early stages of site visits, tribal personnel participation was substantial and enthusiastic. Within a few months, however, that participation had declined and only the consultants were going out into the field. As enthusiasm waned and participants remained unavailable, I attempted to survey tribal individuals concerning their lack of interest. In response, one elder asked to take us to some sites based upon a personal evaluation of cultural significance. Over the course of several months, we proceeded to include visits to places along the Stillaguamish River that had not been documented in our archival research. All of the original participants were now again in attendance, enthusiastic and eager to pursue tribal history.

At certain sites, the elder took me aside to explain personal feelings. The elder described physical sensations whenever we neared a significant spot, asserting that ancestors were most likely buried here. The elder described feeling very warm and placed hands on mine so that I could confirm the heat. We also visited various landscape markers that were claimed to be significant because they communicated significance to the elder in a way that was described as "powerful feelings." It was clear that the other participants respected the elder's knowledge of significant sites as they strongly supported that requests for the sites be included. The sites were authenticated by obvious connections to the elder's knowledge, both ethnohistorical and spiritual. These cultural resource designations were considered to be as valid as any of the sites we had included based solely on archival and archaeological data.

If I pushed for explanation, the elder could or would not explain what was happening, dismissing such encounters with the uncanny as inexplicable. For the professional consultants these sites introduced technological challenges for interfacing and cross-referencing the archival data and mapping within the undocumented dimension of the computer program. Eventually, however, the uncanny sites gained equivalent research weight. During a construction project the following year, one of the elder's designated sites was confirmed as the location of multiple tribal burials more than 150 years old.

SOCIAL CONSTRUCTIONS OF AUTHENTICITY

Within Western constructs of both the social and natural sciences, empirical measurements of accuracy, reliability, and validity are the most acceptable. Anthropologists recognize that scientific acceptance does not always convey meaning cross-culturally (Harkin 1994, 194), and consequently, those of us who work outside our own cultures are admonished to be cautious when seeking to "understand complex, multiple perceptions of reality" (Lomawaima and McCarty 2002, 2). In this vein, there have been anthropological cross-cultural investigations into the notions of validity and authenticity that have sought to clarify cultural contrasts in meanings. These investigations have variously demonstrated that notions of authenticity tend to be historically specific (Raibmon 2005), culturally specific (Grady 1998), power-driven (Sheffield 1997), and market-driven (Steiner 1994, 1995), as well as socially negotiated (Eco 1990, Bendix 1997). Groups of people, through a process of social agreement over time and space, appear to select and impose culturally specific criteria for determining what is authentic, valid, and real.

For anthropologists who not only write about Native Americans but also interact with them, issues surrounding the authenticity of ghosts and the privacy of sources raise concerns about these peoples' sacred belief systems and the ethical representation of their cultures. Consequently, numerous silences exist within cultural studies, from both those who study and also their subjects (Krupat 1992, 30–31). Scholars of history, anthropology, and the arts have also been put under the microscope over the past several decades regarding their biases within critiques of representation (Myers 1988, 610). Ethnographers have been criticized for producing works that purport to describe reality without including or explaining their intervention in the group they study. Because of such criticisms, ethnographers have become more aware of positioning themselves within their writing and, thus, they frequently choose to remain silent on many issues. The reasons anthropologists have avoided analyzing Native American ghosts could be related to our new increased awareness and/or to our degree of involvement with our subjects. Even as I write about this effort to more fully explain the appearance of ghosts in the Stillaguamish landscape, I am faced with an uneasiness that does not stem from any dominant Western social science explanations, such as my repressed white guilt regarding "Indians" (Bergland 2000, 11) and/or its consequent obsessions (16–22). My discomfort has more to do with the imposition of such explanations upon the attempts to understand other cultures.

Interpretations of cultural phenomena are generally considered strengthened by cross-cultural comparison and explorations into the interpretations of others, including literary critics. As James Cifford wrote, "There are no natural or intrinsic disciplines. All knowledge is interdisciplinary" (1997, 59). However insightful it was to learn from the writings of William Apess, I felt uneasy with the subsequent applications of Western interpretations, such as Freud's assertions about loss and mourning (Brogan 1998, 19–29), which were being applied to the conjuring of "Indian" ghosts. Loss and mourning do not increase my understanding of the Native elder's preference to rely on the presence of ghosts as an overriding measurement of accuracy and validity. This is true especially because ghosts have been documented on the Northwest Coastal landscape since the 1700s during the exceedingly prosperous Indigenous times of maritime trade, rather than solely during the postcolonial times of so-called loss and mourning.

Openly writing about the details of Native American cultural hauntings actually has little to do with my subconscious or that of any tribal members. Instead, it is the very introduction and application of the subconscious that drives my uneasiness. The explanatory power of the unconscious introduces an additional layer of Western discourse and social construction to the uncanny (Ricoeur 1970). Psychoanalytic speculations about Native spirits and other spiritualities are mostly disregarded by those who support them. Apess and the elder I accompanied would likely agree that imposing dead European authorities, such as Freud and Marx, into analyses of Native American ghosts serves to merely extend the dominant discourse of the dead, rather than explain it. The insight I acquired from exploring literary criticisms of American ghost literature is not diminished, but it becomes culturally selective if I'm asked to apply Western theories and analyses. I am unable to completely dispose of my anthropological lens when addressing the ideas of others.

My unease also has to do with a conscious responsibility to ethically represent the ghosts of others. My feelings arise from interacting with people who share their lives with me, hope to have their beliefs understood by me. Because I provide them a requisite voice, they trust that I will get it right. I become the "ghost as go-between . . . moving between one culture and another" (Brogan 1998, 6), straddling the margins of borders and boundaries the way ghosts are portrayed in the literature as doing. I not only work in intercultural spaces, I work in the space between writing fiction and writing ethnography, simultaneously creating cultural artifacts and critiquing them, analogous to that which the literary critics have determined for the subconscious conjuring of "Indian" ghosts in American literature.

This is where my uneasiness comes from. Unlike the "Indian" ghosts who are treated by literary critics as mere metaphors of mediation, ethnographers materially exist in the mediation of cultural exchange. They not only observe from a distance, but also participate within the social negotiations of meaning. In American literature, ghosts slip easily back and forth between cultures and contexts with few personal consequences. Outside of that literature, actual people and their cultural knowledge cannot. When the analyses of "Indian" ghosts taken from works of literary art turn on the social theories of Marx and Freud for their existences, then they, too, beg the old ethnographic questions: Whose art? Whose culture? Who gets to decide?

ETHNOHISTORIC EVIDENCE

Within the analyses of Native American ghost literature, "ghosts tend to materialize when the old social bonds have loosened" (Brogan 1998, 20). Evidently, that is when the subconscious kicks in. Yet, a significant component of the dominant historic discourse demonstrates that ghosts materialized routinely on the Northwest Coast during the years when the "old social bonds" of the Indigenous peoples were at their strongest, not loosened. Both Native peoples and the factual evidence of the dominant discourse (Jewitt 1807, Suttles 1998) agree on this. During the maritime fur trade of the late 1700s and into the 1800s, West Coast Native societies continued along preexisting lines, and their interaction with the European fur traders actually intensified traditional patterns (Cole and Darling 1990, 119). The effects of earliest contact have been shown to be generally beneficial and culturally stimulating (Drucker 1943, 27; Wike 1951, 106); there were virtually no violent conflicts between European traders and Northwest Coast "Indians" (Cole and Darling 1990, 127). Cultures went on as before the arrival of foreigners (Coppock 1969, 133); it was change that the "Indians" directed, and therefore their culture remained intact (Fisher 1977, 47).

Unlike during the maritime fur trade on the Northwest Coast, conflict was common on the Northeast Coast between eastern Iroquois "Indians" and white trapping parties, who posed a direct economic threat (Fisher 1977, 39). Absent such outside conflict, Northwest Coast ceremonies, rites of passage, and ritual paraphernalia flourished during the profitable trade era. This is well documented. Most of these practices continue today, though not unchanged. We know that ghosts played significant roles in Northwest cultures for decades before colonization, with its resultant losses and mournings that may or may not have conjured ghosts in other parts of North America. In spite of differences in cultural beliefs among specific Indigenous groups, Native American ghosts on the Northwest Coast have generally contributed significantly to Indigenous peoples' existence and survival.

According to Harkin (1994), the people living on the Northwest Coast conceive of individual personhood as connected to forms and stages of being, beyond the living individual (193). In contrast to Western ideas such as body versus soul or individual versus society, these forms and stages of being are not opposites but rather are interconnected and continuous (196). Temporality is thus expanded and extends beyond the individual person's lifespan. Death is but one stage of being, and various rebirths are possible (197–205). Birth, or rebirth, of the soul depends on the relationship between the world of living humans and other (antithetical) worlds. Ghosts play a role in most such transformations, as they occupy an underworld that is a stopping-off point on the way to rebirth (202). The underworld is known as the land of the dead, and the continued existence of the society of the living depends on it (204). Some individual Northwest groups believe in dual souls, with one soul becoming a ghost while the other begins the process of reincarnation (202). The fundamental fact of Northwest Coastal existence is transformation from one world to another (205). An important part of such fundamentalism, or way of being, requires the living to remember the dead (207). Harkin elaborates: "The act of remembering the dead, remembering ancestors, paradoxically ensures their continued life. The existence of the house, lineage or clan can only be maintained by the consciousness of the living. This memory is a duty to the mythical ancestors and other predecessors" (207).

Northwest Coast rituals are routinely performed in observance of this duty. Today, potlatches are "still linking the living and the dead through various forms of ceremonial exchange and strong emotional bonds" (Kan 1986, 208). Sergei Kan (208, n.10) further quotes Joyce Wike: "A continuity in the relationship of the dead to the living is one important reflection of the familiar Northwest Coast emphasis upon inherited position, ancestral pride, and the recognition of gene-alogies. The nature of this continuity is structured by the belief that the rewards and the status of ranking of real life are maintained or intensified in life after death. Existing along with these beliefs . . . are ideas that physical and ritual contacts with the dead will insure personal success" (Kan 1986, 98, quoting Wike 1952).

Despite decades of attempts by the Canadian and U.S. govern-ments, the Christian church, and many missionary groups to outlaw Indigenous physical and ritual contact with the dead, Northwest Coast potlatches, spirit dancing, and traditional winter ceremonies persisted, albeit underground and out of notice of the dominant authorities (Kew 1990, 476). However, once outside threats dimin-ished, participation increased. As Kew noted, "Since the 1950s, the absolute number of dancers has grown rapidly" (1990, 479).

Within contemporary Northwest Coast ceremonies, the ghosts of the dead are rigorously cared for, ritually fed and clothed (Kew 1990, 479; see also Bierwert 1999, 183–86), and, although some of the rituals have incorporated elements of Christian services, they mostly preserve Indigenous beliefs about the dead and rely on ritu-alists to attend to the dead and their possessions (Kew 1990, 476).

The living bodies of Native people in this region remain inextri-cably linked to the world of ghosts and souls. Their very bones, in life and after death, sustain and determine the futures of their lin-eages (Mauzé 1994, 202; Kelm 1998, 85). Should human bones be disturbed, they are strictly and dutifully attended to with a cer-emonious and respectful reburial. A synedochical reinforcement of caring for bones is expressed in nearly all Northwest Coast shared ceremonies, such as the First Salmon Ceremony, which requires the return of salmon bones into the water, thus ensuring the salmons' revival (Gunther 1926, 615).

The Stillaguamish people have never waivered from their resolute duty to their ancestors' remains—not before, during, or after colonization; not as their land was being confiscated; and not while they mourned their dead or faced the dispersal of their communities. They have spent the last 150 years of white settlement continually reburying the bones of their dead, which have been repeatedly disturbed by development and farming and/or flood control projects along their river.[3] The reasons they give for reburial are confined to heritage, tradition, and duty. This calls for a less dichotomized explanation of ghosts, one that relinquishes the meta-narrative of outside domination and replaces it with ongoing culturally specific knowledge and truths (Krupat 1992, 43–44; Boyd 2006, 350). Measurements of reliability, validity, and accuracy are culturally specific (Grady 1998, 254–55), and each culture will determine and assert its own expressions and measurements of authenticity (Raibmon 2005, 207).

AUTHENTIC GHOSTS

As Paige Raibmon has concluded, "The notion that all things Aboriginal were of the past was a critical element of the colonial discourse of authenticity" (2005, 202). Over time, the dominant discourse asserted modernity to be exclusively associated with the West. Loss became associated with cultural others, those who retained their underlying "authentic being" but were in constant danger of losing it through the processes of colonization (Bendix 1997, 26). Not only was the past a critical element of the dominant discourse during Native American colonization, but it remains a critical element of the contemporary dominant discourse regarding Native American authenticity and validity.

The past continues to play a major role in substantiating evidence used for authenticating Native peoples' existences. Today, many examples of ongoing "Indian" policy making, such as the 1990 Indian Arts and Crafts Act, have found themselves mired in the subjective cultural criteria used to authenticate people and objects.

Enforcing this act and others requires that American Indian identity either "is/is not" (Sheffield 1997, 147) authentic by relying on the amount of "Indian blood" one has inherited form the past. Persistently, the resolutions of contemporary land and resource disputes rest upon legal tests of authentic past identity such as speaking the Indigenous language, wearing traditional dress, and adhering to original customs (Clifford 1988, Tollefson 1992, Barsh 2008, Harmon 2008. Treaty rights, such as Makah Tribal whaling rights, are disputed on the basis that the tribe no longer hunts whales using paddles and canoes or handmade harpoons and lines instead using modern equipment to hunt (Raibmon 2005, 2). As Apess first asserted in 1835, the dominant discourse of American Aboriginals' dead-past is alive and well and still considered a reliable, valid, and legal substantiation of "Indian" authenticity.

The actual semantic concept of authenticity, however, is a semiotic conundrum, described by the semanticist Umberto Eco as "a process of instinctive procedures based mostly on social agreement" (1990, 200). It is precisely its prerequisite social agreement that confines the concept's definition to culturally specific meanings. For the Native elder who approached me, authentic ancestral ghosts exist in the material world with physical proof. In Euro-Western thought, ghosts exist outside the material world, being found only in the imagination and/or the subconscious. However, within the study of logic, the absence of evidence is not evidence of absence (Sagan 1995). In other words, in order to assert that ghosts do not exist in the material world, one must have examined an absolutely genuine material ghost and confirmed its authenticity with the same proof techniques that "one uses to say that the reproduction differs from the original" (Eco 1990, 192). A lack of authenticity cannot be defined without confirming the authenticity of its opposite, in this case a material ghost.

CONCLUSION

As an anthropologist working in the field, exchanging ideas with Native Americans, I am situated between two domains. One is the non-Western domain of multiple realisms that contain "irreducible elements" (Faris 2002, 102) existing outside of Western science, and the other is the domain of the Western black-and-white belief system of empirical truths.[4] I know that the Native elder knows that neither of us can adequately explain the appearance of ghosts. We each search for what anthropologists call "secondary explanation" (Boas 1940), wherein both the elder and I must rethink our respective cultures' understandings of the situation. We know we do not fully share the same realisms. The ghosts of ancestors were included in the historical dialectics of the Stillaguamish and all Northwest Coast people long before the historical dialectics of their colonial displacement and discursive impoverishment. For this reason, the elder's reliance on the authentic physical appearance of ghosts is not merely a reaction to the dominant discourse, although it may articulate with the dominant discourse as needed for survival. Native Americans on the Northwest Coast incorporated portions of the dominant discourse in order to make a living and avoid starvation. Raibmon writes, "Aboriginal people did not exercise much control over the terms of this discourse, but they often manipulated it to their benefit" (2005, 198). Potlatches, intertribal gatherings, heredity rights, and other traditional ways of Native life were interwoven within the new labor constraints of tourism, harvesting by migrant laborers, and trinket manufacturing that were thrust upon Native peoples as they were forced to adhere to their newly imposed identities as peoples of the past. Raibmon continues, "Despite colonial claims to the contrary, the authenticity of Aboriginal life lay not in the mindless mechanical reproduction of age-old rituals, but in the fresh generation of meaningful ways to identify . . . within a changing and increasingly modern age" (199).

Like potlatches, intertribal gatherings, and other traditions, ghosts have not been surrendered but have instead been consciously re-articulated within the new circumstances and identities of the modern age. When they are not making overt appearances in Native American literature, ghosts are covertly segregated into the long-houses, smokehouses, and private lives of Northwest Coast peoples. While Native ghosts may now travel by automobile to the supermarkets of today (Boyd, this volume, 185), they have been mostly silenced by the dominant discourse. Still, they have retained their traditional significance and resilience as vital components of the regeneration of Indigenous existence. Along with the spiritual beings of the dominant society, they are now forcibly segregated into the private domain of religious existence where they are shared with other believers, as a matter of personal and communal salvation.

The Western discourse of the dead as it is continually used for authenticating Native American identities resonates comfortably with my understanding of Western culture. Yet, it provides merely one half of my understanding when negotiating meaning between cultures. If asked to explain my understanding of Native ghosts, how they function, what they represent, their empirical irreducibility, or their psychological source, I must slip into the domain of Western concepts of understanding, wherein the world is knowable and thus "conquerable" (Eng and Kazanjian 2002, 17–19). And I must ignore those domains in which the world is seen to be constantly unfolding. My attempts to explain Indian ghosts will fail, but I know that they are more than creations of loss and melancholia or "reactive inventions of what remains with which to rewrite the past" (4). I also recognize that when Native Americans attempt to resist the imposition of such Western hegemonic meanings, their resistance is also redefined by the dominant discourse.[5]

Anthropology has chosen to remain mostly silent on analyzing Native American ghosts, not merely in order to ethically respect the cultures they study, but also to recognize the differing categories of understanding that exist outside Western rhetoric, many of which are yet to be established. By recognizing ghosts on the Stillaguamish landscape, the elder remained duty-bound as a Coast Salish person to honor and protect the ancestors according to traditions. While we were immersed in the dominant discourse of past history and archival documentation, the elder introduced the ghosts to me. The appearances of ghosts in the field subverted the dominant discourse. It was not done as an act of resistance or subconscious urgings, but to convey authentic cultural knowledge within "spiritual considerations of ancestral place" (Miller 1999, 45). Acknowledging ghosts is acknowledging concern and caring for the dead and remembering the ancestors to "paradoxically" ensure their continued life and the lives of tribal lineages. It is an act of cultural survival, and as such, one of the goals of our joint project.

By borrowing theories of Freud and Marx from social science, literary analyses of Native American ghosts have enabled more insightful anthropological analyses. These literary analyses have unintentionally revealed the ongoing roles that European colonizers continue to play in cultural haunting. When literary critiques incorporate Western social sciences, new perspectives on old ideas are more easily recognized. For Western audiences, the murkiness of ghosts is dissipated by imposing Marx and Freud into the discourse. Applying Western social theories to the appearances of ghosts provides more familiar and authoritative interpretations for Western audiences than do the interpretations of non-Western peoples.

Under the explanatory umbrella of Western social science, Indian ghosts become universalized entities that all function in the same way and appear for the same reasons. The historic specificities of diverse cultural ghosts become homogenized within a generalized Western subconscious as a creative response to repressed guilt and loss through the psychological release of writing. Discussing writing about culture, Clifford (1988, 22) has concluded: "Translations of culture, however subtle or inventive in textual form, take place within relations of weak and strong languages that govern the international flow of knowledge." The result is often a promulgation of the dominant discourse because "engagement with colonial agents and categories—whether acquiescent, collaborative or defiant—further entrench colonial hegemony" (Raibmon 2005, 10). Ethnographic texts underwent intense examination several decades ago for these reasons and were determined to be in crisis. Because analyzing cultures within Western modes of knowledge reifies the analyses, ultimately we learn more about the analyzer than about the cultures being analyzed.

Literary critics have now picked up the ethnographic slack and determined that using Native voices in ghost stories is an attempt to destabilize the realism of the colonizing powers. However, these critics introduce other colonial realisms, such as displacement (Bergland 2000, 3), invisibility (Brogan 1998, 30–31), and silence (71). If these new colonial realisms are to be accepted, then within their newly introduced dialectics, "the older realism is already enacting a form of censorship" (Wood 2002, 11). Though reinterpreted, the constructs of the dominant discourse remain in control. Native Americans remain displaced, invisible, and silent, as dead or ghostly as in the previous colonial discourse. To communicate meaning within this new realism, Western realities and material ideas are still required to define the ghosts, if only to elucidate their irreducible elements through more acceptable irreducible Freudian analyses.[6] There is no easy way for the Native elder or me, the anthropologist, to comprehensively explain what was experienced during visits to the sites along the river. Within the re-articulated dialectics of neocolonial discourse, the term "ghost" is being semantically reduced because of its continued contingency on dominant Western discourse for definition and validity, wherein essentialist ideas, such as "authenticity" and "subconscious," remain dependent upon social agreement for their meanings (Eco 1990, 200).

NOTES

Acknowledgments. *I thank the anonymous reviewers for providing useful comments and suggestions, and also thank the editors of this volume. In addition, I am grateful to representatives of the Stillaguamish Tribe for their input and guidance in completing the final draft. At their request, the word "Indian" is displayed in quotes wherever it appears, to set out its many incongruities. Portions of this essay were presented during the October 2004 Annual Meeting of the American Society for Ethnohistory, with Kathleen Brogan and Renée Bergland included as session discussants.*

1. The Stillaguamish Tribe of "Indians" has resided for centuries in Northwest Washington State. They live along both branches of the Stillaguamish River and share its name. According to linguistic documentation for the Coast Salish peoples, the Lushootseed word stem for Stillaguamish signifies "people of the river" (Suttles and Lane 1990, 501). Archaeologically, the river and the tribe's prehistoric cultural remains are known as the Olcott sites and are recognized as one of the oldest assemblages documented for North America (Baenen 1981, Miss and Campbell 1991). After European contact in the 1700s, it is believed that the Stillaguamish people participated within the Pacific maritime fur trade complex that included their

closest neighboring tribes as well as Russian, British, Spanish, French, and U.S. participants (Suttles 1998, 167). By the time they signed the settlement treaty in 1855, the Stillaguamish Tribe had been decimated by disease. Those who survived refused to leave the river for the "Indian" reservations designated by the U.S. government (Lane 1973, 22). Instead, they lived in their traditional villages from the saltwater to the mountains but were eventually forced to move upriver away from the two mouths of the Stillaguamish River by the encroachment of Scandinavian settlers during the late 1800s (Goodridge 1906, 984–85; Louise 1932). Within several decades, however, the entire river had been logged off and developed by the Scandinavian immigrants and other homesteading entrepreneurs. Most of the earliest European arrivals married resident Native women and raised their families while farming, fishing, and logging up and down both branches and stems of the river (Anderson 1957). In the ensuing decades, much of the Stillaguamish Tribe's traditional culture was distanced and almost all of their traditional cultural resources were usurped. Little documentation of the tribe's past exists. Within the sparse record, a few archival river maps provide traces of former "Indian" occupation, and early records of exploration provide historical details. The tribe reclaimed a small parcel of reserved land near the river when it received formal federal recognition in 1976.

2. For a comprehensive study on Indigenous GIS mapping projects in Canada and the United States, see Chapin, Lamb, and Threlkeld (2005).

3. There are numerous accounts of Stillaguamish efforts to rebury their dead. See Nels Bruseth (1926), Affidavit of James Dorsey (1926), Deposition of Sally Snyder (1955), and Robert H. Ruby and John A. Brown (2001), and newspaper accounts in the *Arlington Times*, "Everett Indians Locate Burial Plot," November 29, 1968; the *Everett Herald*, "Right to Indian Burial Site Involves Soul, Reality, Conflict,", April 8, 1976, and "Discovery of Bones Sparks Controversy," August 2, 1981; and the *Seattle Times*, "Tribes Praise Reburial Effort," July 30, 2005.

4. For an interesting analysis of the scientific and occult truths that have been debated within the history of anthropology, see Peter Pels (2000).

5. One area of Native ghost analyses that did produce an overabundance of ethnographic, historic, and popular literature is composed of the hundreds of publications addressing the Ghost Dance phenomenon (see Osterreich 1991). It seems safe to suggest that this overproduction of over-analyses may have been a part of the overreaction to re-secure the dominant discourse by reining in the "Indian" attempts to thwart it.

6. Ironically, Gilbert Ryle has labeled the human unconscious: "Freud's ghost in the machine" (Ricoeur quoting Ryle 1970, 353).

WORKS CITED

Anderson, Burton Laurence. 1957. The Scandinavian and Dutch Rural Settlements in The Stillaguamish and Nooksack Valleys of Western Washington. PhD diss., University of Washington, Seattle.

Apess, William. 1836. Eulogy on King Philip as Pronounced at the Odeon, in Federal Street, Boston. In *Our Own Ground: The Complete Writings of William Apess, A Pequot*, ed. Barry O'Connell, 163–274. Repr. Amherst: University of Massachusetts Press, 1992.

Baenen, Jim. 1981. Stillaguamish, Snohomish, Snoqualmie, and Duwamish. In *Inventory of Native American Religious Use, Practices, Localities, and Resources*, ed. A. R. Blukis Onat and J. L. Hollenbeck, 395–472. Institute of Cooperative Research, Inc. Report prepared for Mt. Baker-Snoqualmie National Forest, Contract #53-05M6-0076N.

Barsh, Russel Lawrence. 2008. Ethnogenesis and Ethnonationalism from Competing Treaty Claims. In Harmon, *The Power of Promises*.

Bendix, Regina. 1997. *In Search of Authenticity: The Formation of Folklore Studies*. Madison: University of Wisconsin Press.

Bergland, Renée L. 2000. *The National Uncanny: Indian Ghosts and American Subjects*. Hanover NH: University Press of New England.

Bierwert, Crisca. 1999. *Brushed by Cedar, Living by the River: Coast Salish Figures of Power*. Tucson: University of Arizona Press.

Boas, Franz. 1940. *Race, Language and Culture*. New York: Macmillan.

Boyd, Colleen E. 2006. That Government Man Tried to Poison All the Klallam Indians: Metanarratives of History and Colonialism on the Central Northwest Coast. *Ethnohistory* 53 (2): 331–53.

Brogan, Kathleen. 1998. *Cultural Haunting: Ghosts and Ethnicity in Recent American Literature*. Charlottesville: University Press of Virginia.

Bruseth, Nels. 1926. *Indian Stories and Legends*. Arlington WA.

———. 1972. *Indian Stories and Legends of the Stillaguamish and Allied Tribes*. Fairfield WA: Ye Old Galleon Press.

———. 1918–1949. Bruseth Papers. University of Washington Archives Accession No. 228, Box No. 1, Folder No. 3.

Chapin, Mac, Zachary Lamb, and Bill Threlkeld. 2005. Mapping Indigenous Lands. *Annual Review of Anthropology* 34: 619–38.

Clifford, James. 1988. *The Predicament of Culture: Twentieth Century Ethnography, Literature and Art*. Cambridge MA: Harvard University Press.

———. 1997. *Routes: Travel and Translation in the Late Twentieth Century*. Cambridge: Harvard University Press.

Cole, Douglas, and David Darling. 1990. History of the Early Period. In Suttles, *Northwest Coast*, 7:119–34.

Coppock, Henry Aaron. 1969. Interactions between Russians and Native

Americans in Alaska, 1774–1840. PhD diss., Michigan State University. University Microfilms International. Ann Arbor.

Dorsey, James. 1926. Affidavit entered in the Court of Claims Case No. F-275, Claimants' Exhibit E.

Drucker, Phillip. 1943. Archeological Survey of the Northwest Coast: Bureau of American Ethnology Bulletin. No. 133, pp. 17–132.

Eco, Umberto. 1990. *The Limits of Interpretation.* Bloomington: Indiana University Press.

Eng, David L., and David Kazanjian. 2002. Introduction: Mourning Remains. In *Loss: The Politics of Mourning.* Berkeley: University of California Press.

Faris, Wendy. 2002. The Question of the Other: Cultural Critiques of Magical Realism. *Janus Head* 5(2): 101–19.

Fisher, Robin. 1977. *Contact and Conflict: Indian and European Relations in British Columbia, 1774–1890.* Vancouver: UBC Press.

Goodridge, Gardner. 1906. Gardner Goodridge. In *An Illustrated History of Skagit and Snohomish Counties,* 984–85. Chicago: Interstate Publishing.

Grady, C. Jill. 1998. Huichol Authenticity. Ann Arbor MI: University Microfilm International.

Gunther, Erna. 1926. An Analysis of the First Salmon Ceremony. *American Anthropologist* 28:605–17.

Harkin, Michael E. 1994. Person, Time and Being: Northwest Coast Rebirth in Comparative Perspective. In *Amerindian Rebirth: Reincarnation Belief Among North American Indians and Inuit,* ed. Antonia Mills and Richard Slobodin. Toronto: University of Toronto Press.

Harmon, Alexandra. 2008. Introduction: Pacific Northwest Indian Treaties and International Historic Perspective. In Harmon, *The Power of Promises.*

———, ed. *The Power of Promises: Rethinking Indian Treaties in the Pacific Northwest.* Seattle: Center for the Study of the Pacific Northwest in association with University of Washington Press.

Jewitt, John Rodgers. 1807. *A Journal Kept at Nootka Sound, One of the Surviving Crew of the Ship Boston, of Boston, John Salter, Commander, Who was Massacred on the 22nd of March, 1803. Interspersed with Some Account of the Natives, Their Manners and Customs.* Printed for the author. Boston.

Kan, Sergei. 1986. The 19th-Century Tlingit Potlatch: A New Perspective. *American Ethnologist* 13 (2):191–212.

Kelm, Mary-Ellen. 1998. *Colonizing Bodies: Aboriginal Health and Healing in British Columbia 1900–50.* Vancouver: UBC Press.

Kew, Michael J. E. 1990. Central and Southern Coast Salish Ceremonies. In Suttles, *Northwest Coast,* 7:476–80.

Krupat, Arnold. 1992. *Ethnocriticism: Ethnography, History and Literature*. Berkeley: University of California Press.

Lane, Barbara. 1973. Anthropological Report on the Identity, Treaty Status and Fisheries of the Stillaguamish Indians. In *Political and Economic Aspects of Indian-White Culture Contact in Western Washington in the Mid-19th Century*. Unpublished report in the author's possession.

Lomawaima, Tsianina K., and Teresa L. McCarty. 2002. Reliability, Validity, and Authenticity in American Indian and Alaska Native Research. In ERIC *Digest*. ERIC Identifier: ED470951.

Louise, Sister Mary, O. P. 1932. Eugene Casimir Chirouse, O.M.I. and The Indians of Washington. Master's thesis, Seattle: University of Washington.

Mauzè, Marie. 1994. The Concept of the Person and Reincarnation among the Kwakiutl Indians. In *Amerindian Rebirth: Reincarnation Belief among North American Indians and Inuit*, ed. Antonia Mills and Richard Slobodin, 177–91. Toronto: University of Toronto Press.

Miller, Jay. 1999. *Lushootseed Culture and the Shamanic Odyssey: An Anchored Radiance*. Lincoln: University of Nebraska Press.

Miss, Christian J., and Sarah K. Campbell. 1991. Prehistoric Cultural Resources of Snohomish County, Washington. Report Prepared for the Washington State Office of Archaeology and Historic Preservation. Northwest Archaeological Associates.

Myers, Fred R. 1988. Locating Ethnographic Practice: Romance, Reality, and Politics in the Outback. *American Ethnologist* 15 (4):609–24.

Osterreich, Sally Anne. 1991. *American Indian Ghost Dance 1870–1890: An Annotated Bibliography*. Westport CT: Greenwood Press.

Pels, Peter. 2000. Occult Truths: Race, Conjecture, and Theosophy in Victorian Anthropology. In *Excluded Ancestors, Inventible Traditions: Essays Toward a More Inclusive History of Anthropology*, ed. Richard Handler, 11–41. Madison: University of Wisconsin Press.

Raibmon, Paige. 2005. *Authentic Indians: Episodes of Encounter from the Late Nineteenth Century Northwest Coast*. Durham: Duke University Press.

Richardson, Judith. 2003. *Possessions: The History and Uses of Haunting in the Hudson Valley*. Cambridge MA: Harvard University Press.

Ricoeur, Paul. 1970. *Freud and Philosophy: An Essay on Interpretation*. trans. Denis Savage. New Haven CT: Yale University Press.

Ruby, Robert H., and John A. Brown. 2001. *Esther Ross: Stillaguamish Champion*. Norman: University of Oklahoma Press.

Saga, Carl. 1995. *The Demon-Haunted World: Science as a Candle in the Dark*. New York: Random House.

Sheffield, Gail K. 1997. *The Arbitrary Indian: The Indian Arts and Crafts Act of 1990*. Norman: University of Oklahoma Press.

Snyder, Sally. 1955. Deposition entered in the Indian Claims Commission Docket No. 207.

Steiner, Christopher B. 1994. *African Art in Transit*. Cambridge: Cambridge University Press.

———. 1995. The Art of the Trade: On the Creation of Value and Authenticity in the African Art Market. In *The Traffic in Culture: Refiguring Art and Anthropology*, ed. George E. Marcus and Fred R. Myers, 151–65. Berkeley: University of California Press.

Suttles, Wayne, 1990. *Northwest Coast*. Vol. 7 of *Handbook of North American Indians*, ed. William C. Sturtevant. Washington DC: Smithsonian Institution.

———. 1998. The Ethnographic Significance of the Fort Langley Journals. In *The Fort Langley Journals, 1827–30*, ed. Morag Maclachlan, 163–210. Vancouver: UBC Press.

———, and Barbara Lane. 1990. Southern Coast Salish. In Suttles, *Northwest Coast* 7:485–502.

Tollefson, Kenneth D. 1992. The Political Survival of Landless Puget Sound Indians. *American Indian Quarterly* (Spring 1992): 213–35.

Wike, Joyce Annabel. 1951. The Effect of Maritime Fur Trade on Northwest Coast Society. Ann Arbor MI: University Microfilms International.

———. 1952. The Role of the Dead in Northwest Coast Culture. In *Indian Tribes of Aboriginal America: Selected Papers of the 29th International Congress of Americanists*, ed. Sol Tax, 3:97–103. Chicago: University of Chicago Press.

Wood, Michael. 2002. In Reality: Cultural Critiques of Magical Realism. *Janus Head* 5(2):9–14.

Acknowledgments

The coeditors of this volume gratefully acknowledge the financial support provided by the Office of the Provost at Ball State University.

Contributors

Colleen E. Boyd is an associate professor of anthropology at Ball State University. She received her PhD from the University of Washington.

Michelle Burnham is a professor of English at Santa Clara University. She received her PhD from the State University of New York, Buffalo.

Victoria Freeman is in the final stages of completing her PhD dissertation on the historical memory of the Indigenous and colonial past of Toronto and is the coordinating director of the University of Toronto Initiative on Indigenous Governance.

Geneva M. Gano is a visiting assistant professor of American studies and Latino studies at Indiana University. She received her PhD from the University of California, Los Angeles.

C. Jill Grady is a research associate at the Laboratory of Anthropology/ Museum of Indian Arts and Culture in Santa Fe, New Mexico, and a tribal consultant. She received her PhD from the University of Washington.

Sarah Schneider Kavanagh is currently completing graduate studies in education at the University of Washington. She received her bachelor's degree in American studies from Wesleyan University.

Cynthia Landrum teaches in the Native American Studies Program at Portland State University. She received her PhD in history from Oklahoma State University.

Allan K. McDougall is a professor emeritus and adjunct research professor of political science at the University of Western Ontario. He received his PhD from the University of Toronto.

Lisa Philips is a professor and the chair of the Department of Anthropology at the University of Alberta. She received her PhD from the University of Texas.

Contributors

Coll Thrush is an associate professor of history at the University of British Columbia. He received his PhD from the University of Washington.

Adam John Waterman is a visiting assistant professor in American studies at Macalester College. He completed his PhD in American studies at New York University.

Index

Index

anthropology, 184; and colonialism, 190; and human remains, 204, 227–28, 271; internalist, 248–49n114
Assignack, Francis, 244n58
Austin, Mary, 53n40
Australia, xxxiv, 215
authenticity: anthropologists and, 284–85; colonial discourse of, 290, 291

Baker, Robert, 139
Bakhtin, Mikhail, 56
Baldoon (Hooker), 129–31
Baldoon Mystery, xxiv–xxv, 120–47; epistemologies, 131, 141–42, 147; possible culprits, 143, 145, 149n11; social context, 124–25, 147; versions: baldoon.com, 140–41; Chatham-Kent website, 147; Darroch (1997–2005), 138–40; Gervais-Reaney (1976), 133–36; Hooker (1900), 129–31; Jones (1861), 121–23; kent.net, 140; Lauriston (1952), 131–33; McDonald (1905), 123–27, 148n5; McDonald (1915), 127–29; Natilli (2004), 138; Parrish-Grant (1999), 136–38
The Baldoon Mystery (McDonald), 127–29
Baldoon settlement, 118
Baquedano-López, P., 120
Barnum, P. T., 101–2
Barrows, Willard, 88–89, 90, 99
Bass, Sophie Frye, 74–75
Basso, Keith, 54
Batesville IN, xiii
Beacon to the Ancestors Foundation, 234
Bear Butte, 257, 258

Bell, Michael Mayerfeld, xii
The Belledoon Mysteries (McDonald), 123–27, 148n5
Benedict, Ruth, 148n4
Benjamin, Walter, 112n2, 113n10
Benn, Carl, 229
Bergland, Renée L., ix–x, xvi–xvii, 10, 159, 171–72, 281
Berkhofer, Robert, 167, 170, 178n73
Bierwert, Crisca, 55, 282
Black Hawk: burial of, xxiii–xxiv, 95–97; death of, 92–93; destruction of remains, 111–12; dismemberment of body, xxiv, 99–103, 116nn30–31; grave, 88–89, 95–96, 99; haunting by, 104, 112; life of, 93–95; repatriation of bones of, 109–10; theft of body, xxiv, 98–99, 101, 104, 105, 108; widow of, xxi, 105, 110–11
Black Hawk War, 94
Black Hills, 257–58
The Blair Witch Project, vii–viii
Blazing the Way (Denny), 74
Boas, Franz, 272
Bobiwash, Rodney, 239n5
Botimer, Dorothea, 272–73, 274
Bourne, Randolph, 26
Boyd, Colleen E., vii–xl, xxvii, 40, 181–205
Boyle, David, 224
Brandao, J. A., 219
Brant, Joseph, 218
Braude, Ann, xvii
Braudel, Fernand, 57
Brébeuf, Jean, 211
The Bridge (Crane), 30
British Columbia, xiv–xv, xxxv–xxxvi
Brogan, Kathleen, xix–xx
Brooks, Van Wyck, 30

306

Iowa State Historical Society, 85, 86, 87, 88, 92
Ireland, 199–200, 202, 205n10
Iroquois, 278n51
Irving, Washington, ix
Irwin, Lee, 259–60

Jackson, Andrew, 96
Jacobs, Jane M., xxxiv, 212, 222, 236, 237
Jeffers, Robinson, xxii–xxiii; anti-war sentiment of, 26–27, 35, 45; interest in dance, 52n25; interest in genealogy, 38; on Native American genocide, 33, 44, 46, 47, 53n40; view of World War I by, 26–28; works: "Apology for Bad Dreams," 45–46, 48; "The Coast-Range Christ," 27; "Come Little Birds," 44–45; "Hands," 46–47; "Natural Music," 27, 35; "New Mexican Mountain," 31–32; "A Redeemer," 29–30, 33, 40; "Shells," 33, 39; "Shine, Perishing Republic," 28; "Tamar," xxii–xxiii, 33–44, 48–49; "The Torch-Bearer's Race," 37; "The Truce and the Peace," 27. *See also* "Tamar"
Jesuit Relations of 1636, 211
Jews, 14–15
Johnson, Alex, 244n58
Johnson, Leo, 219
Johnson, Pauline, 244n58
Johnson, Samuel, xxx–xxxi
Johnston, Darlene, 224, 228, 231
Jones, Augustus, 210
Jones, Peter, 210, 220, 228, 244n58; *History of the Ojebway Indians*, 121, 241n30, 243n46
Jones, Peter Edmund, 244n58
Jordan, James, 96, 99, 105, 116n30

Kaukkonen, Rauna, xxxii
Kavanagh, Sarah Schneider, xxv–xxvi, 151–78
Kellogg, David, 63
kent.net, 140
Keokuck, 92–93
Kikisebloo, 64, 65
King, Stephen, vii, xv
knowledge: and beliefs, xxvii; and history, 235–37, 248n105; social, 190
Kohl, Johann Georg, 216
Kuts, Melanie, 264
Kwakwaka'wakw, xxxv–xxxvi

LaCapra, Dominick, 231
Ladysmith, British Columbia, xv
Lakota: epistemology of, 260–61; spiritual beliefs of, 256, 257–59, 264–68; and Wounded Knee, xxviii–xxix, 262–63. *See also* Plains Indians
Landrum, Cynthia, xxviii–xxix, 255–78
landscapes. *See* place
language: and alterity, 38–39; Fou-cauldian-Marxist model of, 281; and oral tradition, 242n31
Lauriston, Victor, 131–33, 147
law, 108
Lawrence, Bonita, 221
Lawrence, D. H., 30, 176n30
The Legacy of Conquest (Limerick), 162
LeJeune, Paul, 225, 228
Levi, Primo, 15
Levinas, Emmanuel, 4, 6, 11–12, 15–16
liberalism, 3, 4, 6, 12, 13–14
Liebman, Laura Arnold, 14
Limerick, Patricia Nelson, 162
Lincoln, Abraham, 89, 90

www.ingramcontent.com/pod-product-compliance
Lightning Source LLC
Chambersburg PA
CBHW022347280326
41935CB00007B/105